BACK TO THE

Edited by BARRY W. HOLTZ

SOURCES

Reading the Classic Jewish Texts

A TOUCHSTONE BOOK
Published by Simon & Schuster
New York London Toronto Sydney Tokyo Singapore

TOUCHSTONE

Simon & Schuster Building
1230 Avenue of the Americas
New York, New York 10020
Copyright © 1984 by Barry W. Holtz
Published by Summit Books
First Touchstone Edition 1992
TOUCHSTONE and colophon are
trademarks of Simon & Schuster Inc.
Designed by Edith Fowler
Manufactured in the United States of
America

4 5 6 7 8 9 10
Pbk.   8 9 10

Library of Congress Cataloging in
Publication Data
Main entry under title:
Back to the sources

Includes bibliographical references
and index.
1. Judaism—History—Sources—
Addresses, essays, lectures.
I. Holtz, Barry W.
BM496.5.B33   1984   296.1   84-8452
ISBN 0-671-45467-6
ISBN 0-671-60596-8 Pbk.

Acknowledgments

Since this book, in a very real sense, is about the enterprise of teaching and learning, I find it hard not to say a few words of thanks to some of the teachers who taught me both about the classic Jewish texts and about the discipline of reading itself. In particular I am thinking of Joseph Lukinsky, my first important teacher in Jewish literature, who introduced me to the textual tradition; Jesper Rosenmeier, with whom I studied a very different body of religious texts as an undergraduate at Tufts University; and Allen Grossman, poet, critic, theorist in religious literature, who was my teacher and graduate advisor at Brandeis University a decade ago and whose influence remains with me still.

If I began to name the many friends who have taught me about the texts discussed in this book, the list would be endless. But three who are contributors here have been both colleagues and teachers and have helped me enormously in planning the structure and approach of this volume. For those very helpful conversations, my warm thanks to Alan Mintz, Ed Greenstein, and Art Green.

When *Back to the Sources* was first being planned, I had the benefit of wise counsel from a number of friends. In particular my gratitude goes to Richard Siegel, Michael Strassfeld, Bill Novak, and Michael Paley. A special word of thanks to Nessa Rapoport, who has been for many years a steady guide and supporter and who helped me out with this project when I most needed it.

Others too numerous to name have greeted this project with interest and given me words of assistance and support. I must single out Marc Bregman for his help with the Midrash chapter, Sylvia Ettenberg for her kind encouragement, Linda Holtz and Chuck Distler for their humor, energy, and warmth. Also thanks to Ruth Mandel and Laurie Ottenstein for their unflagging assistance in helping prepare the manuscript.

Quite obviously this book is a joint endeavor and it goes without saying that I owe a special debt of gratitude to all the contributors. They grasped the need for such a book immediately and gave the essays their intelligence, care, and enthusiasm, often taking time away from their strictly academic work to write the essays for this project.

There are three people to whom I owe my greatest thanks. First, this book would never have come to fruition without the energy, support, and vision of my editor at Summit Books, Arthur H. Samuelson. He helped me conceive and develop the project and he nurtured, guided, and believed in it through many permutations. Second, my friend and colleague at the Melton Research Center, Edy Rauch, has given unstintingly of his enormous abilities in helping me talk out the book, in listening to my concerns and questions, and in never complaining about the times that this book may have impinged on my normal work routine. It is a great privilege to be able to work with him and learn from his wise insight. Finally, Bethamie Horowitz has probably heard more about this book than a person need bear. She accepted it with her characteristic grace and patience. More than that, she has listened actively and well, given me advice in great measure, and never faltered in her concern, affection, and reliable good humor. Without her it might never have happened.

for my parents,
Melvin and Meryl Holtz,
with love and with thanks

Contents

First page of Genesis from an early printed Bible, Prague, 1518.

Introduction:
On Reading Jewish Texts

BARRY W. HOLTZ

The most famous story in all of rabbinic literature is a story about the study of texts:

> It happened that a certain heathen came before Shammai and said to him, "Convert me on condition that you teach me the entire Torah while I am standing on one foot." Shammai drove him away with the builder's measuring stick that was in his hand. He then came before Hillel who converted him. Hillel said to him, "That which is hateful to you, do not do to your neighbor. This is the entire Torah; the rest is commentary—go and learn it."
>
> —BABYLONIAN TALMUD, Shabbat 31a

Generally this tale is told as a way of emphasizing Judaism's concern with ethical behavior through the key principle of loving one's neighbor. It has become almost an apologetic text as well, used to show that Christianity does not have a monopoly on love as a religious category. Shammai is seen as the unbending spoilsport; Hillel's message of love is presented as the Jewish Golden Rule, and since the rabbinic master pre-dated Jesus, Jews also get the benefit of being able to say, we got there first. Indeed, Hillel's message of "love your neighbor" fits nicely with the events of the story. He, after all, is the one willing to answer the heathen's question. His message is exemplified by his actual behavior. He greets the willing convert with open arms.

And yet one feels there is more to it than that. Perhaps after all

11

Shammai is on to something. Can one really learn the entire Torah standing on one foot? Shammai's anger does not seem so inappropriate —Torah, he tells his questioner, is a complicated, serious matter. It requires patience and more than a little dedication. In fact, Torah *cannot* be learned on one foot, or in one hour. Perhaps not in one lifetime.

Hillel, too, has his reservations. He may be a more generous sort— perhaps a bit of a soft touch in fact—but his answer is not so simple either. The rest is commentary, but the commentary cannot be ignored. When both feet are finally resting on the ground, then the task really begins—"go and learn it."

In the Jewish tradition statements about study countlessly multiply. Across time and space they abound without end. One can say with little hesitation that Torah and its study is the dominant religious preoccupation throughout the history of Judaism, at least until modern times, and for many even now. From the statement in the Mishnah (200 C.E.*) concluding a list of commandments with *"talmud torah k'neged kulam"*— the study of Torah is equal to them all—to Franz Rosenzweig's preoccupation in the twentieth century with the "Book" and how we must confront it, the focus remains constant. The world, according to the ancient rabbis, rests on three pillars—study, worship, and good deeds. And which of these is the greatest? Study—since from study the others can be deduced.

Torah for the Jewish tradition is a multifaceted term. On one level it refers to the first five books of the Bible, the content of the scroll found in any synagogue. In another more expanded sense, Torah is the Hebrew Bible as a whole. But Torah stands for more than one text or one book. Torah is revelation, the entire revelation and the entire activity of Jewish study throughout the generations. When the rabbinic sages speak of the Written Torah and the "Oral Torah" (the Oral Torah being the commentaries and holy texts of later generations) as *both* being given at Mount Sinai, they mean to suggest that all Jewish study is Torah and all Torah has the validity of revelation. Its authority rests with God, but its agents are human beings. Throughout time Jews have always seen their primary occupation as being part of this devotion to study, this ongoing revelation.

The great texts discussed in *Back to the Sources* are the record of the Jewish concern with Torah. We begin with the Written Torah itself, but Judaism spans far more than just the Bible. Jewish literature, as one of

---

* Jewish sources prefer to use C.E. (common era) rather than the Christian-oriented A.D. (anno Domini—in the year of our Lord).

the authors in this volume suggests, should be seen as a kind of vast inverted pyramid. The Bible is at the base, but the edifice expands outward enormously—midrashic literature, the Talmuds, the commentaries, the legal codes, the mystical tradition, the philosophical books. All this literature is Torah.

In the individual chapters of *Back to the Sources,* we have tried to demonstrate how this body of literature can be of interest to the contemporary reader, even to the reader who has no prior commitment to the religious teachings embodied in those texts. It is our contention that the Jewish textual tradition is one of the great literary achievements of human culture, representing a system that is unique, important, and deeply compelling to anyone interested in literature itself. The classic Jewish texts are as much "classics" as the works of Greek and Roman culture, and although they are far less known, they are as enduring, as challenging and no less profound.

Through this literature the reader can penetrate into the minds of people who devoted themselves to the seriousness of language and the sanctity of human experience. These texts represent a record of their struggles with the meaning of law, the nature of interpretation, the conflict of faith and reason and the elusive power of the divine. In reading them we come face to face with those issues that form the universal core of all great literature, as we see those concerns refracted through the lens of the particular consciousness of the Jewish literary imagination.

To the contemporary reader the Jewish textual tradition is unusual in that virtually all of it is based on the single originating point of the inverted pyramid, the Bible. In that sense Jewish literature is strikingly unique: it is creative, original, and vibrant, and yet it presents itself as nothing more than interpretation, a vast set of glosses on the one true Book, the Torah. In ways far beyond what Hillel could have imagined, the rest is commentary.

This fundamental fact about Jewish literature and its history is expressed elegantly by Gershom Scholem, one of the giants of modern Jewish scholarship, in his essay "Revelation and Tradition as Religious Categories in Judaism." ★ The rabbis of the tradition, according to Scholem, believed that:

> Truth is given once and for all, and it is laid down with precision. Fundamentally, truth merely needs to be transmitted. The originality of the exploring scholar has two aspects. In his

★ In *The Messianic Idea in Judaism* (New York: Schocken, 1971), pp. 282–304.

spontaneity, he develops and explains that which was transmitted at Sinai, no matter whether it was always known or whether it was forgotten and had to be rediscovered. The effort of the seeker after truth consists not in having new ideas but rather in subordinating himself to the continuity of the tradition of the divine word and in laying open what he receives from it in the context of his own time. In other words: Not system but *commentary* is the legitimate form through which truth is approached.

Scholem may be correct, yet the modern mind cannot help but wonder. Conditioned as we are to the importance of ideas such as "originality" and "creativity" it is hard for us to imagine a world where such terms are of little value. *Commentary*—and only that?

In this skepticism we are, no doubt, more than merely victims of the narcissistic inclinations of the present age. For the problem of "originality" has been with Western culture at least since the rise of romanticism a century and a half ago and our image of the "creative" person (particularly the poet seeking the *new* phrase or the composer the *new* musical turn, but also the religious soul seeking *new* insight), conditions the way we look back on the texts of another time. W. Jackson Bate,★ writing about English poetry, studies the birth of the ideal of "originality" in the mid-eighteenth century:

> . . . the spread of the idea of "originality" into the fringes of behavior and into stock value or stock response was only a symptom of the grip that the ideal was beginning to take on the center of the intellect itself. For the concept of "originality" meshed with so many other things in life aside from the arts . . . that the conscience was trapped by it. . . . By the 1750s some of the least original minds of the time were beginning to prate constantly of "originality," thus setting a precedent with which the intellectual has since been condemned to live.

And so this particular concern has been with us for some time now. When we look at a tradition that saw itself as commentary—that is, "unoriginal"—it seems difficult to comprehend.

To understand the consciousness of the traditional texts in this regard, we must never forget the great sanctity with which they endowed the Torah itself. Torah, as is discussed elsewhere in this volume, is more than just another book. The traditional writers saw Torah as God's very word and because of that, it itself is eternally "original." The commen-

★ *The Burden of the Past and the English Poet* (New York: Norton, 1970).

tators do not invent something new; they discover what the Divine Author had always intended. The problem of intentionality, one of the great issues in modern theories of reading and criticism (that is, can we —or should we even try—to discover an author's intentions in writing a particular work), becomes irrelevant to the traditional mind which sees a perfect Author behind the Torah. Of course every interpretation that ever will be was known at Sinai, was intended by God. Isn't this within God's power?

But things are probably more complex than that, too. It is hard to believe that originality was irrelevant to the classic commentators. They were human, too, and the tradition values the great and creative interpreter, the person capable of the *new* insight, the *hiddush,* to use the laudatory term from the traditional literature for a creative point of commentary.

The rabbinic writers, however, surely approached their task with a degree of humility uncommon to our age. In fact, part of the purpose of statements such as "Torah, Mishnah, Talmud and Aggadah—indeed even the statements some bright student will some day make to his teacher—were already given to Moses on Mount Sinai" (quoted from Midrash Tanhuma by Scholem in the essay mentioned above) may have been made to instill humility in generations of rabbis as they took up the mantle of their interpretive role. And to a great extent these warnings served their purpose.

But we know also of students vying with one another at the *yeshivot,* the traditional academies, and we know, too, of the natural human pride that goes with the "well-made thing," as a good *hiddush* can certainly be. One episode from the Babylonian Talmud reveals that the rabbis combined the sense of humility mentioned above with an equally clear feeling for the power of their own interpretive activities. In discussing a particular legal precedent, one sage, Rabina, asks another, Ashi, does this teaching we are considering apply to Hiyya or Oshaia, the great redactors of an important early law code? Yes, Ashi replies. What about Rav and Samuel? Rabina asks, referring to two sages of a later generation. Yes, to them, too, Ashi declares. And what about us, Rabina continues, does it apply in a case stated by you and me? What are we, Ashi shoots back, mere "cane cutters in a bog?" Of course it applies to us, too!

To be sure the idea that the teachers of each generation must be seen as legitimate and significant—no cane cutters in a bog, they—is coupled with the rabbinic tradition's great veneration for the weight of earlier precedents and the great learning of the generations past. But the rabbis carry with them as well a deep sense of personal pride and accomplishment. Even if they are merely uncovering the old, it is a task that requires talent, dedication, and the sharp tools of the imagination.

Dwelling too long on problems of rabbinic self-definition or the issue of originality in traditional literature may be missing the point, however. The question is less to determine if the rabbis thought they were doing something "new" when they wrote the classic texts, than to consider what this enterprise is all about on its own terms.

Let us consider, then, the issue of the relationship of Torah to the vast body of literature that attempts to comment upon, elucidate or explain the Torah—that is, the great traditional texts of postbiblical history. Or, to use the language of the tradition, let us ask: what is the connection between the Written Torah and the Oral Torah? In place of the modern issue of originality I would suggest that the Oral Torah had a different goal: namely a special kind of *interaction*.

The rabbis throughout Jewish history were essentially *readers*. The text was the Torah; the task to read that text. We tend usually to think of reading as a passive occupation, but for the Jewish textual tradition, it was anything but that. Reading was a passionate and active grappling with God's living word. It held the challenge of uncovering secret meanings, unheard-of explanations, matters of great weight and significance. An active, indeed interactive, reading was their method of approaching the sacred text called Torah and through that reading process of finding something at once new and very old.

For the rabbis all interpretations are essentially old—they are already known at Sinai after all. And yet this antiquity, this essential "unoriginality," does not seem to limit or hinder the rabbinic reader. Indeed, it seems to inspire him to even greater heights of "originality." The antiquity of Torah is its great allure. Rather than inhibit the interpreter with a sense that there is nothing new under the sun, it encourages his daring and resourcefulness.

We should not forget also that the "reading" performed by the rabbinic tradition had a level of day-to-day practical significance that rarely affects the way we read. Rabbinic interpretation was intimately connected with law; it touched people in all aspects of their lives. Hence it had a level of urgency that was of great moment.

Yet the distinctive energetic quality of the traditional texts does not come simply because of their concern for immediate issues of law. We find the same liveliness in the nonlegal texts as well. Rather it is the interactive, dynamic spirit of Torah and commentary, of exchange and response that accounts for the richness of the classic texts.

By "interactive" I mean to suggest that for the rabbis of the tradition, Torah called for a living and dynamic response. The great texts are the record of that response, and each text in turn becomes the occasion for later commentary and interaction. The Torah remains unendingly alive because the readers of each subsequent generation saw it as such, taking the holiness of Torah seriously, and adding their own contribution to the story. For the tradition, Torah *demands* interpretation.

Interestingly, this way of thinking about reading—that it is active, that it calls forth response and dialogue on the part of the reader—has much in common with certain trends in contemporary writing about literature. Critics such as Stanley Fish and the late Roland Barthes (who sees at the heart of interpretation "the dialogue of two histories and two subjectivities") have brought many of these ideas to the forefront of current writing about the way we think about literature and the act of reading. Thus Wolfgang Iser, in an influential essay, "The Reading Process: A Phenomenological Approach," * talks about the way that reader and work are intimately interconnected:

> Whatever we have read sinks into our memory and is foreshortened. It may later be evoked again and set against a different background with the result that the reader is enabled to develop hitherto unforeseeable connections. The memory evoked, however, can never reassume its original shape. . . . Thus, *the reader,* in establishing these interrelations between past, present and future, actually *causes the text to reveal its potential multiplicity of connections.* [my italics]

In similar fashion the later interpretive texts of the Jewish tradition show the "multiplicity of connections," of meanings and directions inherent in Torah. Moreover, as many writers have pointed out, the importance of the text served to bring unity to the Jewish people scattered throughout many lands in exile. In the absence of nationhood the text, as George Steiner has put it, became our homeland.

The relationship of text and commentary becomes even more evident and graphic with the birth of Jewish printing in the fifteenth century. The Talmud is printed with its major commentaries arranged around the page; the Bible, too, is printed in an edition known as Mikra'ot Gedolot, with the great commentators' words bordering the page, a kind of gathering of the minds, each with its own personality and

---

* In *New Directions in Literary History,* ed. Ralph Cohen (Baltimore, Maryland: Johns Hopkins University Press, 1974), pp. 125–47.

contribution to make to the enterprise of discussion and interaction. (For more on this see Chapter Four.)

The connection between contemporary literary criticism and the traditional texts is not an exercise in apologetics. Rather it may let us see that although the rabbinic tradition is very old, its way of understanding reading and interpretation may be less foreign to us today than we might have thought. Surely, there are many differences and we should not minimize them: the faith statement of the classic texts in the divinity of Torah is not the least of them. But we today need not relegate these texts to the dustbin of antiquarian history.

I have been speaking about "reading" the classic Jewish texts (and also, of course, about the way that in the Jewish tradition texts tend to be "readings" of other, earlier texts), but we must also consider ways in which our idea of reading might differ markedly from other such notions in the past. In fact, traditional Jews rarely speak about *reading* texts at all; rather, one talks about *studying* or *learning* these sacred books. Thus we must ask: is the difference between reading and learning something more than merely a matter of terminology?

Although I have argued above that reading may be a good deal more active an occupation than we usually think, it is nonetheless a solitary activity. We sit *alone* with a book as we read. Learning or studying can imply something very different. It is important to remember that most traditional Jewish "reading" occurs in a social context—the class, or the study session. In the chapter in this book on the Talmud, we see a detailed picture of the traditional study environment: often in the world of the *yeshiva,* Jewish learning is carried on in a loud, hectic hall called the *bet midrash* (study house) where students sit in pairs or threesomes, reading and discussing out loud, back and forth. The atmosphere is nothing like the silent library we are accustomed to. Reading in the *yeshiva* is conducted in a room with a constant, incessant din; it is as much talk as it is reading; in fact, the two activities of reading and discussion are virtually indistinguishable.

Reading thus becomes less an act of self-reflection than a way of communal identification and communication. One studies to become part of the Jewish people itself. As much as prayer, study is a ritual act of the community. The sociologist Samuel Heilman, in *The People of the Book* (Chicago: University of Chicago, 1983), talks about these learning environments as providing a "sentimental education" in which Jews gain access to the values of their tradition and live out those values by the very act of study. Through the study discussions, Jews actually replicate the world of the Talmud. It is as if distinctions of time and place are erased, and the participant is catapulted back to Rabbi Akiba's academy 1,800 years in the past. The learner joins in the discussions, voices his opinion, is defended or refuted by the legendary teachers and students of other ages and takes his place in the continuum of the tradition.

There is much to be said for such an understanding, since it gives a taste of the rich emotional world connected in a very close way to the classic Jewish texts. These are not only books that one reads or rereads and sets on the shelf. They live, too, in the context of hours of human repartee, of struggle and illumination in community. Part of the great allure of study for Jews over the centuries must have some connection to this interpersonal domain. Thus the texts are "interactive" in two senses: in the way reading is lively and dialogic; and in the way we get to speak to our companions when we study, debate, and ponder the texts aloud.

Moreover, the texts are bound to the lives of individual Jews in ways beyond reading and studying. The entire liturgical structure of the Jewish year resounds with echoes of the great sources. First and foremost is the role of the prayerbook (see Chapter Eight), the daily instrument of worship, which contains within it quotations and allusions to the Bible, to Talmudic sources, to poems of the Middle Ages, rituals of Kabbalah and even to the philosophy of Maimonides (in the popular hymn known as Yigdal)!

But the texts have connections beyond the prayerbook. Each Sabbath, as is discussed elsewhere in this book, a portion from the Torah and from the Prophets is chanted in the synagogue. On certain holidays one of the Five Megillot (scrolls) is read: Song of Songs on Passover, the Book of Ruth on Shavuot (the festival that is celebrated seven weeks after Passover in the early summer), Ecclesiastes on Sukkot (the festival of booths, the fall harvest holiday), Esther on Purim, and Lamentations on the Ninth of Av, the summer fast day commemorating the destruction of the Temples. The holiday of Passover uses the Haggadah, a work of rabbinic literature, as the central text for the Seder meal and on Hanukkah we sing medieval liturgical poems and recite a passage from a rabbinic law code. The texts are always there—throughout the year and throughout the life cycle, in the rituals for birth, bar mitzvah, marriage, and death. The marriage document, for example, read out at the wedding ceremony, reminds us of our ties to the textual tradition of the past —it is written even today in Aramaic, the language of the Talmud.

Thus the texts are connected to study and to prayer. They formed the basis of meditation for the mystical tradition (it is not surprising from all this that letter-mysticism is central to the Jewish method of contemplation!), and they live in the daily, weekly, and ongoing rituals of the Jewish people.

Jewish study and learning, we have suggested, are not merely the activities of the library or the reader in isolation, but rather live in social and religious contexts. A particularly significant feature of the religious context is the fact that traditional learning is invariably done with a master, someone who can guide one's encounter with the text and help make sense of what may be arcane, confusing, or beyond one's grasp. The teacher in such an environment has a special kind of authority— different, I believe, from the role of a teacher in a normal American school or university—because the traditional texts themselves are based to a great degree on a sense of the authority of wisdom. Such an attitude may go back to ancient days when the Oral Torah really was oral and learning was a kind of discipleship. Although the texts have long been written down, we still venerate the learned teacher, and the texts them- selves reinforce this, representing the tradition as a human chain in which one builds on the teachings and insights and legal judgments of the sages who have preceded us.

Thus the solitary reader is at a considerable disadvantage. Not hav- ing the social context of fellow students, not having the reliable authority of the wise master, he is very much left to his own devices and may, in fact, be stuck in his own peculiar quicksand. Add to this yet another problem: namely, that the great classic texts are all composed in other languages—generally Hebrew or Aramaic—and we have another barrier that is intimidating indeed.

Reading the texts in translation is not simply a matter of losing the "flavor" of the original. Many traditional commentaries rely on word- plays, as does the Bible itself (see the discussion in Chapter One, Biblical Narrative, for example). The classic texts count on the richness of asso- ciation that can only be captured in the Hebrew original. In these and in many subtle ways, the translated text is extremely disadvantageous. Moreover, English is a language that carries with it a host of essentially Christian associations. When we read words such as "grace," "sin," or "charity," it is hard to view them as entirely neutral—these are terms that carry with them the weight of Christian context and interpretation. Indeed, to translate, for example, the Hebrew word *tzedakah* as "char- ity" (the usual translation) one misses the point that the Hebrew word comes from the root meaning justice and righteousness: giving to the needy is a requirement, a matter of doing what is right. "Charity" comes from the Latin *caritas*—love or caring; the idea there is that the giving depends on the good will and deep feeling of the giver, not on the *obligation* to act with *tzedek*—justice.

Because Judaism has always stressed the sanctity of the specific language of the Bible, translation has been viewed with a certain degree of ambivalence. Although in rabbinic times an Aramaic translation of the Torah was declaimed alongside the biblical text in public readings (a practice still observed among Yemenite Jews), it was the Hebrew original that was venerated and preserved.

This sense of the sacred quality of the language begins with the Bible itself. God speaks, and through language the world comes into being. Jews, at least since rabbinic times, have taken the holiness of the language with great seriousness. A Torah scroll must be transmitted with each letter correct and intact, otherwise it is considered unfit for use in the worship service, and this and other tokens of care, even in our time, indicate the particular importance of the original text. The importance of language is reflected also in the fact that interpretation was adduced sometimes from the numerical dimension the letters of the Hebrew language. Since each letter also stands for a number, words could be associated through their numerical equivalency, as well as through conventional semantic connections. Thus the thirty-nine categories of work forbidden on the Sabbath, for example, could be deduced by the numerical values of certain verses in the Bible. This mode of interpretation, known as *gematria,* begins in the Talmudic age and continues as a style of reading—somewhat playful to be sure—throughout later Jewish history, particularly in the mystical tradition.

Obviously, *gematria* is rooted in a sense of the special status and quality of the Hebrew language. The words of the Torah are so deep, so mysterious, that interpretations can be gleaned through many signs and hints. Numerical equivalency is just one technique open to the traditional reader.

One of the contributors to this volume, Edward L. Greenstein, has pointed out elsewhere:

> Throughout history the Christian church has always heard its Scripture in translation while the Jewish synagogue has chanted its Bible in Hebrew. . . .

> After all, Jewish exegesis of Scripture has traditionally found great significance not only in the *sense* of the text but quite as importantly in its configurations of Hebrew phrases, words, even letters. . . . The ancient rabbis displayed an understandable antipathy to any sort of Bible translation. But the transla-

tions that were produced . . . endeavored to transfer word for word, particle for particle, each meaningful component of the original.★

Thus the contemporary reader approaching the classic texts in translation is facing an additional burden in trying to penetrate to their meaning.

The fact that many of these texts remain untranslated only partially explains another phenomenon, however. That is, why such a rich body of literature—the classic Jewish texts—remains by and large so unknown to the contemporary audience. It is our contention that these texts represent a great source of richness, depth, and profundity—a contribution to world literature that any educated reader, Jew or non-Jew, should have cognizance of. Why, then, is this literature so unfamiliar?

Clearly, part of the answer is that until recent times this was *anything but* a hidden body of writings. Jews were educated to learn these texts from an early age. Even the more arcane texts were familiar to large numbers of Jewish students, and learning had always been seen as a lifelong process in the world of traditional Judaism.

With the entry of Jews into the mainstream of Western culture almost two hundred years ago, much of this changed. There still was a large community of educated Jews who continued to study these texts, but with the rise of secularization, this number began to shrink. The newly secularized Jews came to see these texts as repositories of all that was dated, "religious" and "unmodern"—for most, it was impossible to separate the text from the context of the "old world." The seriousness of the texts as literature and as wisdom was lost in the headlong rush into modernity. In that sense it is interesting that recently there seems to be a turning back to a serious reexamination of the classic texts. For some this has gone hand in hand with the rise of a Neo-Orthodoxy in American and world Jewry, symbolized to a certain degree by the so-called *baal teshuvah* (returner) phenomenon both here and in Israel.†

Moreover, the rise of interest in adult study within the non-Orthodox sector of the Jewish population has also confirmed a revitalized concern for the books of the Jewish past. Perhaps with the success of the battle of the immigrant generation to become Americanized, a later generation can turn back toward what had been rejected. Perhaps the ancient

★ "Theories of Modern Bible Translation" in *Prooftexts: A Journal of Jewish Literary History,* vol. 3, no. 1 (January 1983), pp. 9–41.
† For more on this the reader might look at Janet Aviad's *Return to Judaism* (Chicago: University of Chicago Press, 1983).

texts no longer stand for the past or for the enemy that must be over-come. And certainly reaction to the destruction of the Holocaust, as well as renewed self-awareness owing to the rise of the State of Israel, have also led people back to searching for the roots of their lost Jewish past.

I have been speaking of the reasons for the invisibility of the classic Jewish sources to the contemporary reader. Aside from these factors that have been discussed above, something else should be mentioned as well. Jews and non-Jews alike have not known about these texts because of certain abiding attitudes about them that have remained in the Christian world. There has been a kind of ongoing prejudice against the Jewish texts that is almost theologically inherent in Christianity itself. To begin with, Christians have traditionally read the Hebrew Bible in a "typo-logical" fashion—events were viewed as mere "shadows," precursors of their fulfillment in the person and meaning of Jesus. The Hebrew Bible was called the "Old" Testament (a term never used in traditional Jewish sources) to contrast it with the fully realized "New" Testament. The effect of such an approach is to undercut the validity *in its own terms* of the Jewish Bible, but more than that there is the implication that Jewish creativity must have ended with the "Old" Testament to make way for the new world heralded by the rise of Christianity.

Thus any Jewish writing after the Bible is seen as necessarily insig-nificant. Judaism can have no contribution because, according to this view, it has been surpassed by the new religion and its teachings. Hence the persistence of Jewish literature—and Judaism itself—becomes a kind of ongoing embarrassment for Christianity. Perhaps that is why the Church burned the Talmud in the Middle Ages—as an attempt to deny the very existence of a living Jewish tradition.

This attitude has found expression in numerous denigrating state-ments about Jewish literature that can be found in Christian theological writings. One common idea is that Judaism at the time of Jesus was in a state of extreme degeneration. This great creative period of rabbinic Judaism is described thus by Calvin:

> Matters had come to such a pass with these people, so great and widespread were the abuses, so thoroughly had the high priests extinguished the pure light of doctrine through their negligence or malice, that there scarcely remained any respect for the Law.

And oddly enough, some twentieth-century historians have perpetuated the same outlook. Karl Adam, a German Catholic writer, speaks of the world of rabbinic Judaism as "a world which was falling in ruins" as do numerous theologians and instructional manuals used for religious education.*

This attitude extends to the Jewish literary productions after the time of Jesus. Christian writers of the past and even in our own time speak of "the inveterate sterility of Israel" or "the fate of Judaism . . . with its extravagant programme and barren achievement."†

Thus the widespread ignorance about the classic Jewish texts has its roots in numerous factors, but some of them are deeply entrenched in a particular kind of consciousness or attitude about Judaism itself.

The reader who wishes to turn to the Jewish sources, therefore, is fighting against numerous impediments: the problem of language, the problem of learning without community, the problem of old negative attitudes, both Jewish and Christian. We have hoped in *Back to the Sources* to make some small contribution to overcoming these difficulties. One should remember, however, that the way we are talking about reading the classic texts in this book differs markedly from the approach to the written sources evident throughout most of Jewish history. Before the nineteenth century—with some very few exceptions—Jews looked upon the Bible and to a lesser degree the other great sources, such as the Talmud, as holy documents, containing within them the wisdom of God's truth. As is discussed in Chapter Two, study for traditional Jews was not a mere intellectual endeavor, it was an act of devotion. To use the traditional language, learning was a *mitzvah,* a divine commandment, and in studying, Jews saw themselves as performing a holy act ordained by God.

In both the Jewish and non-Jewish world, however, rumblings of change eventually began to be felt. Spinoza, for example, in the seventeenth century sought to explore the authorship of the Bible, claiming that only part of it derived from the hand of Moses. But it was not until the nineteenth century that a change in attitude toward the classic texts seriously bloomed. The Christian scholar Julius Wellhausen was the first to popularize the notion that the biblical text was composed of various strands of traditions, different sources reflecting different periods of composition. Even in the Jewish world (where Wellhausen's ideas were greeted with great suspicion) the nineteenth century saw the rise of

* The first two sources are from Jules Isaac's study, *The Teaching of Contempt* (New York: Holt, Rinehart and Winston, 1964).
† These quotations are discussed in *Europe and the Jews* by Malcolm Hay (Boston: Beacon Press, 1950).

"Wissenschaft des Judentums"—a movement advocating "scientific" study of and critical research into the classic texts.

Wissenschaft was, to a certain degree, tied to the Haskalah (Enlightenment) movement within European Jewry and represented for some a way to identify with Judaism and still retain connection to the allure of Western European secular culture. There was in addition a kind of apologetic aspect to Wissenschaft—Jews were going to demonstrate to the non-Jewish world that classic Jewish literature had a legitimacy of its own, and Jewish scholarship could be as rigorous and critical as anything being done in the world of non-Jewish research.

It would be fair to say that the writers in this volume have all been deeply influenced and affected by the tradition of Wissenschaft scholarship. And yet the work that they are doing today reflects a different approach as well. These scholars have tried to combine Wissenschaft's emphasis on critical methodology with a deep concern for the richness and personal relevance of the classic sources. They have attempted to use the techniques of contemporary scholarship to elucidate the inner depth of the classic texts. But they have neither gone the route of apologetics, nor have they viewed the texts as museum specimens needing dissection —both of which having been paths for some earlier scholars. Rather they have tried to follow and expand the direction of writers (such as Gershom Scholem) who have combined rigor with a deep appreciation for the intelligence and significance of the classic sources. And they have tried to penetrate and explore the religious meaning of the classic texts for the person seeking insight and wisdom today.

This book, moreover, is an attempt to deal with the great texts in a popular, nonacademic context. We live in a time, as I have argued earlier, where there is great and renewed interest in the textual tradition. The growth of Jewish studies in universities is only one manifestation of this significant phenomenon. The opening up of Jewish learning to women—who throughout most of Jewish history had very little opportunity for advanced study—is another. Our goal in this book is to be accessible, but to speak with seriousness and without condescension. We have tried to ask what is the enterprise of the great texts? How do they work? How might they speak to a modern reader? Our goal is to fascinate, to illuminate, and in a modest sense, to inspire by revealing something of the marvelous edifice of the Jewish textual tradition. In each chapter we have also tried to provide some bibliographical guidance for the reader who wishes to explore more in and about the great texts that have been discussed.

The great inverted pyramid of the textual tradition, mentioned earlier in this chapter, has formed the model for the structure of this book. We begin with the Written Torah itself—the Bible. Since the Bible is the point upon which all later texts rest and since it is, from a literary point of view, so vast and multifaceted, the Bible chapter is divided into three different sections representing three significant genres of biblical literature. The section on Biblical Narrative serves also as an introduction to the Bible as a whole, its component parts and its structure and content.

The next great layer of the pyramid is the literature of rabbinic Judaism. The best-known of rabbinic books is the Talmud, discussed here in Chapter Two. The Talmud has formed the core of the curriculum of Jewish study for hundreds of years. Even today in traditional Jewish circles mastery of Talmud is considered the height of intellectual achievement, and a firm knowledge of Talmud is essential to attain a level of religious credibility. Accompanying Talmud on the same level in the pyramid is the other great literary opus of rabbinic civilization— the sermons and interpretative commentaries on the Bible known as Midrash. Here we see the imaginative play of the rabbinic mind, as it expands the single point of the Torah into a myriad of possibilities through exegesis and speculation.

At the next level of the pyramid we find the literary productions of the medieval period. The most familiar of these texts are the commentaries on the Bible by figures such as Rashi and Ibn Ezra. Although the medieval commentators differ from their midrashic predecessors, their writings build the rabbinic period and represent yet another expansion of the ancient interpretative impetus. In medieval Jewish philosophy, however, we see a new dimension added to the literary chain. Philosophy was one of the great occupations of Jewish writers in the Middle Ages, keeping alive the Western philosophical tradition at a time when it was virtually ignored by Christian Europe. Philosophers such as Maimonides and Halevi responded in their own fashion to the textual tradition that preceded them, asking a different set of questions and speaking in a different style, yet keeping their connection to the tradition by the seriousness with which they view the significance of Torah.

The medieval period also sees the flowering of the mystical tradition within Judaism in the publication of the Zohar and other texts with a kabbalistic perspective. In modern times, for many years, Kabbalah was seen as an interesting, but aberrant, secondary enterprise of the textual tradition. But in our century, scholarly researchers have made clear the centrality of Kabbalah to the whole of Jewish religious consciousness. Mysticism was not an unusual and insignificant detour, but formed an essential brick in the edifice of the traditional literature and religious practice.

Kabbalah finds new expression in the eighteenth century with the birth of Hasidism. Perched midway between the medieval and modern worlds and in some ways representing a bridge from the former to the latter, Hasidism was brought to the awareness of the non-Jewish world in the twentieth century mainly through the writings of Martin Buber. But it should be noted that both Kabbalah and Hasidism represent a direct link back to the rabbinic texts that first gave birth to the interpretive tradition. The Zohar, for example, has quite appropriately been called a "mystical Midrash" and the Hasidic texts examined in detail in Chapter Seven are homilies of a style very familiar to a reader of rabbinic texts. As the pyramid expands, new ideas enter the consciousness of the writers, but the preoccupation with Torah remains a constant.

Finally we have a chapter on the prayerbook, a book that begins in rabbinic times and has continued to expand and grow along with the pyramid of the classic texts. The prayerbook both resembles and differs from the other texts in the tradition in that it represents a work that was not only meant to be studied, but was essentially intended to be prayed. Yet it, too, in its many allusions to other texts of the tradition, in its excerpting of sections from the Bible, and its interesting interplay with change and history represents a fitting culmination to the entire textual tradition.

It is obvious that many texts in the traditional library are not discussed here. A list of potential chapters could be endless—such is the nature of the rich Jewish textual tradition. We have been forced by necessity to impose limitations. To begin with, we eliminated books that did not seem to be "texts" in the traditional sense of that term. I have in mind here works of modern theology in particular. Obviously, thinkers such as Buber, Rosenzweig, Soloveitchik and Heschel are major figures of Jewish thought in this century. But these works are generally accessible to the contemporary reader and do not have that air of strangeness or unfamiliarity that books like the Talmud and the Zohar possess. Works of a modern literary sort were also eliminated; much as the poetry of Bialik or the novels of Agnon are admirable, they, too, seemed inappropriate in a collection of classic texts.

Some texts were subsumed under other categories—in particular the chapter on Talmud served to deal with the ongoing legal tradition in Judaism and therefore discusses the medieval codes and the responsa literature. Other texts seemed inappropriate because insufficient examples now exist in English translation or where, as in the case of medieval

Hebrew poetry, it is virtually impossible to capture the nature of material without studying the texts in the original. *Back to the Sources* tries to
deal with the essential classics and with those texts that contemporary
readers may find particularly compelling. The explosion of interest in
mysticism in our own time influences, quite obviously, the inclusion of
texts from the mystical tradition (Kabbalah and Hasidism) which a generation ago might not have found its way into a book of this sort. Thus,
although not every text of the tradition is covered here, we have tried to
present a picture that fairly represents the breadth of the literary tradition.

It is clear that no book can replicate the experience of study and
good discussion; nor can any essay reproduce a living teacher before the
reader's eyes. *Back to the Sources* may, one assumes, be used by groups
of students both with and without teachers. But the solitary reader was
primarily in mind as we prepared this book. Reading the classic texts is,
finally, the clearest and most direct access to the very nature of Judaism
itself. This may not be the easiest of endeavors but turning back to the
sources has great rewards. In one of the classic midrashic texts this
matter is addressed with a parable:

> What is the difference between the Written and the Oral Law?
> To what can it be compared? To a king of flesh and blood who
> had two servants and loved them both with a perfect love. He
> gave each of them a measure of wheat and each a bundle of
> flax. What did the wise servant do? He took the flax and spun
> a cloth. He took the wheat and made flour. He cleaned the flour
> and ground, kneaded and baked it, and set it on top of the
> table. Then he spread the cloth over it and left it until the king
> would come.
>
> The foolish servant, however, did nothing at all. After some
> time, the king returned from a journey and came into his
> house. He said to his servants: my sons bring me what I gave
> you. One servant showed the wheat still in the box with the
> bundle of flax upon it. Alas for his shame, alas for his disgrace!
>
> When the Holy One, blessed be He, gave the Torah to Israel,
> he gave it only in the form of wheat—for us to make flour
> from it, and flax—to make a garment from it.
> —SEDER ELIYAHU ZUTA, Chapter 2

And thus, as we read the texts of the tradition, we, too, join in the
process called Torah—we are turning wheat into bread, flax into gar-

ments. Torah, in that case, is ultimately about transformation. The Midrash quoted here makes a significant point: the gift of the Written Torah, if it remains unstudied, untransformed by learning, is of as little use as "wheat still in the box." Reading the texts is work; like all acts of transformation it takes effort, but the goal is to create that which is useful out of that which is only in potential—garments from mere flax, bread from wheat.

But how is Torah "useful"? Surely, for the rabbis, part of that had to do with law, norms of behavior by which Jews have lived their lives for centuries. But I think it means something else as well. As we have said, reading as understood by the tradition is not a passive enterprise. It involves one's whole self; it forces involvement, passion, and self-reflection. Ultimately, it may lead one toward change.

Torah, therefore, for the Jewish tradition is a lifelong pursuit. Not a day without Torah, assert the rabbis. In some sense there is not a moment without Torah, since it informs the way one conducts even the smallest details of life.

The traditional literature recognizes the difficulty of this endeavor, as well as its rewards and fascination. In a striking allegory the Zohar, the great classic of Jewish mysticism, describes the enterprise:

> Torah may be compared to a beautiful and stately maiden who is secluded in an isolated chamber of a palace, and has a lover of whose existence she alone knows. For love of her he passes by her gate unceasingly and turns his eyes in all directions to discover her. She is aware that he is forever hovering about the palace and what does she do? She thrusts open a small door in her secret chamber, for a moment reveals her face to her lover, then quickly withdraws it. He alone, none else notices it; but he is aware it is from love of him that she has revealed herself to him for that moment, and his heart and soul and everything within him are drawn to her.
>
> So it is with Torah, which discloses her innermost secrets only to them who love her. . . . Hence, people should pursue the Torah with all their might, so that they might come to be her lovers.
>
> —ZOHAR, II, 99a

Ultimately, as the Zohar sees it, the pursuit of Torah is a kind of romance. It fascinates, indeed it may infuriate one with its stubborn difficulties. Yet it remains forever captivating. For the Jewish tradition, reading is more than reading: it is a love affair with the text.

From the Garden of Eden story, Bible manuscript with marginal decorations from Yemen, 15th century.

CHAPTER ONE

Bible

A. BIBLICAL NARRATIVE

JOEL ROSENBERG

We are perhaps used to thinking of the Hebrew Bible, together with the poems of Homer and Hesiod, as *the* literature of the archaic world—without considering that these formed only a fraction of the written discourse of ancient times. Still, it was a highly significant fraction: these volumes represent nearly the sole literary output of the archaic world (pre-500 B.C.E.) that is still continuous with the cultural traditions of the West. This is no accident: it means that these works *generated* a cultural legacy, and that the cultural experience they embody and the literary modes they employ are familiar to the modern Western reader partly because this reader has learned to read, to some extent, through their eyes.

Biblical literature has fared somewhat better than its Hellenic companions. Epic and didactic poetry largely passed out of Western literary tradition as active forms around the eighteenth century—roughly the era that marks the beginning of modern prose fiction. The Bible still has a wide readership, however, if, to be sure, not largely a literary readership. Its subtle ways of indirection, in any case, make biblical narrative more akin to modern fiction than to the works of Homer or Hesiod.

By virtue of its general accessibility to readers, its ability to generate thought and interpretation, its pungent wit, and its keen eye for the complexities of human motivation, biblical literature becomes the instant possession of its users. Not that it is ever possessed fully, or that it unlocks all of its secrets, even after several readings. The Bible is a mischievous companion, and one soon finds that its words speak on several levels at once. One may usefully accustom oneself to reading each verse through the latticework of commentary, but the text still coheres remarkably without commentary. It flows through cycles of generations with an ever more realistic spiral of thematic development, and at no point does it break the linear continuity of generational succession. Biblical time seems relentlessly forward moving, but it is the resistances, the folds, the wrinkles in that time—that is, the narratives themselves—that more strongly command one's interest. The reader soon feels drawn into biblical issues, as the participant in an unfolding conversation with the text. This process shows how the Bible is more than a work of literature—it is a system of lore, one with the capability of generating an ever-widening system of further lore. Yet it is also only itself: an elegant and soft-spoken narrative with many beginnings and many endings, a lucid exposition of dilemmas that seem very familiar, even when read for the first time.

But it is the specific mischief that the text plays on the reader that best conveys its unique properties. For while biblical narrative unfolds in a plain and ingenuous voice, its sticky surface soon becomes apparent. Details are omitted that we must fill in with the imagination—or perhaps leave unfilled. Characters' thoughts are concealed, and their actions and words admit of several interpretations. Options seem closed off by choices the characters make, but consequences of the choices are often delayed for several story cycles. Turns of phrase become significant and wordplay seems to multiply. The forward movement of fictional time yields, on closer reading, to a more subtle interplay of flashback, repetition, quotation, allusion, dream-vision and waking, prospective and retrospective glance, fade-out and fade-in—all of which make time seem to proceed in a mottled and disjunctive fashion. Non sequiturs and digressions complicate the screen of discourse, and stories sometimes suspend their actions at particularly tense and weighted moments, only to pick them up at a later stage, creating a text riddled with gaps, discontinuities, and irresolution. Characters come to the fore out of nowhere, and disappear just as abruptly. Even key characters are kept in view only as long as they are useful to the plot.

Above all, motifs return; all action seems haunted by predecessors. A universe of echoes and resemblances emerges, and characters and eras seem to struggle to free themselves from the grip of sameness and from the fugal counterpoint woven by repetition. And when resolutions come, as in places they must, they do not let the text yield its prerogatives of mystery making and complication. To read biblical narrative is to submit oneself to a lesson in *how* to read.

BIBLE AND THE COMPONENTS OF BIBLICAL NARRATIVE

The Hebrew Bible, though roughly equivalent to what Christianity (with its "New Testament") calls the "Old Testament," is called by Jews the "TaNaKh," after the initial letters of its three chief parts: *Torah* (Instruction), *Nevi'im* (Prophets, namely, the historical and narrative Former Prophets, and the poetic and oracular Latter Prophets), and *Ketuvim* (Writings). The Christian arrangement of the books, based on the Septuagint (Seventy—so-called because tradition held that it was produced by seventy scholars), a Greek translation, differs somewhat from that of the Masoretic (Traditional) Hebrew version. The Hebrew Bible is also called *Mikra'* (Lection or Proclamation), largely because of its public recitation in the synagogue, although the term *mikra'* can also mean an individual biblical verse, or a short text. Similarly, the term *Katuv* (Written) can mean all of Scripture, or a short segment. The five books of Moses, called collectively the Pentateuch (from Greek words meaning five volumes), Jews also term the *Humash* (pentad, fivefold entity). The Pentateuch is divided into fifty-four weekly synagogue readings, each known as a *parashah* (division, plural *parshiyyot*) or a *sedra* (order), each about five chapters in length; certain *parshiyyot* are staggered with adjacent ones in nonleap years of the Jewish calendar. There is an older triennial cycle of divisions no longer in general use. Each *parashah* is coupled with a selection from the *Nevi'im,* called in Hebrew a *haftarah* (lit. departure, more correctly conclusion, completion). Although the division into biblical books is at least as old as the Septuagint (third century B.C.E.) the exact form of the Jewish canon was not fixed until the first or second century C.E. The present division into chapters and verses, as well as the vowel markings of the Hebrew text, originated in late antiquity and the Middle Ages. (For a listing of the contents of the Hebrew Bible by book, see chart on page 34.)

THE HEBREW BIBLE

There are thirty-nine books in the Bible. The bulk of what we call "biblical narrative" forms one continuous story, running from Genesis through 2 Kings—what Jewish tradition calls "the Torah" and "Former Prophets." Other biblical books are partly or wholly narrative, and some of these, such as Ruth, Jonah, Esther, and the prologue and epilogue of

TORAH

Genesis	Leviticus	Deuteronomy
Exodus	Numbers	

NEVI'IM

Joshua	Jeremiah	Micah
Judges	Ezekiel	Nahum
1 Samuel	Hosea	Habakkuk
2 Samuel	Joel	Zephaniah
1 Kings	Amos	Haggai
2 Kings	Obadiah	Zechariah
Isaiah	Jonah	Malachi

KETUVIM

Psalms	Lamentations	Ezra
Proverbs	Ecclesiastes	Nehemiah
Job	Esther	1 Chronicles
Song of Songs	Daniel	2 Chronicles
Ruth		

Job, are written in the same, wry, laconic style that characterizes much of Genesis through Kings. This is not to say that all this material had a single author, or that it comprises literature of a single type. The compositeness of biblical narrative has long been recognized, and, indeed, is part of its art. There are remnants of myths, of stories accounting for the origin of human customs and place-names, of family sagas, tribal legends, national epic, royal history, wisdom or morality tales, prophetic calls and missions, satires, parables, archival histories, and cultic stories. These various genres, moreover, are interwoven with much material of a nonnarrative character: genealogies, itineraries, laws, poems, songs, riddles, prophecies, and epigrams.

To approach biblical narrative, therefore, is to confront a rich interweave of modes, requiring us to read, as it were, with two kinds of vision: one, analytic, the other, synthetic. The analytic side of our reading experience involves sensing the unique character of each unit of narrative or tradition, trying to picture its origin and transmission prior to emergence in a literary text, and picturing the human and social context in which it had its original meanings (the "life-setting," to use the prevailing term in biblical studies). Analytic reading may also involve studying common rhetorical and stylistic features of the text, such as repetition, quotation, narrative action, fictional time, character, causality, physical detail, dénouement. The synthetic side, on the other hand, involves understanding a given unit's role in the finished composition we know as the Bible, to note what precedes and what follows it, to trace the permeation of its verbal and thematic echoes in related episodes and stories, to study the timing of its montage in sequence and, above all, to see it as an unfolding story, to evaluate what it adds to the cumulative narrative we have read so far, holding in mind its contents as we proceed to the next units. One must, at the same time, accustom oneself to an almost cubistic art, whose nearest analogue in modern times is perhaps the documentary movie—a weave of voices, memories, and events whose mutual tensions must be felt, even as they merge into a polyphonic whole.

Ancient and medieval readers of the Bible, Jewish and non-Jewish alike, saw its origin as divine: the word of God, as communicated to His prophets and His people Israel. The five books of Moses, in particular, were understood as communicated by God to Moses at Sinai, even if some parts of this Torah were understood as recapitulated and written down by Moses during Israel's post-Sinaitic wanderings. That Moses' own death would be recorded by the prophet himself was a notion consistent with premodern conceptions of Moses' prophetic capabilities, but premodern readers were not, in any case, troubled by inconsistencies of narrative or temporal logic in the Torah. On the contrary, such inconsistencies were spurs to the interpretive imagination, and precisely because the text was seen as transcendent in origin, the interpreters were accustomed to see all biblical moments as simultaneous: verses could be compared or contrasted entirely out of context; the whole of Scripture (Torah, Prophets, and Writings alike) was seen as a vast sea of tiny, discrete insights, each with its own independent career in the history of the various biblical faiths; and Jewish interpreters often appealed to the dictum "There is no 'before' or 'after' in Torah" (Talmud Pesahim 6b). So even premodern readers had their own types of "analytic" reading. Certain medieval commentators, on the other hand—such as Maimonides in his effort to coordinate Scripture and philosophy in *The Guide of the Perplexed,* or the Zohar author in his attempt to find in Scripture a theosophical and mystical map of divine Being—offered synthesizing and systematic readings of Scripture that were, in fact, powerful challenges to the traditional world on whose riches they drew.

Little by little, readers of the Hebrew Bible came to develop something akin to a modern approach to the text. Abraham Ibn Ezra, a twelfth-century Spanish-Jewish commentator (see Chapter Four) seemed troubled that a detail in the story of Abraham's wanderings (Gen. 12.6), reflected a reality subsequent to Moses' lifetime (". . . and the Canaanite was *then* in the land"—i.e., "then," but no longer, though in fact Canaanites were in the land of Israel long after Moses). It was not until the seventeenth century that more secularly minded readers, such as the philosophers Spinoza and Hobbes, wrote with considerable self-assurance that at least part of the Pentateuch had to have been written after Moses' lifetime. In 1753, French scholar Jean Astruc developed one of the first "source" theories for the book of Genesis, based on the different uses of the divine names. His contemporary, J. G. Eichhorn, called "the father of Old Testament criticism," noticed further diversities of style and vocabulary that led to additional refinements in biblical source criticism.

Since the nineteenth century and the studies by German investigator Julius Wellhausen, biblical scholarship has tended to assign the "authorship" of Biblical narratives to four major sources (whether these are *persons* or *schools* is still a matter of debate): "J" (or Yahwist, for its use of the divine name YHWH); "E" (or Elohist, for its use of the divine name Elohim); "D" (or Deuteronomist, understood as the source of Deuteronomy and editor of Joshua through Kings); and "P" (or Priestly writer, source of the cultic laws of the Torah and material of a genealogical and archival nature). These sources were dated roughly to the ninth, eighth, seventh, and sixth centuries B.C.E., respectively. These categories have, in recent years, come under question, both because of changes in our assumptions about Israelite religion and history, and because the separation into sources does little to explain the larger unities that exist in biblical narrative.

Biblical scholars have thus come to speak increasingly of a biblical "redactor"—i.e., an editor who merged the various alleged sources into their present arrangement. Originally, the concept of a redactor arose as a sort of convenient hypothetical being to assign any verse or text that did not fit the style or outlook of the known sources. Redactors (whether there was one or several will not concern us here), if they were visualized as persons at all, were seen as bland, uninspired bureaucrats who were concerned only with smoothing over discrepancies, adding a variant tradition here and there, and supplying a continuous temporal schema to the whole.

Many investigators, however, have come to see that the hand of the redactor in the composition may have been more far-reaching than has been customarily recognized. To a redactor we may credit not only the conflation of sources and the chronological arrangement, but far more complex patterns of symmetry, repetition, coincidence, thematic development, and stylistic modulation that make the redactor's activity a more "literary" art than hitherto acknowledged. Recognition of this art has led some biblical scholars into a deeper appreciation of Midrash and of premodern biblical commentators (see Chapters Three and Four), who, with their belief in the unity of the text and the nonsuperfluous nature of each detail, as well as their keen generalizations on biblical rhetoric and style, have been able to render incisive judgments about the literary design of the text, even though they did not see themselves as literary critics. By viewing the text as a "teacher" par excellence, they conditioned their readers to take no detail for granted, to treat no repetition or allusion as casual, and to see no part of the text in isolation from the whole. It is with a similar respect for the unity and pedagogical purposefulness of the biblical text that Franz Rosenzweig, the German-Jewish philosopher and biblical translator, somewhat puckishly coined the much-cited equivalence between the scholarly designation "R" (for the German term *Redaktor*) and the Hebrew designation *Rabbenu*—our teacher.

SOME CHARACTERISTICS OF BIBLICAL NARRATIVE

Beginning students of the Bible experience some initial difficulties in being comfortable with fragmentary insights. Yet concentration on the detail at the expense of the whole, on the text's techniques and processes at the expense of its message, is, to some extent, a necessary first step in learning to read biblical narrative.

Let us start our exploration, at any rate, by learning how to deal with a fragment of text. We will survey here certain general features of biblical narrative through the medium of short examples. Later we will try to synthesize and expand our insights.

Wordplay. The essential untranslatability of the Hebrew Bible stems largely from its saturation with extensive and subtle wordplays. These are often associated with namings of children or places as, for example, the following:

> . . . and she called his name "Cain" (*Kayin*), saying: "I have begotten (*kaniti*) a person with YHWH's help!"
> —GEN. 4.1

. . . therefore, one called its name "Babel," for there YHWH confounded (balal) the language of all the earth.

—GEN. 11.9

Sometimes these namings have multiple meanings, for example:

. . . and Abraham called the name of that place [Mount Moriah] "Adonai-yireh," whence it is said today: "On the Mountain of YHWH*, yera'eh!" [cf. Yeru-Salem!]

—GEN. 22.14

which can mean:

He (God) appeared.
It (a ram) was provided.
One should appear—for the Jerusalem pilgrim festivals.

One should note that this example is a culmination of a pattern of plays throughout the story on the roots r'y (see) and yr' (fear). This type of verbal echo is called a *Leitwort* (leading word), and often supplies important keys to the meaning of the text, often binding texts located far apart. The use of the *Leitwort* can be better appreciated by readers of Hebrew, which like all Semitic languages places greater emphasis on consonants—usually three root letters—as bearers of the concept represented by the word. But not all instances of the *Leitwort* involve the root letters or their normal sequences. Metathesis (the switching of letters) allows considerable variability to a *Leitwort,* as scholars have shown †— the interplay of the words *bekhorah* (birthright) and *berakhah* (blessing) in the Jacob cycle; of *levenah* (brick) and *navelah* (Let's confuse . . .) in the Babel story, and sometimes even plays involving several words:

". . . in suffering you shall eat of [the earth] all the days of your life" *(kol yemē hayyēkha)*.

—GEN. 3.17

. . . and the man called his wife's name "Eve" *(Havvah),* for she was mother of all living *(em kol hai)*.

—GEN. 3.20

Wordplays thus often involve etymologically unrelated words, e.g., 'ed (mist), 'adamah (soil), 'adam (human being), tardemah (deep sleep) and

* YHWH in these translations is a rendering in English of the four-lettered biblical name of God usually translated LORD.
† Scholarly authorities will not be footnoted in the present article, though where appropriate, certain investigators will be mentioned by name. Most will be found in the bibliographical supplement following this essay.

dam (blood) in Genesis 2–4, *Ya'akov* (Jacob), *Yabbok* (the river Yabbok), and *vayye'avek* (there wrestled) in Genesis 32. In certain cases, a verbal repetition can supply an ironic twist to a story, even binding stories otherwise thought to be unrelated.

Understatement and selective overstatement. Biblical narrative is notable for its extreme economy. Rarely does it present more than the bare minimum about a physical setting, character, or speech. Almost nothing is known about the physical features of a character (we know that Sarah was beautiful, Saul was tall and handsome, and Absalom was long-haired and handsome, but beyond such general, though thematically significant, notations, we have few clues as to how characters looked— as the immense variability in the history of biblical illustration will attest). Rarely do more than two characters converse in a biblical scene at once. Rarely does the narrator interject his own commentary on the action. And most important, rarely are a character's thoughts or motives explained. One of the most poignant examples of this understated style is the following:

> And Isaac said: "Here are the fire and the wood, but where is the lamb for the burnt offering?" And Abraham said: "God will provide Himself the lamb, my son."
> —GEN. 22.8

Abraham here is a model of tact. Not only does he conceal his own inner torment about the impending sacrifice, but he manages to leave his answer ambiguous enough to anticipate either of two outcomes: God "will provide Himself the lamb," namely, "my son," *or* God "will provide himself the lamb" from some other source, as indeed turns out to be the case.

The selectivity of biblical narrative is especially evident in places where it most conspicuously violates the norm of verbal economy. When Abraham is confronted by an angry and distressed king of Gerar, who demands why he had passed his wife off as a "sister," Abraham's answer is unusually verbose, appropriately for one who speaks in a state of nervous agitation to a person of higher social standing, who bears a power of life and death:

> "I thought, 'Surely, there is no fear of God in this place, and they will kill me on account of my wife.' And besides, she is indeed my sister, the daughter of my father, though not of my mother, and she became my wife. And when it happened that God caused me to wander from the house of my father, I

said to her: 'Let this be the kindness you shall do for me: in whatever place we come to, there say of me, "He is my brother." ' "

—Gen. 20.11–13

Non sequitur, anticipatory information, and resumptive repetition. Frequently in the Bible details crop up that seem to have no clear relation to the surrounding narratives. One useful example, shown by Nahum Sarna, is this seemingly superfluous information amid the genealogies that precede the Abraham cycle:

Abram and Nahor took for themselves wives—the name of Abram's wife was Sarai, and the name of the wife of Nahor was Milcah, daughter of Haran [father of Milcah and Yiska]. *And Sarai was barren, having no child.*

—Gen. 11.29–30

This last line is unusual amid a type of discourse that records the *birth* of children. It is only in the unfolding of the next ten chapters that the importance of belated offspring to Sarai (Sarah) comes to be known, and thus her initial childlessness, set against the complex vicissitudes that imperil the conception, birth, and succession of Isaac, make this otherwise obscure gloss the thematic underpinning of the entire Abraham cycle! Moreover, the proximity of the item to the reference to Nahor's wife Milcah is no accident. After the narrowly averted sacrifice of Isaac in Genesis 22, Nahor and Milcah inexplicably return to focus:

It happened after these things that Abraham was told: Behold, Milcah, she, too, has borne children to your brother Nahor: Uz, his firstborn, Buz, his brother, and Kemuel, father of Aram; and Kesed, and Hazo, and Pildash, and Yidlaf, and Bethuel. Bethuel begot Rebecca. . . .

—Gen. 22.20–24

Again, it is unclear initially what point this dry genealogical gloss should have following one of the most volatile of biblical stories, or why, after Abraham is promised "innumerable" descendants, a birth should be recorded in connection with Abraham's *brother.* It is not until Genesis 24—the story of the courtship of Rebecca for Isaac—that the point of this information becomes clear: the births to Nahor include the father of Isaac's future mate, and so indicate the continuation of Abraham's lineage through Isaac, a matter that has been held in suspense throughout the cycle.

Sometimes the anticipatory information summarizes a scene that is about to be retold from a slightly different angle:

> The sons of Rimmon of Beeroth, Rechab and Baanah, went off, and arrived in the heat of the day at the house of Ishboshet, while he lay abed at noontime. They came into the house disguised as wheatbearers, and they struck him in the ribs. Rechab and Baanah escaped. . . .
>
> —2 SAM. 4.5 6

followed by the variant:

> They came into the house while he was lying on his bed, in his bedroom, and they struck him and killed him, and lopped off his head, and they returned by way of the wilderness all night.
>
> —2 SAM. 4.7

Or the anticipatory information summarizes a scene that is about to be told in more detail:

> Joab sent and told to David all the matters of the battle . . .
>
> —2 SAM. 11.18

followed by Joab's more specific instructions to the messenger. Note that these sequences interrupt the smooth flow of narrative time by backtracking and starting over. They may have originated in variant versions of the same episode which the redactor, conflating into a single account, sets forth as supple shifts in perspective of a single, omniscient narrator. When the summarizing information *follows* the more detailed account, it is sometimes called "resumptive repetition"—as, for example, the following:

> Miriam the prophetess, sister of Aaron, took up the timbrel in her hand, and all the women went forth after her, with timbrels and writhings, and Miriam sang responsive choruses with them: "Sing unto YHWH, for truly He has been exalted! Horse and its rider He has thrown into the sea!"
>
> —EXOD. 15.21

which ensues upon the more detailed "Song of the Sea" presented in vv. 1–18. In context, first Moses and the men sing, later Miriam and the women.

Redundancy and repetition. The last few examples illustrate a phenomenon long noticed by readers of the Bible, namely, that events or motifs often occur more than once in the same story or story cycle. Adam names his wife twice. Noah is twice commanded to load the ark, once with "two of every kind," and once with seven pairs of every clean beast, and two each of every unclean. Abraham passes his wife off as a sister twice. Hagar is driven out of Abraham's household twice. Jacob "supplants" his brother Esau three times. Joseph is sold both to Midianites and Ishmaelites. The Israelites in the desert rebel against Moses no less than seven times. Balaam tries three times to drive his donkey forward and three times to curse Israel. The Ten Commandments are given twice. Saul is elevated as king three times. And so on.

Some presence of this pattern is rooted in the rhythms of the folktale (the Balaam sequences, for example). Other aspects are the result of patterns in tradition formation. Biblical narrative is based in part on an oral tradition, and the biblical redactor, culling several versions of the same tradition, skillfully wove them into a continuous story. We need not, as biblical source critics do, assign two versions of a story to two "authors," because it was not always at a literary level that the differences arose, but at the oral stage. It is a process one is familiar with in everyday life: one rarely tells a joke, for example, the way one heard it. In the telling process, there is a kind of natural erosion, in which certain details fall away and others are substituted out of the teller's own imagination. In this manner, many versions of the same legend arose in ancient Israel, and in time some versions acquired a fixed oral or written form. When the time came to collect Israel's sacred literature into definitive canons, the collectors paid their respects to different regions and historical memories by harmonizing the variants into a single framework.

But in doing so, the biblical redactors often made use of the redundancies to great *literary* advantage. In an example shown by Edward Greenstein,★ the confusion as to whether Joseph was transferred to Ishmaelites (Gen. 37.25–27) or Midianites (Gen. 37.28, 36) is sustained throughout the story of Joseph's descent into Egypt, so as to create a blurred sense of the human causality in the descent and thus better throw into relief the clarity of the *divine* plan underlying Joseph's descent. In fact, the Ishmaelite/Midianite ambiguity reaches all the way back to the Abraham cycle, where we read that Abraham had children by two concubines, Hagar (Gen. 16.21), ancestral mother of the Ishmaelites, and Ketura (Gen. 25.1), ancestral mother of the Midianites, and in both cases expelled the heirs rival to Isaac.

★ In K. R. R. Gros Louis, et al., *Literary Interpretations of Biblical Narratives,* vol. 2 (see bibliographical section that follows the present article).

The rivalry or opposition of Jacob and Esau is told at least seven ways:

as a conflict in the womb:

> . . . and Rebecca [Isaac's wife] conceived. The children chased each other around in her womb. She said: "How can I stay alive this way?" And she went and inquired of YHWH, and YHWH said to her: "Two nations are in thy womb, two nationalities will emerge from inside of thee. And one people will be stronger than the other—the elder will serve the younger."
>
> —GEN. 25.21–23

as a conflict at birth:

> When her days of bearing fell due, behold, there were twins in her belly! The first one came out all red, with a coating of hair, and they called his name "Esau." And afterward, his brother came out with his hand grabbing Esau's heel *(ekev)*, and they called his name "Jacob" *(Ya'akov*, lit. "He supplants").
>
> —GEN. 25.24–26

as a descriptive profile:

> And the boys grew. Esau was a cunning hunter, and man of the field. Jacob was a quiet man, dwelling in tents.
>
> —GEN. 25.27

as opposed preferences of the parents:

> Isaac loved Esau, because he ate of his hunter's quarry (or: [Esau's] quarry was at his [father's] command), but Rebecca loved Jacob.
>
> —GEN. 25.28

as the sale of a birthright:

> Jacob was cooking a stew, and Esau came in from the field feeling faint. Esau said to Jacob: "Let me swallow, please, some of that red, red stew!" And Jacob said: "Sell me, first, your birthright," . . .
>
> —GEN. 25.29ff.

as the theft of Isaac's blessing:

> When Isaac grew old, it happened that his eyes grew blind, and he summoned Esau his elder son and said to him . . . "Behold, I have grown old. I know not when I might die. So now, take up your hunter's tools, your bow and arrow, and go out to the

field and hunt for me a quarry, and make for me cooked food the way I like it, that I might eat, so that I may bless you personally before I die." Rebecca was listening to Isaac's words to Esau his son . . .

—GEN. 27.1ff.

Finally, the conflict resurfaces at the end of the Jacob cycle, after Jacob, having spent twenty-one years in exile to avoid the anger of his brother, returns with his vast household to the land of his birth. His wrestle with a mysterious stranger at the river Yabbok (usually understood as an encounter with God or a divine emissary; rabbinic commentary identifies him as the guardian angel of Esau) is an echo or omen of the wrestle left unresolved nearly a generation earlier. When Jacob and Esau finally confront each other face-to-face, their contact is unexpectedly friendly and a reconciliation occurs (see Gen. 32–33). The multifaceted conflict and its mysteriously simple dénouement form part of the outer framework of the Jacob cycle. The inner core is Jacob's sojourn with Laban and the vying of Jacob's wives, which, each in its own way, mirror the brother battle.

Possibly each version of the brother battle was originally coined separately in ancient Israel's lore, but in the biblical composition they are skillfully laid out end-to-end, to tell a consecutive story, and roughly in an order of increasing complexity. Biblical narrative, one could say, is a kind of Midrash collection, containing the voices of many anonymous sages. The grand narrative sweep of Genesis through Kings can be seen to be made up of hundreds upon hundreds of tiny *tradita,* discrete units of lore that have been skillfully orchestrated into stories, the stories into cycles, and the cycles into books and complexes of books.

Ambiguity. We have already seen examples of the Bible's tendency to conceal details and motives in its narration. We should now look at two examples where still deeper levels of ambiguity are evoked.

The first I have chosen from the story of Balaam (Num. 22–24), and it concerns the identity of Balaam. Rabbinic tradition knows of Balaam as a Midianite (based on Num. 31.8), speaks of him as "the evil Balaam" *(Bil'am harasha),* and tries to portray each divine revelation to him in the light least complimentary to the prophet himself. But within the actual story, no details are given as to his nationality. He recognizes YHWH as his God, and speaks humbly and obediently before God throughout. And while he takes on the questionable commission from Balak to curse Israel (Num. 22.4–12), he states firmly that he can say nothing that is not put into his mouth by God, and indeed, his prophecies are pristinely pro-Israelite, including the famous litany *mah tovu ohalekha Ya'akov* (How good are your tents, O Jacob!). At worst, Balaam could be faulted for his impartiality. When finally before his fourth and final prophecy (oracles against the desert nations) he is confronted by an angry King Balak, he repeats his insistence on the controlling will of God in his prophecy and concludes by saying: "And now, behold, I'm going to my people" (Num. 24.14). But what people? It is not until chapter 31 that he is associated with the Midianites, and there the reference to him seems out of place. Could Balaam be a renegade Israelite? Or could he simply be a foreigner who happens to believe in Israel's God? The name "Balaam" (Heb. *Bil'am*) could mean in folk etymology "without a people," and the ambiguity of Balaam's origins is, in fact, never resolved.

The other example comes from the aftermath of the Golden Calf episode. In the course of describing Moses' activities at the Tent of meeting, the text says: "And YHWH spoke to Moses face-to-face, as a man might speak with a friend. . . ." (Exod. 33.11), and then inserts— as if by way of amplification—the following dialogue:

> Moses said to YHWH: "See, you say to me, 'Bring up this people [from the wilderness,]' but you have not made known what [sign] you will send with me. You have said: 'I know you by name, and you have also found favor in my sight.' Now, if I have found favor in your sight, please make known to me your ways. . . ."
>
> —Exod. 33.12–13

The ensuing conversation eventually leads to the following words from God:

> "I will cause all my goodness to pass over in your presence, and will call out the name YHWH before you, and I will be gracious upon whomever I will be gracious, and show love to whomever I will show love. . . . You cannot see my face, for a human being cannot see me and live. . . . Behold, here is a place beside me—stand by the rock, and when my glory passes by, I will put you in the hollow of the rock, and shield you with my hand until I pass. When I take away my hand, you shall see me from behind—but my face will not be seen."
>
> —Exod. 33.19–23

The words are simple enough, but how this is to serve as the answer to Moses' question is left concealed in the mysteries of Israel's ancient lore, and its interpretation again is left up to the reader.

Etiology, hidden causality, and reciprocal justice. Etiological stories in the Bible—stories that show the origins of names, realities, or customs —are well known. Frequently, a story will end with the phrase "and to this day, this place is called such-and-such," or "and to this day, people do such-and-such." But more often, stories conceal causal patterns that are presented without a "to-this-day" formula, but are to be inferred from the details of the narration or dialogue itself. The Garden story, which we will examine in depth later, is a veritable lexicon of cultural etiologies (including a small number of implied etiologies): origin of the pathways of human settlement (the "four rivers," Gen. 2.10–14), of plant fiber clothes (Gen. 3.7), of animal skin clothes (Gen. 3.21), of sexual knowledge, social and sexual inequality, pain in childbirth, human toil, breadmaking, death, and burial. The primeval history (Gen. 4–5) recounts the ascendance of farmers over shepherds, the origin of bloodshed and blood vengeance, the founding of cities, the rise of skilled crafts, the origin of prayer, the origin of the primordial heroes, the shortening of the human life span. The Flood story (Gen. 6–9) recounts the origin of animal sacrifice, of meat eating, of the rainbow, of viticulture and drunkenness, of sexual immorality, of the overall relation and differential fortunes of the three continents. The post-Flood primeval history (Gen. 10–11) recounts the spread of the family of nations, the origin of language variation and cultural misunderstanding, and the rise of the Semitic family of peoples. The ancestral histories (Gen. 12–50) recount, among other things, the origin of certain Israelite sanctuaries, of certain geographical peculiarities (near the Dead Sea and Sodom), of circumcision, of the prohibition on eating the thigh sinew of an animal, of demographic realities. The Exodus, Sinai, and Wilderness narratives recount the origin of Passover; of the Ten Commandments and most of Israel's cultic and legal codes; of the central sanctuary and its priestly institutions; and so forth. While a large majority of etiological examples come from Genesis, the Bible carries the etiological impulse well into the monarchic narratives (cf. 2 Sam. 2.16, 6.8, 18.18, 24.1ff.).

A more interesting phenomenon is where one story sets up a causal pattern resolved in another. Abraham's expulsion of an Egyptian slave, Hagar, leads to the birth of a child, Ishmael, whose descendants, living as a border people, the Ishmaelites, would be partly responsible for the sale of Joseph into Egyptian slavery, and indirectly, for the eventual descent and enslavement of the entire people Israel. This sojourn in Egypt was already prophesied to Abraham in Genesis 15.13ff., in the episode immediately preceding the first Hagar episode. His driving out of the children of Ketura (Gen. 25.6) leads to the rise of the Midianites, descendants of Ketura, who likewise play a role in the sale of Joseph to Egypt (Gen. 37.28, 36).

Jacob's deception of his blind father is balanced by Laban's switching of his older daughter Leah for his younger daughter Rachel on Jacob's wedding night. Pharaoh's drowning of Israelite newborn males is balanced by God's slaying of the Egyptian firstborn males and the drowning of Pharaoh's troops. David's adultery with Bathsheba and murder of Uriah is balanced by the sexual violation of David's daughter Tamar by David's son Amnon, the murder of Amnon by his half-brother Absalom, the appropriation of David's concubines and kingdom by Absalom, and the slaying of Absalom by David's own servant Joab. (See 2 Sam. 11–19.)

Divine justice seems to make the punishment a mirror of the crime, but rarely is punishment visited immediately—if Exodus 20.5 is a guide (". . . for I, YHWH, am a zealous God, visiting the iniquity of the parents on the children, to the third and fourth generation . . ."—with the sense of "as late as the third and fourth generation"). Divine plan seems based on a complex system of moral bookkeeping, to which the literary design of the narrative accords with great subtlety. One could be tempted to call this reciprocal justice "karmic," but it lacks the complex metaphysics of the Hindu concept. Put most simply: persons are free to act as they will, but their actions are fateful. One cannot calculate the consequences of one's actions on future generations. This is essentially a moral doctrine.

Symmetry. We have already seen examples of motifs that repeat or stand in balance. When this involves a *series* of elements that invert and play backward, we can say that the text is symmetrical. Symmetry appears at all levels in the Bible, from the individual sentence (this example pointed out by J. P. Fokkelman)

Shofekh	*dam*	*ha-adam,*
("A shedder	of blood	of a human
a	b	c

ba-adam	*dammo*	*yishafekh.*
by a human	his blood	will be shed.")
c'	b'	a'

—Gen. 9.6

to a segment of narration, to a story, to a story cycle. More often than not, the symmetry is broken by certain thematic configurations (in the Garden story, an etiological sestet, itself a symmetry; in the Abraham cycle, the Hagar and Akedah stories), which, in a sense, cut a swath through the symmetry and establish a more dynamic progression of events. Symmetry in the Bible is rarely a straitjacket. What is especially remarkable is the biblical editor's ability to establish a symmetry of elements while simultaneously moving the story forward.

What symmetry *means* is harder to figure out. It is, to be sure, a natural pattern of human thought limited to no particular culture. (There are symmetries in the *Iliad,* in *Beowulf,* and in folktales worldwide.) It may possibly have served as a memory device for storytellers. And as a redactor's activity, it lends design and proportion to the whole and creates a lively pattern of internal interpretation in a story or cycle, whereby elements in the second half of a symmetrical array complete, deepen, reverse, or otherwise supply some new angle on those in the first. It is especially suitable to the patterns of reciprocal justice discussed earlier. Still more pertinently, the symmetrical array is sometimes a *parenthetical* structure—where each successive inner layer answers a question or problem established by its predecessor. Again, this suggests a type of discourse that has characteristics both of *story* and of tradition-ary *riddle.*

Nonrepetition. Just as there is repetition and paralleling in biblical narrative, so also there is a tendency under some circumstances to *avoid* strict repetition where it might be expected. Even in the Creation story, whose pattern of daily repetition of creative acts has mistakenly been termed "monotonous" by source critics eager to demonstrate "priestly" authorship, there is a supple alternation of verbs ("created" on the odd-numbered days; "made" on the even-numbered days; both together in the creation of man) and a steadily increasing complexity, autonomy, and variegation in the created works of each successive day that makes the total composition anything but monotonous.

Pharaoh's account to Joseph of his dreams is in different words from the narrator's (see Gen. 41.1–7 and 17–24), and there again, while Pha-raoh's version is slightly more verbose (appropriate, perhaps, to one in a state of agitation), there seems nothing about his specific verbiage that would be particularly "Pharaonic" (as opposed to "narratorial"). On the other hand, in places, a slight variation in wording between two versions of the same event can carry great narrative significance. Aaron's account of the making of the Golden Calf, for example, is ambiguous on his own role in the affair (note wordplay here and below):

"I said to them: 'Whoever has gold, part with it!' They gave it to me, and I cast it in the fire. Out came [*vayyetze*] this calf."
—EXOD. 32.24

whereas the narrator had been more precise:

Aaron said to them: "Part with gold rings from the ears of your wives, of your sons, and of your daughters, and bring them to me!" . . . He received it from their hands, and fashioned [*vayyatzar*] with a stylus, and made of it a molten calf. . . .
—EXOD. 32.2, 4

Nonverbatim repetition is thus not always a purely stylistic device for avoiding monotony. It is carefully calibrated to character, setting, and context. It can reveal ways in which a character avoids or distorts reality. And it serves as a way of covering all bases linguistically (an important ingredient in the biblical conception of "truth"), while still keeping the language simple and direct.

Type-scenes and typology. A type-scene is a convention for telling a story, a fixed mode or sequence of action by which an event unfolds, in accordance with readers' expectations and traditional storytelling devices. One could call it a stereotyped scene, but rarely does the biblical author employ a type-scene without introducing an unusual twist to the convention.

Some common biblical type-scenes include the following:

The "wife-sister" episodes (GEN. 12.10–20, 20.1–18, 26.1–16)
Conceiving of a child by a barren woman (GEN. 18.1ff., 25.19ff.; JUDG. 13.1ff.; 1 SAM. 1.1ff.)
Hero's (or his proxy's) meeting with a future bride at a well (GEN. 24.10ff., 29.1ff.; EXOD. 2.16ff.)
Divine appearance at an unknown or anonymous sacred place (GEN. 15.1ff., 16.9ff., 17.1ff., 22.15ff., 28.10ff., 32.1ff., 32.22ff.; EXOD. 3.1ff., etc.)
News of disaster (1 SAM. 4.12–22; 2 SAM. 18.19–19.1; JOB 1.14–21)
Family reunion (GEN. 33.1ff., 45.1ff., 46.28ff.; 2 SAM. 14.28)
Discovery of a crime in the midst of the community (NUM. 15.32–36, 25.1–15; JOSH. 7.1ff.)

Israel's rebellions in the wilderness (Exod. 15.24–26, 16.2–36, 32.1ff.; Num. 11.1ff., 12.1ff., 13.25–33, 14.1ff., 16.1ff., 20.1ff.)

Divine inspiration of a military hero (Judg. 13.25, 14.5ff., 15.14ff., 16.25–31; 1 Sam. 10.1ff., 11.1ff.)

Call of a prophet (Exod. 3.1ff.; Judg. 6.11ff.; 1 Sam. 3.1ff.; Isa. 6.1ff.; Jer. 1.1ff.; Ezek. 1.1ff.; Jonah 1.1ff., etc.)

To take the last example: investigators have noticed certain basic features to narratives portraying the call of a prophet. The prophet is often addressed in a time of historical crisis. He is visited unexpectedly by God or an emissary while going about his daily business. He is given a commission or task to perform. He hesitates and complains that he is unworthy of the charge, or otherwise unready. He is reassured by the divine voice, and finally he is given a sign that God is with him in his new endeavor. If the biblical author adhered mechanically to this pattern, the scene would not arouse much interest. Fortunately, the examples we possess exhibit a wide range of variation, as a comparison of the prophetic call examples cited above will show—such that it is virtually impossible to tell which is the "original" of the pattern, and which are the "innovations."

If one turns from these examples to Genesis 18.1–15 (which, properly speaking, is an "annunciation" story), one finds a subtle reworking of the prophetic-call scene to a new purpose. Abraham and Sarah are shown going about their daily business, when they are confronted by three strangers making their way to Sodom and Gomorrah. Unbeknownst to Abraham, they are divine emissaries, and he simply greets them with the same warm hospitality and generosity he would show to any strangers. Instead of being overtaken by a vision of God, he must take the initiative to invite the visitors to stay for a meal, and he implores them, seemingly against their wishes, to partake of his food and shelter.

A brief scene follows in which Abraham and Sarah prepare the meal, the visitors are served, and they eat with Abraham standing by them. When the visitors are about to leave, they ask where Sarah is and state that within a fixed period of time, she will conceive the long-awaited child, Isaac. Sarah laughs (the word for laughed, *vattitzhak*, is of the same root as the name Isaac, *Yitzhak*), and wonders how a couple so advanced in age can conceive a child. God (who now speaks directly with Abraham, rather than through the visitors) states that nothing is impossible for God, and that a child will, indeed, arrive. The prophetic "encounter" is thus an episode of hospitality; the "commission" is not to deliver a word but to beget a nation; the "hesitation" is a laughing incredulity that such a task is possible: The "reassurance" is given, but through the complications, perhaps, of nomadic etiquette, which prohibits strangers (even divine emissaries) from conversing directly with a man's wife (even God himself seems to obey this restriction). The "sign" is withheld, because this event, like so much else in the Abraham cycle, is a test of faith!

In addition to type-scenes, the Bible is saturated with a looser permutation of symbolism that we can call *typology*. This is the tendency of characters and scenes to mirror one another. The term "typology" has perhaps most often been applied to Christianity's reading of the "Old Testament" as a prefiguration of the events of the "New Testament," but the tendency toward typology is at least as old as ancient Israel, and some of our most compelling typologies come from within the Hebrew Bible itself. The parting of the waters of Creation anticipates the parting of the Reed (or "Red") Sea for Israel. The escape of Noah in an ark *(tevah)* anticipates the escape of the infant Moses in a cradle *(tevah)* on the Nile. The descent of Abraham to Egypt in time of famine and his exit from Egypt with great wealth anticipate the events of the Exodus story. The building of the desert tabernacle anticipates the building of the Temple in the days of Solomon. And so forth. The biblical world is permeated with allusions and resemblances. Signs and portents inhabit the biblical household. Biblical personages enact figures of action that will outlive them. It is this cross-referentiality of the generations that makes each biblical moment a timeless—and, paradoxically, autonomous—image. Eve and Adam are forever tasting the forbidden fruit, Cain raising a rock against Abel, Abraham finding a ram behind a bush, Jacob dreaming at Bethel, Joseph losing his tunic, Moses casting his staff upon the Reed Sea, Balaam stalled on a balking donkey, Rahab the harlot hiding the spies of Israel, David singing psalms, Elijah listening to a "still, small voice," Isaiah prophesying the recovery of King Hezekiah, Jonah pouting on a hillside, Esther interceding for her people, Daniel sitting peacefully with lions.

This separability of each moment, the divisibility of all biblical narrative into discrete units of tradition, suggests the way the Bible lived for Jews and Christians in postbiblical times. The Bible's most fundamental trait is perhaps its quotability, and indeed, it was probably in the quoted state—bit by bit, verse by verse, moment by moment—that the Bible lived in people's imagination in the days before there was a Bible.

A Short Walk through a Biblical Narrative Text

Having viewed some basic features of biblical narrative, let's now take a specific story for a more extended analysis. I'll use the Garden story (Gen. 2–3), though for reasons I'll go into later, I won't begin at the beginning. The reader can see the overall structure of the story diagramed in the chart below. The textual moment we'll focus on here is a segment that stands more or less at the midpoint of the story: the dialogue between the serpent and the woman (Gen. 3.1–6). You should keep a text on hand to refer to, as well as the diagram.

The Structure of the Garden Story *

a   Headnote: "These are the generations . . ." (2.4)

   b   No field economy: ". . . no man to till the soil" (2.5–6)

     c   Man given life, installed in Garden (2.7–17)

       d   Man prefers woman over beasts (2.18ff.)

         e   Names *(ish/ishah)* express equality (2.23)

           f   Etiological summary: "Therefore, etc." (2.24)

             g   Human couple "naked and unashamed" (2.25)

               h   Serpent promises "eyes will be opened" (3.1–5)

                 i   Transgression (3.6)

               h'   The couple's "eyes are opened" (3.7a)

             g'   They experience shame (3.7b–10)

Post-mortem on the event—a sub-symmetry:

         x   God questions man; man points to woman (3.11–12)

           y   God questions woman; she points to serpent (3.13)

             z   [Serpent is silent]

             z'   God passes judgment on serpent (3.14–15)

           y'   God passes judgment on woman (3.16)

         x'   God passes judgment on man (3.17–19a)

           f'   Etiological summary: "For dust thou art . . ." (3.19b)

         e'   Names *(adam/havvah)* express inequality (3.20)

       d'   Man and woman wear skins of beasts (3.21)

     c'   Man expelled from Garden, denied immortal life (3.22–24)

   b'   Field economy begins (implied; cf. sub-palist. and 23b)

a'   Birth of a child completes one generation (4.1)

* From Joel W. Rosenberg, "The Garden Story Forward and Backward: the non-narrative dimension of Gen. 2–3," *Prooftexts* 1:1 (January 1981), 1–27.

We are told first that "The serpent was subtler than every beast of the field that the LORD God had made." Earlier in the story (Gen. 2.18–25), the text had recounted how God fashioned all the animals, like man, from the soil, and brought each creature to the first human being "to see what he would call it." That passage had dealt, in a roundabout way, with how the first human being found his female companion—this discovery in a sense constituting man's *rejection* of the animal kingdom in favor of a human companion. We can, then, see the serpent's action in chapter three as constituting a kind of *response* by the animal kingdom as a whole to man's effort to rise above the animals. The Garden story's nearest analogue in ancient Near Eastern literature, the epic of *Gilgamesh*, portrays a similar pattern: Gilgamesh robs the animal kingdom of its beloved companion, Enkidu, by having a woman seduce the wild man; later in the epic, Gilgamesh, in turn, has a trick played on him by a serpent, who steals the hero's elixir of immortality, thus serving a kind of poetic justice for Gilgamesh's earlier trick. Genesis 3.1, in any case, must be seen in the context of the creation of the animals by God, and the "rejection" of the beasts by man.

That the serpent is "subtler" than any beast suggests that he occupies a kind of middle ground between man and beast, the better to insinuate himself into human affairs. The Hebrew word *'arum* (subtle) is a play on the unrelated word *'eyrom,* pl. *'arummim* (naked), which had described the first human pair in the preceding verse (2.25). The overtone of naked is appropriate to a serpent, who moves around without limbs and who sheds his skin periodically. (The English word "subtle," which came from a Latin word *subtilis,* meaning slender, unadorned, rarefied, actually can mean both "naked" and "clever".) That the serpent is a beast of the *field* coincides with the larger design of the story, which begins (2.4ff.) by surveying the empty space that will eventually be cultivated fields, and ends with the expulsion of the human pair from the Garden of Eden—an enclosed, continuously nourished, and protected space—to the open fields and scrubby earth that man must henceforth till by the sweat of his brow (see Gen. 3.16–24).

Let's return to the center of the story. The serpent now speaks: "Truly, has God said: You shall not eat from any tree of the Garden?" We are accustomed to hearing these words as spoken in a kind of astonishment. Behind his ingenuous manner, the serpent picks his words wisely. The word *kol* has a double meaning: "any" and "every." The serpent thus could be suggesting, incorrectly, that God has prohibited *all* trees of the Garden, or he could be conveying a sense of the seeming unfairness that God should prohibit any *one* tree. This two-in-one challenge is important to our understanding of the woman's answer, for she feels compelled to say (see below) "we may *surely* eat" *('akhol no'khal),* an emphasis that registers her defensiveness over the serpent's innuendo. The word *kol,* one should note, is a *Leitwort* (such as we have discussed earlier in this chapter), occurring in the text of Genesis 2.1–3.24 no less than twenty-two times, not to mention other plays on the letters *kl,* such as the verb *'akhol* (eat), which occurs in various inflected forms throughout the story.

The woman's full reply is as follows: "From every tree of the Garden we may surely eat; but from the tree which is in the midst [or: middle] of the Garden, God has said: 'You shall not eat from it, nor may you touch it, lest you die.' " Ambiguity haunts her words. Again the word *kol* can suggest both *all* trees or any *one* tree. The word "tree" itself *('etz)* can be both an individual and a collective noun, leaving unclear whether it is one or several trees that God has prohibited. The word "in the midst of" *(betokh)* is interpreted by the medieval commentator Rashi to mean "in the middle of," but again, the borders of the prohibition are made no clearer by this word.

The prohibited tree, one should note, is *not* called "Tree of the Knowledge of Good and Evil," a name that appears only in Genesis 2.9 (". . . and the Tree of Life was in the midst/middle of the Garden, and the Tree of the Knowledge of Good and Evil") and in God's prohibition to the man in Genesis 2.16–17: "Of every tree of the Garden you may surely eat; but as for the Tree of the Knowledge of Good and Evil, you may not eat from it, for on the day that you eat of it, you shall surely die." We note that the woman partly duplicates the words of this prohibition, as if quoting oral lore about a scene at which she was not present, but her changes are significant: the command is changed from singular to plural; a new prohibition is added (" 'nor may you touch it' "); and, most significantly, the penalty clause (" '. . . you shall surely die' ") is changed from legal admonition to an expression of fatherly concern (" '. . . lest you die' "). Clearly, the woman's imperfect knowledge of the prohibition leaves her open to new assaults on her somewhat garbled interpretation.

The serpent proceeds to the core of his challenge: "You shall not surely die, for God knows that on the day you eat of it your eyes will be opened, and you will be like God, knowing good and evil." His initial words can actually be read as a *correction* of her quotation: "No: 'You shall *surely* die!' "—but the ambiguity of syntax allows it to be construed, as well, as a refutation of her fears. The serpent then suggests that the prohibition stems from God's desire to hoard knowledge. We should note here that whereas the deity is called throughout the story *YHWH 'Elohim* (the LORD God), in the dialogue He is called only *'Elohim* (God), a word that can likewise mean "gods, angels, divine beings." The serpent insinuates that there is a vast caste system in the cosmos, and that the border between God, god, and nongod is not so clear as the woman thinks. Significantly, the word *venifkehu* (. . . will be opened . . .) has as its last two syllables the word *kehu* ('Take!), thus adding a bit of subliminal urging to his message. The expression "God knows" insinuates that God himself has eaten of the forbidden tree.

Finally, the scene shifts to the woman's thoughts: "The woman saw that the tree was good for food, that it was a delight to the eyes, and that the tree was desirable to contemplate [or: desirable for becoming intelligent], and she took of its fruit and she ate, and she gave also to her husband with her, and he ate." This verse is unique for its complete emphasis on the woman's perspective in the scene: the serpent has receded completely, as if he had been only a figment of her imagination in the first place, and as if it were the thoughts that now reign in her that lead her to partake of the tree. Moreover, the man is represented as if he had been there all along, a mere appendage to her thoughts and deeds. His thoughts are not presented at all, as if to trivialize his own motivations for joining her in the transgression. Whether it was the tree's delightful appearance, the taste of its fruit, the serpent's blandishments, the woman's coaxing, or simply the man's passive acquiescence that led to his eating, the result is the same. That the woman is here presented as the active figure will make clearer the nature of her punishment in Gen. 3.16, where she is made subordinate to the man (as women will generally be shown throughout the rest of the Bible, with certain notable exceptions).

Myths about the origins of the world's evils through the curiosity of a woman are frequent in the ancient world, as for example, the story of Pandora. But in the Garden story, she is also seen as the originator of *ordinary* life, namely, of the familial life cycle and the pattern of labor and division of labor that attends the production of children. Though the first human pair will be denied personal immortality, they will obtain a kind of qualified immortality that results from establishing a new generation, a new link in the chain of generations without which generational continuity and history as such are impossible. Though Adam and Eve are barred access from the mysterious "Tree of Life" (mentioned only in Gen. 2.9 and 3.22), the human family tree that will grow and ramify in the coming chapters constitutes a kind of temporal "Tree of

Life." Immortality will hinge on teaching and providing for a successor
generation.

Let's pause here to think about the literary modes we've seen at
work in this passage—recalling those outlined earlier in this essay—and
also try to relate the passage to the broader framework of the story. We
can see, first of all, that the passage revels in wordplay. The musical
reverberation of the word *kol,* which occurs throughout Genesis 1–3; its
ambiguity as both "every" and "any"; the ease of its confusion with the
verb *'akhol* (eat); the presence of *keḥu!* (Take!) in *venifkeḥu* (shall be
opened); the explicit return of both "take" and "eat" in verse six
(. . . and she took . . . and she ate); the play on *'eyrom* (naked) and *'arum*
(clever); the veritable haggling between the woman and the serpent over
the "correct" reading of the divine command in Genesis 2.16–17—all of
these devices indicate how saturated the passage is with verbal echo and
double meaning.

The larger structure of the Garden story, as the diagram shows,
sandwiches the central narrative episode of the temptation between bits
of verbal and etiological lore. The first human being, seeing his first
human companion, had exclaimed a name for the woman (*'ishah!*
woman!) which in effect required his own renaming from *'adam* (human
being, earthling, soilborn/soilbound) to *'ish* (man as a social being, and
as companion to woman):

> "This one, this time,
> bone of my bone, flesh of my flesh,
> to this one shall 'woman!' [*'ishah*] be called,
> because from 'man' [*'ish*] this one was taken!"
>
> —GEN. 2.23

The man's triumphant acceptance of his own social nature is now
to be tested in the story that follows. A further signal that we are making
a transition to a dramatic episode is the etiological rubric that tells us this
is a "marriage": "Therefore does a man [*'ish*] leave his father and his
mother, and cling to his woman [*'ishto*], and the two of them become
one flesh" (Gen. 2.24). Now, it happens that the word *'ish* (man) is used
just twice more in the entire story. We'll encounter it in the central
episode of the story, the transgression itself: ". . . and she took from its
fruit and she ate, and she gave also to her man with her, and he ate"
(Gen. 3.6). And we'll encounter it again when God pronounces punishments upon the woman: " '. . . and toward your man [*'ishekh*] will be
your longing' " (Gen. 3.16). In every other reference in the story, the
man is called *ha'adam* (the human being). So wordplay isn't simply a

decorative device, but is essential to the story's overall meaning: the brief episode of social freedom enjoyed by the first human pair (during which time the man is *'ish*) is shown, in the story's total design (see diagram) to be but a tiny interlude in a career otherwise marked by drudgery, dependence, and servitude to the ground (*'adamah*) from which the human being (*'adam*) was taken.

Only in the prime of life does the human being go by the name of "man" in the social sense (*'ish*), and this turns out to be only his own preferred designation, not a word that expresses his biological identity. The "punishments" meted out by God to the man, woman, and serpent (Gen. 3.14–19) are in effect simply statements of our normal biological realities: enmity between man and beast, childbearing, pain, toil, difficulty of raising food from the earth, eventual return to the earth at death. To each of these woes there is a positive aspect, the most important of which is that without procreation, we (later generations) would simply not exist. Perhaps for this reason, the man, though he learns he is eventually to die, and in the meantime to live under hard labor, chooses a new name for his companion that expresses the positive and life-affirming aspect of the new reality:

> The human being called his wife's name "Eve!" [*havvah!* Life-bearer!], for she was "Mother-of-all-Living."
> —GEN. 3.20

In this manner, the story's wordplay comes full circle. The contrasting words for man (*'adam/'ish*), and the contrasting words for woman (*'ishah/havvah*)—not to mention the play on all these names in the word *nahash* (serpent)—express as totality a kind of symbolic anthropology of the human species, locating it midway between divinity and beast and showing its life to be comprised of distinct life cycles: a period of abject dependence, followed by a brief interlude of "independence," followed by a period of wise interdependence.

In the full design of the story shown by the diagram, the narration is governed by linguistic and textual realities throughout. The story's beings, in a sense, are made to discover the meanings of their names. To change a name is to change reality. The giving of a name, here, as throughout the Bible, always signals a major transition in being and consciousness. So the story is not simply a historical event, it is a *paradigmatic* event, typically repeated in every lifetime: the normal change in our awareness of our personal and social reality, as we progress through life. The story of an expulsion from a paradisic "Garden" is thus a kind of metaphor, a parable of human maturation. The episode of the woman's temptation by the serpent is a kind of parable-within-a-parable: it translates the loss-of-innocence theme into a moral context; it makes the event the fruit of a "transgression." This grafting together of anthropological with moral lore is perhaps the story's main point.

With such an overdeveloped verbal sense, it would seem that the Bible would have no hesitation about lavishing physical description on its characters and scenes, but in fact the opposite holds true. We are struck by our passage's extreme economy of description. It's as if all that verbal preoccupation robbed the story of its physical detail. We're given no clues as to the dialogue's physical setting, other than its apparent location near the forbidden tree. We've been told very little beforehand about the Garden itself, other than its rich supply of "every tree pleasant of sight and good for food" (Gen. 2.9) and its apparent location near the fount of four cosmic rivers (Gen. 2.10–14). We aren't shown where the serpent is when he tempts the woman. Is he seen, or only heard? Does he face her, or speak from the side, or from behind? Is he prone or upright? (Only later in Gen. 3.15 do we learn that he had not yet received his crawling posture.) Is he, perhaps, as Western art and iconography would have it, coiled around the forbidden tree? We also have no idea what the woman looks like, other than the notion (Gen. 2.25) that she and her mate had no clothes. Was she beautiful? How old did she appear? Was her hair long or short, her skin light or dark? We can't know these things, and the absence of such details suggests that they are indeed irrelevant to the story's meaning. Since our familiar physical realities had not yet been ordained, it's far better to leave the physical description of Paradise and its denizens to the reader's imagination.

The same is true of the episode's temporal setting: we have no idea how long the couple resided in the Garden before their temptation— perhaps, as rabbinic legend has it, no more than a day; or, on the other hand, perhaps days, weeks, months, years, even aeons. Though the story's characters may be conscious of the orders of cyclical time created by God in Genesis 1.14, they do not yet have historical time. The way that the human couple have been passing their "time" is therefore of no interest to the storyteller.

The same is true of the way the characters' thoughts are represented. Though we can surmise certain things about the woman's state of mind from her words to the serpent, we have no detailed information about her thoughts prior to verse six, and even there we are given no clear understanding of how the woman's thoughts, reported only in Gen. 3.6 ("The woman saw that the tree was good for food, that it was pleasant to the eyes and delightful was the tree to contemplate [or: to make one wise] . . ."), relate to the temptation dialogue that has preceded. This ambiguity suggests, as we have noted, that the confrontation with the serpent could be a figment of the woman's imagination, a dialogue with her own more "beastly" nature. Most important, we are not told anything about the man's position in the action, other than (Gen. 3.6) his passive reception of the forbidden fruit which the woman holds forth. As already noted, it is as if the man had been there all along. The irrelevance of the factors leading up to the man's temptation suggest that the only thing we need to know about the man is the outcome of his decision: that he took the fruit and that he was as guilty as his companion in the transaction. It is of the nature of temptation to be irrelevant to the material fact of one's guilt.

Referring again to our diagram (the diagram is ultimately no substitute for the narration itself, but it helps us understand its major movements), we can see how the Garden story is, like many or most biblical stories, composite in origin. It is woven together out of small bits of traditionary lore: namings, etiological summaries, implied etiologies, poem fragments, epigrams, and here and there, as in the "temptation" scene, some actual narration. The creation of man from the soil; the creation of the Garden; its location at the fount of cosmic waters; the creation of beasts from the soil and their naming by the man; the creation of woman from man's rib; the poetic strophes of man's first naming of woman; the etiological summary; and so forth—all can be shown to be independent folk motifs (called, in rhetoricians' language, "topoi") that could well have been borrowed from other stories or lore. This composite merging of themes not only gives us a coherent and connected narrative, it requires us to read the story on several levels at once: it is a fable about the human life cycle (all of its stages have been represented: birth, adolescence, leaving of the "parental" household, marriage, sexual awakening, procreation, labor, and death); about the differences between beast, man, and divinity; about the origin of human society, its economy, culture, and technology (recounting in the process the origin of clothes, agriculture, breadmaking, toolmaking, subordination of woman and beast to man); and about disobedience to God and its consequences. While the temptation scene is homogeneous and self-contained, it takes its position in a complex collage of cultural themes.

Among these broader cultural issues, the most important is perhaps the story's accounting of the origins of the impulse to cooperate with one's successor generations. This is an impulse we tend to take for granted, but without it no culture, no civilization, no morality can exist. Human wisdom is cumulative in character and requires a kind of commonwealth in time, making use of the experience of each generation, each historical moment. A storyteller, seeking a concrete and familiar way to embody this problem would quite understandably see the conceiving or bearing of children as a pivotal symbol for the complex process of generational continuity. The choice of this theme is evident in the story's framework. Genesis 2.4 states: "These are the generations of heaven and earth, once they were created. . . ." The word *toledot* can be translated either as "generations of . . ." or as "story of, history of . . ." The first verse that follows the Garden story (Gen. 4.1) states: "And the man 'knew' his wife Eve, and she conceived and she bore *(vatteled)* Cain. . . ." Again, wordplay—here on two levels: the word "knew" harkens back to the Garden story and its theme of knowledge; the word "bore" *(vatteled)* back to the original headnote about "generations" *(toledot)*. The Garden story's main concern, therefore, is childbearing, and the story's "temptation" episode may thus be about the moment of sexual awakening that will lead to it.

The reader may, at this point, experience a complicated mixture of questions and reservations about this way of reading a biblical story. Can a simple fable speak on such complicated levels? Isn't this something we're reading into the text? If the biblical author wanted to justify the grounds for procreation, why would he represent such a praiseworthy act as marital cohabitation (something in fact *commanded* in Genesis 1.28: " . . . Be fruitful and multiply . . .") as a transgression? And besides, who says the temptation episode refers to *sexual* temptation? No such thing is mentioned in the text itself!

To attempt a partial answer: yes, a simple fable *can* speak on such complicated levels; and yes, this *is* something we read into the text. Every biblical narrative text is qualified by its context, and therefore it is quite an appropriate procedure to interpret a narrative in the light of nonnarrative materials that surround it. It is only in the light of its nonnarrative framework that the temptation scene can be about sexual temptation, and a commanded action can turn into a transgression. If this introduces contradictions into our understanding of God's will, it is because a biblical author (or perhaps the tradition itself) experienced genuinely contradictory feelings about the nature of procreation: we want it and need it, but it brings along so much that we don't want, as other biblical stories demonstrate: sibling rivalry; domestic strife; children who don't walk in their parents' ways, and so forth. That is why it is an interesting and worthwhile subject of story and reflection in the first place. So it's quite appropriate that even God would be represented as ambivalent on the matter, though of course one wouldn't *say* as much.

It is far easier, and far more suggestive, to let the reader draw his or her own conclusions.

A related problem that readers experience is the conflict of biblical and modern sensibilities. Modern readers often feel the need to choose sides in a debate for or against what they view, all too monolithically, as "the biblical point of view." The fact is that even the biblical editor experienced a conflict of sensibilities and chose to represent it dialectically—that is, by weaving together different sources, different modes of human discourse, and different literary styles and allowing them to clash. I'll have more to say about this method in my section on "What Biblical Narrative Is Saying," but meanwhile we should exercise caution lest we draw hasty conclusions about the Bible's "sexism," for example, or its "nationalism," or its "puritanism," or any other ism we care to ascribe to it, from our latter-day perspective. Every biblical story has a silent content that belies these tidy categories, and even in so simple and straightforward a narrative as that recounting the serpent's temptation of the woman, we can find multiple and possibly contradictory meanings. While there's always the possibility that we're overinterpreting, we can still incur the alternative danger of prematurely choosing a single "correct" reading—which, in its own way, is a form of overinterpretation as well. We must remain imaginatively alive to all possibilities, while reserving definitive judgments until we gain a cumulative impression of many texts.

One final structural observation about the Garden story will clarify our contextual understanding of the temptation scene: its symmetry. We notice (see diagram) that within the story's symmetry, there is a second symmetry, somewhat asymetrically off-center to the first. The two symmetries actually are very different, both in structure and meaning. The larger one has a center term; the smaller one does not. The larger one changes meaning radically from one term to the next, while the smaller one is built up from the same repeated action: denial. The larger one, despite its compositeness, has the shape of a story, while the smaller one more closely resembles a proverb. In this manner, we can see that the Garden story includes a commentary on itself, tucked unobtrusively into the midst of its dramatic action. The fact that the smaller symmetry lacks a center term is perfectly suited to the story's events; since the center of the story is the transgression, the little cameo of denial has as its center the "nothing" each denier hopes his or her share in the unseemly matter to be. Since each denial is matched by a corresponding "punishment," ordaining in the process our present-day biological realities, perhaps this short transgression is really about us, and about our attempts to minimize our involvement in our fate. The temptation and transgression scene, by contrast, is part and parcel of the story, its mythic center, and it, too, is more or less a symmetry: for each action, there is a consequence; for each definition, there is a counterdefinition. Seen this way, the central action, the transgression, can be an event both lamentable and historically meaningful.

I began these remarks on the Garden story with its central episode rather than with its beginning, in order to emphasize that biblical stories are often best understood from the center outward. A step-by-step commentary is misleading because it encourages us to think that the story's sequential progression is its only meaningful pattern. *Finding* the center of a story, of course, is no easy task—it may be the fruit of a long trial-and-error process for determining the shape of the whole. Perhaps I could have usefully presented this discussion from the reverse perspective, from the periphery of the story inward, or even presented a fully sequential commentary. The point is that we don't discover a biblical story's principles of order on the first, or perhaps even on the tenth reading. It is repeated exposure to the story—repeated savoring of its details and incongruities, extended reflection on its preoccupations and obsessions—that gives us our sense of its structure and meaning. Perhaps this matter can point us to the *first* steps in approaching the text as well. Since we can't determine either the borders or the center of a story overnight, we should begin with those details that exert the greatest tug on our attention, and move from there to the adjacent details and from there to the least adjacent. If we proceed on the assumption (a fairly safe one when we're dealing with the Bible!) that all elements are interrelated, we may eventually discover that interrelation in a manner that best accords with our own unique reader's instincts. So while there might be right and wrong methods in interpretation, there is no right or wrong order in which to pursue it. One can begin virtually anywhere in the text, as long as one remains concerned for the whole. At any rate, having surveyed in some depth a single story, it is now to the whole that I want to dedicate the concluding phase of our discussion.

WHAT BIBLICAL NARRATIVE IS SAYING

Given the enormous variety of subjects and literary forms in the Bible, and the long span of time in which the Hebrew Bible as we now know it gradually coalesced, it is impossible to distill *the* message of biblical narrative. Attempts to generalize yield only moral and theological truisms that do violence to the Bible's special way of talking. Biblical narrative rarely moralizes. It explores moral questions, to be sure, but it is in the wit and nuance of the specific moment that one is to find the narrative's intelligence most concentrated. This intelligence steadfastly withholds itself from stating "messages." It allows its messages to arise from silences in the narrative. In a sense, it is *weighing* messages, in that discordant voices in the tradition are allowed silently to clash, even as the narrative plunges inexorably forward.

This is not to say that the text lacks a point of view, or that it has no overarching design. It *is* possible to speak of "preoccupations" in biblical narrative, and as such to determine what the narrative is saying. It is *perhaps* possible to do so without doing violence to the Bible's way of talking, but the best summary of biblical narrative is the narrative itself. For readers who wish to determine what the narrative is saying beyond itself—and to serious readers, this is a lifetime discipline—I will try to suggest some guidelines for starting out.

First, the narrative from Genesis through Kings conceals the identity of its own speaker, or speakers. This is important, because it should discourage speculation on the identity of "the author," even if it is disguised as "the redactor." We are immeasurably closer to the *intelligence* of such an author than we are to his or her *identity*. This is so whether we regard that author as an individual, a school, a succession of authors, or the collective voice of an oral tradition. The only attributed "author" in this narrative corpus is Moses, and only for the bulk of Deuteronomy. Properly speaking, the Moses who speaks here is still a character, and his speeches are one long quotation within the larger narrative. The silence of the text about its own speaker is thus all-embracing, and it could mean many things—that to cite a speaker is unimportant, or that the speaker is God, or the tradition, or the people, or the sages, or "we," the readers.

Our sense of authorship, needless to say, likewise shifts in meaning with our choice of narrative unit and our definition of the scope of the unit. It is equally admissible to treat as a self-contained composition the Garden story, Genesis, or some larger combination of biblical books, up to the whole of Genesis through Kings. When we deal with the largest possible unit, what we look for is different from what we look for in a smaller composition. Yet the absence of an identified narrator, or of an attributed author, redactor, or patron, is consistent throughout, and may be part of what the narrative is saying.

Second, the narrative in some sense purports to be history. This we assume from its concern for chronology, its inclusion of archival material, its interest in political and military events, its preoccupation with etiology and long-range causality. Indeed, in its effort to supply a multiplicity of traditionary voices, the narrative anticipates the modern genre of documentary history, but it cannot be said to resemble history in the modern sense, in which the weighing of evidence by scientific criteria, a clear attribution of sources, and a general skepticism about what can be known prevail. In that the text itself sometimes refers the readers to other sources now lost (the "Book of Yashar," "The Chronicles of the Kings of Judah and Israel"), we must assume that it makes no pretense to being comprehensive history, as comprehensive as its chronological scope may seem. It is a highly selective presentation of events and may represent a very partisan and polemical perspective in relation to the culture of its milieu. So we should beware of an expression like "the biblical view of . . .," insofar as the makers of the Bible understood themselves to be abridging, distilling, and epitomizing far more complex domains of experience.

Unfortunately, we have very few independent corroborations of the factuality of biblical events—the stela of Pharaoh Merneptah, the inscription of King Mesha of Moab, and the annals of Sennacherib offer interesting perspectives on the Exodus, the reign of King Ahab, and the Assyrian conquest, respectively, but they can hardly be viewed as "parallel" sources. The spade of the archaeologist has turned up much valuable evidence from which to construct a picture of daily life and material culture in the biblical period, but few literary texts comparable to the Bible. The El-Amarna letters, for example, which represent the experiences of Canaanite kings in the era preceding Israel's Exodus, offer no independent corroboration of biblical events, apart from recording a general civil unrest in Canaan that accords with the breakdown of Egyptian and Canaanite power described in the Bible.

For better or for worse, the Bible's narrative, law, prophecy, and poetry are all we possess of a subjective view of ancient Israelite history. As such, it is invaluable, and the domain of history it claims for itself must be taken seriously in reconstructing life in ancient Israel. We may even assume that the reigns of kings recorded there, and certain of the key events and personalities, had much basis in fact. But we must distinguish between the Bible's chosen historiographic territory, and the somewhat different reconstruction of life in biblical times afforded by modern historical method. And in other respects—in its claim to represent a voice of divine revelation, in its function as a law book, and in its creation of a sense, if not the substance, of tradition and lore—the Bible is something quite other than a work of history or literature.

Third—and this flows from the preceding sentence—the narrative and nonnarrative materials of the Bible must not be read in isolation from one another. I have already shown how genealogical information can shape a narrative cycle, and similar subtleties may be seen in the interpenetration of narrative and law: the law of circumcision is placed into a cycle preoccupied with childbirth (Gen. 17, in the context of Gen. 12–25); the laws of Passover are intertwined with the Passover narrative; the Ten Commandments twice serve as a legal preamble (Exod. 20; Deut. 5), the initial laws of the Sinai covenant deal with release from slavery, as the narrative context demands; the laws of the Tabernacle are interwoven with the stories of its origin and inauguration, the laws of sin-offerings with stories of transgression, and the laws of disease control and purification with stories of plagues. It is often unclear whether the Bible uses narrative as a didactic prop for the laws, or the presentation of laws as events in the narrative. For a full understanding, we must be prepared to read the text both ways. The situation is analogous with narrative and poetry: sometimes the poetry seems to punctuate the narrative; at other times the narrative seems to be a commentary on the fragmentary poems. This dual valence, this sense of the interdependence of the tradition's various modes of discourse, may likewise be part of what the narrative is saying.

Finally, there are very distinctive and idiosyncratic properties to the kind of history the Bible purports to tell. It is, for example, in some sense a *world* history, insofar as it sets Israel's history against the events of Creation and the primordial generations of mankind. But its views of world history are bleak and repetitive: the surrounding nations are shown to have experienced one disaster after another, in accordance with their immoral and tyrannical societies. The principal motif of Genesis 2–11 is "curse," whereas that of Genesis 12–50 is "blessing." Israel and her ancestors are portrayed as having reversed the decay of human history and returned to the blessed and pristinely optimistic state of the Creation (Gen. 1.1–2.3).

From Exodus onward, the interplay of blessing and curse is more evenly mixed and more explicitly intertwined with the laws of the Sinai Covenant: blessing rests in performance of God's commandments and precepts, and curse arises from their abandonment. But this sense of reciprocal justice is already present in Genesis—I have offered examples of its operation there. Again, it is important to stress that the narrative withholds itself from moralizing; its scheme of justice emerges silently from the spare and almost calligraphic description of events. But the depiction of blessing and curse as contingent upon human choice, as rooted in a covenant between a human community and God, as dependent upon moral behavior, is unambiguous.

Biblical scholars have noticed two somewhat conflicting religious ideologies in the Bible, where the nature of the Israelite Covenant is concerned. One ideology they have termed a "conditional" covenant, and have associated it with the Sinai revelation, the premonarchic tribal confederation, and the antimonarchic prophetic movements of the tenth century B.C.E. onward. This covenant essentially stipulates that when Israel performs the will of God, she will enjoy God's blessings, and if not she will be cursed and will suffer natural and political disasters. Most important, it views Israel's tenure of the promised land as contingent on her fluctuating worthiness (like all other nations of Canaan) in the sight of God.

The other ideology, termed an "unconditional" covenant, has been associated with the Davidic monarchy and the nationalistic sentiments of the Solomonic era. The Abrahamic covenant of Genesis 17 has been associated with this ideology, though the author of Genesis 17 has been held to be Exilic or post-Exilic. Genesis 17 promises the land of Canaan to the descendants of Abraham as an "everlasting possession" (Gen. 17.8), and inaugurates an "everlasting covenant" (Gen. 17.19) with a yet-unborn Isaac. This "Abrahamic" covenant (symbolized by the sign of circumcision) bears a strong resemblance to the "everlasting" covenant between God and the house of David proclaimed in 2 Samuel 7.

Genesis 15, on the other hand, describes another type of Abrahamic covenant, remembered in rabbinic tradition as the "covenant between the [sacrificial animal] parts." It foretells the Exodus to Abraham, though without mentioning by name either Israel or Egypt: God explains that his descendants "will be strangers in a land not their own for 400 years," that their hosts will oppress them, that He will judge the oppressors and send forth Abraham's progeny with great wealth, and above all that in the meantime, "the iniquity of the Amorite (Canaanite) is not yet complete" (Gen. 15.16). This covenant's association with the Exodus, with reciprocal justice, and with a cycle of iniquity reflects more of the conditional view.

One wonders, of course, why the two senses of covenant, so opposed as they seem to be, coexist so intimately throughout the Bible, including the poetry and prophecy. (Is not the familiar distinction we tend to make between prophets of doom and prophets of consolation— sometimes the same prophet!—analogous to that between the covenants?) Obviously, they represent a polarity that lies at the heart of ancient Israelite history. In the final text we possess of the narrative running from Genesis through 2 Kings, both ideologies are skillfully interwoven and alternate almost in the fashion of a sonata. Wherever you find the unconditional perspective, the conditional is not far out of view. In a sense, both survived in later Judaism as different domains in the national and religious experience of the Jew: the conditional view oriented to everyday reality, to matters of law, justice, and ethics; the unconditional to utopian reality, to the realms of hope, dream, and prayer. If one believes moral struggle to be everlasting, then the two covenants are not in contradiction. The full trajectory of Genesis through Kings, at any rate, seems to be saying this.

To return for a moment to Genesis 15: the text speaks of a "fourth generation" *(dor reviʿi)* returning to the land to dispossess the Canaanite inhabitants (Gen. 15.16). This concept of a four-generation cycle of justice has a kind of inverse counterpart in the following motive clause attached to the second of the Ten Commandments:

> ". . . For I, YHWH, your God, am a zealous God, visiting the iniquity of the parents on the children, up to the third and the fourth generation among those that hate me, and doing kindness to the thousandth generation among those that love me and keep my commandments."
>
> —Exod. 20.5

Variants of this statement appear in Exodus 34.7, Numbers 14.18, and Deuteronomy 5.9. It appears to say, not that punishment for transgressions is certain to be visited upon the transgressor's own and immediately succeeding generations, but that it could be visited *as late as* the third or fourth generation, when those generations persist in the crime.

A suggestion of this pattern is already present in the Garden story, where the first human couple, instead of immediately dying for eating of the forbidden fruit, incur a delayed retribution, reflected in their long-term pattern of life, their awareness of mortality, and their loss of children through death and exile, as a concrete foretaste of the mortality they themselves will undergo. Every patriarch in Genesis lives out an echo of this pattern—experiences a foretaste of mortality through the presumed loss of a child. But Abraham and Isaac, at least, are portrayed as living unusually blessed lives, and the Canaanites of their era by and large behave toward them with uncommonly fair and courteous demeanor. (They behave, indeed, like a people whose "iniquity . . . is not yet complete.") The pattern is true also of Jacob, but to a lesser degree.

While each of the patriarchs experiences trials, Jacob's are unusually harsh: twenty-one years of exile from the land of his birth, turbulent relations with Canaanites (Gen. 34), blood guilt upon his children (ibid.), severance from his favorite son for at least fourteen years in his old age, including several years of famine, and finally, a death which, if occurring under conditions of reconciliation and good fortune, is still a death in exile in Egypt, the land of his descendants' servitude. Life decisively declines for this family in the third generation following Abraham.

I pointed out earlier that there seems to be a subtle causal relation in Genesis between Abraham's treatment of Hagar, Ishmael, and the sons of Ketura, on the one hand, and the role of the Ishmaelites and Midianites in the descent of Joseph, and thus of Israel, into Egypt, on the other. The initial Hagar episode (Gen. 16) stands, in fact, at the center of a symmetrical array of stories, bracketed between the two covenants (Gen. 15 and 17), and follows immediately upon the prophecy of the sojourn in Egypt. Hagar herself is an Egyptian, so that there is, as Martin Buber has shown, a circular correspondence between Abraham's oppression of an Egyptian and the Egyptians' oppression of his descendants. Israel's descent into Egyptian servitude in effect begins in the third and fourth generation after Abraham, and in that Moses lives in the fourth generation after Joseph, the period of Amorite/Canaanite (and Egyptian) "iniquity . . . not yet complete" coincides with the period of the ancestors' iniquity not yet expiated. This pattern is only visible when we read Genesis and Exodus as a continuous narrative, and its alleged sources as working together harmoniously in a single text.

Closely related to this hidden causal patterning is the narrative's penchant for surprise factors and sudden reversals. Two very common phenomena in the narrative are the ascent of younger offspring to power, and the pivotal role of women in the action. Both express the text's apparent delight in circumventing the most revered human conventions of power, status, and inheritance in order to highlight God's disregard for the trappings of human vanity, and to portray God as one who restlessly juggles the fortunes of persons, families, and nations in an effort to right the equilibrium of moral justice. God's action here is even seen as demonically playful, as in Hannah's song:

> Yea, a crafty God is YHWH; by Him much mischief is
> contrived,
> The bows of mighty men are smashed; they that stumble have
> grown strong,

> Those sated with food are hirelings, the hungry are [hungry] no more,
> The barren woman has borne seventy, the mother of many is forlorn,
> YHWH causes death and causes life, brings down to Sheol and raises up,
> YHWH disinherits and makes wealthy, humbles as He elevates,
> Raises the pauper from the dust, from dungheaps lifts the destitute,
> to scat them among princes, vouchsafes them the Throne of Glory!
> Truly, YHWH's are the world's extremities, on which He founds the world!
>
> —1 Sam. 2.3b–8

The obscure word *alilot,* which I here translate as "mischief" (some translators render: ". . . by Him is judged the mischief [of human beings]!" or simply: "by Him are judged all deeds"), is cognate to the word *hit'allalti* ("dealt mischievously") in the verses: "YHWH said to Moses, 'Go to Pharaoh, for I have hardened his heart, and that of his servants, so that I may place these signs in their midst, and so that you may tell into the ears of your child, and the child of your child, how I dealt mischievously in Egypt, and how I placed my signs into their midst, so you will know I am YHWH' " (Exod. 10.1–2). The "you" in this command conspicuously shifts from Moses to another subject, the "you" of later generations who would commemorate and retell the story of the Exodus. The turbulence and arbitrariness of God's action against sinners is balanced by the stability and security of those generations who "remember slavery in the land of Egypt." The nexus of the generations, which seems so fragile and so imperiled throughout the patriarchal narrative cycles and in numerous other stories, especially in 1/2 Samuel, is described in Exodus 10.1–2 and similar passages, as preserved and nurtured by education and tradition.

Paradoxically, that type of cultural continuity seems conspicuously *absent* in biblical narrative. Each generation is represented as having squeaked through. It is not to the narrative that we must turn, in order to find a concrete vision of generational continuity, but to biblical law, the subject of the next section in this chapter. There, a society is outlined in which the presence of elders, judges, magistrates, scribes, sages, and storytellers, and a system of education and jurisprudence are presupposed. The stories, by contrast, portray an undercommunicating and miscommunicating social milieu, in which generational discord and discontinuity are ever a threat. In a sense, without that tension and turbulence, there would be no biblical narrative: its characters would recede into the serene continuity of a genealogy. Narrative and poetry record the exceptional; genealogy and law record the norm. The exceptional is invoked to justify the norm.

So there is a hidden participant in biblical narrative, an onlooker who is perhaps at the same time a hidden character. The Bible's relentlessly "chronological" progression (despite the quirks and unevenness of narrative time) anticipates a continuation of the tradition it purports to depict, outside the borders of the text, by the future generations who read and retell. Their closest analogue in the text is not the narrative hero but the narrative background. Though much of the Bible's narrative focuses its interest on individual leaders, especially Moses, Saul, David, and Solomon, the people and their local leaders are ever their foil. They hover in the background like a chorus. They clamor for this and that. They run after temptations, they forget, they grow wanton. Such an unconscious and haphazardly navigating body politic, however, can only be perceived for what it is by an enlightened readership—that is, by members of a conscious and rationally navigating body politic. Someone is teaching someone else about the repeated failure of a society to govern itself. The text invites a readership concerned with the problems of both personal and communal self-governance. Kings, after all, are made from the ground up.

In this way, biblical narrative predicts its own interpretive history, while at the same time binding its readers to its world by a connection deeper, perhaps, than even law or genealogy: the force of parable and analogy. So the people Israel and their representative body, "the elders," are present even alongside Moses at Mount Sinai, when God decides to speak face to face:

> "Face to face YHWH spoke to you on the mountain and out of the fire. . . ."
>
> —DEUT. 5.4

> [The elders] saw the God of Israel. Under his feet, it was like the very heavens for brilliance. But upon the notables of the children of Israel, He did not put forth His hand. They saw God, and they ate, and they drank.
>
> —EXOD. 24.10–11

I think a lot about those elders, and about what they might have seen—most of which, of course, is tantalizingly withdrawn from view.

In the end, this phantom Sanhedrin (to borrow the rabbinic term for the later Israel's legislative body) who, from the standpoint of Israel's tradition history, may be older than Moses, turns out to serve as an admirable metaphor of biblical narrative itself: a body of anonymous observers, who, having coalesced to produce biblical tradition, merge, finally, with the narrative's postexilic and postbiblical interpreters. The text is a full portrait of the body, in several senses of the term: individual, household, national. This text's oneness out of many, its own resemblance to a body of conflicting impulses, its implicit confusion of past, present, and future are perhaps what enabled the kabbalists of a later era to read the Bible's very human and largely unmetaphysical narratives as mysteries of the inner life of God. As perhaps they are.

WHERE TO GO FROM HERE

The past decade or so has represented an enormous expansion of literary studies of the Bible. Until then, biblical scholarship had concentrated its interest on highly technical questions, such as those raised by *source criticism* (study of how various books, segments, and strata in biblical literature originated, and how they coalesced), *form criticism* (study of genres, oral storytelling patterns, and folk motifs in the Bible), *tradition history* (study of how traditions arose in ancient Israel and coalesced at the preliterary level), *redaction criticism* (study of how the Bible was edited into books, collections, and canons), and an offshoot of form criticism, *rhetorical criticism* (study of rhetorical patterns and repetitions in the text). More will be said about these disciplines later, but it should be noted that in spite of the great amount of useful information they've produced, they are not the best place for the beginner in the subject to start, in order to gain a literary sense of the Bible. Their profusion of verse, half-verse, and even quarter-verse references, their propensity for catalogues, lists, and diagrams, their tendency to slice up the text into hypothetical components, their excess of abbreviations and symbols render their discourse a forbidding thicket for the untrained. On the other hand, there are ways of making use of them, after one gains some experience in reading the Bible and biblical criticism.

The most accessible literary studies of the Bible have, as one might expect, been written by people involved in the study of (nonbiblical) literature, especially literary critics and literary artists. Actually, a very palatable and still useful work called *The Literary Study of the Bible* (Boston, New York, Chicago: D. C. Heath, 1899) was written by Richard

G. Moulton, a professor of English at the University of Chicago, as early as the turn of the century. Moulton explored a wide range of literary types and techniques in a pleasingly nontechnical style. Later, worthwhile popular introductions to biblical literature, such as Mary Ellen Chase's *The Bible and the Common Reader* (New York: Macmillan, 1952), Chase's sequel, *Life and Language in the Old Testament* (New York: Gramercy, 1955), and Maurice Samuel's *Certain People of the Book* (New York: Alfred A. Knopf, 1955) have more or less become classics of their kind. Samuel, in particular, takes upon himself the burdens of interpretation (which introductions to the Bible generally shy away from) with a great deal of empathy and imagination. In more recent times, Elie Wiesel's *Five Biblical Portraits* (Notre Dame, Ind.: University of Notre Dame Press, 1981) proceeds along lines similar to Samuel's, i.e., explores biblical characters, though neither work can properly be called an introduction to the literary study of the Bible.

The first chapter of Erich Auerbach's *Mimesis: the Representation of Reality in Western Literature* (Garden City, N.Y.: Anchor Books, 1955) contains a study of the story of Abraham's "sacrifice" of Isaac (Gen. 22) in comparison to Book 19 of Homer's *Odyssey*. This essay likewise has attained the status of a classic in the field of literary study of the Bible. In a different vein entirely is Roland Barthes' essay "The Struggle with the Angel: Textual Analysis of Gen. 32.22–32," in his book *Image, Music, Text* (New York: Hill and Wang, 1977). It is fortunate that Barthes, who was one of the subtlest and most interesting of French literary critics, managed to include the Bible among his many interests before his untimely death in 1980, but this essay, because of its difficulty, is not recommended for the beginner in either Bible or literature. The essays of Edmund Wilson's *Israel and the Dead Sea Scrolls* (New York: Farrar, Straus, & Giroux, 1978) began as articles in *The New Yorker,* and include a lengthy piece entitled "On First Reading Genesis."

Herbert N. Schneidau's *Sacred Discontent: The Bible and Western Tradition* (Berkeley, Los Angeles, and London: University of California Press, 1977) is a worthy discussion of the Bible's thematic impact on Western literature, which manages to communicate a great deal of interest about biblical narrative along the way. Northrop Frye's *The Great Code: The Bible and Literature* (New York and London: Harcourt Brace, Jovanovich, 1982), is in its own way, an approach to the same subject Schneidau deals with, but this time set in the context of an elaborate theory of literature begun in Frye's earlier works, especially *The Anatomy of Criticism* (Princeton, N.J.: Princeton University Press, 1957). Again, not for the beginner! Frye's view of the Bible, by which he means the Bible of Christianity, is a richly imaginative construction, but static, ahistorical, theoretical. In fact, there are no actual studies of biblical texts in this work. A planned sequel will handle that.

Probably the best work on biblical narrative by a literary critic, if not the best book on the subject altogether, is Robert Alter's *The Art of Biblical Narrative* (New York: Basic Books, 1981). In addition to a great variety of specific interpretations of biblical stories, written both sensibly and sensitively, Alter conveys a lively and informed sense of the intellectual issues currently at stake in literary study of the Bible. He draws our attention, in the process, to a wide variety of narrative techniques and literary phenomena in the Hebrew Bible, arising in exposition, dialogue, type-scene construction, characterization, and composite artistry. Alter has the advantage of being grounded both in the history of Western fiction and in the history of Hebrew literature. Lucidly and gracefully written, this is a highly useful and informative book for both scholars and beginners. Its generally favorable reception among biblical scholars and lay readers alike confirms this.

Some interesting uses have been made of the Bible by philosophers and literary critics on their way to saying other things. Among the most fascinating of these ventures: Nietzsche's *The Antichrist,* found in Walter Kaufmann, ed., *The Portable Nietzsche* (New York: Viking Press, 1968); Kierkegaard's *Fear and Trembling/Sickness Unto Death* (Garden City, N.Y.: Anchor Books, 1954); Sigmund Freud, *Moses and Monotheism* (New York: Random House, 1939, and later eds.); Kenneth Burke, *The Rhetoric of Religion* (Berkeley and Los Angeles: University of California Press, 1970); George Steiner, *Language and Silence* (New York: Atheneum, 1970); also, George Steiner, *After Babel: Aspects of Language and Translation* (New York, Oxford, London: Oxford University Press, 1975); Leszek Kolakowski, *The Keys to Heaven/Conversations with the Devil* (New York: Grove Press, 1972); Franz Rosenzweig, *The Star of Redemption* (New York: Holt, Rinehart & Winston, 1970); Ernst Bloch, *Atheism in Christianity* (New York: Herder and Herder, 1972); and Michel Serres, *The Parasite* (trans. L. R. Schehr; Baltimore and London: The Johns Hopkins University Press, 1982). None of these works can be called easy reading, but their energy, inventiveness, and exceptional style shine through the obscurities.

This is the place to mention interpretations of the Bible in modern fiction, poetry, and drama: Thomas Mann's *Joseph and his Brothers* (New York: Alfred A. Knopf, 1934–44) heads the list, of course, with its masterful, expansive, finely drawn recreation of life in biblical times. Lesser known is Mann's fictional treatment of Moses, *The Tablets of the*

Law (New York: Alfred A. Knopf, 1945, 1964), a briefer, essaylike work of great beauty and significance. Anthony Burgess's *Moses: A Narrative* (New York: Stonehill, 1976) is a long, narrative poem, quite good in places; Burgess's command of the Queen's English is in its usual top form. James Michener's *The Source* (New York: Random House, 1965) is a typically encyclopedic fable of successive eras of history at an archaeological site in northern Israel and includes several long episodes of life in biblical times. Archibald MacLeish's *J.B.* is a 1959 verse drama based on the book of Job. Stefan Heym, an East German writer who lived for a time in the United States, has written *The King David Report* (London, Melbourne, and New York: Quartet Books, 1977), a novel about David and Uriah the Hittite. Another novel on this subject is Moshe Shamir's *The Hittite Must Die* (New York and London: East and West Library, 1965), written originally in Hebrew.

Treatments of biblical themes, of course, abound in modern Hebrew and Yiddish literature. Shlomo Rosenberg's "The Birth of Solomon," David Frishman's "Sinai," H. N. Bialik's "King David's Cave," and Haim Hazaz's "The Bridegroom of Blood" can be found in Joseph Leftwich's anthology *Yisroel: The First Jewish Omnibus* (New York and London: Thomas Yoseloff, 1963). The bulk of Bialik's *Aggadot ha-Melekh David* (found in *Kol Kitve H. N. Bialik,* Tel Aviv: Devir, 1938, 1951) remains, alas, as yet untranslated, as well as Pinhas Sadeh's fine, offbeat novel *Mot Avimelekh va'aliyato hashamayma bizro'ot immo* (The Death of Abimelech and his Ascent to Heaven in the Arms of his Mother, Jerusalem: Schocken, 1975), a tale whose basis is Judges 9.

Unusual and noteworthy interpretations of biblical stories have been produced by contemporary theologian Arthur Waskow in *Godwrestling* (New York: Schocken Books, 1979). In a category by itself is Franz Kafka's *Parables and Paradoxes* (New York: Schocken Books, 1970), which includes a number of parables on biblical themes. As for treatments of biblical themes in Jewish poetry, one should above all consult T. Carmi, ed., *The Penguin Book of Hebrew Verse* (New York: Penguin Books, 1981); S. Y. Penueli and A. Ukhmani, eds., *Anthology of Modern Hebrew Poetry* (Jerusalem, 1966); R. F. Mintz, *Modern Hebrew Poetry* (Berkeley: University of California Press, 1966, 1981); S. Burnshaw, et al., eds., *The Modern Hebrew Poem Itself* (New York: Schocken Books, 1966); and Howard Schwartz and Anthony Rudolf, eds., *Voices Within the Ark: the Modern Jewish Poets* (New York: Avon Books, 1980).

One can see that outside the professional world of biblical scholarship, literary interpretation of the Bible has been around for a long time. Quite new, however, is the sudden intensification of interest in literary approaches to the Bible among biblical scholars themselves within the past ten to fifteen years. An early, fairly readable and nontechnical expression of this interest is Kenneth R. R. Gros Louis, et al., *Literary Interpretations of Biblical Narratives* (Nashville and New York: Abingdon Press, 1974). This has been followed up by a sequel, K. R. R. Gros Louis with James S. Ackerman, eds., *Literary Interpretations of Biblical Narratives,* Vol. 2 (Nashville and New York: Abingdon Press, 1982). These volumes include some noteworthy essays, among others, by Gros Louis, Ackerman, and Edward Greenstein. James Barr's *The Bible in the Modern World* (New York: Harper and Row, 1973) contains a useful chapter on "The Bible as Literature." One should also note the sophisticated treatment by D. Robertson, "Literature, the Bible as," in *The Interpreter's Dictionary of the Bible,* Supp. Vol. (Nashville: Abingdon, 1978).

Underlying this surge of literary interest among biblical scholars is a growing disillusionment with the historical-critical method inherited from nineteenth-century biblical scholarship, and with so-called "diachronic" approaches, namely, approaches that seek to reconstruct the development of a biblical story *through time,* by determining the underlying literary strata, preliterary oral forms, and tradition history. Ironically, one of the pioneering works in diachronic method, Julius Wellhausen's *Prolegomena to the History of Ancient Israel* (1883; trans. and repr., Gloucester, Mass.: Peter Smith, 1973) was an exceptionally well-written and nontechnical book, still useful today in characterizing biblical narrative. Similarly, Herman Gunkel's *The Legends of Genesis* (1901; repr., New York: Schocken Books, 1970) was an equally readable short introduction to the methods of form criticism, the study of preliterary oral forms in the Bible. Gunkel's monumental German-language commentary on Genesis (1901), for which *The Legends of Genesis* was originally written as an introduction, served as a vast reservoir of parallels between the Bible and world literature and mythology. Gunkel's *The Folktale in the Old Testament,* first published in 1917, has recently been published in English by the Almond Press in England.

Useful summaries of historical-critical method in study of the Bible, both source- and form-critical, are offered by Herbert F. Hahn, *The Old Testament in Modern Research* (Philadelphia: Fortress Press, 1966) and H. H. Rowley, *The Old Testament and Modern Study* (London, Oxford, New York: Oxford University Press, 1961), as well as the older work, H. W. Robinson, *Record and Revelation* (Oxford: Oxford University Press, 1938). Good general introductions to the Bible include R. F. Pfeiffer, *Introduction to the Old Testament* (New York: Harper and Row,

1948); O. Eissfeldt, *The Old Testament: An Introduction* (New York: Harper and Row, 1965); E. Sellin and G. Fohrer, *Introduction to the Old Testament* (Nashville: Abingdon, 1965); A. Bentzen, *Introduction to the Old Testament* (Copenhagen: G. E. C. Gad, 1967); and, on a less technical level, Samuel Sandmel, *The Hebrew Scriptures* (New York: Oxford University Press 1978), and Sandmel's shorter work, *The Enjoyment of Scripture* (New York: Oxford University Press, 1972).

Counterposed, however, to the so-called diachronic methods is a newer "synchronic" method, which seeks to read a biblical story as a whole system, regardless of its composite sources and its preliterary history. Ample discussion and applications of this method can be found in M. J. Buss, ed., *Encounter with the Text: Form and History in the Hebrew Bible* (Philadelphia/Missoula, Mont.: Fortress Press/Scholars Press, 1979); Robert Polzin, *Biblical Structuralism: Method and Subjectivity in the Study of Ancient Texts* (Philadelphia/Missoula: Fortress Press/Scholars Press, 1977), Robert Polzin, *Moses and the Deuteronomist* (New York: Seabury Press, 1980); R. C. Culley, *Studies in the Structure of Hebrew Narrative* (Philadelphia/Missoula: Fortress Press/Scholars Press, 1976); R. Polzin and E. Rothman, eds., *The Biblical Mosaic: Changing Perspectives* (Philadelphia/Chico, Calif.: Fortress Press/Scholars Press, 1982); R. Barthes, F. Bovon, et al., *Structural Analysis and Biblical Exegesis* (Pittsburgh: The Pickwick Press, 1974). In a less structuralist vein is the very useful collection, R. Friedman, ed., *The Creation of Sacred Literature* (Berkeley and Los Angeles: University of California Press, 1982).

In a similar spirit to that of the synchronic approach are a number of books written by persons from outside the field of Bible or literature, most notably, Edmund Leach, *Genesis as Myth and Other Essays* (London: Jonathan Cape, 1969), a study of the Bible from the standpoint of structural anthropology, and Steven J. Brams, *Biblical Games: A Strategic Analysis of Stories in the Old Testament* (Cambridge, Mass. and London: MIT Press), a very readable and accessible study of biblical narrative from the standpoint of modern game theory. Anthropologist Mary Douglas's *Purity and Danger: An Analysis of the Concepts of Pollution and Taboo* (London: Routledge & Kegan Paul, 1978), while not about biblical literature per se, has some interesting things to say about biblical thought categories in her chapter on the dietary laws of Leviticus, as does her "Deciphering a Meal," in *Dedalus* (Winter 1972).

Extended textual studies in the synchronic mode have tended to be somewhat disappointing. Take, for example, the work of Dutch scholar J. P. Fokkelman, *Narrative Art in Genesis* (Amsterdam: Van Gorcum, Assen, 1975) and *Narrative Art and Poetry in the Books of Samuel, vol. 1:*

King David (Amsterdam: Van Gorcum, Assen, 1981). Fokkelman is an imaginative and ingenious interpreter of biblical narrative, but his books are exasperatingly meandering and numbingly technical. He exhibits a nice sensitivity to wordplay, formal patterns, and plot ironies, but in the end, especially in the book on King David, the reader is left preferring the simplicity and elusiveness of the text to the explanatory pyrotechnics of the interpreter. The same can be said of C. C. Conroy's *Absalom Absalom! Narrative and Language in 2 Sam. 13–20* (Rome: Biblical Institute Press, 1978), which seems to confuse the mechanistic cataloguing of verb tenses, action patterns, and narrative strategies with the empathy and insight that great literature generates in readers. A more successful, if still uninspired, interpretation of the David story is D. M. Gunn's *The Story of King David: Genre and Interpretation* (Sheffield: *Journal for the Study of the Old Testament,* supp. series, 1978), appealing partly because it argues its points with a certain "biblical" economy.

Perhaps one of the best literary studies by a biblical scholar working in a synchronic mode is Michael Fishbane's *Text and Texture: Close Readings of Selected Biblical Texts* (New York: Schocken Books, 1979)—concise, balanced, erudite without bullying, and in general, informed by a coherent philosophy of the biblical text and a clear sense of what one can learn from it. His chapters on the Jacob cycle and the Eden motif are particularly groundbreaking and suggestive treatments (based on longer, more technical studies in academic publications). Of similar caliber are the various studies by Robert Polzin (see above), who manifests the rare capacity for insights that are both trustworthy and exciting. His study of Job in *Biblical Structuralism* and of Deuteronomy in *Moses and the Deuteronomist* are among the best new interpretations of these works.

Fishbane, it should be noted, has been strongly influenced in his work by the biblical translations and scholarship of Martin Buber and Franz Rosenzweig, who advanced a theory of *Leitwörter,* thematically important words that echo through a text and supply guidelines for interpretation. The Buber-Rosenzweig German translation of the Bible is gradually being rendered into English by Everett Fox, whose Genesis translation was recently issued by Schocken books. Of Buber's various writings on the Bible, *Moses: the Revelation and Covenant* (New York: Harper and Row, 1958) and *On the Bible: Eighteen Studies* (New York: Schocken Books, 1968) are the most accessible. His *The Kingship of God* (New York: Harper and Row, 1967) is at present out of print, probably because of its difficulty, but it is a worthwhile and important book about a much misunderstood biblical theme and its reputation is currently on the rise among biblical scholars.

In theory, there should be no such thing as "Jewish biblical scholarship," since impartial study of the Bible should not advance the views of a particular religion. Nevertheless, by generally *refraining* from advancing some of the biases of Protestant scholarship (especially the Hegelian Christianity inherent in Wellhausen's "Documentary Hypothesis" —see my chapter), modern Jewish interpreters have created a distinctive scholarship of their own. Foremost in this vein was Benno Jacob, whose masterful German commentary on Genesis is perhaps the best of its kind in our century. The English abridgment of this work by his son Ernest I. Jacob and his grandson Walter Jacob (*The First Book of the Bible: Genesis,* New York: Ktav, 1974) is an inadequate and superficial approximation of the original—we badly need an unabridged version.

Similarly opposed to Wellhausen was the Italian-Jewish Semiticist Umberto Cassuto, who taught during the latter part of his life at Hebrew University. His planned commentary on the Torah was left unfinished. The work he did complete—*From Adam to Noah* (Jerusalem: Magnes Press, 1972), *From Noah to Abraham* (Jerusalem: Magnes Press, 1964), and *A Commentary on the Book of Exodus* (Jerusalem: Magnes Press, 1974) —conveys a sufficient sense of his method: a good command of intra-biblical parallels, a respect for the integrity of the text, an awareness of fine points of grammar and lexicography, and an effective use of medieval Jewish commentators. For biblical interpretation more or less exclusively based on the medieval commentators, see the very useful and illuminating work of Nehama Leibowitz, *Studies in Bereshit (Genesis), Studies in Shemot (Exodus),* etc. (Jerusalem: World Zionist Organization, 1972 onward). I should reiterate here that Midrash and medieval Jewish commentary should be standard equipment in any study of biblical literature. See the articles on these subjects elsewhere in this book.

Not all Jewish biblical scholars, it should be noted, reject the methods or results of source-criticism. In a more mainstream vein are the following excellent works: Nahum M. Sarna, *Understanding Genesis* (New York: Schocken Books, 1970) and Moshe Greenberg, *Understanding Exodus* (New York: Behrman House, 1959). Both are part of a series sponsored by the Melton Research Center of the Jewish Theological Seminary, and each has an accompanying student's workbook and teacher's guide.

Contemporary English-speaking Jewry has long needed a one-volume Torah commentary to replace the stodgy, bombastic, synagogue edition, *Pentateuch and Haftorahs,* edited by J. H. Hertz. That need has now been well served by W. Gunther Plaut and the late Bernard J. Bamberger (with essays on the ancient Near East by William Hallo) in their work *The Torah: A Modern Commentary* (New York: Union of American Hebrew Congregations, 1982). It now sells for around $30, which for an 1,800-page work of such high quality is a real bargain. Though the book was published by the Reform movement, its importance and appeal will transcend the divisions of American Jewry.

The Plaut–Bamberger work is based on the new Jewish Publication Society translation, which at present may be the best English translation available. I prefer it to the Revised Standard Version, the New English Bible, and the Jerusalem Bible, and a host of lesser translations. Everett Fox's Buber-Rosenzweig translation, mentioned earlier, may prove a serious rival, but one is really talking about two opposed theories of translation—essentially, contextual vs. literal. The NJPS falls into the former category, and my own biases lead me to prefer this method, but I look forward to pleasant surprises from Fox.

Some important standard commentaries on individual biblical books include the following series: *The Anchor Bible, The Westminster Old Testament Library, The International Critical Commentary,* and *The Interpreter's Bible.* Among major reference works, one should above all note *The Interpreter's Dictionary of the Bible.*

Among histories of ancient Israel, one should keep in mind John Bright, *A History of Israel* (Philadelphia: Westminster, 1948 and later eds.), Martin Noth, *The History of Israel* (New York: Harper and Row, 1958), Roland deVaux, *The Early History of Israel* (Philadelphia: Westminster, 1978), and Norman K. Gottwald, *The Tribes of Yahweh: A Sociology of the Religion of Liberated Israel, 1250–1050 B.C.E.* (Maryknoll, N.Y.: Orbis Books, 1979).

Noth's *A History of Pentateuchal Traditions* (Englewood Cliffs, N.J.: Prentice-Hall, 1979) remains the most important work in the field of tradition history, alongside G. von Rad's *The Problem of the Hexateuch and Other Essays* (Edinburgh: Oliver and Boyd, 1966) and Albrecht Alt's *Essays on Old Testament History and Religion* (Garden City, N.Y.: Anchor Books, 1968).

In the field of rhetorical criticism, one should note J. J. Jackson, ed., *Rhetorical Criticism: Essays in Honor of James Muilenberg* (Pittsburgh: Pickwick Press, n.d.), which includes a bibliography of the writing of the discipline's originator, James Muilenberg. Muilenberg in certain ways anticipated the approaches of the synchronic method.

The best anthology of ancient Near Eastern literature (important to study of the Bible for comparative purposes) is James A. Pritchard's *Ancient Near Eastern Texts* (Princeton, N.J.: Princeton University Press, 3rd ed., 1969), which also has been abridged as *The Ancient Near East:*

An Anthology of Texts and Pictures (Princeton, 1971) and *The Ancient Near East, Volume II: A New Anthology of Texts and Pictures* (Princeton, 1975).

Important journals in biblical studies include *The Journal of Biblical Literature* and *Vetus Testamentum,* two publications devoted to diachronic method that have in recent years included articles of a more synchronic type. *Semeia,* on the other hand, was created explicitly for studies in a synchronic and structuralist mode. *Society of Biblical Literature Seminar Papers,* an annual publication issued in connection with the society's conferences, often carries articles of literary interest. *Biblica* and *Interpretation* are also quite useful, as is the British *Journal for the Study of the Old Testament.* Somewhat more accessible to the lay reader are articles that sometimes appear on biblical topics in the *Journal of Jewish Studies,* the *Harvard Theological Review,* and *Prooftexts: A Journal of Jewish Literary History.* The biblical articles in the *Hebrew Union College Annual* are diachronic studies of generally high quality.

The following books on the Bible are ones that I have not made use of in my own work on the Bible, but which should be mentioned here, without attempt at evaluation:

James L. Crenshaw. *Samson: A Secret Betrayed, A Vow Ignored.* Atlanta: John Knox Press, 1978.

E. M. Good. *Irony in the Old Testament.* Philadelphia: Westminster, 1965.

David M. Gunn. *The Fate of King Saul: An Interpretation of a Biblical Story.* Sheffield: JSOT Press, 1980.

Jacob Licht. *Storytelling in the Bible.* Jerusalem: Magnes Press, 1978.

Jack M. Sasson. *Ruth: A New Translation with a Philological Commentary and a Formalist-Folklorist Interpretation.* Baltimore: Johns Hopkins University Press, 1979.

Certain readers may wish to pursue more general reading on the nature of narrative. The most useful to the study of the Bible are the following: Claude Lévi-Strauss, *Structural Anthropology* (Garden City, N.Y.: Anchor Books, 1967); Roland Barthes, *Image, Music, Text* (cited above); Albert Lord, *The Singer of Tales* (New York: Atheneum, 1965); Wayne C. Booth, *The Rhetoric of Fiction* (Chicago: University of Chicago Press, 1961); Vladimir Propp, *The Morphology of the Folktale* (Austin: University of Texas, 1968); Boris Uspensky, *A Poetics of Composition* (Berkeley: University of Calif., 1973).

The foregoing should more than suffice the ambitious reader. Naturally, you don't need to read every single book on this list in order to become an informed reader of the Bible. The main factor is continued direct exposure to biblical texts themselves, along with ample time to reflect. It is, properly speaking, a lifetime task to learn how to become the kind of reader of the Bible that the biblical authors anticipated. So, take your time. Let the text flirt with you. And let your best guide be your own reader's instincts.

COURTESY OF THE LIBRARY OF THE JEWISH THEOLOGICAL SEMINARY OF AMERICA

From Deuteronomy 24, Bible manuscript from Spain, 15th century.

B. BIBLICAL LAW

EDWARD L. GREENSTEIN

For the ancients, religion was already to a certain extent what it should become for us—practical poetry." With this insight the German poet of the romantic period, Novalis, provides a useful perspective on the Bible: what we now call religion embodied in antiquity, not a segment or area of life, but an entire world view that permeated, ordered, and shaped the full range of human behavior. Religion was not a distinctive sector of experience but an ingredient of all experience. Perhaps on account of its pervasiveness, religion was not distinguished in the Bible by a name of its own; there is no word for "religion" per se in biblical Hebrew. The Bible encompasses a variety of genres: stories, hymns, proverbs, prayers, laws, prophetic speeches, and more. Yet the particular religious world view of the Bible cuts across these diverse materials, organizes them, and gives them unity. Even such discrete genres as laws and narratives may interrelate. In fact, we shall see that the civil and ritual laws of the Bible are informed and given distinctive shape by two great mythic stories: the Creation and the Exodus.

TORAH AND LAW

The most sacred part of the Jewish Bible, the Torah, or Five Books of Moses, presents an integrated—though not necessarily consistent—picture of God, the world, the peoples that populated it, and the rules by which one people, Israel, was to live in it, with heavy emphasis on the last-named category. The Torah has for good reason been called "the

83

Law." The bulk of its material (the latter half of Exodus, Leviticus, a good part of Numbers, and the core of Deuteronomy) comprises the regulations by which Israel is to fulfill its duties to God. The title "Law," however, is of Greek, not Hebrew, origin and derives from the word *nomos,* "law." This is familiar from the name of the fifth book of the Torah, *Devarim* in Hebrew. This Hebrew name means "words" and is taken from the first words of the book: "These are the words that Moses spoke to the Israelites across the Jordan. . . ." But in the Greek translation of the Bible adopted by the Christian Church, the book was entitled *Deutero-nomos* (Latin, *Deuteronomium,* English, Deuteronomy), which describes its contents as a review of the law, a "second law." ★

The Hebrew word *torah* does not strictly mean "law." The fact that it does not is crucial to its role in Judaism. Hebrew does employ words for a "statute," a "ruling," and, of course, *mitzvah,* a "commandment." But the word *torah* itself means "instruction" or "teaching." The laws of the Torah are one of its means of teaching; they are the specific behaviors by which God inculcates his ways—what we call values—in his human creatures. If we are to understand these values we must read the laws, in a sense, as a sort of body language that outwardly symbolizes something of much deeper significance.

Biblical law's didactic function is all the more striking when we notice that, contrary to the common view, the Torah does not encompass a complete code of law. It is selective, illustrative, paradigmatic. Its arrangement is imbalanced. Some laws are repeated twice or more; laws we would expect to find are often absent. Moreover, with the exception of the cultic rites of Deuteronomy, there is no evidence that the Torah's laws circulated in ancient Israel as a practical guide or anthology of precedents. (There is evidence to the contrary, more on which later.) This appears less surprising when we compare the fate of the famous Code of the great king Hammurapi of Babylon, from the eighteenth century B.C.E., five centuries before Moses. Hammurapi had his laws incised on a tall black monument and erected it inside a shrine. He sought to impress the gods with how responsibly and fairly he had been governing the lands that the gods had placed in his charge. But of the thousands of legal documents that have been unearthed from ancient Mesopotamia, not one clearly cites this great Code for authority! *The Torah's laws, too, seem to have served less as a tool for the judiciary than as a vehicle for religious instruction.* The religious character of the law is further

---

★ This name in turn derived from the phrase *mishneh torah,* "double [copy] of the *torah,*" in Deut. 17.18.

suggested by the fact that once God had declared what the law was, the task of disseminating the law was entrusted to the tribe of Levi, the priests:

> They shall teach your rulings to Jacob and your teaching to Israel.
>
> —DEUT. 33.10

The various norms that God commands the Israelites in the Torah were calculated to instill abstract values through concrete acts.

GOD AS KING

In a carving atop the monument bearing Hammurapi's Code, the god of justice, Shamash (Sun), hands the monarch the insignia of power, imparting to him the values that he will embody in his legislation. In the epilogue to his Code, Hammurapi proudly boasts of

> Just laws which Hammurapi, the able king, has set up so that the land will adhere to honest administration and good governance. . . . So that the strong does not harm the weak, to provide justice for the orphan and widow . . . have I inscribed my precious words on my monument, set them up before my statue, "The King of Justice."

As Hammurapi's statement shows, ancient Near Eastern law outside the Torah differentiates between principles of justice and the laws themselves. But in the Torah God dictates the laws directly, without human intermediation.

Indeed, for Deuteronomy the king must take special pains to consult God's law:

> It will be when [the king] sits on the chair of his kingship, he shall have a copy of this teaching written on a scroll by the levitical priests. It shall be with him and he shall read out of it all the days of his life so that he learns to revere the Lord his God, to keep all the words of this teaching and these statutes, to do them.
>
> —DEUT. 17.18–19

The Torah conceives of God as Israel's true king. This concept is manifested in a number of ways: by the story of the Torah from Genesis through Exodus, by the nature of the Covenant, and by the symbolism of the *mishkan* (God's palace among the Israelites). We shall examine each of these in turn.

First, the Torah's narrative establishes the Lord's right to rule, his legitimacy, as it were. God creates and controls all lands and all peoples. Out of the many peoples, he covenants with one, Abraham and his descendants, promising them the land of Canaan and numerous progeny. The people of Israel cannot remain in the land that will be called Israel until they have accepted the laws of God. Jacob's name became Israel only after he had wrestled with God (Gen. 32.22–32). In order to ensure that Israel will accept his laws, God places the Israelites in a position of indebtedness: he creates a famine and thereby forces Jacob and his sons to descend to Egypt, where they are enslaved; then God liberates them magnificently. By hardening Pharaoh's heart and extending the number of plagues in Egypt to ten, the Lord impresses both the Egyptians and the Israelites with his power (see Exod. 10.1–2). When the Lord splits the Reed Sea★ for the Israelites to cross and then drowns the pursuing army of Egypt, he earns the Israelites' trust (Exod. 14.31). He further increases their dependence by sending them into the wilderness where they will need him to provide water and food— manna and quail. When he brings the Israelites to Mount Sinai to impose his laws upon them, he reminds them that he has been their benefactor:

> You have seen that which I did to Egypt. I have carried you on
> the wings of eagles and I have brought you to me.
> —Exod. 19.4

And just as he begins to present the Ten Commandments, he declares:

> I am the Lord your God who have taken you out from the land
> of Egypt, from a house of slaves.
> —Exod. 20.2

That God coerced the Israelites into accepting the regimen of his commandments finds vivid expression in a Midrash of the classic rabbis (see Chapter Three for more on Midrash). In Exodus 19.17 the Torah states that at Sinai the Israelites "stood up at the bottom of the mountain." The word for "bottom," however, denotes literally "underneath." How could the Israelites be standing *underneath* the mountain? The word, felt the rabbis, contains a fuller tale. The Lord raised the mountain over the Israelites' heads and, threatening to drop it, asked the

★ What is usually called the Red Sea is termed the "Reed" Sea *(yam suf)* by the Bible.

Israelites if they would accept the obligations of the Torah. Displaying a profound instinct for survival, the people responded, "All that the Lord has spoken, we will do" (Exod. 19.8).

GOD AS A COVENANT PARTNER

The Torah conceives of Israel as God's slaves or, more properly, vassals. In order to free the Hebrews from their Egyptian bondage, the Lord has Moses command Pharaoh: "Release my people that they may serve me in the wilderness!" The Hebrew verb for "to serve" or "worship" *(avad)* also lies at the base of the word for "slave" *(eved)*. The word for slave also denotes "vassal," and the Torah models the God-Israel relationship on that of a mighty king and his vassals. The overlord furnishes sustenance and protection, the vassals owe exclusive devotion —worship of one God; and acts of fealty—observance of the commandments. In fact, as modern scholars have long noted, the covenant between the Lord and the Israelites hews to the pattern of an ancient Near Eastern vassal treaty. Such a treaty is imposed after an overlord conquers or performs some great favor for lesser kings. He then commits them to provisions of allegiance; they must, for example, come to his aid in war. After spelling out the vassals' obligations, the overlord invokes "the great gods of heaven and earth" to pronounce blessings for loyalty and curses for betrayal. That the biblical covenant follows the form of ancient vassal treaties is most obvious in the books of Leviticus and Deuteronomy, where the corpus of laws concludes with lengthy series of blessings and curses. For example:

> Blessed be you in the town, and
> blessed be you in the field.
> Blessed be the fruit of your womb,
> and the fruit of your ground,
> and the fruit of your cattle, the
> calving of your oxen, and the fecundity
> of your sheep.
> Blessed be your basket and your bowl.
> Blessed be you in your entering, and
> blessed be you in your exiting . . .

> Cursed be you in the town, and
> cursed be you in the field.
> Cursed be your basket and your bowl.
> Cursed be the fruit of your womb and
> the fruit of your ground, the calving

of your oxen, and the fecundity of your sheep.
Cursed be you in your entering and
cursed be you in your exiting . . .
(Deuteronomy 28.3–6. 16–19)

If Israel serves God faithfully, adopting his ways, they will dwell securely in a "land flowing with milk and honey"; but if they rebel, they will be exiled and their land devastated.

Israel's anxiety over satisfying God and holding onto its land reverberates in the Torah's first story about people, the Garden of Eden story. The Lord commands the man and woman to do one thing: refrain from eating of the tree of the knowledge of good and evil. They violate this single prohibition and are expelled from the garden.

Christian tradition reads this story as evidence of "original sin," the irreparable flaw in human nature that can be redeemed only by God's sacrifice of his only son. In the context of the Torah, however, the man and woman leave the mythical garden to live a mundane existence in the real world. They do not "fall" from grace. Although the Lord of Israel may make severe demands and pronounce terrifying threats, he is characterized in the Torah as

> a God loving and kind, slow to anger and greatly devoted and faithful; staying devoted to thousands [of generations], tolerating crime, betrayal, and sin; [yet] he will not call [the guilty] innocent, innocent, tendering the crime/punishment of fathers on sons and on sons-of-sons, on the third [generation] and on the fourth.
>
> —Exod. 34.6–7

According to Deuteronomy, Moses could ply God into forgiving Israel their transgressions by reminding him that they're only human. He would evoke the ancestors who showed outstanding trust:

> Pay mind to your servants, to Abraham, to Isaac, and to Jacob. Do not direct your face to the hardness of this people, nor its wickedness, nor its sinfulness.
>
> —Deut. 9.27

Moses went on to play on God's strikingly human ego:

> Lest the land from which you have taken us out say: "For lack of the Lord's capability to bring them to the land which he promised them, for his hatred of them has he taken them out to have them die in the wilderness."
>
> —Deut. 9.28

The last part of the verse is telling: God doesn't really hate the people, even when they rebel. He wouldn't want it to seem as though he did. Even when the Israelites constructed a Golden Calf, dancing about it and proclaiming, "This is your god, O Israel!" Moses could persuade God to yield his anger and promise a future. God is a *mensch*.

GOD DWELLS AMONG THE PEOPLE

The intimacy of God and Israel implied by their "understanding" is central to the ritual of the Torah. God resides among the people, a king in their midst. The people's prosperity and security depend on retaining God's very presence in their camp (e.g., Exod. 29.45–46; cf. 23.25). At the center of the camp in which the Israelites lived and traveled following the Covenant at Sinai, the Torah prescribes a "tabernacle," literally a "dwelling" *(mishkan)*, for God. (Later, rabbinic tradition utilizes the same Hebrew wordstem to denote the immanent presence of God, the *shekhinah*.) Surrounding the rectangular courtyard of this portable sanctuary the twelve tribes of Israel camp, three on each side. Within the courtyard are a square altar for offerings to God and the sanctuary proper, a rectangular structure in which the priests would serve God in dignified privacy. The backmost, square-shaped chamber of this structure comprises the inner sanctum, the Holy of Holies, God's apartment. The symmetrical shapes of the altar and Holy of Holies symbolize their unique sanctity.

God's apartment is set up as a royal chamber. The ark of the covenant, in which the stone tablets of the law were deposited, was covered by a solid gold seat, God's throne. Ancient Phoenician kings sat on their thrones flanked by winged sphinxes—the Bible's *keruvim*, "cherubim"—and so did the Lord of Israel sit on the throne of the ark, a golden cherub on each side. The apartment was sealed by a veil, embroidered with gold cherubim, a delight for God's eyes. Outside the curtain stood a golden *menorah* or lampstand, penetrating the veil with light; an incense altar, emitting its stimulating fragrance into God's chamber; and a golden table, on which loaves of bread and empty drinking vessels symbolized the priestly concern for God's creature comforts. (In more primitive sanctuaries the ritual functioned to serve the biological needs of the god; the structure of the Torah's *mishkan* conserves the outer form of the primitive paraphernalia.) For Israel, God's immanence found expression in the perception of God as a superperson.

KEEPING THE ENVIRONMENT PURE

The Torah's religion focuses on nourishing the divine presence, providing an environment worthy of God. In order to establish and maintain a holy environment the Israelites had to do two general, yet multifaceted tasks: keep the atmosphere free of impurity and keep the laws of God.

> Holy shall you be for holy am I, the Lord your God.
> —LEV. 19.2

For the Torah God is more than an idea or spirit; God is a physical, though largely invisible presence. In the Garden of Eden, God's afternoon stroll startled the man and woman by its rustling (Gen. 3.8). In Genesis 18, God and two of his messengers, or angels, visited Abraham in human guise. God's locus could be seen in the wilderness and in the *mishkan* by the glowing aura or cloud that enveloped it. When the Israelites freshly completed and consecrated the *mishkan,* this is how the Torah describes the scene:

> The cloud covered the tent of meeting, and the aura of the Lord filled the *mishkan*. Moses was not able to enter the tent of meeting for there resided *[shakhan]* upon it the cloud, and the aura of the Lord filled the *mishkan*. Upon the rising of the cloud off the *mishkan,* the Israelites journey, in all their journeys. But if the cloud does not rise, the Israelites do not journey, until the day of its rising. For the cloud of the Lord is upon the *mishkan* by day, and fire is by night upon it, before the eyes of all the House of Israel, in all their journeys.
> —EXOD. 40.34–38

God's substance is pure, but his purity is sensitive to invisible pollutants in the environment; God will withdraw, as in an allergic reaction, when too many pollutants are drawn too near. Animals brought into the *mishkan* and the people who enter it must be examined for purity by the priests. Some animals are flawed or tainted—impure—by nature, and human beings can become tainted, requiring rites of purification. The concern for purity surrounding God dominates chapters 11–15 of Leviticus, which delineate the various sources of ritual pollution and their antidotes through acts of purification. We shall be looking at some illustrations below.

Some of the important ideas behind ritual purity derive from the themes of Genesis 1.1–2.4, the story of Creation. God created the world by separating out distinct areas and classes from the dark, watery, primeval chaos. Just as that chapter in Genesis is neatly ordered by an arrangement into days and patterned by repeating formulas, so is Creation ordered by divisions: light from darkness, water above from water below, land from water, species of vegetation from species, breed of animal from breed, human from animal, female from male, Sabbath from weekdays. And later, as Genesis runs its course and Exodus carries it further, Israel is distinguished from the many nations, destined to be a treasure among peoples and the priests among nations (Exod. 19.5). The division into species likewise governs the Torah's ritual. As anthropologist Mary Douglas and others have shown, the Torah divides the world into that which is Godlike, pure and holy, and that which is inimical to God, tainted and profane.

When the world was new, the humans were given vegetation for food, not animals. Only after the Flood, as a concession, did God permit people to eat flesh so long as it was not taken live and its blood was removed:

> Every animate being which is live yours may be for eating; like the grassy greens have I given you everything. But flesh with its blood yet in its breath you may not eat.
>
> —GEN. 9.3–4

Blood epitomizes life, and God is life or rather, living-ness. Humans may not expropriate God's element. Before proceeding to discuss purity per se, it will be useful first to explore further this notion of living-ness.

LIFE BELONGS TO GOD

The earliest chapters in Genesis deal with, among many other matters, the boundary between God and human. The main difference between God and human is not appearance. When the Torah states "God created the human in his image, in the image of God he created him, male and female he created them" (Gen. 1.27), the text means that of all the animals he created, only the human occupies the blessed status of resembling God, a clone of the deity. In the Garden of Eden, when the humans assert their difference, the independence of their will from God's by disobeying him, they acquire another trait that makes them similar to God: knowledge. But they also acquire the characteristic that becomes the distinguishing mark of humanness as opposed to divinity: mortality. The boundary between God and human is drawn by the lifeline. Only God lives forever, is always living-ness.

In one of the strangest episodes of the Torah, Genesis 6.1–4, this aspect of God's uniqueness is threatened. The sons of God have cohabited with the daughters of the humans and produced a divine-human hybrid, sharing God's immortality. God recoils and enforces a greater measure of humanness upon the human race. He imposes an upper limit of 120 years on their life span. (The Torah inconsistently has the patriarchs of Israel live longer—Abraham accumulated 175 years. But the great Moses died at 120.)

Because blood, symbolizing life, is the element of God, and the human is a mortal clone of God, the Torah places the highest penalty on the shedding of human blood:

> He who spills the blood of a human, by a human will his blood
> be spilled, for in the image of God did he make the human.
> —GEN. 9.6

Unlike the Code of Hammurapi, which permits the family of a murder victim to accept compensation for the loss of life, the Torah forbids the Israelites to "take a ransom for the life of a murderer who is condemned to die." (Num. 35.31)

In the Torah life is supreme and cannot be treated as a commodity. As Moshe Greenberg has clarified in a major essay, "Some Postulates of Biblical Criminal Law" (see "Where to Go from Here" below), the same consideration underpins the Torah's law of retaliation, which has often been held up as an example of the Bible's primitiveness. Injuries shall be requited

> . . . life in place of life, eye in place of eye, tooth in place of
> tooth, hand in place of hand, foot in place of foot, burn in place
> of burn, wound in place of wound, injury in place of injury.
> —EXOD. 21.23–25

While the allegedly more "advanced" Mesopotamian codes allow for monetary compensation, the Torah cannot place a price tag on life or limb. Conversely, the Mesopotamian codes, reflecting the values of a developed, essentially capitalistic economy, prescribe stiff penalties, even death, for property damages, where the Torah assesses only a fine.

That living-ness is God's foremost quality informs the dietary and other ritual laws of the Torah. Blood, the paramount symbol of life, may not be eaten. While animal flesh is permitted for human consumption, the blood is not. It must be returned to God. In the older strata of Israelite law, as reflected in such passages as Leviticus 17.1–6 and 1 Samuel 14.31–35, an animal could be eaten only after it was ritually slaughtered at some sacred altar anywhere in the land, and the animal's blood drained on the altar. (The Hebrew word for altar, *mizbeah*, denotes a "place of slaughtering.") The Book of Deuteronomy, however, assumes an Israelite society in which there is only one central altar throughout the land. Since it would create an unreasonable hardship to compel Israelites living far from the central altar to go there to slaughter every animal, Deuteronomy introduces profane slaughter, without an altar. The blood of the slaughtered animal must be spilled on the ground, "like water" (Deut. 15.23). The blood belongs to God and may not be ingested by humans.

Animals that themselves consume the blood of other animals may not be eaten by the Israelites. Nor may a kid be boiled in the milk of its mother. The flesh of the young goat may not be cooked in a secondary symbol of life, milk.

MORE ON PURITY AND PURIFICATION

The types of animals that people are permitted to eat, that are "pure"—the term "kosher" is postbiblical—are those that in addition to being vegetarian, fall within the categories that God created in the beginning: those that graze on land, those that wing in the air, and those that flap in the sea. A "pure" animal possesses the major characteristics of its class and does not overlap another category. Land-grazers have split hooves and chew their cud; air-wingers fly; sea-flappers have fins and scales. The pig is tainted because it does not chew its cud; a lobster is impure because it walks, straddling the border with the class of land-grazers. The chicken, which is not mentioned in the Torah, would clearly be tainted and impermissible in the biblical scheme for the same reason. In its postbiblical development, rabbinic Judaism found the chicken "kosher," but it debated whether the chicken is meat or *pareve* (a condition neither meat nor dairy).

Since God created the world in classes, it is not for humans to co-opt God's prerogative and create that which God did not. (The first to spell out this principle was the medieval commentator, Rabbi Joseph Bekhor Shor; see Chapter Four.) Hybrids are proscribed:

> Do not sow your orchard with two kinds [of seed], lest the sum of the seed which you have sown and the produce of the orchard become consecrated. Do not plow with an ox and an ass united. Do not wear mixed-fabric [sha'atnez], wool and flax together.
>
> —DEUT. 22.9–11; cf. LEV. 19.19

The Torah views the combination of species, even if only in appearance, as taboo, a human appropriation of that which is God's alone. Notice that in the case of mixing seeds, a hybrid plant would belong only to God and is automatically consecrated, or holy. Similarly, the high priest, ministering directly to God in the sacred precincts, would wear an outfit made of linen and wool, the taboo fabric. That which is God's alone is also the only substance that can serve as an instrument of rehabilitating the tainted to purity: blood.

Here, for example, is the instructive procedure for how a person defiled by leprosy reinstates himself in the divine presence (Lev. 14.1ff.). A priest slaughters a pure bird, draining its blood into a clay vessel containing water from a running source ("living water"). Into this he dips a live bird, together with cedar wood, crimson, and hyssop, each a scarlet substance that increases the redness of the blood–water compound and enhances its power to absorb the ritual pollution. The priest sprinkles the blood upon the leper and releases the bird, which carries off the impurity. The pollution gone, the leper washes, shaves, washes his clothes, and remains outside his house for seven days, allowing the house, too, to return to normality. Then the leper becomes again *taher* (pure).

This is not the end. In the Torah's view, there are no accidents. God programs every event in nature or history. If a person suffers a disease, such as leprosy, God is assumed to be afflicting that person for some cause, presumably a sin. Later, the Book of Job will react to this theology and point to the saintly Job as an empirical challenge to the Torah's ideology. But for Leviticus, now that the erstwhile leper has been purified, he is fit to bring offerings to God that will redress his presumed offense and restore him to God's favor.

On the eighth day following his purification, he brings two perfect he-lambs, one year-old she-lamb, three smaller measures of flour and oil, and one large measure of oil. The list of ingredients and ensuing rites that the priest performs are not fully explained by the text. They can be decoded, however, by familiarizing ourselves with the "vocabulary" of Leviticus, the basic types of offerings that are laid out in the opening chapters of the book. This ritual comprises, for example, the *asham* of Leviticus 5.17–19, the *hattat* of Leviticus 5.1–6, the *minhah* of Leviticus 2.1–3, and the *olah* of Leviticus 1.10–13.

The priest slaughters one he-lamb, takes the larger measure of oil, and waves them before God, presenting an offering (the *asham*) to expiate the guilt that was presumed to have brought about the affliction in the first place. In order to present the offering, the ex-leper had to become pure so that he could approach God. The general Hebrew term for what we call a sacrifice is *korban*, "something brought nigh" to God. The erstwhile leper had to remain pure, to complete the offerings to God. The priest accomplished this by placing some blood, the Godly substance, on strategic loci of the ex-leper's body: his right earlobe, thumb, and toe. This he then covered with oil, to protect the shield of blood from defilement.

Having expiated the sin through the guilt offering, the worshiper had the priest perform two more rites for him: a purification offering *(hattat),* comprising the she-lamb, and a propitiation offering (*olah* and *minhah*), comprising a he-lamb and flour-and-oil mélange, respectively. Thus, from all this we see that to reinstate oneself in the divine presence one must undergo a metamorphosis of ritual stages: initial purification rendering one fit to approach God, an admission and requital of guilt, a transformation to one's former purity, and a gift to reestablish good relations. The rites make up a dance to the rhythm of a spiritual process.

We have seen that blood, symbolizing life, serves as the instrument of purification. Other items preferred by God are, similarly, things that are fresh, close to the condition in which God made them: the first fruits of the earth and the womb (Exod. 13.1ff.; Deut. 26.5–10); an altar of unhewn stone (Exod. 20.25); unsown ground (Deut. 21.4); free-flowing water (e.g., Lev. 14.5, 52). What defiles the pure are blemishes in the condition of createdness and compromises in the state of living-ness. One may not lacerate oneself (Deut. 14.1) because that would produce a flaw in the divine image. Leviticus, chapters twelve through fifteen, delineates a number of tainted conditions: birthing, skin disorders, bodily discharges. What is involved in each of these is a leak of blood or other life-sustaining fluid. Defilement is caused by contact with death or a life-leak. A woman who gives birth to a son has incurred no crime at all, but she must bring a purification offering after a seven-day period of rehabilitation. She must wait fourteen days after giving birth to a girl because the girl's potential life-leak redoubles that of the mother.

It is important to see that in the biblical mindset ritual pollution and the defilement produced by sin or crime are objective conditions inimical to God. Just as the consequences of our actions affect the world whether we intend them or not, violations of God's code, be they deliberate or accidental, push God away. The entire community needs the nourishment of God, so the entire community shares responsibility for keeping the environment pure. "Expunge the evil from your midst" resounds through the Book of Deuteronomy (13.6 et al.).

WHAT IS DISTINCTIVE IN BIBLICAL LAW

At the outset we noted that the diverse materials of the Torah, law, and narratives too, work hand in glove to transmit and reiterate the Torah's major concerns. The Creation story, we have seen, establishes a basis for the laws of purity, dividing Creation into species and domains. The story of the Exodus from Egypt, the second pivotal story of the Torah, seems actually to shape the subject matter of biblical law. The lessons of the Exodus seem to make the difference between the social laws of the Torah and parallel laws of other cultures.

The laws we find in the Torah do share a good deal in common with those of the Babylonians, Assyrians, Hittites, and other peoples of the ancient Near East. Even the biblical injunction of leaving part of the harvest for the underprivileged to collect (Lev. 19.9–10; Deut. 24.19–22) appears to have parallels in ancient Sumer and Egypt. But the humanitarian laws of Mesopotamia betray no historical self-consciousness. Those of the Bible are often buttressed with a historical or experiential rationale: "Remember that you were a slave in Egypt"; "Love for the alien what [you love] for yourself for you were aliens in the land of Egypt." (Lev. 19.34)

The lessons of the Exodus distinguish a number of laws in the Torah. The Israelites had been slaves, but the Lord set them free. Obviously, a slave need not be locked into his or her lowly status. The Code of Hammurapi assumes different treatment for the slave, the civil servant, and the citizen. With only minor exceptions, such as Exodus 21.20–21, the Torah does not respect differences in social station. The Code of Hammurapi, the Hittite Laws, and other ancient codes impose penalties on anyone who would abet a fugitive slave. Ancient Israelite practice reflects a similar attitude since the Bible reports at least two instances in which Israelites pursued runaway slaves (1 Sam. 30.15; 1 Kings 2.39–40). The Book of Deuteronomy, though, sets a different standard:

> You shall not deliver a slave to his master when he seeks asylum with you from his master. With you let him dwell, in your midst, in the place that he chooses within one of your gates that seems good for him. Do not oppress him.
> —DEUT. 23.16–17

The Torah hardly abolishes slavery. The Bible assumed slavery as a given and gave it a role. A slave was an indentured servant who could repay his debts through labor. Here is how Leviticus 25.39–43 puts it:

When your brother sinks beside you and sells himself to you,
you shall not work him the work of a slave. As a hired-hand,
as a resident-alien shall he be with you; until the year of release
he shall work with you. Then he will take leave of you, he and
his children with him, and he will return to his family, and to
the estate of his fathers will he return. For my slaves are they,
whom I have taken out of the land of Egypt. They shall not be
sold as a sale of a slave. You shall not tyrannize him harshly,
but you shall revere the Lord.

The influence of the liberation from Egypt upon the laws of slavery
stands out in the last sentence. The word "harshly," which recurs in
Leviticus 25 in verses 46 and 53, echoes the narrative in Exodus 1, which
tells that the Egyptians enforced hard labor upon the Hebrews "harshly"
(Exod. 1.13, 14).

The laws controlling slavery are the first civil laws that God imposes
at Mount Sinai, shortly after the Exodus. The law in Exodus 21 limits
slavery to six years. The Book of Deuteronomy, which modern scholars
attribute to a later period, revises and further humanizes the law in
Exodus. Exodus 21.2 speaks of a "Hebrew slave"; Deuteronomy 15.12
speaks of "your Hebrew brother," obliterating the class designation
"slave." Exodus speaks of a buyer's "purchasing" a slave, while Deuteronomy takes the slave's perspective: "If your Hebrew brother *is sold* [or
sells himself] to you." Exodus allows for the release of a male slave, but
Deuteronomy includes the "female Hebrew," too. In Exodus the slave
"shall leave as a freeman" in the seventh year. But Deuteronomy underscores the obligation of the master to free his servant: "You shall release
him as a freeman from you." It continues:

And when you release him as a freeman from you, you shall
not release him empty. Provide, provide for him from your
flock, from your threshing-floor, and from your winepress;
that by which the Lord your God has blessed you, give to him.
—Deut. 15.13–14

Exodus goes into what happens if the master has furnished his slave with
a wife who bears him children (21.3). Deuteronomy omits this contingency entirely because, as Moshe Weinfeld has explained,* the slave is
fully a person and the man for whom he or she works has no cause to
interfere in his or her private life.

Exodus foresees the possibility that a slave may wish to remain with

* *Deuteronomy and the Deuteronomic School* (Oxford: Clarendon Press, 1972), p. 283.

his family (21.5). This cannot occur in Deuteronomy's version of the law. Rather, a slave would only want to stay out of affection for his master (15.16)! In both codes the master pierces the attached slave's ear to mark his status of permanent servitude. The historical symbolism of this act remains moot, but rabbinic interpretation follows the thrust of the Torah's logic. The ear that heard the Lord proclaim (see above) that the Israelites are his servants alone and yet seeks to serve a human master deserves to be disfigured and punished! See the comment of Rashi to Exodus 21.6. (On Rashi's commentary, see Chapter Four.)

In typical hortatory style, Deuteronomy 21 supplements the slave law with two verses (15 and 18):

> You shall remember that a slave were you in the land of Egypt, and the Lord your God redeemed you. For this I command you this matter today. . . . Let it not be hard in your eyes when you release [the slave] as a freeman from you, for double the labor of a hired-laborer has he worked for you. The Lord your God will bless you in all that you do.

The Torah acknowledges the difficulty of holding up a high standard of behavior. People incline to be self-centered and selfish. But the Torah directs the Israelites to hallow their environment and their conduct so that God's presence will dwell among them and provide a constant source of blessing.

How We Read a Biblical Law

In the preceding section, the approach that we took in interpreting biblical laws was characteristically modern. For one thing, we sought to understand the background of biblical law and to appreciate its significance by means of comparing related laws from other ancient Near Eastern cultures. For another, we adopted the critical notion that the Torah may embody a revelation from God, but that revelation was shaped by the people that received and applied it. The Torah was compiled and edited from material that originated at different stages of ancient Israelite history. Thus codes of law in different places in the Torah reflect various sources and may in fact diverge from or even contradict one another.

The traditional Jewish approach exemplified in the rabbinic process of interpretation (see Chapter Three) operates under different assumptions. There the fundamental assumptions regarding biblical law are the following. Although at first blush the laws of the Torah seem sketchy, in fact God has coded all the laws we will ever need into the language of the Torah. It is up to rabbinic interpretation to explain how all the laws that are defined in the rabbinic codes of the classic period derive from the text of the Torah. Because the coding of revelation into the language of the Torah is efficient, no two laws teach the same thing, no two laws contradict each other, all the laws form a consistent system, and—because the rabbis claim to have received the official and authoritative interpretation of the Torah—all are consonant with the beliefs of the classic rabbis. In other words, the meaning of the Torah's laws is not determined through an explanation of their historical and literary contexts—which is what we have done. The Torah's laws mean what the rabbis' traditions, emerging centuries later, say they mean.

To grasp this distinction more clearly, let us read through a biblical law together, interpreting it first according to modern critical methods, then contrasting our interpretation with the rabbinic understanding. The law we shall consider is Deuteronomy 24.10–13.

In ancient times, as is often the case today, borrowers would leave their creditors a pledge as collateral. This is common knowledge and is assumed by the law. Since a poor borrower had little to offer as a pledge, he would typically leave his outer robe with the lender. Deuteronomy wishes to protect the poor borrower from the creditor in two ways. First (24.10–11), to respect the dignity of the borrower, the law restrains the creditor from invading the poor man's home to confiscate the pledge:

> When you lend your neighbor any item, you shall not go into his house to take his pledge as a pledge. Outside you shall stand, and the man to whom you are lending will bring the pledge out to you outside.

It is also implied that the borrower, not the creditor, has the option of selecting the article that will serve as pledge.

Second (24.12–13), Deuteronomy seeks to protect the poor borrower from double jeopardy:

> And if he is a poor man, you shall not lie down in his pledge. Return, you shall return to him the pledge at sundown that he may lie down in his robe and bless you. Then you will merit reward from the Lord your God.

It's bad enough a man must borrow; he shouldn't have to go cold at night, too. In the Land of Israel it is often very warm by day but cold at night. A poor person might have nothing for his blanket but his robe, the article he pledged on his debt. Hence, the law instructs the creditor to return the garment taken in pledge by nightfall, and indirectly by extension, urges all Israelites to be considerate of others. The goal is a modest utopia in which people will bless each other for being kind.

We today are able to discern some of the background of this law because we have material from ancient Mesopotamia and, in this instance, ancient Israel itself that bears upon its significance. To take the latter, more striking evidence first, a Hebrew letter from the seventh century B.C.E. documents a formal complaint by a laborer who alleges that his supervisor distrained his garment for no good reason. Apparently Deuteronomy's worry over the hasty seizure of poor people's garments was not idle.

By comparing a parallel law in the Code of Hammurapi we may better appreciate the humanistic thrust of Deuteronomy's law. The Babylonian law places a monetary fine on the improper distraint of a pledge. This is well and good. But the overriding concern there is *economic* justice—ergo, the imposition of a fine. Deuteronomy takes a *moral* tack, concerning itself with the personal needs of the borrower, his immediate situation. Typically, biblical law cares about people, whereas Mesopotamian law worries over money (see also above).

There is yet another angle by which we can view Deuteronomy's law. We can compare it to a parallel one in the Book of Exodus 22.24–26. After forbidding an Israelite to charge interest on a loan to another Israelite, the text in Exodus goes on to say (22.25–26):

> If you take, take as a pledge the robe of your neighbor, by the setting of the sun you shall return it to him. For it is his only covering, it is his robe for his skin. In what [else] will he lie down? It will be that if he cries out to me [= God], I shall hear, for gracious am I.

Clearly the law in Exodus covers the same ground as that in Deuteronomy. Although Exodus features the melodramatic rhetorical—almost Yiddish-flavored—question, "In what [else] will he lie down?" the contents of the two texts are similar. Both also refer to God's personal concern for the indigent borrower.

Deuteronomy, however, adds another dimension to the law, barring the creditor from barging into the debtor's home. Modern scholars tend to date the law in Deuteronomy later than that in Exodus. Consequently, we would say that the compilers of Deuteronomy found this particular law in Exodus sympathetic and chose to include it in their code as well. But they took the liberty of expanding the law in order to underscore its humanism.

The rabbinic reading of these laws differs not only on the specifics, but even on the general meaning of the laws. The rabbinic approach to

Exodus 22 and Deuteronomy 24 may be found, for example, in the eleventh-century commentary of Rashi (see Chapter Four). The rabbinic method, according to which the Torah does not waste words, sees two different laws here. Exodus refers to a garment worn by day, Deuteronomy to one worn at night. Thus, in the rabbinic interpretation of Exodus 22.25, the creditor must return the garment during the day, taking the phrase "by the setting of the sun" to denote before sundown, in daytime. Then what is the force of "In what [else] will he lie down?" in Exodus 22.26? According to the rabbis, it refers not to a garment at all but to a couch, another article that might have been seized as collateral. Although the rabbinic interpretation may seem to twist the words of the text, to their credit the rabbis grasp the ultimate intent of the law and carry it one step farther. In the Torah's formulation the law seeks to protect a borrower's rights when a pledge is taken. The rabbis do not even allow the taking of collateral on such a debt, which is, after all, just borrowing from a fellow Hebrew. They understand the Torah to refer to a pledge that is seized only after a debtor has failed to pay back a loan on time. In this case, the creditor deserves some protection, too.

Readers who wish to read the laws of the Torah with a historical-critical perspective should consult a modern critical commentary that points out parallel passages in the Torah itself and in ancient Near Eastern sources. Then one has three essential tasks: to see if a law's meaning is suggested by its context, i.e., the surrounding laws in the Torah text; to examine the style and language of the law, to see if certain aspects seem to be emphasized by virtue of repetition or an "extra" phrase; and, third, to see how this particular law may distinguish itself from a law elsewhere in the Torah or in the ancient Near East. If, after consulting a commentary and performing these three steps, one feels confused, there is every likelihood that sophisticated scholars, too, must struggle and puzzle over what that ancient, intriguing text is trying to tell us.

Where to Go from Here

We have attempted in this chapter to survey some of the Torah's ritual and civil laws by connecting them with the two most critical stories in the Torah. The story of Creation describes how God ordered the world by way of categories and infused his creation with life. Israel is commanded to respect and safeguard those categories of God and revere life itself as the property of God. The story of the Exodus from Egypt impresses upon Israel God's concern for the downtrodden and his desire for human freedom. Many of the Torah's laws which distinguish them from the laws of other nations in the ancient Near East seem to exemplify a special regard for the disadvantaged. The Israelites, who know what it means to be a slave and an alien, must see that their slaves and the aliens among them receive the sort of treatment that God had afforded His people.

Yet, it will be obvious to any with even a modest familiarity with the Torah that many areas of biblical religion and law have not even been touched upon here. Accordingly, we append references to sources and studies that can assist the interested reader in going into the subject matter more thoroughly and deeply. The literature written about the Bible is tremendous and continues to swell, so the selections are only representative of what is available in English. One should also consult the reading suggestions following Chapter Three and Chapter Four.

A good text on biblical thinking, including some cultural background, is Frank E. Eaken, Jr.'s *The Religion and Culture of Israel: An Introduction to Old Testament Thought* (Washington, D.C.: University Press of America, 1977). The most comprehensive, insightful, and readable introduction to biblical culture is still Johannes Pedersen's two-volume *Israel: Its Life and Culture* (London: Oxford University Press, 1926–1940). The best discussion of the biblical mindset, though technical, is H. Wheeler Robinson's *Inspiration and Revelation in the Old Testament* (Oxford: Clarendon Press, 1946). A more recent treatment is Hans Walter Wolff, *Anthropology of the Old Testament* (Philadelphia: Fortress Press, 1974).

Antithetical, yet classic, reconstructions of the history of Israelite religion are Julius Wellhausen's *Prolegomena to the History of Ancient Israel* (Cleveland and New York: Meridian Books, 1957) and Yehezkel Kaufmann's *The Religion of Israel* (New York: Schocken Books, 1972). For a theological comparison of the Bible and ancient Near Eastern religion, G. Ernest Wright's *The Old Testament against Its Environment* (London: SCM Press, 1950) provides a helpful perspective. On the parallel between the biblical covenant and ancient Near Eastern treaties, see especially George Mendenhall, "Covenant Forms in Israelite Tradition," *The Biblical Archaeologist Reader 3,* ed. Edward F. Campbell, Jr. and David Noel Freedman (Garden City, N.Y.: Anchor Books, 1970), pp. 25–53.

Good analyses of the biblical cult tend to be technical, such as Menahem Haran, *Temples and Temple-Service in Ancient Israel* (Oxford: Clarendon Press, 1977); Baruch A. Levine, *In the Presence of the Lord* (Leiden: E. J. Brill, 1974); and Jacob Milgrom's *Studies in Levitical Terminology* (Berkeley: University of California Press, 1970) and *Cult and Conscience* (Leiden: E. J. Brill, 1976). On the underlying ideas of the laws of purity in the Torah, see Mary Douglas, *Purity and Danger: An Analysis of Concepts of Pollution and Taboo* (London: Routledge & Kegan Paul, 1966), especially pp. 41–58; and Jean Soler, "The Dietary Prohibitions of the Hebrews," *New York Review of Books,* June 14, 1979, pp. 24ff. For a critical discussion, consult Robert Alter, "A New Theory of Kashrut," *Commentary,* August 1979, pp. 46–52. To negotiate the jargon-laden Book of Leviticus, the commentary of Bernard Bamberger in *The Torah: A Modern Commentary* (New York: Union of American Hebrew Congregations, 1981) is a steady guide.

Concerning biblical and ancient Near Eastern law, Hans Jochen Boecker's *Law and the Administration of Justice in the Old Testament and the Ancient East* (Minneapolis: Augsburg Publishing House, 1980) provides an overall introduction. A historical approach to the laws of the Bible is taken by Anthony Phillips in *Ancient Israel's Criminal Law* (Oxford: Basil Blackwell, 1970). In *The Laws of Deuteronomy* (Ithaca: Cornell University Press, 1974) Calum M. Carmichael compares the laws of Deuteronomy to passages elsewhere in the Torah. More technical studies, taking a comparative and historical approach, are Shalom M. Paul, *Studies in the Book of the Covenant in the Light of Biblical and Cuneiform Law* (Leiden: E. J. Brill, 1970) and Moshe Weinfeld, *Deuteronomy and the Deuteronomic School* (Oxford: Clarendon Press, 1972). The underlying values embedded in biblical law are exposed in Moshe Greenberg's essay, "Some Postulates of Biblical Criminal Law," in *The Jewish Expression,* ed. Judah Goldin (New York: Bantam Books, 1970), pp. 18–37.

For legal and other material from the ancient Near East, the best collection of sources is James B. Pritchard, ed., *Ancient Near Eastern Texts Relating to the Old Testament,* 3rd ed. (Princeton: Princeton University Press, 1969). The slave laws referred to above are found on pp. 167 (Code of Hammurapi, laws 15–20), 190 (Hittite Laws 22–24), 160 (Lipit-Ishtar Code, law 12), and 163 (Laws of Eshnunna, law 50). The laws on collateral are on pp. 170 (law 114) and 176 (law 241). The related Hebrew letter is translated there on p. 568. Ancient parallels to the gleaning laws, alluded to above, are cited from Samuel Noah Kramer, *The Sumerians* (Chicago: University of Chicago Press, 1963), p. 108; and W. O. E. Oesterley, *The Wisdom of Egypt and the Old Testament* (New York: Macmillan, 1927), pp. 79–80.

For specific topics and survey articles in all areas, one will often find useful the entries in *The Interpreter's Dictionary of the Bible,* 5 vols. (Nashville: Abingdon, 1962–1976) and the *Encyclopaedia Judaica* (Jerusalem: Keter Publishing House, 1971), 16 vols. The best guide to the Bible, however, is reading and rereading it, in Hebrew if possible.

From Exodus 15, The Song at the Sea, Bible manuscript known as the Codex Hilleli, 1242.

C. BIBLICAL POETRY

MURRAY H. LICHTENSTEIN

Poetry, as a mode of thought and a mode of expression, a vision and a voice, permeates the writings of the Hebrew Bible. There is scarcely a biblical book that does not contain at least one poetic line or passage. Of course, there are the great blocks of poetry, such as in the 150 Psalms, the oracles of the major and minor prophets, the wisdom poetry of Proverbs and Job, the dirges of Lamentations and the love lyrics of the Song of Songs. But throughout the vast corpus of the Bible's historical narratives—the Pentateuch, Joshua and Judges, the books of Samuel, Kings, and Chronicles—the prose text is irregularly punctuated by poetic utterances which add a distinctive dimension and special substance to the sagas of ancient Israel.

Even among the quintessentially prosaic particulars of ritual law in Leviticus, one finds the poetically formulated divine oracle:

> Through My intimates is My holiness
> to be made manifest,
>
> Before all the people is My glory
> to be perceived.
> —Lev. 10.3

These words serve to silence a bereaved Aaron, stunned by the instantaneous death of two of his sons, who had presumed to initiate unauthorized offerings in the sanctuary and so incurred the divine wrath. Through the medium of this poetic oracle, however, Aaron comes to understand the real reason behind their fiery end. The sons of Aaron had

105

willfully subverted God's sanctuary into a kind of private priestly chapel and appropriated God's rituals as purely private hereditary prerogatives. The poetic line is as stark, direct, and immediate as the divine punishment itself. Here the complementary divine attributes of "holiness" (Heb. *kadosh*) and "glory" (Heb. *kavod*) are made to echo one another in awesome reverberation, even as they do in the more famous poetic vision of Isaiah 6.3:

> Holy, Holy, Holy [Heb. *kadosh*]
> the Lord of hosts,
>
> His Glory [Heb. *kavod*] compasses
> the fullness of all the earth.

Just the opposite of this echoing effect is achieved by juxtaposing the two contrasting terms "my intimates" and "all the people" in the two halves of our couplet. What is now highlighted is the distinction between the priesthood (God's "intimates") and the people on whose behalf they are to render service before God. For it was precisely the failure of Aaron's sons to observe this distinction, to act in accordance with their own special role in Israel, which made their tragic end inevitable. In their presumption, they had at once sinned against God and acted to the detriment of their own people. These two instances of poetic coupling—holiness and glory, priesthood and people—combine to convey, in the most succinct and most pointed manner possible, the complex cause-and-effect relationship between *priestly* behavior which respects and thus reflects God's *holiness,* and the extent to which the *people* come to experience the divine *glory*. More simply put, priests who slight God's sanctity, in effect, deprive the people of the divine presence. As distinct from how it may have been articulated in prose, in this poetic formulation the actual sin of Aaron's sons—in all of its implications—is not so much expressed to their grieving father as it is *impressed* upon him. Aaron is indeed silenced, and one may surmise that his reaction was conditioned not only by the content of God's words, but by their mode and mood, their poetry, as well.

We have seen a single (and by no means unambiguous) instance of the effect of poetry in the Bible, but by citing this unusual verse from Leviticus we have only begged the more fundamental question: what constitutes the phenomenon of biblical poetry? In the pages that follow we will attempt to address that problem by resolving the one, impossibly broad question into three, more manageable parts: biblical poetry—*What is it? How is it? Why is it?* Or, expanding upon these a bit, *what* are some of the distinctive qualities of language, tone, and outlook that characterize biblical poetry; *how* is biblical verse composed, given form and structure; *why* is biblical poetry such a favored and so striking a medium of the divine message?

BIBLICAL POETRY: WHAT IS IT?

Unlike the Greeks, the ancient Israelites have left us no "Poetics," that is, no systematic definition or description of the phenomenon. Indeed, the same may be said for even so basic a notion as logic, which, while clearly in evidence in the words of the Bible, is never spoken of as such. As with their logic, the Israelites seem to have been infinitely less self-conscious about their poetry than the Greeks. It has been rightly observed that there is, in fact, no single word in biblical Hebrew that corresponds to our term "poetry." Of course, there is a variety of terms for different types of poetic compositions, but no one, all-embracing term that speaks of the poetic endeavor as a whole. The Hebrew word *shir* denotes only "that which is sung," unlike the English word "poetry," which etymologically means "that which is made," but which in actual usage goes on to say a great deal more about the nature of what has been "made."

The remnants of Canaanite lore, preserved in and outside of the Bible, have left us no mention of a mythological muse, or a proto-historical first poet. The closest we come are references in Ugaritic (Canaanite) myth to the craftsman god Kothar, whose expertise seems to have embraced, among other things, the making of music, and the female divinities poetically dubbed "swallows, daughters of song." In the Bible itself we only hear the briefest mention of one Yubal, a son of Cain, who is said to have been the "father" of all who play musical instruments (Gen. 4.21). But biblical poetry, no matter how once closely linked to musical accompaniment, was primarily a medium of words, not melody, and remains all the more so now that only its words have survived.

Further obstructing our grasp of what poetry meant in ancient Israel is the almost total absence of any historically reliable data revealing when, why or by whom most biblical poems were composed. While in general, literary critics are accustomed to studying poetry as a specific reflection of a given cultural epoch, or a given period in the life of the poet, the reader of biblical poetry has been left little in the way of historical or biographical information from which to draw any such conclusions. True, the Bible speaks, for example, of individual "Psalms of David" and the "Proverbs of Solomon," but the actual intention of these very general attributions was clearly quite different from what we mean today by precise determination of the authorship of a given work.

Even the poetic oracles associated with specific prophets (whose dates and partial biographies we are given) are not entirely free from scholarly doubts and uncertainties concerning the historical circumstances of their composition. Are the poetic oracles we have today the same as those actually uttered by the prophet, or do they represent the prophet's "polished" literary version of what had been spoken earlier in a less quiet moment and circumstance? What contribution, if any, was made by the prophet's disciples or various other editors to his words, with regard to both what has been preserved for us and what has been omitted from the written record?

We are also left to wonder about the actual role of different poetic compositions in the daily life of ancient Israel. Were the Psalms, in whole or in part, the liturgy of the Temple? Were they composed specifically for this purpose, or was this a later adaptation? How and when were these Psalms recited as part of divine service? Further, by whom and for whom were the various collections of Proverbs made—the royal court? the circle of "Wisdom" teachers? the general populace? Tradition and modern biblical scholarship alike offer their various suggestions on these and related questions, but the biblical record itself retains its silence.

The lack of any biblical pronouncements on the subject of poetry, however, may serve to spur all the more our effort and imagination in uncovering what may be implicit in biblical poems themselves. A particularly helpful approach, as noted in the section of this chapter on biblical narrative, suggests itself from the fact that at times the Bible preserves, alongside a prose historical account, a poetic rendering of the self-same event. Thus, for example, the crossing of the Sea of Reeds as recorded in the fourteenth chapter of the book of Exodus is followed in the fifteenth chapter by the "Song of the Sea," more properly an ancient Israelite victory hymn celebrating the deliverance from Egypt. Even a limited comparison and contrast of these two texts suggests much about the quality of the Israelite poetic sensibility, as it stands in bold relief against the background of its prose counterpart.

The traditional historical narrative of Exodus 14 traces the ordered progression of a complete sequence of events: the massing of the Egyptian troops by the sea; Moses' reassurance of the frightened Israelites; the divine order for Moses to extend his rod over the waters, so that they might be split and the Israelites might cross on dry land; the separation of Egyptians from Israelites by a pillar of cloud; God's splitting of the sea by means of a strong east wind, as Moses extends his arm over the water; the resulting formation of walls of water on either side of a cleared path of dry land; the entry of the Israelites into the sea and their pursuit by the Egyptians; God's infliction of panic and mechanical impediments upon the Egyptians; Moses' extending of his arm over the sea at God's command, signaling the sea's return to a watery state; the drowning of all the Egyptians, their chariots and horsemen, in the sea.

Turning to the first twelve verses of the poem in Exodus 15, which treat the same subject as the prose narrative, we do not find this sequential progression of events, but rather an alternating series of impressions and emotional responses that follow no chronological order. Thus the first verse anticipates the dramatic ending of the prose story:

> (1) Let me sing of the Lord, for He has
> triumphed gloriously;
>
> Horse and driver He has hurled
> into the sea.

What follows in vv. 2–3 is an interruption of the narrative content with a general hymnic passage, making no specific mention of the events themselves:

> (2) The Lord is my strength and might,
> He is become my salvation;
> This is my God, so I will glorify Him,
> The God of my father, so I will exalt Him.
> (3) The Lord is a warrior,
> The Lord Himself.

Of course, the theme of God's prowess as "warrior" pervades and unites the various references to specific divine acts in the poem, but here the epithet is kept general. Yet even in this less specific context, the poet's highly personal references to God as "my strength" and "my salvation" (v. 2) reflect the same intimate involvement as that prompted by the particular deliverance at the Sea of Reeds: "Let *me* sing of the Lord . . ." (v. 1). Thus the first two passages of the poem balance one another in terms of the complementary perspectives of the specific and the general: both the specific acts of God in history ("Horse and driver He has hurled into the sea") *and* the general attributes that are reflected in such divine acts ("The Lord is a warrior") provide the impetus for the poet's personal celebration in song.

The narrative of the poem resumes in vv. 4–5, where specific mention is made of the sinking of Pharaoh's chariotry and officers in the sea.

Here, however, "the sea" and "Sea of Reeds" mentioned in v. 4 are spoken of somewhat differently in the following verse:

> (5) The deeps [Heb. *tehomot*] covered them,
> They went down into the depths
> [Heb. *metzolot*] like a stone.

These two poetic synonyms do more than simply replace mention of the Sea of Reeds so as to avoid its repetition. They are, in fact, richly evocative entities in their own right, appearing elsewhere in biblical poetry as images for the ultimate human experience of distress and peril (see Pss. 71.20; 69.16), and each having broadly cosmic associations, above and beyond any *specific* body of water (see Prov. 3.20; Ps. 107.24). Far more than an imaginative substitution of more exotic terms for the prosaic "Sea of Reeds," they represent the poet's more ambitious attempt to move one particular historical moment, the drowning of Egyptians in the Sea of Reeds, into the broader realm of the universal and the timeless.

With vv. 6–7, we again experience a hymnic interruption, which, strictly speaking, is unrelated to the events of the narrative. But, like the hymnic interlude of vv. 2–3, and the word choice of v. 5, the interruption again serves to set the events into the widest possible context:

> (6) Your right hand, O Lord, is of
> awesome power;
> Your right hand, O Lord,
> shatters the foe!
> (7) In Your great triumph You
> break Your opponents;
> You send forth Your fury,
> it consumes them like straw.

Pharaoh's army is no longer a specific historical antagonist, but now merges with those whom the poet styles "the foe" and "Your opponents"—those who ever have, or ever will, in any way challenge the authority of the divine will. Similarly, no longer is the agent of divine punishment limited to the waters of the Sea of Reeds, or even the cosmic deep, but now extends to God's fiery wrath, which "consumes them like straw" (v. 7). Clearly, nothing is more incongruous or inconsistent with the watery setting of this specific historical event than is the poetic reference to a consuming fire. But that is just the point that the poet makes in our passage—the universal significance of what happened at the Sea of Reeds utterly transcends the particular means of punishment (drowning), as much as it transcends the particular identity of the foe (Pharaoh's army).

The poem refers to the event at hand in vv. 8–10, making reference to the heaping up of the waters into wall-like barriers. In v. 8, the miraculous transformation of the fluid to the solid is strikingly emphasized through the cumulative effect of the poetic synonyms "waters" *(mayim),* "deeps" *(tehomot),* "sea," and, most especially, "that which flows" *(nozelim).* Further, the heaping up of the water and the returning of it to its natural state are accomplished not by "a strong east wind," as in the prose of Exodus 14, but by "the blast of Your nostrils"—the very breath of God. This dramatization of the event from the standpoint of God's personal participation is matched by the intimation we are given in v. 9 into the hearts and minds of the Egyptians, once again spoken of as "foe":

> (9) The foe said:
> "I'll pursue, I'll overtake,
>   I'll divide the spoil,
>   My appetite will be sated by them;
> I will bare my sword,
>   My own hand will disinherit them!"

What a sharp contrast to the repeated, troubling references in the prose (Exod. 14.4, 8, 17) to *God's* having "stiffened" Pharaoh's heart! Here there can be no question as to Egyptian culpability, the "foe" is unequivocally an enemy in thought, word and deed. And the true hallmark of every enemy of God is precisely Pharaoh's short-sighted, even blasphemous reliance solely upon the might of his own "sword" and his own "hand." As the "foe," the act of the Egyptians is so broadened into general human terms as to include *all* attempts at supplanting Israel out of voracious greed, here spoken of as Pharaoh's "appetite." These lines thus anticipate the references in vv. 14–16 to Israel's future foes—Philistines, Edomites, Moabites, Canaanites—whose ultimate fate, like that of the Egyptians, is also described in terms of a likeness to "stone" (cf. vv. 5 and 16).

Further, the enemy's brash declaration of its intent in v. 9 is followed immediately by notice in v. 10 of the very different outcome:

> (10) You made Your wind to blow,
>   The sea covered them;
>   They sank like lead
>   In the majestic waters.

The irony of so dismally failed expectations is heightened by the highly stylized boastful language used initially in v. 9 to proclaim the Egyptian intent. Here the staccato, rapid-fire succession of verbs—"I'll pursue, I'll overtake, I'll divide . . ."—leaves no room whatsoever for doubt or hesitation about the outcome, not unlike the effect of Caesar's famed *veni, vidi, vici* (I came, I saw, I conquered). But the illusion of so automatic a success is rudely dispelled by the unforeseen intervention of Israel's God.

These last specific references in vv. 8–10 to the deliverance at the Sea of Reeds are followed, once again, by a generalized hymnic interlude which conveys the poet's vivid impression of God's awesome power, whenever and however manifested:

> (11) Who is like You, O Lord, among the celestials;
>   Who is like You, majestic in holiness,
>   Awesome in splendor, working wonders!

Almost as an afterthought, these words are particularized by a final reference to the vanquished foe:

> (12) You put out Your right hand,
>   The earth swallowed them.

With this intense reaction, which depicts the earth, no less than the sea, as servants of the divine will, and portrays the power of the Deity no less sovereign above than it is below, we may contrast the relatively dispassionate formulation of the prose of the previous chapter:

> And when Israel saw the great power which the Lord had wielded against the Egyptians, the people feared the Lord: They had faith in the Lord and in His servant Moses.
> —Exod. 14.31

In summary, the poetry of Exodus 15 thus offers an alternative view of what happened at the Sea of Reeds. Its concern is not the logical sequence of events, nor, for that matter, even the complete description (in whatever order) of what transpired. Indeed, surprisingly little of the details recorded in the prose of Exodus 14 finds its way into the poetic version. Missing here are the divine cloud, the twice repeated stretching out of Moses' hand (replaced, significantly, in v. 12, by the extension of *God's* right hand), the dialogue between God and Moses, the immobilized chariot wheels of the pursuers, even the belated but momentous recognition by the Egyptians that "the Lord is fighting for them against Egypt" (14.25).

Rather, the concern of the poem is the creation of an indelible image of the divine warrior triumphant, an impressionistic image built up as a montage of brief glimpses of the Deity in action—in close-up detail and in long-shot perspective—interspersed with appropriately subjective reactions by the poet himself. The effect is heightened by evocative word choice and well-calculated juxtapositions, which serve to move the listener (or reader) in and out of the event, surrealistically overriding the constraints of time and space.

From these distinctive features observed in our poem one cannot adduce the sum total of ancient Israelite poetic art, but we are indeed provided with a useful index for gauging some of the qualities that distinguish biblical prose from poetry. A further opportunity for this kind of synoptic reading is offered by the story of Deborah's victory over the Canaanites, celebrated alike in the prose of Judges 4 and the poetry of Judges 5. Here, too, one's efforts are richly rewarded with specific insights and heightened appreciation of the unique vision and voice of biblical poetry.

An analogous technique which may be applied to highlighting the distinctive mode of biblical poetry is afforded by prose narratives that incorporate poetic compositions as part of their text. Here, too, the very proximity of prose and poetry, even in contexts less directly related than in our previous example, allows us to formulate more clearly what it is that the poetry, and only the poetry, adds to the excellence of biblical prose. So, for example, in the prose tale of Jonah we hear of the prophet imprisoned in the belly of a great fish, but in a decidedly objective and matter-of-fact manner:

> The Lord provided a great fish to swallow Jonah, and Jonah remained in the fish's belly three days and three nights. Jonah prayed to the Lord his God from the belly of the fish.
> —JON. 2.1–2

In the same way we learn of his unceremonial deliverance, vomited up by his former host:

> The Lord commanded the fish, and it spewed Jonah out upon dry land.
> —JON. 2.11

It falls, however, to the so-called "Prayer of Jonah," originally an independent psalm of thanksgiving but presented in chapter 2 of the book as the words of the distressed prophet himself, to convey something of the otherwise unexpressed emotional component of this episode. Only the poem explores the actual experience of those three critical days in the fish, which so transforms the prophet that when ordered a second time to "Go at once to Nineveh," he now complies without either hesitation or duplicity, as before (cf. Jon. 1.2 and 3.2).

This poetic "supplement" inserted into the prose narrative of the book of Jonah not only imparts emotional content to the tale, it does so with a typically "poetic" disregard for the unities and strict proprieties of space and time. The sufferer, Jonah, is at once in "the belly of Sheol" (Jon. 2.3) and in "the heart of the sea" (2.4); he is at once in the land of the netherworld, with its gates bolted behind him forever (Jon. 2.7), and in the depths of the sea, where the waters rise to drown him and reeds are already entwined in his hair (Jon. 2.6). How different this poem is from the ordered, elegantly structured progression of episodes in the prose tale, which allows little or no room for the distractions of such suggestive and sublime ambiguities. The prose author skillfully balances the scene on board ship at sea (Jon. 1) with the scene in the streets of Nineveh (Jon. 3), each presenting a dramatic example of the immediate responsiveness of foreigners to the God of Israel, "who made both sea and land" (Jon. 1.9). The two scenes are made to echo one another in their sharp and ironic contrast to the much slower spiritual progress of Jonah, God's own prophet. Yet there can be no confusing the two locales. In the stark reality of prose, Jonah can only be in *one* place at a time, a limitation to which "the Prayer of Jonah" is not subject.

Equally telling juxtapositions of prose and poetry present themselves in the Hebrew Bible. The "prayer of Hannah" (1 Sam. 2.1–10) purports to have been uttered following the birth and consecration of her son Samuel. But, once again, we have an originally independent psalm extolling the dramatic reversals effected by Divine Providence, here pressed into service to convey the private emotional response of an individual (Hannah) to a specific situation or event. More elaborately, the "Oracles of Balaam" (Num. 22–24) have been adroitly interwoven with narrative sections, creating a veritable tapestry of song and story. In all cases, the distinctly "poetic" vision and voice become all the more apparent from the contrast, and reveal the unique contribution their emotional subjectivity and associative complexity bring to biblical literature.

BIBLICAL POETRY: HOW IS IT?

In the best of any traditional poetry, poetic technique is not some arbitrary set of rules to be followed for their own sake, but a true reflection of shared aesthetic values and a tried resource for effecting their realization. Just so in biblical poetry, we observe various formal techniques of composition, all contributing to the attainment of an ideally conceived, all-embracing sense of *balance*. Clearly, the most readily perceived means of effecting such balance in a given poetic line or longer passage is the poet's propensity for what has been termed "parallelism." Most generally, the latter refers to the balance between the two halves (or at times the three components) of a poetic line, in terms of either structure or language or thought or, indeed, all of these simultaneously. The first three verses of the "Song of Moses" in Deuteronomy 32 offer a striking, if rather extreme, example of the various expressions of balance sought after and achieved by the biblical poet:

(1) Give ear, O heavens, let me speak;
> Let the earth hear the words
> > of my mouth!
(2) May my message fall like the rain,
> May my utterance drop
> > like the dew;
> Like showers on young growth,
> Like droplets on the grass.
(3) For it is the Lord's renown
> I will proclaim;
Ascribe greatness to our God!

In the first verse the poet exhorts the eternal pair of cosmic opposites, heaven and earth. Ancient Near Eastern myth and poetry alike personify and specifically pair off these spatial extremes, which frame the world of human existence. Here, however, their juxtaposition is only part of a larger pattern in which *all* of the elements of the poetic line are paired off just as naturally through the use of poetic synonyms. The specific verbs "to give ear" and "to hear" are indeed synonymous, and in fact constitute a highly traditional word-pair employed as synonyms elsewhere in biblical poetry and reflected in the poems of the ancient Canaanite precursors of the Israelites. More approximate as synonyms are the terms "let me speak" and "the words of my mouth," which, as verbal form and noun, balance one another conceptually as cause and effect, or intention and fulfillment.

What we experience here, however, is not simply a matter of corresponding synonyms or related terms bridging the two halves of the poetic line, but also the resulting *parallelism of thought,* the echoing of a single sentiment, producing what has aptly been called "thought-rhyme." By the conclusion of the poetic line, everything expressed in its first half is balanced by some counterpart in the second, be it specific word or general idea. Just as this first verse manifests *internal* balance in the correspondence of its two poetic half-lines, it also features a kind of *external* balance between its opening and concluding words which serves to frame the verse as a whole. Thus the verse begins with the verb "give ear" (*ha'azinu,* deriving from the word for "ear," *ozen*), and ends with the phrase "words of my *mouth*" *(peh),* artfully balancing at the two extremes of the verse the physical organs of hearing and speech, the two reciprocal organs of communication.

In the second verse of our poetic passage the balance between its various constituent elements becomes somewhat more complex. We begin, as before, with the simple juxtaposition of synonyms or conventionally associated items. Thus the verbs "fall" and "drop," and the nouns "rain" and "dew" (another classical word-pair going back to pre-Israelite poetic tradition) create the same kind of perfectly symmetrical balance as observed in the first verse, as do "showers" and "droplets," "young growth" and "grass." More nuanced, however, is the relationship between the terms "message" and "utterance." While the latter refers literally to "that which is said," the term here translated "message" (Heb. *lekah*) suggests more particularly "that which one should grasp" from the words of another. Here a balance is struck not between two simple synonyms, but between two reciprocally related phenomena, the words that one speaks and the essential message that they contain. Rather than follow the example of the first verse, which juxtaposes a closely related verb ("let me speak") and noun ("the words of my mouth"), the poet has opted for a more subtle combination of terms: "message," referring to inner content, and "utterance," referring to external form.

Even more elaborate is the kind of structural balance we see in the second verse. Here the poet has not only created internal balance between the two *halves* of a single poetic line, as in the first verse, but has also succeeded in achieving external balance between two *whole* poetic lines as well:

> (2) a. May my message fall like the rain,
> May my utterance drop like the dew;
> b. Like showers on young growth,
> Like droplets on the grass.

While, as already observed, the respective halves of (a) and (b) balance one another, so, too, (a) is balanced by (b). That is, the parallel phrases "like showers on young growth" and "like droplets on the grass" pick up on, expand, and further echo the preceding parallel phrases "like the rain" and "like the dew." Indeed, the cumulative effect of this rhythmic repetition of the terms "rain," "dew," "showers," "droplets" is not unlike that of the very raindrops of which the verse speaks! In the case of the two halves of (a) and the two halves of (b), the balance is completely symmetrical, in that everything in the first half is balanced by something in the second. But the balance created between (a) and (b) is, by the same token, asymmetrical, in that only one part of (a), its short similes, finds representation in (b).

Interestingly enough, we do not actually sense anything wrong in verse 2. That is, the asymmetry is neither jarring nor even perceptibly incongruous. The seeming paradox is explained by the fact that in the second verse, as in the first, the poet achieves balance between the halves of the poetic lines, and between the whole lines themselves, by means of something other than parallelism alone. This is the effect of the poetic device referred to by biblical scholars as "meter," or, more generally, rhythm. This formal aspect of biblical poetry is perhaps the least understood, or at least the least agreed upon among scholars, and it is clearly the most difficult of all the Bible's poetic techniques to convey adequately in translation.

Simply put, it may be said that in the Hebrew of the second verse of the "Song of Moses" both poetic lines are of approximately the same length, and consequently, they are symmetrically balanced in sound, if not in sense. This rough equivalence in length holds whether one counts the syllables of the words in each line (or in the halves of each line), or whether, using another system, one reckons the number of essential words in each. However we choose to conceptualize the technique in question, its effect, like that of parallelism, is perceived by the listener (or reader) as balance. And just as with parallelism, the poet will at times opt for the creation of asymmetrical balance, quite often deliberately lengthening the first half of the poetic line—in syllable-count, word-count, or both—relative to the second. What remains constant, however ever, is that the aesthetic of rhythmic balance is realized to the satisfaction of the biblical poet, if not always to the complete comprehension of his latter-day readers or professional students.

While not all biblical examples of poetic parallelism are as highly symmetrical as those observed in the opening lines of the "Song of Moses," nor all metrical, or rhythmic, patterns as regular, the use in our passage of both parallelism and meter as mutually reinforcing techniques for creating poetic balance is indeed typical of biblical poetry. Parallelism, as the *qualitative balance of sense units* (be they specific words, grammatical forms or constructions, concepts or images), and meter, as the *quantitative balance of sound units* (be they syllables or words), do not, however, exhaust the resources of the biblical poet. As will be seen presently, also to be taken into account is the elegant *structural balance of compositional units* (be they stanzas or strophes), through which the poetic masterbuilder creates the architecture of his poem.

What parallelism and meter are to poetic lines, compositional structure is to whole groups of poetic lines that share a combination of common theme, style, imagery, vocabulary, metrical pattern, or like elements. Thus, for example, the first three verses of the "Song of Moses," taken together, constitute a discrete, coherent structural unit introducing the long poetic composition that follows. The uniform content (here the poet's announced intention to sing God's praises before all, and for the benefit of all), clearly unites the individual poetic lines. Indeed, only in these three verses, and nowhere else in the entire poem (some 43 verses in length), do we hear the poet's personal voice. Even more strikingly, the structural unit is given more precise definition by the verbal and stylistic features with which the passage both begins and ends, here a verb of speaking employed in the first person (v. 1 "Let me speak"; v. 3 "I will proclaim"), together with an imperative, or command form (v. 1 "Give ear!"; v. 3 "Ascribe!"). This use of patterned repetition to frame, as it were, a given structural unit, as in our text, is a particularly effective means of imparting internal balance to that unit. Elsewhere, however, the same technique is also employed to create external balance between more than one such unit within a complete poem. Poetic structure thus reflects the same aesthetic ideal of balance as evident in both parallelism and meter, and may serve equally well as the technical means for its realization in biblical poetry.

The few lines we have been considering from the "Song of Moses" suffice to highlight the role of balance, in all of its richly diversified expressions, as a unifying element underlying the various techniques of biblical poetry. It is, however, in longer, more elaborate literary units, and especially in complete poetic compositions, that the particular effect of structural balance is best appreciated. The reader might wish to examine on his or her own, for example, the Twenty-ninth Psalm, a biblical poem often singled out both for its marked traditionalism and for its consummate art.

BIBLICAL POETRY: WHY IS IT?

The last of our three questions about biblical poetry is in many
ways the most difficult to address. It is one thing to perceive a distinctive
outlook and a distinctive style, but quite another matter to fathom what
special needs these poetic modes of thought and expression actually
filled. As has often been observed, the vividness of poetic language, and,
more specifically, the regularity of meter and parallelism, make biblical
poetry especially memorable, functioning almost as a kind of mnemonic
device. Clearly, the capacity to preserve and transmit tradition suggests
one indispensable function of poetry in the Bible, but it does not exhaust
the possibilities raised by our question.

It would, perhaps, be edifying to assume, as some have, that the
noblest or most profound spiritual insights of ancient Israel simply had
to be expressed in what was deemed its noblest idiom. The theory,
however, falls short of the actual practice. What of the ancient "Song of
Lamech" in Genesis 4.23–24?

> (a) Adah and Zillah, hear my voice,
>   O wives of Lamech, give ear to my speech.
> (b) I have slain a man for wounding me,
>   And a lad for bruising me.
> (c) If Cain is avenged sevenfold,
>   Then Lamech seventy-sevenfold.

Within these three poetic lines parallelism and meter impart classical
balance, and the passage as a whole is likewise artfully structured. Note,
for example, that in the original Hebrew, lines (b) and (c) are not only
conceptually related, but are also formally coordinated, each being introduced by the particle *ki* (which cannot be rendered uniformly by any
one English equivalent). Also present is the characteristically shifting
focus observed in other biblical poems, here a specific application in (b)
juxtaposed to a general truth in (c), accompanied by the movement
between a generalized relationship of "man" and "lad" in (b), and a
specific relationship of ancestor (Cain) and descendant (Lamech) in (c).
But while all of these observations on the "poetic" nature of this passage
may hold true, it is equally true that the brutal braggadocio expressed
here is neither noble nor profound.

Obviously, I have selected an extreme case, one whose "poetry" I
calculated to fall on deaf ears in a culture such as ours, in which (nomi-
nally, at least) vindictiveness is not esteemed as the admirable quality

one celebrates in song. To be a bit more fair to Lamech and his song, this fragmentary passage in Genesis does not stand within any explanatory narrative context, so that the morality or aptness of its sentiment cannot, in fact, be judged. What we have here may well be a relic from some now vanished heroic epic, preserved in the fourth chapter of Genesis, not for its sublime truths, but for its venerable antiquity. To be sure, this tantalizingly terse vignette from the life of Lamech succeeds admirably in drawing with precision and economy the emotional contours of an outspoken personality who would have otherwise been relegated to a silent slot in the genealogy that precedes the passage. Nevertheless, the essential point remains valid, namely, in ancient Israel the poetic mode does not seem to have been restricted exclusively to what we might consider the cause of spirituality or aesthetics.

A less disquieting, but perhaps equally surprising function of biblical poetry is related to the conduct of warfare. Thus, for example, in the "Song of Deborah," an ancient victory hymn preserved in Judges 5, we hear the poet, speaking for all Israel, implore:

> (12) Awake, awake, O Deborah!
> Awake, awake, *strike up the chant!*
> Take your captives, O son of Abi-
> noam!

The reference here seems to be to some poem celebrating a spectacular victory of the past, to be sung before the battle and so inspire confidence or bolster morale. One is reminded of the tradition that in 1066, at the Battle of Hastings, the heroic "Song of Roland" was recited for the benefit of William the Conqueror and his troops. Whatever its basis in fact, the tradition, like our passage from the "Song of Deborah," suggests that our own notion of what constitutes a "congenial" setting for the recitation of poetry be kept as broad as possible.

It is thus no inherently "elevated" quality that singles out biblical poetry as the favored voice of ancient Israel's most enlightening visions and the principal medium of divine revelation itself. Rather, a possible answer to the "why" of biblical poetry is more likely to proceed from our appreciation of its peculiar genius for effecting the direct, immediate involvement of its audience in a kind of emotional dialogue with both its form and content. One might even say that biblical poetry is actually created as the end result of dialogue. No biblical poem derives from a vacuum, the private work of some lone, idiosyncratic individual recording his own musings, or renderings of reality, primarily for his own edification. As one composing "traditional" poetry, the poet participates in, and is in constant dialogue with a literary tradition from which he draws and to which he adds. Thus he never quite composes alone. His audience, as bearers of tradition, constitutes his collaborator, who interacts with the poet by bringing to his words definite expectations that lend them both shape and substance.

Indeed, the biblical poet is hardly ever out of communication, or dialogue, with someone. It may be as prophet, alternately consoling and rebuking his troubled people; it may be as teacher addressing his instruction with words "O my son"; or it may be as worshiper approaching the Deity, now with bitter complaint, now with grateful words of thanksgiving. Biblical poetry is, in fact, much like biblical religion; it is a relational phenomenon. It both derives from interaction and has the marked capacity to generate more of the same. Thus, for example, in the classical "Song of Deborah" of Judges 5, the poet cannot be content to remain an impassive narrator of events which are to him so personally engaging:

> (9) My heart is with Israel's leaders,
>   With the dedicated of the people—
> Bless the Lord!

This exuberant sense of involvement, or dialogue, with his subject also embraces personal invective:

> (15–16) Among the clans of Reuben
>   Were great decisions of heart.
> Why then did you stay among the sheepfolds
>   And listen as they pipe for the flocks?
> Among the clans of Reuben
>   Were great searchings of heart!

The audience of this poem could not, and cannot remain unaffected by the poet's interaction with his subject, which by its very nature reaches out to include all who hear his lingering question and await its answer.

In like manner, the wisdom poetry of the Bible effectively exploits this same potential for personal involvement as a mode of instruction. Thus the poem of Job does not formally, or didactically expound its profound insights into the nature of divine justice or the limits of human wisdom. Instead, its themes are developed at length through the sustained personal interaction between Job and his "comforters," as well as our own interaction with the various players in this drama. We become intimately aware of their individual temperaments and closely follow their shifting moods, especially as these result from the nature of the ongoing dialogue—the reasoned calm of Eliphaz in chapters 4–5, his ruffled aggressiveness in chapter 15, and ultimately his unbridled hostility in chapter 22. What engages us so directly is not simply the clash of ideas, but also the clash of the personalities espousing those ideas, and our own fluctuating sympathies with respect to these individuals. The dialogue in the book of Job is as much the message as the medium. Indeed, of prime interest in the book is precisely our emerging appreciation of the limits of human dialogue, in which people "talk at" one another, as opposed to a direct and immediate encounter with the Deity.

Prophecy favors the poetic voice for much the same reason. It too relies on poetry's unique way of achieving immediate, intimate rapport. What is the ultimate concern of the prophet, if not the empathetic dialogue between God and Israel, and what better "sensitivity training" than the interaction between the prophetic word and the popular sensibility? Isaiah, of course, never hesitates to avail himself of poetry's lyricism and sonorous beauty, but he is, I think, never more successful in his mission as prophet than when he draws upon the poetic resources for both reflecting and generating personal involvement. The "Song of the Vineyard" (Isa. 5) is a case in point:

> (1) Let me sing for my beloved
>   A song of my lover about his vineyard.
>   My beloved had a vineyard
>   On a fruitful hill.
> (2) He broke the ground, cleared it of stones,
>   And planted it with choice vines.
>   He built a watchtower inside it,
>   He even hewed a wine press in it;
>   For he hoped it would yield grapes.
>   Instead, it yielded wild grapes.
> (3) "Now, then,
>   Dwellers of Jerusalem
>   And men of Judah,
>   You be the judges
>   Between Me and My vineyard:
> (4) What more could have been done for My vineyard
>   That I failed to do in it?
>   Why, when I hoped it would yield grapes,
>   Did it yield wild grapes?"

The language here is decidedly not "poetic" in our sense of featuring elevated diction, or sublime imagery, or lyrical mood. Nor is it particularly distinguished in terms of the specifically biblical canons of internal and external symmetry or the various other forms of poetic balance, especially parallelism. Rather, the unique success of the "poetry" in this passage rests on its manifest power first to create a highly emotional dialogue, and then to involve us personally as parties to it. The poet begins speaking with detachment about his beloved's vineyard, but before long his voice becomes submerged in that of his distraught intimate, the God of Israel. Then poet and subject as one draw us into the situation with the direct appeal: "*You* be the judges." As we share their sense of outrage, as Judah and Jerusalem once shared their sense of outrage, there emerges the ultimate dialogue between one's "selves"—the highest to which we might aspire and the lower levels at which we actually function. It is precisely the capacity for such inner dialogue that the poet, as prophet, seeks to implant in the consciousness of his audience. And it is precisely for its marked facility at conducting and generating more than one kind of dialogue at any given time that the prophet turns to poetry as the voice for his vision.

Biblical literature is, of course, primarily "religious" literature: whatever its particular subject, its underlying theme remains the relationship between God and Israel. And the Bible's most consciously religious literature, the genre most specifically designed as a vehicle of rapport between man and God, is prayer. Not surprisingly, therefore, prayer presents some striking instances of the unique role played by poetry in the Bible. By contrast, the petitionary prayers of, for example, Eliezer (Gen. 24.12–14), Moses (Exod. 32.31–32) and Hezekiah (2 Kings 19.15–19) are all formulated in elegantly simple and straightforward prose. While as expressions of sincere religious sentiment they cannot be faulted, they nevertheless leave one wanting for precisely the kind of religious effect of which poetry is capable. As we begin reading these heartfelt prayers addressed to God, we are "outsiders," which is to be expected. By their conclusion, however, we remain outsiders still, and the problems of the petitioner remain his, and his alone. Not so in the poetry of the prayerful Fifty-first Psalm, which also speaks to God in highly personal terms but which, in the process, embraces the larger world of which we too are a part. Thus, even as the petitioner acknowledges his many private transgressions, he succeeds in redirecting our attention from any particular infractions of the moment to the broader, more universal dimensions of human guilt and remorse:

> (7) Indeed I was born with iniquity;
>   With sin my mother conceived me.

What we have here in this deliberate blurring of temporal, and even generational, lines is not simply the kind of hyperbole, or figurative speech, which one expects in a poetic mode. It is, rather, an equally "poetic" attempt at widening the circle of interested parties. The motivation of petitioner and poet alike is even more transparent in the explicit promise

> (15) I will teach transgressors Your ways,
>   That sinners may return to You.

Finally, the pleas for private restoration are balanced by the all-inclusive national aspiration

> (20) May it please You to make Zion prosper;
>   Rebuild the walls of Jerusalem.

The poetic vision and voice of Psalm 51 effectively transform a private petition into what is experienced as a dialogue of shared religious concern, conducted simultaneously between worshiper and Deity, poet and audience, Israel and the world.

WHERE TO GO FROM HERE

The phenomenon of biblical poetry remains greater than the sum of its parts—its what, how and why. The present essay could, at most, aim at introducing the reader to the kinds of questions one might ask, and provide, by example, some ways of approaching these questions. This introduction to biblical poetry will, it is hoped, be read as an invitation to reread in full those biblical texts cited in the discussion by name or only in brief excerpts, and more importantly, to consider any or all of the great number of poems that had to go unmentioned entirely.

Thus, as indicated earlier, the same kind of comparative study undertaken here with respect to the prose narrative of Exodus 14 and the "Song of the Sea" in Exodus 15 may also be applied to Judges 4 and 5, which likewise treat a single historical event in both prose and poetry (the "Song of Deborah"). In beginning this exercise in isolating distinctively poetic perspectives and techniques (what we have called the "vision" and "voice" of biblical poetry), one should consult a recent scholarly commentary on the book of *Judges,* such as that in the *Anchor Bible* series (Garden City, N.Y.: Doubleday, 1975). This kind of critical commentary calls necessary attention to the numerous uncertainties that still challenge biblical scholars as to the original form and meaning of individual words and even whole verses of this chapter. Comparison and contrast of any three or four different English translations of a given passage will suffice to indicate the scope of these uncertainties. Clearly, whether one is reading biblical poetry in the Hebrew, or in a reliable English translation, appreciation of both form and content must be preceded by some awareness of the considerable gap that exists between a modern Western reader and an ancient biblical text. The gap is not only geographical, chronological, and linguistic, but most especially, cultural as well. An up-to-date commentary—including the items cited in its bibliography—offers a guide to what biblical scholarship has done to narrow that gap, and prepares the reader for the kinds of problems involved in producing an accurate translation of a given passage in the "Song of Deborah" or elsewhere.

As a next step, one might consider the poetic structure of the passage in Judges 5. Can we detect here the same kind of alternating pattern of historical references and hymnic reactions as in Exodus 15? If so, does the poet succeed in creating the same kind of "shimmering" effect, passing back and forth between the particular and the universal, the time-bound and the timeless? By determining what the victory hymns of Judges 5 and Exodus 15 have in common, we are well on the way toward recognizing the two as belonging to one genre, or class of poetry, distinct from other genres.

In reading Judges 5 or any other biblical poem, close attention should be paid to the parallel structure of the individual poetic lines, trying, in each case, to determine what kinds of balance—verbal, stylistic, conceptual, and so on—the poet has achieved through his juxtaposition of the halves of a poetic line. It is also important to resolve the poem into its larger discrete units. One should look for some telltale change in subject matter, speaker, or style as a guide to where one unit ends and another begins. As we have seen, close attention to the *repetition* of words and phrases aids us in recognizing distinct patterns, patterns that constitute the internal organization of the poem. While we may be used to reading poetry in which the poet has supplied us with neat divisions into stanzas and like units, in biblical poetry the burden rests with the reader to detect more subtle indications of structure and plan. It may even be helpful to set aside for the moment the printed format of your translation and write out the poem for yourself, clearly marking off the units and divisions you have decided upon by some system of stanzas, spacing, or indentation.

Recognizing the individual components or sections of a biblical poem, however, is only a beginning, not an end, in its fullest appreciation. There must also be some attempt to understand the conceptual relationship between the various parts of the poem. Here one might look for symmetry or balance in form, which mirrors some kind of symmetry or balance in content—two structurally balanced units that echo one another in sentiment, two that complement one another, two that contrast, or two that express cause and effect. A key focus in determining the relationship between the parts of a poem to the whole is provided by the idea of a *progression*. Is there any discernible movement in setting or mood from the beginning of the piece to its conclusion, such as, for example, the movement from the celestial to the earthly realm that a reader will observe in Psalm 29?

These and other approaches to the reading of biblical poetry will be greatly facilitated both by a proper translation and by any number of specific works devoted to the appreciation of biblical literature. The English translation that is quoted throughout this study (but departed from, on occasion, better to illustrate a given point) is the new rendering by the Jewish Publication Society, now available in three volumes: *The Torah* (2nd ed., 1967), *The Prophets* (1978), *The Writings* (1982). Aside from its accuracy and clarity, this translation is unmatched in the honesty with which it indicates to the otherwise unsuspecting English reader the existence of real difficulties in the original Hebrew text and the gaps in our present knowledge.

Much has been written on the various aspects of biblical poetry—its history, stylistics, theology—and much more will doubtless be written in the future by biblical scholars and literary critics alike. Unfortunately, a great deal of the bibliography of our subject is restricted to highly technical discussions in professional journals not readily accessible or known to the general reader. One very useful resource for locating such studies, including quite a few that deal directly with some of the texts discussed here (e.g., Exodus 15, Deuteronomy 32, Judges 5, Psalm 29, and so on), is the annotated bibliography (covering the years 1915–72) found in the reprinted edition of a classic work on biblical poetry, G. B. Gray, *The Forms of Hebrew Poetry* (New York: Ktav, 1972); see the "Prolegomenon" by D. N. Freedman.

Here are the names of some of the older, book-length appreciations of biblical poetry that are especially directed at the more general reader (listed in order of publication date):

R. G. Moulton. *The Literary Study of the Bible*. Boston, N.Y. and Chicago: D. C. Heath and Co., 1899.

E. G. King. *Early Religious Poetry of the Hebrews*. Cambridge: Cambridge University Press, 1911.

P. C. Sands. *Literary Genius of the Old Testament.* Oxford: Clarendon Press, 1926.

D. B. Macdonald. *The Hebrew Literary Genius.* Princeton: Princeton University Press, 1933; reissued 1968.

T. H. Robinson. *The Poetry of the Old Testament.* London: Gerald Duckworth & Co., 1947; repr., 1960.

While some of these studies are obviously outdated, especially with regard to the comparative study of biblical and Canaanite poetry, much can still be gained from their specifically literary perspectives and often illuminating examples. Of these works, the most reliable and objective is the last-named study by T. H. Robinson.

A more recent treatment, which presents an admirably comprehensive survey in a brief format, is the article "Biblical Poetry" in the *Encyclopaedia Judaica* (vol. 13, P-Rec, pp. 671–81; see bibliography on pp. 692–93), written by J. Muilenburg. For a most interesting look at how different generations have understood the formal techniques of biblical poetry, see J. L. Kugel, *The Idea of Biblical Poetry: Parallelism and Its History* (New Haven and London: Yale University Press, 1981, esp. pp. 96–286). A more general and popularly oriented appreciation is available in S. Sandmel, *The Enjoyment of Scripture* (London, Oxford and New York: Oxford University Press, 1972), chap. 7, "Verse and Poetry."

The cultural background of a good deal of the imagery found in biblical poetry is strikingly illuminated by comparative material from the ancient Near East and world literature in T. H. Gaster, *Myth, Legend and Custom in the Old Testament* (New York and Evanston: Harper and Row, 1969). For a representative collection of poetic texts from the ancient Near East (in English translation), see J. B. Pritchard, ed., *Ancient Near Eastern Texts Relating to the Old Testament* (Princeton: Princeton University Press, 3rd ed. with supp., 1969). In the latter, note especially the renderings of Ugaritic myths and legends by H. L. Ginsberg, which present most of what has survived of ancient Canaanite poetry in what is clearly the most reliable English translation. These texts contain the closest parallels yet discovered to the formal and stylistic features of biblical poetry, and their ongoing interpretation by scholars is a perpetual source of revitalization to the study of our subject.

First page of the early printed Soncino Talmud of 1483.

CHAPTER TWO

Talmud

ROBERT GOLDENBERG

> When the persecutions of Hadrian were over, our Sages gathered at Usha: R.★ Judah, and R. Nehemiah, and R. Meir, and R. Yose, and R. Simeon ben Yohai, and R. Eliezer the son of R. Yose the Galilean, and R. Eliezer ben Jacob. They sent a message to the elders of the Galilee, saying, "Let whoever has learned come and teach, and whoever has not learned come and learn." They gathered together, learned and taught, and did as the times required.
>
> —SONG OF SONGS RABBAII 2.16

Although this story appears only in a relatively late source, it reflects the central motive of the rabbinic movement from the time of its first appearance in Jewish life. Convinced that Jewish life could recover from its defeats at the hands of Rome only through renewed dedication to "Torah," rabbis organized themselves to spread their teaching, gain disciples, and achieve the largest possible role in Jewish life. Of all the books that ancient rabbis have left behind, the most revealing, the most challenging, and the most rewarding is the Talmud.

The word "Torah" was just placed in quotation marks to call attention to its special meaning. For the ancient rabbis, as mentioned in the Introduction, "Torah" meant far more than the five books attributed to Moses that Jews customarily call by that name. For them, Torah was

★ The standard abbreviation for Rabbi or Rav ("Rav" was the title of ordination in the ancient Babylonian Jewish community).

the Divine Wisdom which had existed before the world came into being (see Prov. 8.22–31), indeed, the blueprint according to which Creation had followed its proper course. Torah included all possible knowledge of God's will, of the life the Creator intended for the Chosen People to live. All things, from the most trivial to the most sublime, were within its realm.

Basing this notion on certain hints in the text of Scripture, ancient rabbis taught that the revelation granted to Moses had been delivered in two forms, a smaller revelation in writing and the larger one kept oral. This "Oral Torah" had been transmitted faithfully by the leaders of each generation to their successors, by Moses to Joshua, and then to the elders, then to the prophets, to the men of the Great Assembly, to the leaders of the Pharisees, and finally to the earliest rabbis. Thus only these rabbis knew the *whole* Torah—written *and* oral—and only such knowledge could qualify anyone for legitimate leadership over the people of Israel.

The earliest rabbis saw themselves, as noted, as heirs to the Pharisees. This ancient sect has acquired a terrible reputation, primarily because of the intense hostility to it expressed in a few chapters of the New Testament. What the Pharisees aimed at, however, was essentially the extension of holiness from the limits of the Jerusalem Temple to a wider range of everyday life. They sought, for example, to eat all their meals, not only sacrificial foods, in a state of Levitical purity; this concern, which will be reflected in the sample passage below (pp. 132–133), had the effect of putting much routine activity under the regulation of laws originally intended for special events. On the one hand, this tendency produced the concern for ritual detail that underlies the early Christian critique of Pharisaism, but on the other it turned life into an inexhaustible supply of opportunities to fulfill divine law and thus to sanctify life.

Associated with the Pharisees were the scribes, also attacked in the New Testament as pettifogging, self-righteous hypocrites, but also open to more charitable understanding. The scribes were men who devoted their entire lives to the study and teaching of Holy Writ and to the unending development of new techniques for interpreting it, again a religious style open to corruption, but again one founded on an unexceptionable premise. The scribes were Jews who considered the Scriptures a source of infinite wisdom, and saw no better way to spend their lives than in study.

The rabbinic movement can be understood as combining these two impulses; it sought to merge studiousness with a sense that the laws of Scripture should be expanded to cover all of life, not limited to their own originally intended contexts. Beginning in the Land of Israel, the rabbis sought to carry this conception of Jewish life to the entire Diaspora, that widespread dispersion of Jewish communities that had begun in Babylonia in the sixth century B.C.E., and had been growing ever since. Within a century of the destruction of the Temple in the year 70 C.E., rabbis had started organizing the "Oral Torah," and were preparing it for permanent transmission:

> R. Akiba [d. 135] was like a worker who took his basket and went outside. He found wheat and put it in; he found barley and put it in; he found spelt and put it in; he found lentils and put them in. When he came into his house, he set aside the wheat by itself, the barley by itself, the beans by themselves. R. Akiba did likewise, and made the whole Torah into separate rings.
>
> —AVOT D'RABBI NATHAN, ch. 18

This rather odd story expresses the rabbis' conception of how their own literature began to grow. Rabbi Akiba, the great martyr-hero of the early second century, is described as the first compiler of "Oral Torah." Much like a gleaner who sorts the day's collection after his return home, Akiba is credited with initiating a process in which numerous miscellaneous fragments of transmitted lore were organized and collected under subject headings ("rings") of various kinds. This earliest codification of rabbinic teaching began, it is said, early in the second century; although this part of the tradition cannot be verified, it is certain that by the turn of the third century the Mishnah ("Recitation," "Recapitulation," that is, of the Oral Torah) was complete.

The Mishnah is the core document of the Talmudic tradition. Composed in very terse language and arranged topic by topic over a wide range of subjects, the Mishnah looks much like a code of Jewish law, though it probably is something other than that. Full of unresolved legal disputes and liberally sprinkled with nonlegal materials (stories, interpretations of Scripture, and so on), the Mishnah probably represents an early attempt to reduce the Oral Torah to an official compilation, to prepare some authoritative statement of the minimal amount of learning a disciple had to acquire for admittance to advanced rank in the rabbinic movement. The Mishnah is thus the earliest teaching-text, the oldest curriculum of Jewish learning in the world today.

The Mishnah is divided into six Orders, each dealing with a broad area of Jewish life. These in turn are divided into smaller topical sections called *massekhtot* ("webbings," usually translated "tractates" or "treatises"); there are sixty-three of these in all. The tractates of the Mishnah vary in length, and within each Order are generally arranged according to size. Each Order and almost every tractate is called by a one-word name that reflects its dominant theme.

The first Order of the Mishnah is called *Zera'im* (Seeds), and deals mostly with agricultural law (tithes, first-fruits, and so on). The first tractate, however, is called Berakhot (Blessings); it deals with the life of prayer in Judaism, both regular daily prayer and prayer for special occasions, and presumably was placed at the beginning of the entire work because it seemed an appropriate way to start it out. A good way to see what the Mishnah as a whole is like is to see how it begins.

MISHNAH BERAKHOT, CHAPTER ONE

1. From what time [may people] recite the evening Shema?★ From the hour that the priests come in to eat of their Heave-offering, until the end of the first watch; [these are] R. Eliezer's words, but the Sages say, Until midnight. R. Gamaliel says, Until the first light of dawn. There was a case when his sons came back from a feast; they said to him, "We have not recited Shema." He said to them, "If the first light of dawn has not appeared, you are obliged to recite." And not only [in] this [case], but [in] every [case where] the Sages have said "Until midnight," the commandment [applies] until the first light of dawn: the burning of fat parts and [prescribed] limbs [on the altar]—the commandment [to do so applies] until the first light of dawn; all [sacrifices] which are to be eaten for [only] one day —the commandment [to do so applies] until the first light of dawn. If so, why did the Sages say "Until midnight"? In order to keep a man away from transgression.

2. From what time [may people] recite the morning Shema? From [the time one can] distinguish between blue and white. R. Eliezer says, Between blue and green. And he [must] finish it by sunrise. R. Joshua says, Within three hours [of sunrise], since it is the way of princes to arise at the third hour. One who recites from this hour forward has not lost anything; [he is] like a man reading in the Torah.

3. The House of Shammai say, In the evening every man [must] recline and recite, and in the morning, they [must]

★ For an explanation of what "reciting Shema" is, see Chapter Eight.

stand, as it is said, "When you lie·down and when you rise up" (Deut. 6.7). But the House of Hillel say, Every man reads in his [own] way, as it is said, "And as you go along the way" (Ibid.). If so, why does it say, "And when you lie down and when you rise up"?—At the hour that people [generally] lie down and the hour that people [generally] rise up. Said R. Tarfon, "I was once travelling and I lay down to recite according to the opinion of the House of Shammai, and I endangered myself on account of robbers." They said to him, "You deserved to lose your life, since you violated the opinion of the House of Hillel."

4. In the morning [one] recites two blessings before [Shema] and one after it, and in the evening two before it and two after it, one long and one short. At a place where they said to lengthen, he is not permitted to shorten; [where they said] to shorten, he is not permitted to lengthen. [Where they said] to seal off [a blessing, with the words "Blessed art Thou . . ."], he is not permitted not to seal off; [where they said] not to seal off, he is not permitted to seal off.

5. [People] make mention of the Exodus from Egypt at night [as well as by day]. Said R. Eleazar b. Azariah, "Behold, I am as one seventy years old but I was never worthy [to prove] that the Exodus from Egypt should be mentioned at night, until Ben Zoma offered this interpretation, as it is said, 'In order that you remember the day of your leaving the land of Egypt all the days of your life' (Deut. 16.3): 'The days of your life' [would mean] the days; 'all the days of your life' [includes] the nights." But the Sages say, "The days of your life" [means] this world; "all the days of your life" includes the days of the Messiah.

Even without stopping to explain all the technical details of this chapter (some of that will be done below), the reader can learn much from examining it. First, the text takes very much for granted. The reader of this chapter must already know what "reciting Shema" means, and is expected to agree that the recitation must take place twice a day, since it seems that only details of hour and posture remain to be clarified. References to entirely unconnected matters of cultic ritual are added without any effort to explain them, and indeed one such reference (to the time that priests eat Heave-offering)* is crucial to the very first

---

* Heave-offering (Hebrew terumah) was a kind of religious tax on fresh produce that people gave to the priests. It had to be kept undefiled, and could not be eaten by persons who had become impure.

sentence in the chapter. Technical concepts like "seal off a blessing" similarly are mentioned with no effort to explain what they mean. It is of course true that the Mishnah is a large work, and that many of these phrases are explained more fully elsewhere in it. Still, the text as it stands here makes no reference to such explanations. One simply begins at the beginning, and one is expected to make one's own way.

Second, disagreements are never resolved. The text reports that the "Houses" of Shammai and Hillel do not agree concerning the proper posture for reciting Shema, but it fails to indicate how one really ought to recite it. It reveals that R. Tarfon's colleagues shared the Hillelite opinion, but not why, or whether they considered that everyone should share this preference. Similarly, the different time limits in paragraphs 1 and 2 are simply allowed to stand side by side. No single answer is ever declared authoritative, and in fact several of them are couched in extremely vague or exotic terms and never clarified at all.

Third, nonlegal materials (several stories, the Midrash of Ben Zoma) are regularly used to support or to illustrate legal opinions. Such a "proof" is quoted in full in the last paragraph but then rejected anyway. Indeed, the Sages' interpretation of Deuteronomy 16.3 implies that the Exodus from Egypt is not part of the evening Shema after all, though even that is never clearly stated, nor is the implied disagreement ever resolved. Thus the relationship between the rules and the supporting materials in this chapter remains unclear.

In other words, while the Mishnah *looks like* a code of rules for Jewish life, it apparently *is* something else. It requires more elucidation than it supplies, and it fails to tell how its contents might actually be put into practice. It is, however, a remarkably seductive text: anyone studying these chapters will almost inevitably frame a list of questions for further inquiry—What is "reciting Shema" anyway? Why evening? Why morning? Why do these authorities disagree like this, and who are they, anyway? How has each arrived at his opinion, and how are those who would be their disciples actually supposed to act?

The Mishnah serves extremely well for the training of disciples or for the education of a community. It covers the main themes of Jewish life, and it does so in a way that teaches the most important point of all: Jewish life is a life of constant study; one's Jewish learning is never complete while any part of it remains unexplained or incompletely integrated with the rest. Thus the Mishnah almost at once gave rise to a tradition of careful, detailed text-study that has continued down to the present.

From Mishnah to Talmud

Within a generation of its first appearance toward the turn of the third century C.E., the Mishnah had become the central text of the Oral Torah.* In the Galilee, and increasingly in Babylonia (today part of Iraq) as well, groups of rabbis and their disciples would gather to study its tractates, clarify their meaning, and apply their instructions to situations arising in their own lives. These study groups, which apparently began as informal arrangements meeting in people's homes, are the ancestors of the academies of Talmudic study *(yeshivot)* that are still the centers of rabbinic training today.

Over succeeding generations, as rabbis continued their study of Oral Torah, a tradition of commentary and explanation began to grow. The first generation applied itself chiefly to clarifying passages of the Mishnah that seemed obscure, but this work was soon accomplished, and rabbinic attention moved on to other concerns: extracting general principles of action from the particular rules that the Mishnah supplies, or expanding the collection of recorded precedents and actual applications of Mishnah-law in functioning rabbinic courts. Soon a new body of Oral Torah began to accumulate with the Mishnah as its core: the first generation discussed the Mishnah; the second generation continued this discussion, but also discussed the comments of their predecessors; the third generation discussed the Mishnah, both sets of earlier comments, and also their relationship to one another; and so on for several hundred years.

This rapidly expanding mass eventually became an object of study in its own right, called *talmud* in Hebrew and *gemara* in Aramaic; both words mean "study," and both had had other meanings before they became the names for the post-Mishnaic rabbinic tradition. The "webbing" of the Oral Torah grew ever tighter, as traditions attached to different passages of Mishnah came to refer to one another, or to draw connections between related Mishnaic materials that do not themselves express these links. Attention came to be drawn to the various sayings attributed to a given rabbi in the hope of detecting the hidden principles that held his teachings together, or alternatively to find apparent contradictions in his rulings and then to resolve them. As new materials were produced by successive generations, it became necessary to decide where

* Note that a "text" can be oral.

to fit them in. Thus the Talmudic tradition became more and more tightly organized, while at the same time newly created materials always threatened to dismember this organization at its seams. When, after centuries, this process of steady accumulation and slightly less steady organization finally came to a halt, the books now called the Talmud★ remained as its monument. All modern forms of Jewish religion stand on this foundation.

There are two Talmuds. The earlier, the Jerusalem or Palestinian Talmud (it was really produced in the Galilee), dates from the first half of the fifth century. It takes the form of an extremely loose and elaborate commentary on selected tractates of the Mishnah. Proceeding paragraph by paragraph, it offers a jumble of textual elucidation, case precedents and other stories, moral instruction both general and specific, theological speculation, legends about Bible characters and later people too, and so forth. It shows signs of insufficient editing: transitions, both within arguments and also between sections, are weak, and parallel discussions appear in widely separated sections with no reference to one another, each sometimes duplicating, sometimes contradicting the others. The first English translation of the Jerusalem Talmud has just now begun to appear, and it will run to numerous volumes and thousands of pages.

Yet the Jerusalem Talmud is barely half the size of the Babylonian. Dating from a century or two later, the Babylonian Talmud shows the result of more leisurely and more skillful preparation. The arguments in the legal sections are far more elegantly presented, with points made more trenchantly and with the help of a much larger arsenal of standard technical terms and rhetorical devices. The narratives in the Babylonian Talmud also tend to be smoother and more elaborate. In general, studying the Babylonian Talmud tends to be more challenging, but also more gratifying. It is frequently difficult, but the Jerusalem Talmud is often just obscure.

The complete Babylonian Talmud was issued in English translation several decades ago by the Soncino Press. It is currently available in several different formats.†

★ Unfortunately, the word "Talmud" has two meanings. It can refer to the *gemara,* that is, to the huge mass of rabbinic discussion of Mishnah that accumulated after that text appeared, or it can refer to the composite works—Mishnah plus *gemara*—that usually go by that name. This ambiguity sometimes became deceiving because the two meanings are so closely related.
† A short list of translations and other study aids appears at the end of this chapter.

A Talmudic Glossary

In preparation for examining a sample passage from the Talmud, it may help to explain a number of terms.

Mishnah—As already mentioned, this is the name of the earliest major rabbinic book, though the term also is used to denote a single paragraph of that collection. The Mishnah as a whole is arranged like a code: a *mishnah* (i.e., a single paragraph) is part of a chapter, a chapter part of a tractate, a tractate part of an Order. Every passage of the Talmud ostensibly belongs to the discussion of one *mishnah* or another. The central status of the Mishnah in the rabbinic tradition is reflected in the fact that the Talmud has a special set of technical terms for quoting from it, terms that ought not to be used when other rabbinic materials are cited.★

Tosefta (Aramaic, supplement)—A collection of older traditions similar to the Mishnah, this work concentrates on materials that the editor(s) of the Mishnah chose not to include. The Tosefta is arranged like the Mishnah into Orders and tractates, but its relationship to the Mishnah is hard to determine. Certain sections seem like commentaries on the parallel sections in the Mishnah, others seem more like alternate versions of the Mishnah itself, others seem to have almost nothing to do with the Mishnah, almost no connection at all. These different sorts of relationships can appear within one tractate, in unpredictable sequence. For scholars, therefore, the Tosefta is noteworthy because it sheds some light on the development of the materials appearing in the Mishnah itself, but there will be little further occasion to mention it here.

Baraita (Aramaic, outside)—A *baraita* is a piece of tradition appearing in one of the Talmuds but attributed to a rabbinic teacher who lived in the time of the Mishnah or even earlier. All such early traditions, though not part of the Mishnah itself, were held by later teachers to be authoritative in some way,† but since they often contradicted one an-

---

★ This does not mean, to be sure, that the contents of the Mishnah always determined the actual law.
† In general, the various periods in the history of the rabbinic tradition (Mishnaic, Talmudic, early medieval, late medieval, etc.) are arranged hierarchically in order of age. Though this rule was often disregarded, there was a general tendency for every age to accept as binding the texts and the decisions of its predecessors.

other, and since later teachers also often felt free to disregard them, the exact nature of that authority is hard to determine. At the very least it can be said that no such tradition could simply be ignored. If a *baraita* was quoted in the course of a discussion, its meaning and its implications necessarily had to be explored. Any later teacher could strengthen the authority of his opinion by quoting a *baraita* in its support.

Tanna (Aramaic, repeater)—The Tannaim, as they are collectively known, were the authorities whose work is assembled in the Mishnah; the name reflects their characteristic mode of teaching—repeating Oral Torah. The first century or so following the destruction of Jerusalem is thus known as the Tannaitic period, and the Mishnah, the Tosefta, and certain other books are called Tannaitic literature. The shorthand for the preceding discussion of *baraita* could therefore be this: the Talmuds consider any fragment of Tannaitic tradition worthy of their most serious attention.

Amora (Aramaic, discusser)—The Amoraim are the rabbinic teachers of the post-Mishnaic era whose traditions are found in the *gemara* part of the Talmuds themselves. The Amoraic era was thus the successor to the Tannaitic. In theory, the Amoraim simply expanded on the Tannaitic foundation of Judaism, but in fact the several centuries of Amoraic activity saw the rabbinic tradition enter into a decisively new phase, as the preceding description of the Talmud tried to suggest.

Halakhah (Hebrew, law; derived from the verb *to go*)—The *halakhah* is the set of rules often known as "Jewish law" that governs Jewish life. It must be kept in mind, however, that the *halakhah* embraces far more than the term "law" usually suggests in English; its subject matter is much broader, and much Jewish "law" is in principle unenforceable. Who, for example, really knows which kitchens in a given community are kosher, or which members of that community secretly violate the Sabbath?

Although the Mishnah only looks like a law code, nevertheless, most of its content pertains to the *halakhah;* although the Talmud only looks like a commentary on the Mishnah, the same can be said of it. The earliest public role in the Jewish community that rabbis were able to achieve was as judges and community officials. *Halakhah* naturally became their chief concern, a concern that fit their theological conviction that Judaism essentially amounts to learning precisely what the Torah commands and then *doing* it.

Aggadah (Hebrew, discourse)—Any nonhalakhic Talmudic discussion can be labeled *aggadah*. The term sometimes has the more specific meaning of rabbinic narrative, either stories about Bible heroes or about great rabbis of earlier generations. More broadly speaking, however, *aggadah* also embraces moral exhortation, theological speculation, and a great, miscellaneous variety of folklore. Despite its primary concern for *halakhah,* the Talmud is large enough to contain great quantities of *aggadah* sprinkled seemingly at random among its pages.

Finally, a picture of a page of the Talmud, and then a sample passage. The attached illustration (see page 140) depicts the very first page of the Babylonian Talmud, just as the analysis that is to follow will examine the Talmud's very first discussions. As the picture makes clear (see Schematic Drawing and Key, pages 141–42), even the layout of a page of Talmud reflects its character as discussion. In the middle of the page, set in larger type, are the oldest stages of the conversation, the Mishnah and the *gemara* themselves. The first word is enclosed in an ornate frame (this is true for every tractate), and then the first Mishnah is printed out in full. On the fourteenth line, set off by the enlarged Hebrew letters *gimmel-mem* (for *gemara*), the Mishnah ends and the Talmudic discussion begins; it will continue for fifteen pages and will include numerous and wide-ranging digressions (see below). Then *mishnah* number two is printed, and the Talmudic discussion resumes.

Surrounding the Talmudic text are the two most famous of the medieval commentaries. To the right is the commentary of Rashi (*Rabbi Shlomo Itzhaki,* 1040–1105), the master of Jewish commentators. In the course of his life, Rashi produced commentary on almost all the Bible (see Chapter Four) and almost all the Talmud, and to this day no traditional Jew will study either of those sacred texts without having Rashi at hand. Indeed, starting with the first printings of the Talmud in the late 1400s, almost every edition that has ever appeared has put Rashi right next to the central text, as he appears here. In this page, which stands to the left of the binding, Rashi is on the right, but on alternate pages he stands on the left. Thus, Rashi is always at the center of the volume, at the "heart" of the study of the Talmud.

On the right here, in the outside column, are the Tosafot (Heb., supplements). Originally amplifications of Rashi's comments by his own disciples and successors, the Tosafot developed over the next few generations into a vast interconnected set of specific queries. Where Rashi tries to keep track of the discussion on any specific page, the Tosafot seek to connect it with some other discussion elsewhere. Where Rashi seeks simplicity and clarity, the Tosafot aim at complexity—but often produce obscurity. Much of the Talmud's reputation for overcomplicated, "hairsplitting" dialectic derives from the Tosafot and their attempt to combine all Talmudic literature into a single, integrated whole.

מאימתי

קורין את שמע בערבין. משעה שהכהנים נכנסים לאכול בתרומתן עד סוף האשמורה הראשונה דברי ר׳ אליעזר. וחכמים אומרים עד חצות. רבן גמליאל אומר עד שיעלה עמוד השחר. מעשה ובאו בניו מבית המשתה אמרו לו לא קרינו את שמע אמר להם אם לא עלה עמוד השחר חייבין אתם לקרות ולא זו בלבד אמרו אלא כל מה שאמרו חכמים עד חצות מצותן עד שיעלה עמוד השחר...

First page of the Tractate Berakhot in standard edition of Talmud.

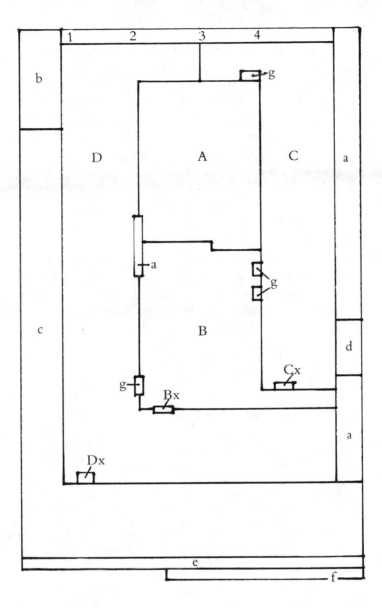

KEY TO SCHEMATIC DRAWING

Heading:

1. The letter *bet,* indicating page two, side one. There is no page one; see the text, page 143.
2. "Berakhot"
3. "First Chapter"
4. "From When"; most chapters of the Mishnah, and therefore of the Talmud, are named after their first words

continued

This was undeniably a worthy aim, but it has sometimes turned the Talmudic conversation into a gathering where everyone is talking at once.

Beyond Rashi and the Tosafot, at the margins of the page, numerous other voices enter the discussion: cross-references to other Talmudic sources, a key to quotations from the Bible and another to the great codes of Jewish law, additional briefer commentaries from medieval and even recent centuries. Off the page altogether, at the back of every volume of Talmud, even more such materials can be found. Commentaries and codifications of the Talmudic tradition have kept the Oral Torah alive up through the present.

In the upper left-hand corner of the sample page can be seen the Hebrew letter *bet,* indicating that this is page two. No Talmudic tractate has a page one; the book always begins, so to speak, on the second page. An old explanation of this practice has it that by starting on page two, by not learning page one first, you know from the very beginning of

---

KEY TO SCHEMATIC DRAWING *continued*

Major blocks of print:
   A. Mishnah Berakhot 1:1. Note the ornate design surrounding the first word.
   B. The beginning of the *gemara*. The *gemara* pertaining to this *mishnah* will continue until page 9b.
   C. The commentary of Rashi (1040–1105)
   D. The comments of Tosafot (Rashi's descendants and disciples)
On Rashi and the Tosafot, see the text, page 139.
In keeping with the early custom of printers, the first word on the next page is indicated for the *gemara,* Rashi, and the Tosafot. This custom is especially helpful with the sort of complicated page layout the Talmud tends to present. These words are indicated in the small boxes Bx, Cx, and Dx.

Other blocks of print:
   a. Cross-references to other passages in the Talmud
   b. Cross-references to medieval codes of Jewish law. These codes include the *Mishneh Torah* of Maimonides★ (1135–1204), the *Great Commandment-book* of R. Moses of Coucy (13th century), the *Four Turim* (Rows) of R. Jacob b. Asher (d. 1340), and the *Shulhan Arukh* of R. Joseph Caro★ (1488–1575). The two starred codes are discussed in the text, pages 161–63.
   c. The comments of R. Nissim Gaon (d. 1062)
   d. A textual emendation by R. Joel Sirkes (1561–1640)
   e. Notes by R. Akiba Eger (1761–1837)
   f. An anonymous comment, possibly added by the original printers of this edition (Romm, Vilna, 1880–86)
   g. Key to quotations from the Bible

your studies that you will never "know it all." More to the point, early printers assigned the number one to the very elaborate title page which they placed at the beginning of each volume, and then began the text with page two.* Furthermore, Hebrew books in those days numbered leaves, not pages. Thus every page number belonged to both sides of the sheet that carried it, and source references would have to cite "folio x, side a" or "side b." The standard way of citing the page just pictured therefore became "Berakhot 2a"—the first side of the second numbered sheet in tractate Berakhot. Since almost every edition of Talmud since the invention of printing has maintained a standard pagination, there is no need to specify edition or source beyond this number. "Berakhot 2a" will be the same in any edition a reader is likely to consult.

A Sample Passage: Berakhot 2a–3a

The following sample passage was taken from the Babylonian Talmud; since that one is "the" Talmud—the more authoritative, the more accessible, the more interesting—it seemed appropriate to draw our sample from it. The passage will be translated in full, without omissions, to give the full flavor of the Talmudic style of discourse. There will, however, be interruptions for explanation or elaboration; the text itself will be printed with indented margins, so any such interruptions will be easy to identify. The passage chosen is the very beginning of the Talmud, Berakhot 2a–3a; it is thus attached to the chapter of Mishnah that was translated above.

This entire section purports to be a discussion of the very first phrase in the Mishnah: "From what time may people recite the evening Shema? From the hour that the priests come in to eat of their Heave-offering. . . ." After a few introductory queries, the passage will present several definitions of the time when Shema may be recited and will raise certain questions concerning the relationship of these definitions to one another. It may seem that this is all a practical discussion, an effort to decide when in fact the time for Shema arrives and then to produce convenient tests for determining whether that moment has come.

It is important to keep in mind that this is not at all the true purpose of the passage. Two facts make this clear: the practical question at hand

---

* Most modern books are similar. Very few actually have a page one containing part of the body of the text.

(When should Shema be recited?) is never explicitly resolved, while the answer accepted by later tradition—Shema may be recited when the stars first appear—actually is provided in this passage but receives no particular attention. The Talmud both ignores the practical question and also answers it without noticing! If one may personify a text in such a way, its mind is clearly on something else.

It will be easier and more appropriate to discuss that "something else" after the sample passage has been examined.* For now, let it just be noted that the relationship of all these opinions to one another—which rabbi holds which view, which definition refers to an earlier hour, and so on—will turn out to be of greater interest than the practical matter of determining the law.

> GEMARA. Where is the Tanna standing that he teaches "From when," and further why is it that he starts with the evening? Let him start with the morning! The Tanna "stands" on Scripture, as it is written, "When you lie down and when you rise up" (Deut. 6.7), and he teaches thus: When is the time of the Shema-recitation of lying down? From the time that the priests come in to eat of their Heave-offering.

(The "I" in the next sentence can be understood as the editor adding his own observation to the ongoing discussion. Since all this material did in fact originate as oral give-and-take, such semiparenthetical remarks could very easily be inserted as extended treatments of any particular *mishnah* continued to develop. There is usually no way to determine who any given "I" is, or when any such insertion actually found its way into the text.)

> And if you like I can say he learns [this] from [the story of] the creation of the world, as it is written, "And it was evening, and it was morning, one day." (Gen. 1.5)

The Talmud begins simply, with an attempt to fill in the gaps in the Mishnah's presentation. Assuming that the author of the Mishnah must surely have biblical warrant for his rules—a warrant the Mishnah itself makes no effort to provide, and indeed for which it seems to feel no need—the *gemara* quotes the relevant verses from the Torah. Thus, the mutual independence of Written Torah and Oral Torah, which the Mishnah so clearly establishes in its very first chapter, appears to the

---

* For people who can't wait, an outline of the entire section appears below, on pp. 155–56.

Talmud a weakness that it equally quickly sets out to rectify. On the other hand, the basic terms of the Mishnah's discussion—the need to recite Shema at all, the connection with Heave-offering—are once again simply taken for granted.

Having identified the Tanna's biblical warrant, the Talmud proceeds to question his consistency in applying it.

> If so, later on, where he teaches "In the morning one recites two blessings before it and one after it, and in the evening he recites two blessings before it and two after it" (Mishnah 1.4), let him teach about the evening first!

People normally live their lives from morning to night; that is the natural way to conceive a "day." Yet our *mishnah* begins with a question about the evening Shema! The *gemara* began by demanding an explanation of this odd procedure, and by way of explanation provided a pair of biblical verses that reverse the sequence and put evening or "lying down" before morning. But now it turns out that the Tanna himself goes on to disregard these same precedents, because in *mishnah* 1.4 he treats the morning before the evening! What's going on?

The answer to this question has to do with literary techniques. The biblical verses induced the Tanna to start with the evening, but he did not wish to keep skipping back and forth. Thus, once he began to speak (in 1.2) of the morning, he decided to complete that discussion before he returned to his first topic. In technical language, this is called a chiastic structure, and rabbinic literature employs this pattern in a variety of ways.

> The Tanna began with the evening and then returned to teach about the morning *[in 1.2]*; as long as he was treating of the morning he explained matters pertaining to the morning, and then he turned back and explained matters pertaining to the evening.

Having thus defended the Tanna's editorial methods, the discussion turns to the substance of the law:

> The Master said, "From the time the priests come in to eat of their Heave-offering." Now when do priests eat Heave-offering? From the time the stars come out. Let him teach "From the time the stars come out"! *[By proceeding as he does]* he teaches us something extra by the way: Priests eat Heave-offering from the time the stars come out.

This paragraph clearly implies that Shema may be recited from the hour of the appearance of the stars, yet as already mentioned, this crucial conclusion is left implied, as though it was not worth stating. Instead, the question about Shema is now simply forgotten, and this mention of the stars becomes the pretext for a complex digression. The editors of the Talmud apparently sensed this was odd, and expressed their discomfort in the form of a question about the *mishnah* itself: why, if the point here is that one recites Shema when the stars come out, did the Tanna proceed so obliquely? They answer once again in terms of literary technique. By answering the question so indirectly, the Tanna was able to teach two things: (1) recite Shema when the stars come out, and (2) that is also the time when priests should eat their Heave-offering.

This brief digression, however, now leads to a longer one: after showing one lesson the Tanna teaches "by the way" (namely, that priests eat their Heave-offering when the stars come out), the Talmud now goes on to point out another. It is necessary to know that certain kinds of levitical impurity could be removed simply through an act of ritual immersion, while in other cases the individual being purified was obligated as well to bring a special offering to the Temple. This purification-sacrifice was called "expiation."

> And he teaches us [as well] that [lack of] expiation does not hold back [a priest from eating Heave-offering, as impurity itself would], as it is taught, "And when the sun sets he shall be clean" (Lev. 22.7)—sunset holds him back from eating Heave-offering, but expiation does not hold him back from eating Heave-offering.

In other words, a defiled priest who has properly bathed himself becomes "clean" as soon as that day ends at sunset. Even if he still owes an expiation-sacrifice, his impurity has been removed. He must, of course, offer the sacrifice at the first opportunity, but he may have his share of sacred foods at once.

The formula "it is taught" used in the preceding paragraph normally introduces a *baraita*. This particular *baraita* comes from Sifra, an ancient Midrash★ on Leviticus.

The digression now continues. It should be noted that the Hebrew term for sunset literally means "when the sun comes," and possibly reflects the old conception that the setting sun goes home after its long day's race. Such an expression, however, could equally well be taken to mean sun*rise,* the time when the sun *leaves* its "home" and comes back

★ See Chapter Three.

into the world. This ambiguity explains the perplexing discussion that now unfolds.

> And from what [do we infer] that "and when the sun sets" means sunset and this "he shall be clean" means at the end of the day? ([2b] Perhaps it refers to the appearance of [the sun's] light [the next morning], and "he shall be clean" means "he can now cleanse himself [with the appropriate sacrifice]." Said Rabbah the son of R. Shela, "If so, Scripture should say, 'he shall thereafter become clean.' What is the meaning of 'He shall be clean'?—With the [new] day, as people say, 'The sun has turned to evening, and the day is clean.' "
>
> This [teaching] of Rabbah b.* R. Shela was not known in the West [i.e., the schools of the land of Israel], and they raised the question, Does this "and when the sun sets" refer to sunset, so that "he shall be clean" means with the [new] day? Perhaps it refers to the appearance of [the sun's] light and "he shall be clean" means "the man can now cleanse himself."
>
> But then they resolved the matter from a baraita; as it is taught in a baraita: "The sign for the matter is the emergence of the stars." You can deduce that [Scripture] refers to sunset, so that "he shall be clean" means with the [new] day.

It is typical of the Talmud that a digression that really has nothing to do with the subject at hand is treated in the same thorough manner as the central theme of the discussion. The motif of "the emergence of the stars" has led to consideration of the proper sequence of acts required for a defiled person's repurification, and thus to the claim that an expiation-sacrifice, though obligatory, is not a prerequisite for the purification itself. The Talmud now supports this assertion by every means at its disposal: extremely painstaking analysis of a single biblical verse, citation of a relevant baraita, reference to a presumably well-known popular slogan reflecting the favored interpretation. Along the way, it becomes clear as well that not every rabbi knew all pertinent traditions. In the absence of Rabbah b. R. Shela's elegant inference—it depends on the absence of a single letter from the Hebrew text of the Bible—the rabbis of "the West" had to reach the conclusion in a much less direct way, by citing a baraita of no clear relevance (the sign of what matter? What is this baraita talking about?) and then simply saying that it proved their point!

---

* An abbreviation for ben or bar ("son of" in Hebrew and Aramaic, respectively). The expression is translated fully in the preceding paragraph, where this rabbi is mentioned for the first time.

The discussion now returns to the actual subject—the precise definition, for purposes of reciting Shema, of the onset of evening.

The Master said:

(This usually is a general formula for reintroducing any text previously
quoted in the discussion, though the phrase appears without this meaning just a few lines above. Normally, the text thus introduced was
previously incidental to the discussion, but now becomes central. In the
present case, the text in question turns out to be our *mishnah* itself.)

"From the hour that the priests come in to eat of the Heave-
offering." But throw these *[together]*:

(A standard formula for introducing a second text which seems to contradict the one already under consideration.)

From what time *[may people]* recite the evening Shema? From
when a poor man comes in to eat his bread with salt until the
hour he gets up at the end of his meal.
The final part *[of this new text]* certainly differs from our
Mishnah *[which provides a much later end-limit]*; shall we say the
beginning contradicts our Mishnah *[as well]*? No; a poor man
and a priest *[represent]* one measure *[of time]*.

That is, the *mishnah* speaks of priests and the *baraita* speaks of "a poor
man," but these definitions of the earliest time for Shema do not conflict
because the two events in question coincide: they represent the same
"measure" of time. This response, however, gives rise to further complications, but note that the relevance of the *baraita* about "the sign for
the matter" has now been clarified.

But throw these *[together]*: From what time *[may people]*
begin to recite the evening Shema? From the hour that people
come in to eat their bread on Sabbath eves; *[these are]* R. Meir's
words, but the Sages say, From the hour that the priests have
the right to eat their Heave-offering. The sign for the matter is
the emergence of the stars. And even though this matter has no
proof it has a *[Scriptural]* indication, as it is said, "And we
worked at the task, while half of them held spears, from the
first light of dawn until the emergence of the stars" (Neh.
4.15). And it says, "So they were for us a guard by night, and
a workforce by day" (Neh. 4.16).

Before the real work of determining the mutual relationship of all these
"signs" can proceed, the cited sources once more provoke a digression

that must first be cleared away. If the aim is to show that night is considered to begin with the appearance of the stars, then surely verse 15 makes that clear. Why bring in verse 16 at all? The answer is that verse 15 by itself might be taken to describe only these particular workers' personal habit; only verse 16 explicitly identifies their working hours as "day" and their idle hours as "night."

> Why "and it says"? If you say it becomes night when the sun sets, but these [people worked] late and [resumed work] early, come and hear: "So they were for us a guard by night, and a workforce by day."

(The phrase "come and hear" is a very common formula used to introduce a text intended to prove a point or resolve a dispute. This can be a biblical citation, as here, or a rabbinic saying taken from some other context.)

The discussion now returns to the real, underlying question: How do all these different definitions of the time for the evening Shema compare?

> [If] you assume that a poor man and "people" [represent] one measure [of time], and if you say that a poor man and a priest [represent] one measure [of time, as was indeed just proposed] then the Sages agree with R. Meir! You must rather infer that a poor man [represents] one measure and a priest [represents] a different measure. No; a poor man and a priest [represent] one measure [of time], while a poor man and "people" do not [represent] one measure [of time].

In the name of various authorities, different Tannaitic traditions are cited to determine the time "night" begins. This is necessary because all take the beginning of "night" to be the point after which the evening Shema may be recited. These various limits, however, are expressed in terms that have nothing to do with reciting Shema or with one another! They speak of priests becoming cleansed and eating their Heave-offering, poor people eating their humble daily meal, "people" in general starting their Sabbath meal, and so on. Only one of these definitions—the appearance of the stars—directly concerns "night"; all the rest refer to apparently familiar social and cultural arrangements which no one here stops to clarify. For this proliferation of definitions to make any sense at all, it must be assumed that the various authorities disagree, and that each has found some well-known custom that illustrates his particular opinion. Otherwise they all have indulged in a terrible game of obfuscation, giving numerous unclear answers to the basic question when one simple answer would have done. Part of the Talmud's task here, then, is to clarify the disagreements that these traditions presumably report.

The present complication arose because the Talmud tried to eliminate an apparent contradiction between two such traditions by saying that a poor man and a priest (that is, the time such people begin their evening meal) represent one time limit and not two. They could be identified in this way because the two limits in question are both reported anonymously, and therefore can be taken to express the consensus of "the Sages," not some individual's divergent opinion. On the other hand, Meir's term "people," initially taken as a generality embracing all other terms (the point of his answer would then lie in its reference to the Sabbath), in the end is understood as having a specific meaning of its own. While this interpretation may seem less attractive than the first, it means that the earlier contradiction need not be resolved anew.

This extravagantly "Talmudical" discussion actually reflects a basic conflict of principles. Two assumptions have been working here—that (a) different named authorities give different answers to the same question because they in fact disagree, but that (b) all anonymous answers are consistent with one another, even when they seem to differ. The Talmudic authorities knew well that exceptions to both these principles could be found (some will presently be cited), but they preferred to uphold them whenever they could. Needless to say, these principles pull the discussion in opposite directions: one multiplies disagreements, while the other seeks to deny them. This tension is the root cause of the complicated discussion now underway.

But *do* a poor man and a priest *[represent]* one measure? Throw these *[together]*:

From when *[may people]* begin to recite the Shema evenings? From the hour that the day becomes holy on Sabbath eves; *[these are]* R. Eliezer's words, but R. Joshua says, From the hour that the priests become cleansed in order to eat of their Heave-offering. R. Meir says, From the hour that the priests immerse themselves in order to eat of their Heave-offering. (R. Judah said to him, "But do not priests immerse themselves while it is still day?") R. Hanina says, From the hour that a poor man comes in to eat his bread with salt. R. Ahai (some say R. Aha) says, From the hour that most people come in to sit down *[to their meal]*.

And if you say that a poor man and a priest *[represent]* one measure, then R. Hanina*['s opinion]* and R. Joshua*['s opinion]* are the same. Must you not rather infer that the poor man's measure is one *[thing]* and the priest's measure is another *[thing]?* You must infer *[this after all]*.

Thus finally the tension between the two working principles is resolved: once both "priest" and "poor man" are identified as the opinions of specific, named authorities, it can be taken for granted that they refer to different time limits. The anonymous statements that gave rise to this extended discussion may now be allowed to differ, since each can now be traced back to a different early master—the *mishnah* to Joshua and the original *baraita* to Hanina. Why, in the course of transmission, each opinion came to be separated from the name of its author, so that both seemed anonymous statements expressing a single consensus, is apparently not a question that arouses concern. It is just assumed that such things happen.

Once the Talmud has thus resolved the technical question it found so bothersome, it moves on to another of the same kind; the substantive question of when actually to recite Shema will never receive such careful consideration. In the following question, "them" refers to the same two criteria, the priest and the poor man.

> Which of them is later? It makes sense that the poor man must be later, for if you say that the poor man is earlier, R. Hanina*['s opinion]* is the same as R. Eliezer*['s]*.★ Must you not infer that the poor man is later? You must infer *[this]*.

The Talmud's consideration of the Mishnah and its implications will go no farther, but there are a few concluding details before the discussion actually ends.

> The Master said: "R. Judah said to him, 'But do not priests immerse themselves while it is still day?' " R. Judah speaks well to R. Meir! R. Meir *[can]* say to him as follows: "Do you suppose I am speaking on *[the basis of]* your *[conception of]* twilight? I am speaking *[on the basis of]* R. Yose's *[conception of]* twilight," as R. Yose said, "Twilight is like the blink of an eye; this one comes in and this one goes out and it is impossible to grasp *[the moment]*."

As Leviticus 22.7 makes clear (see above), immersion for the removal of impurity must precede *sunset,* while Shema must be recited at the time

★ Author's note: I do not understand the logic here myself. Tosafot suggest there is simply a limit to the number of distinctions one can make, but this seems implausible so late in a discussion where so many have already been introduced.

"when you lie down," that is, after *night* has begun. Thus, it is clear that immersion comes before the time for Shema, and in fact Meir proposes that the priests' immersing themselves be the sign to onlookers that the time for Shema has arrived. Judah's objection is that between the time for immersing and the time for Shema there is an intermediate stage called twilight which is not appropriate for either activity; it is no longer day, but it is not yet night. Meir's rule for Shema will lead people to perform the recitation before the proper time.

Meir's response grants Judah's logic, but denies his premise. Judah assumes that "twilight" lasts a substantial period of time (Rashi in his commentary suggests this is the time it takes a man to walk half a mile), but Meir and their contemporary, Yose, do not agree. On their understanding, "twilight" is really only a logical concept; it is the name people give to the transition from day to night, but it has no duration of its own at all. Since priests always immerse themselves at the last possible moment before sunset, their behavior is indeed a reliable indicator that the time for Shema has arrived.

The composition of this brief exchange requires further comment. This passage, while it *may* begin with an authentic comment by R. Judah, almost certainly does not record R. Meir's actual response. Numerous details suggest this conclusion. For one thing, Judah speaks Hebrew, as does Yose in the final remark attributed to him, while Meir is made to speak Aramaic—and Babylonian Aramaic at that. Furthermore, Yose's description of twilight is introduced with the phrase "as R. Yose *said,*" as though this were a saying of the master received from past generations. Yose was in fact the contemporary of Meir and Judah; if we were dealing here with a live debate between the latter two, Yose's saying would be introduced in different terms. It seems, therefore, that Yose's comment was appended by a later contributor to indicate the basis of Meir's remark,* and that Meir's response itself really shows how someone else thought he could have answered Judah's challenge.

This whole debate is an expansion of an earlier tradition (the introductory "the Master said" makes this clear), an expansion that grew by stages: first someone supplied a defense of Meir's position against Judah's challenge and formulated this defense as though it were Meir's own, and then Meir's defense was reinforced by showing that his contemporary, Yose, agreed with him in his basic dispute with Judah. As is often the case with such expanded traditions, the new materials appear in the

---

* That is why the quotation marks ending the translation of Meir's response to Judah appear before "as R. Yose said."

language of their Aramaic-speaking inventors, while older traditions appear in Hebrew.

The fact that such a debate could have been composed in this way teaches an important feature of the Talmudic tradition. The names of Judah and Meir and Yose function here chiefly as ways of designating specific points of view. These points of view are what matter, not the names. Meir as a historical personage is of very little interest here; his name, along with the others, is used as a label and little more. No doubt these men really lived and as far as anyone knows they really held the opinions attributed to them here. But in the course of time their legal rulings took on an importance that had nothing to do with these teachers as real people, and finally overshadowed their flesh-and-blood humanity until it could hardly be seen. The fact that Judah's disagreement with Meir was continued this way by later generations shows how important the disagreement remained, while the fact that it was continued in the form of a historical fiction shows how unimportant the "reality" of these people came to be.

These considerations, which will be elaborated below, shed light on the Talmud's final question: can these teachers really have said the things attributed to them? In the Talmudic context, this question does not mean, is the attribution to Meir historically reliable, because after all we wish to follow the great man's teaching as he really spoke it? Instead it means, are the teachings attributed to Meir internally consistent, so that we may use them for the purpose of building a more elaborate dialectic, so that we can use the name "Meir" and expect our hearers will know the set of opinions we mean to invoke? Or are they inconsistent, so that the Talmudic technique of labeling rulings with the names of past authorities turns out to be useless?

> [3a] R. Meir's [opinion creates a] difficulty for R. Meir's [other opinion]. Two Tannaim [handed down traditions] according to R. Meir.

Meir's opinion quoted earlier, that Shema may be recited from the hour that people come home to eat their Sabbath meal, conflicts with the opinion quoted just now, that Shema may be recited after the priests have had their ritual baths; the first ruling stipulates a rather later hour than the second. The Talmud concedes the difficulty and simply says that different "reciters" cited traditions in the name of R. Meir which were not in accord with one another. Thus the Talmud grants the existence of unreliable traditions, though the assumption seems to be that traditions are to be considered reliable unless specific evidence casts doubt on them, as here. No consideration is given to the question of which of these two "Tannaim" was right; evidently there is no way to tell.

In the post-Mishnaic age, the title "Tanna" was also given to a functionary in the rabbinic schools whose sole task was to memorize older traditions and then to recite them on command. Unlike the earlier Tannaim, these later ones were figures of low prestige. It was widely recognized that the qualifications for this position were an excellent memory and a general lack of imagination; these had to be people who could be counted on simply to repeat what they had learned, without trying to "improve" it in any way. In the present case, two such Tannaim are said to have transmitted incompatible traditions in Meir's name. The Talmud makes no effort either to explain how this situation arose or to consider its wider implications.

> R. Eliezer's [opinion creates a] difficulty for R. Eliezer's [other opinion]. Two Tannaim [handed down traditions] according to R. Eliezer; or if you like I can say that the beginning [of the mishnah] is not R. Eliezer['s opinion].

Again, an inconsistency is alleged among one man's teachings; in this case, Eliezer's ruling in the last *baraita* authorizes reciting Shema from the onset of Sabbath holiness while the *mishnah* itself, apparently in the name of Eliezer, draws the line at the hour that priests eat Heave-offering. This latter has now been identified as nightfall, while the Sabbath begins with sunset, which is earlier.

At first, the Talmud offers the same solution as in the case of Meir's teachings, but here a second possibility arises. According to the Mishnah, Eliezer, "the Sages," and Gamaliel clearly disagree over the end of the time for the evening Shema. Since Eliezer's name follows hard on the first clause of the text, it is natural to take that clause as reflecting his opinion. But that initial clause treats of the *beginning* of the time for Shema; what if it really represents an anonymous statement of the rabbis' consensus, and not Eliezer's opinion at all? In that case, there is no inconsistency in Eliezer's position; the *baraita* explicitly reports his position, in his name, and the Mishnah has nothing to do with him.

This proposal once again reflects the Talmud's indifference toward the history behind these traditions. The first clause of the Mishnah may or may not reflect Eliezer's real opinion, and in the end the Talmud seems not to care. As long as the internal consistency of the set of opinions attributed to Eliezer can be maintained, the question whether these really were his teachings drops out of sight. The set of opinions must be maintained in its integrity, for it is needed as a stone in the edifice of legal tradition; as a historical record, however, it evokes no interest at all.

This brief discussion marks the end of the Talmud's treatment of the first clause of the Mishnah. As noted, the second clause is undoubtedly to be taken as Eliezer's opinion, so this way of resolving the alleged contradiction in his teaching plays a double role: it completes the first major section of the Talmud and it supplies a transition to the next. In medieval manuscripts and most printed editions, the second clause of the Mishnah is actually copied out here, providing a break in the text and calling attention to the change in subject. The Talmud does not always supply such a clear marker, and there are many passages where it is no longer clear which clause of Mishnah is the one under consideration. Here, however, there can be no such doubt, and this rather lengthy translation/commentary can therefore come to an end.

WHAT WAS THIS PASSAGE TRYING TO DO?

An outline of the first section of the Talmud would look like this:

I. "Where does the Tanna stand?"—Inquiry into the basis of the Mishnah
    A. Biblical warrants
    B. Principles of editorial arrangement

II. Why not just say "from the appearance of the stars"?—a long side discussion about expiation-sacrifices and priests eating their holy foods

III. The first outside source: the poor man
    Solution to problem: poor man equals priest

IV. The second outside source: people/priests
    A. Prooftext from Nehemiah provokes second digression
    B. Solution to problem: poor man still equals priest, but "people" is different

V. The third outside source: Sabbath/priests may eat/immersion (challenged)/poor man/most people
    A. Final proof that poor man and priest are not the same measure
    B. Which is later? . . .

VI. Final matters
   A. Judah's challenge and Meir's response
   B. Meir *vs.* Meir
   C. Eliezer *vs.* Eliezer

Although our *mishnah* seems concerned with fixing the proper rule for reciting Shema, and although the *gemara* seems concerned with clarifying this rule, a look at this outline makes clear that the actual work of determining the proper time for Shema receives almost no attention at all. From the very beginning, and almost as a side point, it is taken for granted that the time for saying Shema begins with the appearance of the stars, but the Talmud never says this, and instead keeps adding more and more opinions to an increasingly complicated mix. In general, the Talmud seems more interested here in understanding all these opinions, and in clarifying their relationship to one another, than in actually choosing one to be the operative rule. (This is not always the case, to be sure, but this passage must be allowed to speak for itself.) Perhaps for this reason, later codes of Jewish law simply disregarded all these Talmudic complications and laid down the rule that Shema may be recited from the time that three stars of medium brightness have appeared in the sky.★

If, then, the Talmud is not primarily interested in determining the law, what is it trying to do? As already hinted, and as its own name implies, the Talmud is a scholastic text. *Its chief purpose is to preserve the record of earlier generations studying their own tradition and provide materials for later generations wishing to do the same.* It is a book produced by and for people whose highest value was the life of study.

Thus, to the extent that the Talmud is concerned with law, its purpose is not really to lay down simple, hard-and-fast rules, but rather to build the law up into an elegant structure, all parts of which are interwoven with all other parts. The aims of this enterprise are clarity and consistency, but not necessarily simplicity. The clarity must be won; it is the goal, not the starting point. The elements of the desired structure are not general principles, but specific, highly detailed rules, usually, though not always, attributed to well-known teachers from previous generations. Each man's teachings must both be internally consistent and also in some way distinguishable from every other man's. The attribution of precisely the same teaching to two different authorities is a redundancy that must be explained (though this is not, on the Talmud's terms, hard to do).

★ There will be more about codes later.

This method for organizing the tradition soon made the dispute between named masters a basic form for transmitting rabbinic legal teaching. Hardly a chapter of the Mishnah is free of disputed rules. Here lies the origin of the argumentative style for which Talmudic reasoning has been famous (or infamous!) for centuries.

These accumulations of rulings attributed to past authorities took on a life of their own. Later teachers would use earlier traditions to support their own opinions. Sets of rulings became the subject matter for later generations' study; the edifice of interconnection became more and more elaborate, and the countervailing distinctions more and more subtle, as time went on. Eventually, as the sample passage above illustrated, the actual historical identity of these earlier authorities lost all relevance. "R. Meir" was simply shorthand for "the opinions attributed to R. Meir," and a rabbi centuries after Meir's time would say, "I agree with R. Meir" but mean, "I share the opinion attributed to R. Meir." As a result, new opinions could begin circulating in Meir's (or anyone's) name, even if he himself had never spoken them. All one meant by identifying an opinion as his was that such a ruling fit into the system generated and transmitted in his name and was therefore to be considered part of that system. For the purpose of later generations, it made no difference at all whether Meir had or had not actually originated the saying under discussion. The process of developing the tradition of rabbinic law could work equally well in either case.

Paradoxically, this withering away of earlier rabbis' historical reality served to liberate historical imagination about them. Parallel to these legal developments there grew legends about these men that seem to heighten our awareness of them as real people, even while the narratives have little or no actual relationship to them as historical personages. Some of the greatest rabbis (Akiba, for example, or especially the earlier Hillel) are known to us almost exclusively through the stories that grew up around them. Great rabbinic leaders thus became both disembodied bearers of an elaborate legal tradition and also heroes of a marvelously rich tradition of legend; meanwhile they had in fact disappeared behind this two-layered screen.

From the historian's point of view, the Talmud thus becomes a terribly frustrating book. It is rich with stories that may—or may not—reflect the way certain events happened, and it is full of legal discussions that may—or may not—report the actual content of early rabbinic scholarly activity. Everything is fascinating, everything is potentially an open window on the past, but nothing can be trusted. At various points in the later development of the rabbinic tradition, leaders needed techniques for overcoming this uncertainty—the present generation is no different in this respect. It will be useful to review some of those earlier techniques, and then at last to raise the question how people of the present generation can approach this remarkable tradition.

THE TALMUD AND ITS OFFSPRING

As has been mentioned, the Talmud tends to assume the tradition is basically reliable: if a given saying is attributed to Rabbi X then Rabbi X said it, and if it is reported that Rabbi X said Y then that is what Rabbi X said. When confronted with evidence that the tradition is not in order —the final sections of the sample passage presented such evidence—the Talmud knows of several standard procedures for removing the resultant discomfort. It can "correct" one of the conflicting traditions, as though to say that one day in the schoolhouse a conflict of this sort arose, but it was found to be the result of a faulty text. The fault was corrected, and now the "official" tradition is once again reliable. The fault itself can be accounted for in several ways: a student was inattentive and got his master's words wrong, or the words were remembered correctly but attached to the wrong context, or the tradition is correct but was temporarily misunderstood, and so forth. More rarely, as in the case above, the Talmud admits that two different versions of a master's teaching are inconsistent, but then leaves both standing. In the sample, this occurred because each had its own authentication; each was transmitted by a different "Tanna," and even though something perplexing had happened here, there was no way to sort things out. Elsewhere, it may be suggested that the master in question had himself changed his mind. One way or the other, the Talmud is satisfied; this is made clear by the simple fact that the rabbinic tradition did not collapse over difficulties of this sort. The teachings of earlier masters were considered to have been reliably transmitted, and occasional discrepancies were handled on the spot, so to speak, with no consideration for their possible broader implications.

With respect to the law, the problem was more difficult. Since rabbinic traditions were considered authoritative, later generations wished to live according to their teaching. How could one do that, however, if the tradition was organized largely according to disputes, and if these were so often left unresolved? In response, the Amoraim developed guiding rules of the sort, "If Rabbi A differs with Rabbi B, follow Rabbi A," or, "If Rabbi C differs with one colleague follow

Rabbi C anyway, but not if he differs with all his colleagues," or, "Follow Rabbi D in matters of X but not in matters of Y."* These rules themselves were sometimes ignored, and later generations took for granted that an explicit ruling found in the Talmud itself must always supersede such general guidelines. Still, they provided an escape from utter confusion. Now in principle, any dispute in the Mishnah, even if the Talmud seems not to resolve it, could be resolved by reference to such rules, and disputes of the Amoraim found in the Talmud itself could be resolved through reference to similar rules worked out by later generations of Talmudic and post-Talmudic masters.

Thus, in the end, the legal content of the Mishnah and then the Talmud became the basis of the continuing tradition of Jewish law, even though these texts originated to serve other ends. This change reflects another, still more fundamental one.

At the time the Talmud was composed, "the rabbis" formed one of the movements in Jewish life. Their influence was steadily growing, to be sure, but the Jewish community as such was not organized around them. Except when they could acquire some part in the community's formal governance (as they did, for example, in Babylonia), they could not count on any *power* over their fellow Jews, and whatever *influence* they could achieve had to be won through the force of their teaching.†
Under these circumstances, the Talmud and its related literature were chiefly the private study texts of a particular group.

In the Middle Ages, however, rabbinic teaching was indeed the basis of all Jewish religious life. "Judaism" was rabbinic Judaism; the other ancient forms of this once-varied tradition had disappeared. Talmudic literature was now public property; not that everyone studied it, but everyone accepted its authority. Talmudic law was more than material for study, it now really was the law of the community. As such, it demanded clarification and application in all sorts of novel situations.

Once again, however, the problem of historical reliability was not a paramount concern. The very authority of the Talmud was taken to imply that its text was trustworthy; you could not base your life on a book if you could not trust it. Later generations naturally knew of the problems recognized in the Talmud itself, but they accepted the solutions it offered as well. The problem of medieval teachers had rather to

---

* A sample list of such rules can be found in the Talmud at Eruvin 46b.
† The distinction between power and influence comes from the work of Jacob Neusner. Professor Neusner is one of the leading scholars of our generation, and by far the most prolific. No list of his works can be complete, but for a sample see the booklist below, pp. 172–175.

do with explaining a text that by now was quite alien to their own day-to-day surroundings, and with applying its law to situations that the framers of that law had not foreseen.

Medieval rabbis developed three distinctive types of literature to meet this need. One was the *responsum* (Heb. *teshuvah*); as the name implies, this had the form of the answer to a question. Medieval Jewry never developed a hierarchy in the formal sense, but still every generation knew who were the truly distinguished teachers, the great men of the time. Other rabbis all over the world would address inquiries to these luminaries whenever they felt unable to solve a problem that had arisen in their own locality. At first, these problems were usually referred to the surviving academies in Babylonia, heirs in the strictest sense to the authority of the Talmud itself. As these began to decline, however (tenth to eleventh centuries), and as centers of Torah-study began to arise elsewhere (in North Africa, then in Spain, then in the Rhineland and Italy), queries were sent wherever local rabbis thought they had found the leaders of their generation. Every great rabbi of the Middle Ages wrote many responsa, and huge quantities of these survive; a computer project in Israel has now begun to collect, classify, and prepare an index to the entire surviving collection.

Every *responsum* is preceded by a question, in which the inquirer describes the situation which has arisen and specifies the legal matter on which he needs a ruling. The question itself will very often include a citation of all relevant Talmudic passages and perhaps even survey possible interpretations of these. The inquiry thus has certain features in common with a lawyer's brief, except that it comes not from one of the two contending sides but from the lower-court judge himself. Similarly, the answer, much like an appellate court's decision, will not necessarily uncover great new amounts of precedent; it will rather provide an authoritative interpretation of texts that the inquirer has already cited.

Over the years, the accumulating body of responsa thus provided a growing collection both of specific precedents based on concrete cases and also of general interpretations of key Talmudic passages, interpretations that might now be applied to any case where these passages were thought pertinent. The availability of fresh responsa in every generation (and they are still being produced today) was the most important factor in keeping Jewish law a living tradition over so many years.

A second type of literature was the *novella* (Heb. *hiddush*). *Hiddushim* were commentaries on the Talmud written without specific reference to a particular case. As time went on, consensus began to develop about which passages of the Talmud were fairly clear in meaning, and which required careful explanation. The greatest scholars in each generation prepared their own explanations of the Talmud, initially for their own students (and very often only orally) but eventually in written form for wider circulation. Many authorities produced both responsa and *hiddushim*, though not all worked with equal comfort in both forms; the responsum was the preferred format of those whose community position required that they issue numerous practical rulings, while commentaries on the Talmudic text attracted those whose lives were spent in more private study.

Finally, and perhaps best known, the Middle Ages saw the appearance of the great comprehensive codes of Jewish law. The three texts underlying Jewish law—the Bible, the Mishnah, and the Talmud—are none of them organized by topic. Anyone wanting to know what the Bible says about the Sabbath will need to read the entire book through or to have access to some modern index of its contents; the text itself provides nothing of the kind. The Mishnah, because it is arranged by tractates, seems better in this regard, except that one quickly learns that not everything concerning the Sabbath is found in the tractate bearing that heading, and not everything in that tractate concerns the Sabbath; the same is true for divorces, or kosher slaughter, or any topic at all.

The Talmud, because of the free-wheeling discussions out of which it was put together, is more like the Bible than the Mishnah. Even with the Talmud it always pays to start the study of some topic with the tractate named after that topic, but it is never safe to use those titles as indicators of the likely content of a specific passage. As with the Bible, if you want to know what the Talmud says about the Sabbath, you have to read the whole thing through—and the Talmud is extremely long. As a result, soon after the Talmud became a closed text, summaries of its legal contents began to appear. Most of these treat only selected topics, while the more comprehensive summaries, like that of R. Isaac of Fez ("Rif," 1013–1103), still follow the order of the Talmud itself; though these formats gather much material into a more concise framework, neither is yet a true code in the modern sense of the term.

The greatest of the true medieval codes is that of Moses Maimonides (1135–1204). Reflecting his philosophical bent (for more on this see Chapter Five), Maimonides' Code, the *Mishneh Torah,* (the Torah recapitulated) begins with a philosophical introduction in which the rudiments of Aristotelian physics and metaphysics are turned into the foundation of Jewish law. Further reflecting its all-inclusive character, the *Mishneh Torah* ends with a section detailing laws concerning the Messiah, how he is to be recognized, and what he can be expected to accomplish. In between, every conceivable topic of Jewish law is treated in its proper place in a carefully worked-out sequence. All Talmudic sources relevant to any subject matter have been gathered and digested by the author and only the outcome of the process actually written down; as a result, the reader finds no summary of ancient discussions, but rather a simple statement of the law in the clearest possible language. Maimonides wrote that the purpose of his code was to make study of the Talmud unnecessary for those who merely wanted to know the law. He was widely condemned for this arrogance and denounced as a threat to traditional Judaism, and he failed to achieve that particular aim. The *Mishneh Torah* is nonetheless one of the most impressive accomplishments in the long history of Jewish thinking.

The code most influential in modern Jewish life—and also the last comprehensive one to be written—is the *Shulhan Arukh* (The Set Table) of R. Joseph Caro (1488–1575). Actually a digest of Caro's own commentary to an earlier, more elaborate code, the *Shulhan Arukh* aims at giving a simple statement of the law as it affects the life of the ordinary Jew; those who enter the banquet hall of Torah can now find its contents laid out ("The Set Table") in elegant simplicity. Unlike Maimonides, Caro simply ignored all areas of the law not currently applicable, though like his great predecessor, he tended to omit all reference to earlier sources or to opinions he had decided to reject.

Caro's code reflected its author's own background. Its law was the law of the so-called Sephardic Jews of Spanish and Portuguese descent; in Caro's own time these Jews lived primarily in Greece, Turkey, and the Land of Israel. The *Shulhan Arukh* gained world-wide acceptance through the work of another, the great Polish rabbi, Moses Isserles (d. 1572). Greatly impressed with Caro's work, Isserles nevertheless saw it would fail among the Ashkenazic Jews of Eastern Europe unless it included and granted legitimacy to their own distinctive customs. He therefore wrote a "Tablecloth" for the Set Table, and it was the composite work thus produced that became the functioning code for observant Jews to our own day.

To be sure, the process of commentary and adjustment has continued. Within Caro's own lifetime, commentaries on his code had begun to appear. Alterations in circumstances have led to modifications of some of his and Isserles' rulings, and new developments have required the application of those rulings in ways and to questions that the authors themselves could never have foreseen. Nevertheless, the phrase "*Shulhan Arukh* Jew" is still used—both in praise and in criticism—to describe those whose conception of Jewish life is centered on carrying out the laws found in this code. Even among those who find this a narrow conception of the wealth that Judaism has to offer, the continuing use of this term testifies to the power of Caro's work four hundred years and more after it was completed.

Perhaps because it was the first compiled after the invention of printing, and therefore circulated far more quickly throughout the Jewish world, Caro's was the last comprehensive code to be drawn up. The history of Jewish (that is, Talmudic) law, however, hardly ended in the sixteenth century. Responsa, as noted, continue to be written, and even the codes retain a life of their own through the new work they have stimulated. Each great code represents an important turning point in the history of the law. Each has given rise to its own commentaries and adaptations, but no code has brought that history to an end.

There is an irony here: the same centuries that saw the composition of these great codes also saw unending opposition to the activity they reflect. There has always been a fear among rabbis that codifying presented a double threat to the authentic tradition: it could distract people from studying the *really* important texts (principally the Talmud), and a truly authoritative code might well freeze the law in a way even the most tradition-minded leaders did not wish to see. These two dangers feed one another. If a code is not to freeze the law, a steady stream of commentary and application will be needed to keep it fluid. But if all that energy is to go into commenting on other people's writing, is it not preferable to keep the focus on the Talmud itself, the truly authoritative text, the foundation of the whole system? The history of Jewish law has revolved around questions of this sort for over a thousand years. The questions themselves can receive no definitive answer, since they involve, among other factors, the question of individual temperament and the accidents of history, but they attest to the continued liveliness of this ancient facet of the Jewish tradition.

WHY STUDY TALMUD, AND HOW?

All that has preceded this point is really only background to what follows. So far the subject has been the Talmud as a text—a sample passage, a description of its origins and its offshoots, and so on—but now it shifts to the act of study. What is it like to study the Talmud? Why did Jews make Talmud-study the central feature of their entire religious tradition? What was the source of the Talmud's fascination, and how can that fascination be made available today?

Jews have studied the Talmud for a great variety of reasons. Many of these can be labeled practical. Of these "practical" reasons, one has already been discussed at some length—the Talmud has been studied in order to extract functioning law from its pages. For most of Jewish history, Jews in various communities have constituted self-governing enclaves within the larger society, and from the time rabbis rose to prominence as leaders of Jewry their legal traditions provided the rules by which these enclaves lived. Thus rabbinic marriage law became Jewish marriage law, rabbinic rules about the Sabbath became rules for all Jews, and so on. The Talmud itself does not always state with precision what these rules are to be, and in the nature of things it could not anticipate new situations in which these rules would have to be applied. Thus study of the Talmud for its law became a chief activity of those in the community who were charged with teaching and enforcing that law.

There were other practical reasons too, however. The Talmud, like the Mishnah before it, has always functioned as a training text for rabbis and their disciples. This "academic" function, as has been noted, may in fact be older than the applied-law function just mentioned. Now, not all rabbis actually served as legal authorities. Some were teachers, or administrators, or political advisors; some, for that matter, were merchants. Anyone, however, who aspired to the title "rabbi," anyone who wished to be part of an ancient chain of tradition, had to become immersed in the "sea of the Talmud." The Talmud therefore served the additional practical function of training religious leaders. Not all so trained thereupon took up the authority now available to them. Some used the training in other ways, and some did not use it at all.

In a rather more specialized sense, the Talmud was also of practical use in the study of Scripture. Among their other intellectual enterprises, the rabbis of antiquity spent a great deal of time reading and explaining the Bible. Their explanations are found scattered throughout Talmudic and especially Midrashic literature. Later generations of Jews—even Jews who never achieved the ability to study the Talmud itself—did study Scripture; the Pentateuch in particular was read through, year in and year out, in the synagogues. Jews needed to know what their holy writings meant, and their ancient rabbis could tell them. This need became especially important in the Middle Ages, when the Bible was constantly being interpreted by Christians in such a way as to undermine the Jews' own traditions. A response was needed, and the Talmud often provided it. (The situation was actually more complicated. Christians too studied the Talmud—often with the help of apostate Jews—and would then quote rabbinic authority in support of their own claims. Jews thus had to develop a double attitude toward the nonlegal aspect of the Talmud: when it was useful to them they cited it to refute the Christians' claims, but when it weakened their position they felt free to repudiate it.* There will be more about the nonlegal side of the Talmud at the end of this chapter.)

Finally, the Talmud has been used in modern times as an important source of scholarly information, and here the contrast between modern and older methods of Talmud study becomes most striking. Use of the Talmud as a source of historical data stands partly still within the realm of Jewish religious activity, but partly outside it as well; to study the history of Judaism is not the same as to study Judaism. To be sure, the two are connected; both depend on the same body of literature, and both are primarily concerned with the same group of people. Those who study the history of Judaism, however, need not practice it; they need not be Jewish at all. Though many important modern-day scholars have seen their studies as part of their own religious lives, these same studies have opened up the Talmud to audiences that in the past could never have entered its world.

Other differences flow from this one. The traditional Jew studies Talmud because it communicates ultimate truth—truth about God, truth about the world, and most important, truth about how God wants the holy community of Israel to live. The modern scholar, on the other hand, approaches the text for information, not "truth." Contemporary academic scholars recognize that the Talmud, like any ancient document, must be studied with critical care; scribes over the many centuries have permitted error to creep into their copies, and even the ancient rabbis themselves occasionally misremembered or misunderstood the traditions they were teaching their disciples (see above, page 154). Modern scholars approach the Talmud seeking the answers to all sorts of questions— usually questions of their own devising—and they have developed techniques for working out more or less reliable answers to these questions. In earlier ages, the pious Jew normally approached this same text with one unchanging question in mind, a question itself received from the past: how does the God of Israel, the Creator of the Universe, want me to live? Questions of historical reliability, or of outside cultural influence, were in the long run irrelevant to this kind of inquiry.

Modern historical consciousness actually makes the traditional in-

* This point was made most explicitly by the philosopher Nahmanides at a disputation in Barcelona in the year 1263.

quiry more difficult than ever. The new types of investigation are not simply "irrelevant" to such a quest, they impede it. How can the Talmud reveal the eternal word of God if it turns out to be the work of third- or fourth-century men living in the fading world of Near Eastern antiquity? How can questions of Jewish law be resolved from a text that may conceal scribal error on every line? These considerations help explain why modern, critical Talmud study was long resisted in traditional *yeshivot* and is still excluded from many of them. Historical relativity in general and text criticism in particular turn out to raise new *religious* issues, issues that earlier masters of the rabbinic tradition never had to face.

Nevertheless, Talmudic study has remained entirely unchanged in a very important respect, and will remain unchanged as long as people engage in it. The Talmud is a book put together by people who saw intellectual activity as sanctifying. They found holiness in their effort to bring rational order to their tradition, and as a result problem solving and disciplined logic became important characteristics of rabbinic discourse. The need to erect a logical edifice for the rabbinic tradition, even at the cost of respect for historical detail (see above, pp. 156–58), reflects the overwhelming devotion to logical elegance and systematic thoroughness that is the chief feature of Talmudic argument. (The system is legal, not philosophical; this must never be forgotten.) This relish for complicated but careful argument is entirely available to the modern reader, and is very much in keeping with modern tastes. In an important sense, it is immune from historical criticism, because it comes from the text of the Talmud, not from the particular individuals who once composed that text. And the text is still there.

This is one of the reasons that Talmud study for many people in the modern world is not a practical activity at all, but rather an important religious experience. Even in the past, for that matter, the *main* reason for the Talmud's preeminence, the chief cause of its central role in Jewish history, was not practical at all. The Talmud was *Torah*. In a paradox that determined the history of Judaism, the Talmud was Oral Torah in written form, and as such it became the clearest statement the Jew could hear of God's very word. This must not be understood too literally. The point is not that God dictated the entire Talmud to later rabbis in the same way some believed the Written Torah had been dictated to Moses, but rather that in the Talmud the Jew could find a clear expression of God's will. The Talmud provided the means of determining how God wants all Jews to live, in all places, at all times. Even if the details of the law had to be altered to suit newly arisen conditions, the proper way to perform such adaptation could itself be learned from the Talmud and its commentaries. Thus this basic text uncovered the fullness of God's revelation to the people of the Covenant. The Talmud revealed God speaking to Israel, and so the Talmud became Israel's way to God. To study Talmud was to converse with the Creator of the Universe.

For this reason, even before the Talmud was complete, ancient rabbis had evolved such a complicated etiquette for Torah study that study became a religious ritual in its own right, indeed, in the opinion of many, the most sacred ritual that Jewish life had to offer.* In its most ambitious expression, rabbinic thinking came to see this activity as not only a way to *move toward* God—it was also a way to *be like* God, for God too studies Torah, taught Rav Judah, three hours a day (Avodah Zarah 3b). In the end, therefore, the *act* of Talmud study was holy beyond the holiness to be found in the words of the text. Jews studied Talmud because the act brought them closer to the divine.

Since Talmudic law does not really govern our lives,† the present generation cannot see a practical usefulness in Talmud study as previous generations saw one. In general, Jews being trained for professional service in the Jewish community learn much or little Talmud, depending on the nature of the profession and also on the segment of the community offering the training. An Orthodox congregation demands more Talmudic training of its rabbi than a Reform one, and any community demands more Talmudic training of the local rabbi than of the executive director of the local Y. "Leadership" in modern Jewish life is no longer a function of Torah-learning.

As a result, the value of Talmud study as religious experience is all the greater for the modern Jewish reader. Some can still accept some version of the traditional conception of revelation, and for these the Talmud can remain "Torah" even while the new problems of history and text are confronted. For others, for those who shy away from such notions, the Talmud remains the historical core of the Jewish religious tradition. Through the Talmud earlier generations speak to their successors and later generations can respond. The Talmudic tradition chronicles a people's ancient quest to find and understand its God. The Talmud offers the modern Jew a living link to the past.

* This point too was first made by Jacob Neusner.
† In Israel, of course, Talmudic law has much greater authority than elsewhere, and even in a country like the United States most Jews still follow traditional Jewish law in matters like marriage, observance of the holidays, and so forth. The difference from the medieval arrangement nevertheless is huge.

". . . And How?"

Beginners especially may find Talmud study a difficult task. The logic can be convoluted, while every page alludes to customs, political arrangements, and so on which were once everyday reality but are now terribly obscure. Worst of all, the whole effort must be made with translated texts, unless the student can master Hebrew and Aramaic even before starting. It must therefore be emphasized that the necessary background can be acquired. People have done so in every generation, and people can do so now. The texts are translated; introductions, explanations, and commentaries have been written; Hebrew has been revived as a spoken tongue. The would-be beginner need only supply the will.

It may also help to bear in mind that Talmud study can be tremendous fun. Like any challenging task, the task of understanding an unfamiliar Talmudic passage is intimidating only until it has once been accomplished. After that, the challenge can be relished, and the task enjoyed. The fact is, after all, that the Talmud is *interesting*. The people represented in it were intelligent, articulate, and dedicated to the remarkable project of helping an ancient tradition survive mortal danger. Their arguments stimulate, their language gives pleasure, the immensity of their achievement provokes awe. There is wit in the Talmud, and humor too. There are wonderful stories, and logic whose disciplined sharpness is breathtaking. The Talmud has been compared to the sea; you never enjoy swimming anywhere until you've gotten used to the water. Getting wet can be uncomfortable at first, but after that "the water's fine"; the pleasure keeps mounting.

But what does it mean to study the Talmud; how is it to be done? In our time, the Talmud exists primarily in print, as a book, and our culture tends to see reading as a private activity. Even the reader of this book probably is sitting alone somewhere, trying to concentrate on its pages. People not reading alone usually are found in large groups, either listening to a lecturer explain a text, or in a classroom, engaged in group discussion. Neither of these settings, however, reflects the manner of Talmud study in the traditional *yeshiva*. There, students study in pairs, reading every word of the text out loud, never going on to the next phrase until they have exhausted the meaning of the one under discussion. The Talmud itself, after all, originated as oral discussion, and still has the form of an elaborate conversation carried on over centuries. Its standard way of citing an opinion is "Rabbi X says . . ."; later generations of rabbinic disciples listened to Rabbi X, and answered back. This mode of study, called in Aramaic *havruta* ("fellowship"), turns text study into dialogue and makes books into tools for overcoming, not strengthening, isolation. It makes the tradition of rabbinic learning a powerful source of community cohesion, a source of speech rather than silence. This activity was usually called not "study" but "learning," and in every Jewish community an invitation to fellowship could take the form of the proposal "Let's learn together." The life of the mind and the life of society were thus made one.★

In the past, it was also taken for granted that one needed a teacher to study Talmud properly. Those pairs of students in the *yeshiva* always know whose disciples they are, and regularly gather to hear "the rabbi" lecture, or to be examined by him one by one. In an extreme statement, ancient rabbis are quoted as having said that even one who has memorized the whole Bible, and the Mishnah too, is still only an ignoramus, a heretic, or even worse, unless he has also "served the Sages," that is, has carried out a proper apprenticeship with a master (Sotah 22a).

The advice still has force, especially for the beginner. The world of the Talmud is an exceedingly complex one; a first entry into it through books is like looking up a word in a foreign-language dictionary. Every choice the dictionary offers is in some sense a translation of the word in question, but only one really captures the correct meaning in context; others may amount to grotesque errors. So too the Talmud's habit of assuming whenever it talks of one thing that the student already understands ten others makes it useful to have access to a teacher who can put everything into a helpful framework, who can say when some term or idea is *mentioned* in place X that it's really *explained* in place Y. Such living sources of guidance have saved countless novice Talmudists from despair.

They are not, however, indispensable. The booklist at the end of this chapter assumes that modern students of the Talmud differ from their predecessors in their way of study just as they differ in their purpose and in their prior training. Those who can find a teacher or a class which suits them in aim and in atmosphere are fortunate to be sure, but the following bibliography is designed for the modern reader who wishes

---

★ It seems to me that solitary study tends to seek meaning, while study *be-havruta* tends to look for implications. When we read by ourselves, and we are satisfied that we have understood, we naturally move on. But when "learning" is a kind of conversation, then there is always more to be said. The rate of progress is more leisurely, the depth of analysis more penetrating. The modern way of "study" and traditional Jewish "learning" are more different, and are different in more ways, than might at first seem the case. See the Introduction to this book for more on this matter.

to sample the Talmud in the way most modern books are read—alone, with ready access to printed study aids, but without the constant presence of a colleague or a guide. Pirke Avot 1.6 (see below) advises "Acquire a companion," but not everyone is so lucky.

FINAL NOTE—THE TALMUD IS MORE THAN LAW

This chapter has concentrated almost exclusively on the legal aspect of Talmudic literature, and this has been so for a number of reasons. For one thing, the Talmud has functioned for much of its history principally as the basis of Jewish law. More people have studied the Talmud to learn its legal content than for any other reason. Second, the Talmud treats matters of law more than it treats any other sort of topic. Other interests too are reflected in its pages, but the Talmud is primarily a law book, just as the ancient rabbis primarily concerned themselves with the study, the application, and the enforcement (when they could) of the law—they would have said the commandments—of the Torah. Finally, this chapter has been concerned not directly with the Talmud as a book, but with the experience of studying that book, and there can be no doubt that the study of Talmudic law is really what people have always meant when they spoke of "learning *gemara.*" Beginners possibly were initiated into Talmud study with easier materials, but only when the legal heart of the literature—the famous gored oxen and their companions—had been reached were people thought to have become "disciples of the Sages."

Nevertheless, the Talmud is not altogether a law book, and a few words, even as an afterthought, should be devoted to its other interests.

The Talmud contains much narrative. Many famous legends about personalities in the Bible make their first appearance in the Talmud. So too many well-known stories about the early rabbis themselves can be found there, as can long narratives about crucial events in Jewish history. In particular, the rabbis' version of the most crucial event of all—the Romans' destruction of Jerusalem and its Temple—takes several pages in tractate Gittin (55b–58b) to recount. More generally, rabbinic narrative includes folklore, stories about angels and demons, and gossip about all sorts of surprising people (Nero became a convert to Judaism, Jesus was an Egyptian magician,★ and so on). Some of these stories really constitute precedents embedded in the legal materials, but the modern reader's interest in them can go far beyond that original use.

★ Much Talmudic discussion of early Christianity was censored out in the course of the Middle Ages and must now be recovered from scattered manuscripts.

The Talmud also contains what would now be called theological speculation. Scattered here and there are brief references to God and how God operates in the world. All things considered, the Talmud for a "religious" text pays remarkably little attention to God, but still a student who works through its entire length will have a considerable notion of how those early Jewish teachers conceived of their Creator. In particular, there is again one quite lengthy section (Hagigah 11b–16a) that contains much of our information about early Jewish mysticism, the so-called Merkavah ("Chariot") movement. Much of this material appears in a format that was discussed above—exegesis of Scripture—but its interest for the modern reader is not limited to that functional aspect.

Finally, the Talmud embodies an entire world view which can perhaps best be embraced by the word "ethics." The Talmud taught the Jew how to live. This includes the working-out of Jewish law, of course, but also much, much more; ancient rabbis knew perfectly well that law can never provide a full set of guidelines for living one's life. One must also, as later teachers put it, be a *mensch*.

This ethical side to the Talmudic tradition appears most clearly in a particular tractate of the Mishnah, one which in fact never received a *gemara* of the standard type at all. Tractate Avot ("Fathers") is an anthology of rabbis' sayings about a great variety of subjects. These appear in no particular order, other than a vague chronological sequence which peters out before the tractate is half finished. Despite its unusual format, however, this tractate is probably the most studied Jewish text of all time.

From an early period, the custom grew of studying one chapter of tractate Avot on each of the Sabbaths between Passover and Shavuot. There are six weeks between these festivals, and originally there were only five chapters in Avot, but this custom became so firmly entrenched that a sixth was added, just to make the study come out even. In fact, the tractate came to be known popularly as "Pirke Avot," the "Chapters of Avot" (in English, commonly, the "Ethics of the Fathers," reflecting the tractate's characteristic theme), after the custom of studying this text every year, a chapter at a time.

Avot begins with a kind of brief history of the entire Jewish tradition as rabbis understood it ("Moses received Torah from Sinai and transmitted it to Joshua; Joshua to the Elders, the Elders to the Prophets," and so on); the entire remainder of the tractate consists of sayings attributed to one rabbi or another, starting with the earliest forerunners of the rabbinate and going up to the early third century. These sayings deal with numerous topics: techniques for Torah study, types of personality, and general ethical advice. For centuries, Jews have lived by the lessons they learned from Pirke Avot, and there is no better way to end this chapter than to quote from that ancient compilation a single remark (2.8) attributed to the founder of the rabbinate after the destruction of Jerusalem, a remark that contains within it the heart of the rabbis' mission in history:

> Rabban Yohanan ben Zakkai . . . used to say: "If you have learned much Torah, take no credit for yourself, for that is why you were created."

WHERE TO GO FROM HERE

Introductions to Talmudic literature. A number of books have been produced which are essentially just handbooks, giving the names of all the Mishnaic tractates, lists of the important Tannaim and Amoraim, and so forth; two of these can be mentioned here:

Moses Mielzener. *Introduction to the Talmud.* New York: Bloch, 1968.
Hermann L. Strack. *Introduction to the Talmud and Midrash.* New York: Atheneum, 1969.

If you already have access to a good encyclopedia, you probably don't need either of these, but if not, you may find one of them handy. Even if you have an encyclopedia, of course, a single, compact volume is easier to handle and carry around.

Other volumes try to evoke the nature of the Talmud, or of the world from which it emerged:

Morris Adler. *The World of the Talmud.* New York: Schocken, 1963.
Jacob Neusner. *There We Sat Down.* New York: Ktav, 1976.
Adin Steinsalz. *The Essential Talmud.* New York: Bantam, 1976.

while one newly issued work is a remarkable introduction to the ongoing significance of the Talmud in the world of Orthodox Jewry:

Samuel Heilman. *The People of the Book.* Chicago: University of Chicago Press, 1983.

On a more scholarly level, the following pair of volumes provide convenient summaries of recent scholarship on the origins and development of the Mishnah and Talmud:

Jacob Neusner, ed. *The Modern Study of the Mishnah.* Leiden: E. J. Brill, 1973.

Jacob Neusner, ed. *The Formation of the Babylonian Talmud*. Leiden: E. J. Brill, 1970.

Introduction to Talmud study. Jacob Neusner has written a volume that takes the reader through the detailed study of a chapter of Mishnah (Berakhot, chapter 8), and then of both the Talmudic chapters based on it. At every step, Neusner tries both to explain the text under review and also to highlight what it is like (as experience and as theology) to study that text. The book is called *Invitation to the Talmud* (New York: Harper & Row, 1973). Much more elementary versions of the same enterprise are to be found in two volumes by the same author called *Learn Mishnah* and *Learn Talmud* (New York: Behrman, 1978). Finally, Neusner has written a short series of lectures in which he considers more thoroughly the theology behind a religion of study and rational, critical discussion; that volume is entitled *The Glory of God Is Intelligence* (Salt Lake City: Brigham Young University Press, 1978).

A more technical guide to Talmud study is Aryeh Carmell, *Aids to Talmud Study* (New York: Feldheim, 1975). This little pamphlet contains chronological listings of Talmudic authorities, a glossary of technical terms, a brief summary of Aramaic grammar (for those who already know Hebrew), and so on. More advanced is Louis Jacobs, *Studies in Talmudic Logic and Methodology* (London: Vallentine, Mitchell, 1961).

The most useful aid of all is the well-known Talmudic dictionary of Marcus Jastrow (there are numerous editions and reprints). This work lists and translates every word appearing in ancient rabbinic literature and usually supplies one or more sample uses of the word, with each sample translated and its source indicated. While more recent scholarship has left many of Jastrow's derivations open to serious question, his translations remain invaluable to any student of ancient rabbinic texts.

Translations of the Mishnah. Three complete translations of the Mishnah have appeared in English. One is part of the Soncino Press translation of the Talmud (see below). Another, almost without commentary, was issued by Herbert Danby (Oxford: Oxford University Press, 1933); the third, more heavily annotated, was prepared by Philip Blackman (New York: Judaica Press, 1964). A new translation by Jacob Neusner will shortly appear through the Yale University Press.

Translations of the Talmud. The entire Babylonian Talmud was translated into English some time ago by the Soncino Press. This translation now comes in several formats, including a bilingual edition (not yet complete) in which each page of the Talmud is printed facing its translation. The Soncino translation has some sketchy notes, but it cannot really be considered an annotated edition designed for students.

A new English translation of the Jerusalem Talmud, the first in that language, has just begun to appear. It is edited by Jacob Neusner and published by the University of Chicago Press. A new translation of the Babylonian Talmud, with the same editor and published by Scholars Press, will follow.

A bilingual edition of tractate Ta'anit was issued some time ago by the Jewish Publication Society of America; the translator was Henry Malter. This volume is less expensive than the Soncino set, but it too is very sparsely annotated.

Possibly more useful to the starter are pamphlets, each translating one chapter of the Talmud and providing for that translation quite extensive annotation, prepared by the Department of Torah Education and Culture in the Diaspora of the World Zionist Organization. Readers wishing to know more about these booklets can contact a nearby Israeli consulate, or write directly to the WZO in Jerusalem.

Similar pamphlets have been published privately by the Gross Brothers Press in New York City; the editor of these is Nathan Lomner.

Finally, an effort called the El 'Am Talmud was begun some years ago. This was to be a fully annotated bilingual edition of the Talmud. Each page was to provide a translation of the text, brief biographies of the rabbis mentioned in each passage, short explanations of the historical and cultural background necessary for understanding the text, and indications of the correct halakhic implications to be drawn from every discussion. One complete tractate (Berakhot) and parts of several others have appeared to date.

Codes and Responsa. Large sections of Maimonides' *Mishneh Torah* have been translated into English as part of the Yale Judaica Series. That same series now also contains a magisterial *Introduction* to the *Mishneh Torah* by Isadore Twersky.

Surprisingly, the complete *Shulhan Arukh* has never been rendered into English, though a nineteenth-century abridgment *(Kitsur Shulhan Arukh)* by Solomon Ganzfried was translated by H. E. Goldin. Unfortunately, the *Kitsur* tends to focus on details of ritual rather than presenting the full richness of the legal tradition. This translation, usually called *The Code of Jewish Law,* can be found in several editions.

Solomon Freehof is a Reform rabbi who has published numerous collections of responsa, both older ones and also more recent halakhic decisions of his own movement. These collections have various titles, all including the word "responsa." Recent Orthodox responsa are collected in J. David Bleich, *Contemporary Halakhic Problems* (New York: Ktav, 1977); Dr. Bleich also edits a column on current responsa in the Orthodox quarterly, *Tradition*. With respect to the Conservative movement, see Mordecai Waxman, *Tradition and Change* (New York: Burning Bush, 1964), Seymour Siegel, *Conservative Judaism and Jewish Law* (New York: Ktav, 1977), and Isaac Klein, *A Guide to Jewish Religious Practice* (New York: Jewish Theological Seminary of America, 1979).

ויקרא

COURTESY OF THE LIBRARY OF THE JEWISH THEOLOGICAL SEMINARY OF AMERICA

First page of Leviticus Rabbah from early printed edition of Midrash Rabbah with penciled notations in margins, Venice, 1545.

CHAPTER THREE

Midrash

BARRY W. HOLTZ

The Talmud, as was shown in the previous chapter, is the best-known of the texts produced by rabbinic Judaism. It has formed the core of the curriculum of Jewish learning for many hundreds of years, and it stands as the foundation upon which later Jewish literature, particularly legal writing, rests. And yet the Talmud does not represent the entirety of rabbinic literature. Another body of work—less familiar but probably more accessible to the contemporary reader—remains to be explored. We are speaking here of the texts known as Midrash, a type of literature so significant that in many ways it can be seen as the central enterprise of almost all Jewish religious writing until the modern period. In this chapter we shall try to explore what Midrash is and why it has had such importance in the history of Judaism.

WHAT IS MIDRASH

To begin with we should make clear that there is no single book called the Midrash. Despite the popular use of the term, one cannot with accuracy use the phrase "the Midrash says," the way we can refer to books such as the Talmud, the Zohar or the Shulhan Arukh. Midrash is a type of literature; it is, as we shall see, a kind of process or activity, but there is no one Midrash. Rather there are collections of Midrashim (plural of Midrash) which were put together at various times and by various editors and authors over the course of many hundreds of years. The great flowering of Midrash was roughly between the years 400 and 1200 C.E. But it is important to note that originally, midrashic literature was oral—sermons preached in the synagogues and teachings of various sages. During the years mentioned, Midrashim were edited, organized, and written down, but midrashic texts often represent traditions a good deal older than the period of the written books.

Unfortunately for non-Hebrew readers, when the Soncino Press published its English translation of the best-known midrashic text, Midrash Rabbah, they called the set *The Midrash,* adding their part to the confusion. In fact, Midrash Rabbah itself is a collection of individual texts collected by different editors at different times. Leviticus Rabbah and Genesis Rabbah, for example, are not the work of the same author, even though traditionally they are published in the same volume or set.

What, then, is Midrash? It is helpful to think of Midrash in two different, but related, ways: first, Midrash (deriving from the Hebrew root "to search out") is the process of *interpreting.* The object of interpretation is the Bible or, on occasion, other sacred texts; * second, Midrash refers to the corpus of work that has collected these interpretations, works such as Midrash Rabbah. There are different types of Midrashim, but before we explore the different categories, it will be useful to talk about the "why" of Midrash: what necessitated the development of this literature, and why it has been so important.

To do so, we must return to two terms mentioned in the previous chapter: *halakhah* and *aggadah.* Halakhah refers to Jewish literature primarily concerned with law and codes of behavior. For Judaism this refers equally to matters of civil law and religious law, for throughout Jewish history *all* law was seen as essentially religious. Thus the requirements for waving the *lulav* (palm) and *etrog* (citron) on the holiday of Sukkot, the laws of marriage and divorce, the ethics of giving charity, and the requirements for returning lost property would all fit under the rubric of *halakhah.*

Aggadah is a looser and more wide-ranging term referring to narrative literature, parables, theological or ethical statements, and homilies. Perhaps the easiest way to understand *aggadah* is to think of it as virtually all the nonlegal literature of rabbinic Judaism. It is, one might say, a kind of "imaginative" literature.

* In that sense the *gemara* sections of the Talmud are a kind of Midrash on the Mishnah (see Chapter Two).

It should be obvious that these are rather artificial distinctions and terms. In fact there is very little in Jewish literature which is either pure *halakhah* or pure *aggadah;* the driest legal texts are often dotted with aggadic asides; and aggadic stories are often brought to teach a point about the law. The Talmud, for example, is often referred to as a legal code, in other words, a purely "halakhic" text. But as pointed out in Chapter Two, nothing could be farther from the truth. More than merely law, the Talmud is also filled with stories and legends, allegories and theological pronouncements. Yet the distinctions, for all their artificiality, are often useful, and the categories of *halakhah* and *aggadah* can give us particular insight into the origins and development of Midrash.

Midrash—the act and process of interpretation—works in both the halakhic and aggadic realms. That is, sacred texts, most notably the Bible, are carefully interpreted, both to derive points of law and to give occasion for theological statements or stories and parables. The aggadic sections of the Bible (such as most of the book of Genesis) can be used to adduce legal practices (we learn about blowing the shofar, the ram's horn, on Rosh Hashanah from the story of the binding of Isaac), and the halakhic sections of the Bible, in turn, are often the occasion for *aggadah* (one of the great aggadic books in all of midrashic literature is a work devoted ostensibly to interpreting the book of Leviticus, despite all the legal minutia about sacrifices that dominate that section of the Bible).

Curiously, both halakhic and aggadic sorts of Midrash seem to develop out of the same set of forces. Primarily we can see the central issue behind the emergence of Midrash as the need to deal with the presence of cultural or religious tension and discontinuity. Where there are questions that demand answers, and where there are new cultural and intellectual pressures that must be addressed, Midrash comes into play as a way of resolving crisis and reaffirming continuity with the traditions of the past. Since Midrash is overwhelmingly the process of interpreting the biblical text, we must look to the Bible first for the kinds of forces that led to the development of the midrashic literature.

What we notice at once is that the very style of the Bible creates a kind of tension that the rabbinic sages were forced to confront. This is particularly striking in the realm of *aggadah,* but as we shall see, the same issue is relevant to halakhic concerns as well, and may in fact even be more crucial there.

As was mentioned in the "Biblical Narrative" section of Chapter One, the literary critic Erich Auerbach some years ago explored the style of the Bible in an influential essay entitled "Odysseus' Scar."* It is an essay worth mentioning again since it has as much importance for the study of Midrash as it does for an understanding of the Bible. In this essay Auerbach compared the Bible to another relatively contemporary work, Homer's *Odyssey,* and noted a vast difference in style between the two works. The primary characteristic of biblical style, Auerbach pointed out, is its laconic nature: very little is said, particularly in comparison to the kind of detail we find in Homer. The Bible is loath to tell us the motivations, feelings, or thoughts of characters. Rarely giving us descriptive details either of people or places, it is composed in a stark, uncompromising style.

Hence in the laconic style of the Bible, we find one significant cause of the necessity for Midrash. Midrash comes to fill in the gaps, to tell us the details that the Bible teasingly leaves out: what did Isaac think as his father took him to be sacrificed? The Bible doesn't tell us, but Midrash fills it in with rich and varied descriptions. Why did Cain kill Abel? Once again the Bible is silent, but Midrash is filled with explanation. How tall was Adam as he walked in the Garden? Look to the midrashic materials, not to the Bible for such details. The human mind desires answers, motivations, explanations. Where the Bible is mysterious and silent, Midrash comes to unravel the mystery. Moreover, there are sections of the Bible that are simply confusing or unclear. Midrash attempts to elucidate confusions and to harmonize seeming contradictions.

Look at the biblical story of Cain and Abel, for example. Halfway into the narrative we read the following verse: "Cain said to Abel, his brother. And it came to pass, when they were in the field, that Cain rose up against Abel his brother and slew him." (Gen. 4.8) Something is wrong here. *What* did Cain say to his brother? The text seems jumbled; the dialogue never appears! A modern translation generally will indicate this difficulty with an ellipsis after the word Abel and a footnote. The contemporary Bible scholar might point out that we obviously have a problem in textual transmission here—somewhere along the line, perhaps, a verse was accidentally dropped by a scribe, and thus we have a faulty text.

But for Midrash this problem is not a difficulty; it is an opportunity. Midrash supplies the missing dialogue. We hear the cause of the enmity between Cain and Abel and the confusion is solved. Thus, according to one source, the story of Cain and Abel is one of petty and foolish

* In Erich Auerbach, *Mimesis* (Princeton, N.J.: Princeton University Press, 1971), pp. 3–24.

jealousy—on both sides. And because of that, murder entered human experience.

Not surprisingly, the laconic style of the Bible has a role in the realm of *halakhah* as well, for the Bible often states matters of law without clarification or detail. We know for example that Jews must observe the Sabbath, but what does that actually entail? The Bible tells us only a few details, such as the prohibition against gathering the manna. It is up to later interpreters to fill in the blanks. Observant Jews today keep separate dishes for milk and meat, but where is that outlined in the Bible? Nowhere, in fact. It was the Midrash of rabbinic Judaism, legal Midrash, that defined the laws. What does it mean to love one's neighbor as oneself? *Midrash halakhah* will explore that problem as well. Thus it is obvious that knowing the Bible alone cannot be the basis for a person's understanding of Judaism. Without knowing the rabbis' interpretation of the Bible, one does not understand either Jewish thought or Jewish practice.

The laconic style of the Bible, however, does not give us the entire picture. Midrash comes into being for another important reason as well —over time any tradition is faced with the problem of discontinuity. The Bible is a very old document. It reflects its time of origin, the world of the early history of Israel. By the time of the rabbis much had changed. The social and political realities of the biblical world had given way to Greek culture, and the influence of Hellenism was crucial in the world of rabbinic Judaism. Midrash arose as an attempt to keep a sense of continuity between the ancient traditions of the Bible and the new world of Hellenistic Judaism.

In the realm of *halakhah* the need for continuity is easy to see. The legal system of the rabbis required new ideas, new interpretations of Torah to deal with the world in which the Jews lived. Probably the most striking factor was the impact of the destruction of the Temple in the year 70 of the Common Era, since so much of Jewish religious life had revolved around the Temple and so many of the laws dealt with the sacrificial cult. With that loss, new legal questions came immediately to the forefront: How should we deal with the loss of sacrifice? How can we expiate sin without the sin offering? What is the role of the priestly class? Thus in one famous midrashic passage we read: "The Temple and its sacrifices do not alone expiate our sins, rather we have an equivalent way of making atonement and that is through deeds of human kindness." This is a radical, but necessary, reinterpretation of the law.

Moreover, the rabbis when examining the ancient texts of the Bible found it necessary at times to reread texts in the light of their own contemporary values and beliefs. The most famous example of such a rereading is the interpretation of "an eye for an eye" in Exodus 21. The rabbis of the Babylonian Talmud could not believe that the Torah really intended us to take this verse literally; thus for them it was clear that the text referred to monetary compensation (Talmud, Baba Kamma 84a).

The same factor applies to the aggadic dimension as well, where we see the discontinuity of changing times influencing the theology and spiritual vision of the rabbinic mind. One striking example is the concept of the soul. Most modern biblical commentators agree that the concept of a soul distinct from the body is foreign to the Bible, certainly to the early sections of the Bible. But what if we ask, does Judaism "believe in" the concept of the soul? Despite the Bible, to say no would be to ignore the myriad references to soul that we find in rabbinic literature and thus to base our understanding of Judaism on the Bible alone. Indeed, we must say that Judaism *does* accept the idea of a soul, an idea that no doubt crept into rabbinic thought under the influence of Hellenism and was "read into" biblical texts that probably never had such a idea in mind at all. To choose just one example, consider the followin midrashic text:

> "Bless the Lord, O my soul"
>
> —Ps. 103.1

What reason did David see for praising the Holy One, blessed be He, with his soul? He said: The soul fills the body, and the Holy One, blessed be He, fills His Universe, as it is said, "Do not I fill heaven and earth? saith the Lord" (Jer. 23.24); let the soul which fills the body come and praise the Holy One, blessed be He, who fills all the Universe. The soul carries the body, and the Holy One, blessed be He, carries His Universe, as it is said, "I have made and I will bear; yea I will carry," etc. (Isa. 46.4); let the soul which carries the body come and praise the Holy One, blessed be He, who carries the Universe. The soul outlasts the body, and the Holy One, blessed be He, outlives the world; let the soul which outlasts the body come and praise the Holy One, blessed be He, who outlives His Universe, as it is said, "They shall perish, but Thou shalt endure; yea all of them shall wax old like a garment. . . . But . . . Thy years shall have no end" (Ps. 102.27f.). The soul is only one in the body, and the Holy One, blessed be He, is the only One in the Universe; let the soul, which is only one in the body, come and praise the Holy One, blessed be He, who is

the only One in the Universe as it is said, "Hear, O Israel; The
Lord our God the Lord is one." (Deut. 6.4)

—LEVITICUS RABBAH, IV,8

It is clear from this text that there is no ambivalence or lack of clarity
about the existence or nature of the soul. It is an idea firmly rooted in
the Midrash of the rabbinic period.

Another and related idea is that of the afterlife. Once again we have
a notion, hazy at best in the Bible (the Bible speaks, for example, of
Sheol, a shadowy, undefined netherworld; but these references are rare
and often in the realm of poetic utterance; see Jacob's remark following
the report of Joseph's death in Gen. 37.35), which is later borrowed
from the Greeks and then through the process of interpretation—Midrash—grafted back onto the Bible.

The soul and the afterlife are only two of the many "external" ideas
that entered rabbinic Judaism through the impetus of Midrash. Another
type of discontinuity addressed by Midrash is in the realm of history
itself. Dramatic and unusual events find their response in Midrash, and
none so strikingly as the midrashic response to the destruction of the
Temple, as much a factor here in the realm of *aggadah* as it is in the
halakhic dimension discussed earlier. After the destruction the people
turned to the rabbis for words of hope and consolation, and out of this
need midrashic texts, such as Lamentations Rabbah, were born. In the
following example from that text, the rabbis use the common comparison of the Torah to a marriage contract (*ketubah* in Hebrew) as a means
of offering hope to a people in despair:

"This I recall to mind, therefore I have hope."

—LAM. 3.21

R. Abba b. Kahana said: This may be likened to a king
who married a lady and wrote her a large *ketubah:* "so many
state-apartments I am preparing for you, so many jewels I am
preparing for you, and so much silver and gold I give you."

The king left her and went to a distant land for many
years. Her neighbors used to vex her saying, "Your husband
has deserted you. Come and be married to another man." She
wept and sighed, but whenever she went into her room and
read her *ketubah* she would be consoled. After many years the
king returned and said to her, "I am astonished that you waited
for me all these years." She replied, "My lord king, if it had

not been for the generous *ketubah* you wrote me then surely my neighbors would have won me over."

So the nations of the world taunt Israel and say, "Your God has no need of you; He has deserted you and removed His Presence from you. Come to us and we shall appoint commanders and leaders of every sort for you." Israel enters the synagogues and houses of study and reads in the Torah, "I will look with favor upon you . . . and I will not spurn you" (Lev. 26.9–11), and they are consoled.

In the future the Holy One blessed be He will say to Israel, "I am astonished that you waited for me all these years." And they will reply, "If it had not been for the Torah which you gave us . . . the nations of the world would have led us astray." . . . Therefore it is stated, "This do I recall and therefore I have hope." (Lam. 3.21)

Leviticus Rabbah is only one example of a midrashic text in which the rabbis spin a web of *aggadah* in response to the terrible calamity of the destruction of the Temple. Here the rabbis are telling the people that an ongoing faithfulness to the Torah will eventually result in God's fulfilling the promises contained in that document. God *seems* to have deserted Israel, but when He returns, God will be astonished by Israel's faithful adherence to His teachings. In that way Midrash tries to bridge the gap between faith and despair, seeking to make sense out of the events of tragic history. Thus, whether it be through historical events or in reaction to the intellectual stirrings of the Hellenistic world, the aggadic aspects of Midrash were as affected by the problem of discontinuity as was the legal realm.

To sum up this discussion of the spiritual and intellectual origins of Midrash, we might graphically picture the roots of this body of literature in the following fashion:

MIDRASH

Aggadah	*Halakhah*
1. Style of the Bible	1. Style of the Bible
a. Motivations, meanings	a. Filling in the gaps
b. Resolving confusions	b. Exposition of detail

2. Discontinuity as times change
   a. Destruction of Temple
      (need for consolation)
   b. New ideas
      (soul, afterlife)

2. Discontinuity as times change
   a. Destruction of Temple
      (loss of sacrifices)
   b. New values
      (eye for an eye)

One further point remains to be made. How could the rabbis do it? How could they have allowed themselves the freedom and flexibility to make such startlingly new interpretations of Torah, to change the laws of the Bible itself? There is no simple answer to this question, particularly because it is asked with hindsight, from the perspective of people who are not within that system but are looking back on top of it, as it were. One cannot really say whether the rabbis were aware that they were changing Torah through Midrash. It is certain that they saw that laws were being reformulated (and perhaps they realized that ideas and values were being changed as well), but the assumption in rabbinic thought is always that new interpretation is implied by Torah itself. As discussed in the Introduction to this book, the idea for the rabbis is that they are only *uncovering* what is already there.

The key point, the point around which everything revolves, is the rabbis' conception of Torah itself. Torah, to the rabbis, was an *eternally relevant book because it was written* (dictated, inspired—it doesn't matter) *by a perfect Author,* an Author who intended it to be eternal. When we keep this essential fact in mind, much of the midrashic process falls into place. The rabbis could not help but believe that this wondrous and sacred text, the Torah, was intended for all Jews and for all times. Surely God could foresee the need for new interpretations; all interpretations, therefore, are already in the Torah text. Thus we have the idea mentioned previously: on Mount Sinai God gave not only the Written Torah that we know, but the Oral Torah, the interpretations of Jews down through time. Midrash, in other words, was already in God's mind when the Torah was conceived. In the words of one famous passage about Torah found in the Mishnah: "Turn it and turn it again, for everything is contained therein."

It is true that not all the rabbis were equally zealous in their pursuit of interpretation. For example, Rabbi Akiba, it has been argued, was more radical in his approach to interpretation than his colleague Rabbi Ishmael. But all the rabbis would subscribe to a doctrine of the eternal interpretability of Torah and we might say that if there is any one dogma of rabbinic Judaism it is that *everything is contained therein.*

It is in this way that we can rightfully call almost all Jewish writing, at least until the nineteenth century, a kind of Midrash. Midrash, as it were, did not end with rabbinic Judaism, but in the legal codes of the Middle Ages and the Hasidic homilies of the nineteenth century, Midrash—the process of interpretation—continues. It is the genius of the rabbis that gave birth to this marvelous tool, and it is through interpretation that Judaism gained its strength in the past and will, some have argued, gain its strength in the future.

Types of Midrash

We tend nowadays to think of the Jewish sermon as a modern invention, something borrowed perhaps from our Protestant neighbors. But in fact, sermons have been preached throughout much of Jewish history. In rabbinic times, sermons were so popular that people would flock from miles around to hear the Sabbath or Festival address of some renowned preacher.

The preacher would enter dramatically after his assistants had "warmed up" the audience, and as he spoke, an underling—acting as a kind of primitive "living loudspeaker"—would repeat his words so that all could hear. We do not have an actual transcript of an ancient sermon in its entirety, but fragments of these ancient sermons, reworked and polished by later editors, form the core of one major type of midrashic literature. Reasonably enough, this body of literature is called *homiletical* Midrash, since it is based, at least in essence, on the homilies preached by the ancient sages.

The classic examples of homiletical Midrash are Leviticus Rabbah and Pesikta De Rav Kahana. Although these texts are available in English, to the untrained reader (particularly if he or she does not have access to the Hebrew original) these texts can seem difficult indeed. Often the logic of the passage is not entirely clear since it depends on wordplays or associations that are not captured by the translation. Moreover, as discussed at length later in this chapter, homiletical Midrash is dependent on certain subtleties of form that add to its complexity and create additional problems for the contemporary reader.

Far more accessible are the works known as *exegetical* Midrashim. Here the oral influence may also be present, but it is far less obvious. The ancient editors of these works assembled, it appears, a set of short, pithy comments on individual verses of the Bible, many of which may have been collected from a variety of sermons or public teachings of the various sages.

One recent writer, James Kugel, in an article entitled "Two Introductions to Midrash," * points out that Midrash is basically a "verse-centered" literature. That is, the midrashist is primarily concerned with explicating a particular verse or set of verses in the biblical text, not a whole book or even an entire narrative. Thus, Kugel points out, the midrashic works in our possession today are misleadingly well organized! They suggest in their line-by-line explication of biblical books that the rabbinic authors are treating the "whole text" of a particular biblical work, where in fact they have edited compilations of bits of sermons or lessons that had been passed along by a kind of oral grapevine. Kugel draws an amusing modern analogy in his description of the relationship between the oral word and the later midrashic work:

> . . . midrashic explications of individual verses no doubt circulated on their own, independent of any larger exegetical context. Perhaps in this sense it would not be inappropriate to compare their manner of circulating to that of jokes in modern society; indeed they were a kind of joking, a learned and sophisticated play about the biblical text, and like jokes they were passed on, modified and improved as they went, until a great many of them eventually entered into the common inheritance of every Jew, passed on in learning with the text of the Bible itself. (p. 147)

The concise nature of the individual statements in this type of Midrash allows us to get an easier handle on some of these texts, and a classic exegetical Midrash like Genesis Rabbah is a good place to begin one's study of this literature.

Among the exegetical texts we find examples of some of the earliest Midrashim, works called Tannaitic Midrash since they date from the period of the "Tannaim," the early sages. Unfortunately, these works—the most famous is called the Mekhilta, a commentary on Exodus—are also called *halakhic* Midrash, even though they are filled with aggadic passages: thus still more confusion for the puzzled reader.

Finally, there is a body of literature known as *narrative* Midrash. In these books we see little connection in a direct or organized fashion to

* In *Prooftexts: A Journal of Jewish Literary History,* vol. 3, no. 2 (May 1983), pp. 131–57.

the task of *explicating* the Bible, but instead there is occasion for stories and legends, either about individual rabbis or about biblical characters. Some of these works are known as "rewritten Bible," since they replicate and expand upon the biblical narrative. Because of the noninterpretive style of the texts, some scholars in fact would prefer not to call these works Midrash at all. A well-known example of narrative Midrash is Pirkei De Rebbe Eliezer.

To make some sense out of the various categories of Midrash, the following chart is suggested. I should add that we have simplified a bit for the sake of clarity. Some midrashic works fall less clearly than we might like into neat categories.

Types of Midrashic Texts ★

Estimated Date	Exegetical	Homiletical	Narrative
Tannaitic period (up to 200 C.E.)	Mekhilta Sifra Sifre		
400–650 C.E.	Genesis Rabbah Lamentations Rabbah	Leviticus Rabbah Pesikta De Rav Kahana	
650–900	Midrash Proverbs Ecclesiastes Rabbah	Midrash Tanhuma Deuteronomy Rabbah	Pirkei De Rebbe Eliezer Tanna Debe Eliahu
900–1000	Midrash Psalms Exodus Rabbah Ruth Zuta Lamentations Zuta		
1000–1200	Midrash Aggadah (by school of Rabbi Moshe ha Darshan)		Sefer Ha-Yashar

★ See article on Midrash in *Encyclopaedia Judaica* for more complete chart.

Late anthologies of Midrash include:
  Yalkut Shimoni
  Midrash HaGadol
  Ein Yaakov

READING A MIDRASHIC TEXT

Before turning to some specific texts we should say a few words about the method of Midrash, particularly in the homiletical and exegetical forms. A great scholar of the early part of this century, Isaac Heinemann, talks about two major characteristics of midrashic style: "creative historiography" and "creative philology." We have alluded to creative historiography before. This is the imaginative filling in of the gaps, the search for reasons, the explication of meaning and motivation. This aspect of Midrash translates well for the modern reader, and it affords us an opportunity through which we can gain insight into the ancient rabbis and their thought. Through the explication of sacred texts, the theology, and the religious and moral concerns of these founders of Judaism become clear.

For the English reader, creative philology is a good deal more difficult to catch. For here we see the rabbis using puns and wordplays, reversals of letters and convergences of sounds. This aspect of explication may be foreign to our sensibility and difficult to capture in translation. The important point, however, is to see this method as something not merely quaint or obscure. In fact the punning is based on the profound seriousness with which the rabbis viewed the sacred text. The unlocking of the Bible's secret mystery was their enterprise, the very holiness of the text is what allowed them to let their imaginations roam —even if it meant interpreting through puns and letter reversals. Moreover, it is essential that we factor out the method from the content. Although the rabbinic method of creative philology may be strange to us, we should learn to take quite seriously the particular point that is being made by the Midrash. It may even be true that the pun can unlock meanings in the Bible for us that we may not have seen before. Learning to "think midrashically" may speak to us more deeply than we realize.

Whether it be "creative philology" or "creative historiography" many Midrashim are based on a so-called "problem" point in the biblical text. Midrash uses as a jumping-off point subtleties in the Bible that may often elude the modern reader. In looking at a midrashic text our first task, then, should be to try to ascertain what is troubling, or inspiring, the midrashic author. Seeing the confusion of the Genesis text about Cain and Abel mentioned above, one does not have difficulty understanding the motivation behind the midrashic attempt to fill in the gaps, nor are we surprised to find the Midrash supplying the thoughts of Abraham and Isaac as they walked up the mountain toward their sacrificial task. But at other times it takes a good deal more concentration to see the "problem" that the Midrash seeks to answer. Partly this has to do with our sense of the word "problem" itself. Thinking about the biblical text as something that "inspires" the midrashic mind may be a more useful formulation than seeing the Bible as littered with problems waiting to be solved. James Kugel uses the term "surface irregularities" to describe the problems discerned by the rabbis' extraordinary ear for the Bible's Hebrew style. Any small oddity of usage, any unusual word or grammatical construction led the rabbis toward an interpretive point. As excellent close readers of text, the smallest nuance of language or character motivation inspired their comments.

Obviously, some of these surface irregularities do not translate well for the English reader. At times, the rabbis may have been responding unknowingly to a problem in the evolution of the Hebrew language itself. The Hebrew of the Bible differs from the Hebrew of rabbinic times, both in vocabulary usage and in points of syntax. The rabbis on occasion read biblical Hebrew as if it were Mishnaic (rabbinic) Hebrew, and thus they may discover problems where none actually exist. It would be similar to our reading Shakespearean English—where the word "fond," for example, usually means "foolish" or "silly"—as if it were modern English, where the same word, "fond," means having warm affection for someone.

Sometimes one feels the rabbis create problems for the sake of having opportunities to write Midrash! Kugel puts it well when he remarks:

> . . . in later midrash there is much material, especially list-making and text-connecting, whose connection with "problems" is remote indeed; in fact, like many a modern-day homilist, the midrashist sometimes betrays signs of having first thought of a solution and then having gone out in search of the problem to which it might be applied. (p. 145)

And yet, despite these provisos, it has long been a tradition to examine Midrash—in particular exegetical Midrash—with an eye toward the problem to be solved. The non-Hebrew reader, however, should be aware that these may not always be evident in translation.

One matter that can make Midrash more accessible, even to the person reading the texts only in English, is to take care to check the biblical verse upon which the Midrash is based in its entirety and in its context. Sometimes the Midrash will only quote the first section of the biblical verse, but its concern may be with the end of the verse, or the verse that follows it. The editions of Midrash that we have often had those biblical verses added to the original midrashic source simply for the sake of the reader's convenience. In the manuscript version, the quotations may not even appear. Although this "shorthand" quotation system is enormously helpful, it can also be misleading. The editor may assume that we know the whole verse or section by heart, and therefore he only need give us the opening as a kind of hint. Suffice it to say—one must check the full verse. At times the rabbis will quote a "prooftext" from some other place in the Bible. Once again, it is important to examine that source and try to determine the point they are making by bringing it into the picture. Some of this is a matter of literary convention—the rabbis used prooftexts as a common way of validating or justifying statements they were making. At other times the particular text quoted may present the reader with a subtle commentary on what the Midrash is saying.

Of course it is important to go beyond the Midrash as only biblical commentary. The rabbis were elucidating the Bible, to be sure, but their interpretations reflect their philosophy, theology, and inner consciousness. Besides marveling at their ingenuity or wit, we must also try to make sense out of what lurks beneath the mere interpretive point. Since the rabbis wrote no philosophy, it is through their midrashic endeavors that we see their entire religious perspective.

Let us now turn to our first text. It comes from Genesis Rabbah and deals with the creation of man. Here is the text:

> "And God said: Let us make man."
>
> —GEN. 1.26

Rabbi Simon said: When the Holy One, blessed be He, came to create the first man, the ministering angels divided into groups and parties, some saying: Let him not be created, and others saying: Let him be created. . . . Mercy said: Let him be created, for he will be merciful, and Truth said: Let him not be created for he will be all lies. Righteousness said: Let him be created, for he will do righteous deeds; Peace said: Let him not be created, for he is full of strife.

What did the Holy One, blessed be He, do? He took Truth and flung him to the earth. The ministering angels said to the Holy One, Blessed be He: Master of the Universe, do you disgrace your own seal. Raise Truth from the earth . . .

Rav Huna said: While the ministering angels were still arguing and disputing, the Holy One, blessed be He, created man. Then He said to them: Why do you argue? Man is already made.

—GENESIS RABBAH, VIII, 5

What do we see in this text? As we have said, in looking at a midrashic text, it is often very useful to consider what is "troubling" the rabbinic writer. To the rabbis there were no inconsistencies, no problems in transmission (as a modern biblical critic might say), there were only mysteries of meaning that needed to be unlocked.

In our text above, the problem, the troubling point, is quite clear. When God comes to create the first person, He says "Let us make man." Who is the "us"? To whom is God speaking? As far as we know from the first twenty-five verses of Genesis, God is alone. Suddenly he addresses someone else. Hence it begins as many Midrashim do with a problem of biblical *language*.

The modern biblical scholar might solve this particular problem by suggesting that God is using the "royal we"—something like the speeches of kings in Shakespeare's plays. By such a formulation there *is* no real problem. The plural is standard biblical usage. But the Midrash chooses another and more literal answer. God must be speaking to *someone,* and to whom else could He be speaking but the heavenly host, the angels. And with that opening the rabbinic imagination begins to operate. The writer of this Midrash begins to envision an entire drama, a grand debate centering around the question of man's creation. The angels are arrayed in parties and companies, disputing and arguing the question. (Is this perhaps a reflection of heated debates among the ancient rabbis? Is the angelic assembly being portrayed in the imagery of the rabbis' own familiar world?)

It is interesting to consider which angels are pictured on man's side and which are opposed. Mercy is seen as an essential feature of a human being's character, but so is falsehood as we see from the comments of the angel of Truth. A similar conflict is seen between Righteousness and Peace. Or, we wonder, are those characters arbitrary? Does it matter to the midrashist which angel is portrayed as being on which side? Is the rabbinic author simply trying to tell us that human beings are jumbled-up creatures, inconsistent and impossible to read? Perhaps the rabbinic sage could just as easily have placed Mercy on the negative side, Truth in support of creation. From this text we cannot be sure.

One thing is clear—we are getting a kind of rabbinic anthropology, a rabbinic philosophy of the nature of human beings, and it is far more complex than we might have assumed. Perhaps, these rabbis argue, it is *not* such a good thing that man was ever created. And perhaps, we wonder, the history of destruction and terror wrought upon early rabbinic civilization bears out such a dark and tragic view of humanity. Another legend in the midrashic literature tells of a debate between the school of Shammai and the school of Hillel that went on for over two years, until it was decided that it was better if a person had not been created. But now that he had been created the best he can do is "search his deeds."

Now, to return to our text, we see a significant conflict. God, who has remained outside the debate at the beginning, takes Truth and flings him to the ground. Why? Perhaps God knows that Truth indeed speaks the truth—for how can Truth not—and the nature of man *is* lies and deceit. But God, it seems, cannot in this case tolerate the truth. He knows what man is and can be, and yet, despite that, God chooses to create man.

With a kind of humor, the Midrash pictures God slipping away unseen, as it were, from the heated debate and in the background creating man surreptitiously. And why? Is it perhaps that God is afraid that the nay-sayers will win? Having started the discussion, God now sees that He may have to bow to those who oppose man's creation? God therefore subverts the debate, overrules it. When the angels look up, it is too late. There is man, already created. It is as if God got more than He bargained for in beginning creation with a discussion, with "Let *us*," and in the long run had to create man on His own after all.

And there is more here. How does this Midrash speak to us today? It seems to me clear that the rabbis, or at least those rabbis who composed this text, were troubled by their sense of the nature of human character. The Midrash reflects a great sense of doubt about the worthiness of our lives in the face of our terrible failings as people. And yet behind it lurks God's almost autocratic will. Human life, this Midrash seems to suggest, makes little sense given who we all are. Our worthiness is suspect, but our lives *must,* in some profound sense, in some way beyond reason or logic, be meaningful—because God has chosen us for existence. Our existence supersedes debate and reason, even truth. And in that we are face to face with a great mystery. Thus, even for the ancient rabbis, human life can seem without point or meaning; from this Midrash in particular we are left to trust that in God's mind there is some sense to our very being, but to us it is beyond comprehension. Indeed, it is even beyond the angels' comprehension.

There is something about this Midrash that strikes the reader as profoundly true. That is, this is not merely an interesting explication of the biblical verse or an interesting insight into the way the rabbis thought. It is rather a statement about the nature of our existence that strikes home. Given the tragedies of our own century, given the little acts of cruelty we see every day, most of us would share the view of this Midrash—if there is some sense to this life, to the way people are, it is beyond our frail capacity for understanding it. It remains "behind the curtain," as the rabbis sometimes put it, in the secret mind of God.

There are times that the midrashic form allows the rabbis to state radical or controversial ideas that they might have been unable to do if they were writing formal "theology." Thus we can see their doubts, their anger and their confusion emerging through some of their interpretations of biblical texts. Our second midrashic source gives such an opportunity:

> "The voice of your brother's blood is crying out to me from the land."
> —GEN. 4.10

> Rabbi Shimon ben Yochai said "This is a difficult thing to say and it is impossible to say it clearly. Once two athletes were wrestling before the king. If the king wants, they can be separated; but he did not want them separated. One overcame the other and killed him. The loser cried out as he died: 'Who will get justice for me from the king?' Thus: 'The voice of your brother's blood is crying out to me from the land.' "
> —GENESIS RABBAH, XXII, 9

The context of this text is a verse from Genesis 4 that comes toward the end of the Cain and Abel story. Cain has killed his brother and God accuses him of murder. But Rabbi Shimon ben Yochai raises another and more difficult point—who is really to blame?

Rabbi Shimon begins by telegraphing his discomfort about what he is going to say through a rabbinic phrase that almost always introduces a text of great interest: "This is a difficult thing to say and it is impossible to say it clearly." Here the rabbi is going to say something that troubles him greatly, challenging his own inner convictions. To express himself "clearly" (but isn't it really to *mask* what he has in mind?) he makes his comment by using a parable. Certainly the parable is obvious—God is the king; the two wrestlers are Cain and Abel. The dying wrestler cries out with great anguish—"Who will get justice for me from before the king?" Why? Because he realizes that it is the king who must be blamed. Had the king wanted to stop the fight he could have. Does the text mean to say: had God wished to prevent the murder He could have? What Shimon ben Yochai is suggesting is that God is to blame for this murder —*He* is the true culprit.

This view is reinforced by an interpretation of the verse in question that involves a play on words. The word in Hebrew for "to me" *(ayli)* can also be understood as "at me." Thus the verse becomes, "The voice of your brother's blood is crying out at me!" Or even better: "at ME!" That is, the dying Abel is accusing God of the murder, and Rabbi Shimon, at least through stacking the deck in the parable, seems to concur.

What is fascinating is that this radical view does not go unchallenged. We have another, later text which seems to be a direct reply to Rabbi Shimon and which envisions another kind of scene, a conversation between God and Cain, the conversation that falls into a "gap" in the biblical text in Genesis:

> Cain said: "Am I my brother's keeper?"
>
> —GEN. 4.9

> You God watch over all of creation and you're blaming me! This is like a thief who steals things at night and gets away with it. In the morning the watchman grabs him and says "Why did you steal those things?" He replied: "I'm a thief; I haven't been remiss in doing my trade, but you're a guard; why did you fail in your duties?" Then Cain said: "I killed him, true, but You created me with the evil urge in me. You watch over everything and You let me kill him. You killed him! You didn't accept my sacrifice and I was jealous." God answered: "What have you done?" The "voice of your brother's blood calls out . . ."
>
> —MIDRASH TANHUMA, on the Torah
> reading for Genesis, Chapter 9

We are not given the name of the rabbi speaking, but his approach seems to be a frontal attack on Rabbi Shimon. Here the whole issue of God's guilt is rejected and the Midrash comes down fully against Cain.

The Cain portrayed in this text is a cagey manipulator. He tries three different approaches in his argument with God, each one designed to draw the blame away from himself. First he tries the analogic approach. The whole situation, he argues, is very much like something else—a thief who steals from under the nose of the watchman. Clearly, it is the watchman who is to blame—the thief was only plying his own trade. Why blame him?

Cain is so glib and the analogy is painted so convincingly that for a moment we do not see the flaw in the logic. Namely, a thief, after all, is a *thief*—he is not an admirable workman plying his trade. He is not just another hardworking fellow, as Cain would have it, who has a kind of friendly competition going with the watchman. Rather he is morally in the wrong. The criminal, in other words, cannot be excused by arguing that he is a good sport, a good workman, or an admirable person. Cain here has more than a little of the shifty salesman to him: if God is the watchman in the Cain parable, it is God who must be blamed for the murder.

Cain then turns to a second, more abstract argument. Who is to blame? Once again, it is God. Here the approach is not quite what Rabbi Shimon argued in our earlier text, but equally it shifts the blame away from Cain. God, according to Cain, created the inclination in man to do evil and therefore, in at least an ultimate way, He is to be blamed. But this argument too is flawed. To always hearken back to origins, to lay the guilt upon God because of the very nature of man may have some validity as a philosophical construct, as an argument to play with, but it abdicates responsibility for any individual human act. To argue that it would have been nicer or neater to have human beings without their inclination to do evil, their baser sides, misses the point. Given our situation, our existence *as it stands,* we must accept responsibility for the deeds we do without arguing, "I should have been made differently."

The third argument is perhaps the most subtle. For here the midrashic Cain goes back to the biblical text itself and points out a problem any reader (including, obviously, the rabbi who authored this Midrash) must feel—why does God accept Abel's sacrifice in Genesis 4.4, but reject Cain's? Is not God the true culprit in the tale by this act of favoritism?

The Midrash rejects all three of Cain's arguments, but in curious fashion. There is no reply from God, no counter argument or debate. Instead Cain is ignored! His case is demolished by God's silent rebuff— "What have you done" (in committing this murder)? God returns and we hear the emphasis on the word *you*. There is no mitigating "I" from the divine, no reply like God's reply to Job, only the stern rebuke of the "voice of your brother's blood calls out to me. . . ."

Thus the rabbinic author rejects Shimon ben Yochai's case. He sees God as beyond human judgment. The responsibility is with Cain. But . . . does he? In even conceiving Cain's arguments we can hear the doubts that our author himself must have had. And in leaving God silent, we are left more than a little up in the air. The point of this Midrash, in all likelihood, is to exonerate God, but the way that the text is composed does leave room for doubt. Perhaps the Midrash means to do two things—answer Shimon ben Yochai's case *and* raise a few doubts of its own. We cannot really know, but in the subtle interplay of discussion and in its desire to take on the crucial issue of human evil and divine culpability, both of these texts touch concerns that live in our minds as profoundly as they touched our rabbinic forebears.

Up to this point we have focused on Midrashim of the exegetical type. Exegetical Midrashim, because of their short, pithy style and their orientation toward dealing with the literary problems inherent in the biblical text, are a good deal easier to handle than the more lengthy, discursive, homiletical Midrashim. These texts (see chart on pp. 188–189), as we have mentioned before, more closely resemble the sermons of rabbinic times, although, once again, it is important to remember that they are by no means exact transcripts of spoken sermons. The Midrashim have been polished, refined, and ultimately edited into the midrashic collections, such as Leviticus Rabbah, that we now have. Scholars have termed works such as Leviticus Rabbah "literary homilies" to distinguish them from their original oral sources, and also to indicate that they seem to conform to a fairly consistent literary form.

In that sense the literary homily represents a unique kind of genre, different from exegetical Midrash, which feels at least somewhat familiar to the contemporary reader in its resembling an unusual but recognizable commentary to the Bible. The homiletical Midrashim rarely, if ever, give a verse-by-verse commentary, and although they may have something in common with a collection of preacher's sermons, their inner structure makes them more dissimilar than comparable to a sermonic collection, like, for example, modern anthologies of sermons written by famous preachers of the past.*

The general approach of the literary homily is to structure each chapter around three basic types of sermon forms. These forms probably resemble certain types of actual sermons from rabbinic times, but our knowledge of practice in the ancient synagogues and study houses is extremely scant. The best-represented and most numerous of these forms is a sermon type known as the proem *(petihta)*. Professor Joseph Heinemann has argued† that the proem may have served as a kind of introductory sermon preached in the synagogue immediately prior to the Torah reading. Heinemann's position is convincing in that the proem form is structured in a "backward" kind of fashion, culminating its *last* sentence with the *first* verse of the Sabbath or Festival reading.

The proem usually begins with a quotation from a place in the Bible far from the Torah reading itself, often from the "Writings," such as Psalms or Job. Then the midrashist weaves a string of verbal connections in which he links this "verse from afar," as it is termed, to the opening verse of the Torah reading of that day. Heinemann believes that we can understand the proem by imagining it as a kind of public performance, designed to entertain as well as to enlighten. The good preacher, as mentioned earlier, would often gather large crowds by his presence, and we can imagine that part of the attraction was to see and hear a master of wit as he wove his midrashic pattern. Some proems (the Tanhuma Midrashim are the best known) begin not with a verse from afar, but with a halakhic question. The midrashist creates his pattern and chain of connections based on that question, once again, leading in its culmination to the first verse of the Torah *parasha*. This type of proem, beginning most typically with the phrase "let our master teach us" may also have represented actual practice—a preacher was asked a question from the floor and then had to improvise a sermon that led up to the Torah reading.

The chapters of the literary Midrashim that we have usually open with a series of proems, all based on the opening verses of the Torah portion. The second type of homiletical form known simply as "body" *(gufa)* then follows. This form is a good deal more variable and less defined than the proem form. Finally, the literary Midrash ends with a "messianic peroration" *(siyum),* which concludes the chapter with some

* Such as collections of the sermons of the seventeenth-century Christian poet John Donne or the American preacher and philosopher Jonathan Edwards.
† "The Proem in Aggadic Midrashim," In *Studies in Aggadah and Folk Literature,* Scripta Hierosolymitana 22 (Jerusalem: Magnes Press, 1971) pp. 100–22.

kind of hopeful message harkening toward the messianic age. Obviously no preacher would (or could!) have delivered an entire set of proems, body, and peroration in one sermon; what we have is a purely literary form created by the later editors for the written work. How much this parallels the living sermons of the time we can never know, but the literary homily that we have has its own appeal for the reader today, with its ingenuity, formalist beauty, and subtle structure.

It would be too lengthy a process to reproduce an entire literary homily chapter here, but we will now look at an example of a short proem from Leviticus Rabbah:

> "And when you shall come into the land, and shall plant all manner of trees for food. . . ."
> —LEV. 19.23

> R. Judah b. Simon began his discourse by quoting "After the Lord your God shall you walk." (Deut. 13.5) But can a man of flesh and blood possibly 'walk after' the Holy One, blessed be He, the One of whom it is written "Your way was in the sea and Your path in the great waters, and Your footsteps were not known" (Ps. 77.20). And yet you say, "After the Lord shall you walk . . . and unto Him shall you cleave."
> —DEUT. 13.5

> But can flesh and blood go up into heaven to 'cleave' to the Shekhinah, the One of whom it is written, "For the Lord your God is a devouring fire (Deut. 4.24) and of whom it is written "His throne was fiery flames" (Dan. 7.9), and of whom it is written "A fiery stream came forth from before Him" (Dan. 7.10)? And you still say "Unto Him shall you cleave!"

> But in fact the Holy One, blessed be He, from the beginning of the creation of the world, was occupied before all else with planting, thus it is written "And the Lord God planted a garden at first in Eden" (Gen. 2.8), and so you shall also— when you first enter the land you should occupy yourselves first with nothing else but planting. Thus it is written, "And when you shall come into the land, you shall plant all manner of trees. . . ."

Rabbi Judah ben Simon begins (literally "opens," *patah,* from which the term *petihta,* "proem," originates) with a "verse from afar," here Deuteronomy 13.5, "After the Lord your God shall you walk." Knowing that the sermon is about the Leviticus reading, "And when you shall come into the land," one understands why it is not difficult to recapture the experience of surprise that Heinemann sees at the core of the proem's art. What could this quotation from Deuteronomy possibly have to do with the agricultural development of the land that is the theme of our Leviticus verse?

The *darshan* (preacher) seems in no hurry to solve this dilemma. Indeed, the literary (or oral, in its original setting) tension between the verse from afar and the sermon-verse (Lev. 19.23) is typically sustained at length throughout the homily. This tension is part of the art and the artistry of the homiletical form—the listener must not make the connection too soon or the *darshan's* performance is diminished.

The midrashist then addresses a problem he discerns in the Deuteronomy verse—in what way can a human being "walk after" God Himself? To our ears the question seems almost overly literal. Of course the Bible is speaking metaphorically here, and the *darshan* knows it. But as we have seen before this typical "overliteralism" is also an opportunity for Midrash to operate, and it allows the *darshan* to spin out his sermon with rhetorical flourish. These Midrashim often set up literary straw men in order to knock them down later; yet part of the fun of the performance is simply this process.

The *darshan* bolsters his questions by bringing a prooftext from Psalms. God's footsteps are unknowable, His path is beyond human scale. How could any person be expected to walk as He walks? Not only can we not walk after God, but cleaving to Him (as the verse in Deuteronomy continues) is also beyond our abilities. God's Shekhinah, His Presence, is all fire—how can a person cleave to fire?

With this question the first half of the proem ends. Curiously, after raising all these questions the *darshan* shifts in another direction. In lengthier sermons the string of connections is sometimes more elegantly or more subtly constructed, but it is not unusual at all to see the kind of transition exemplified here. Once again, the oral nature of the original sermon may explain the abruptness. For the listener—one who does not have the leisure for rereading and pondering the logic of connections— these rapid shifts are far less problematic than for the reader examining the texts under the microscope of close reading. Moreover, the aesthetic of the sermon simply seems to be less concerned with the elegance of transition than we might expect, though clearly there are certain homilies whose tightness of construction is particularly appealing.

Our example is fairly typical, however. The *darshan* answers his original question by pointing out that indeed the Bible gives an important example of how human beings can "walk after" God. For God plants and this is a divine activity that we can emulate. And unlike the earlier examples of God's walking in "great waters," examples that are far beyond human ability, God's horticultural activities are not described in an absurdly supernatural fashion. We have a verse describing God planting a garden in Eden, which is in simple and direct language. (Although the Midrash reads the Hebrew word *mikedem* in Gen. 2.8, usually translated "eastward," in its other sense "at first.")

And by this turn we have reached our sermon-verse, "when you enter the land, you shall plant." Why should we plant? Because in so doing, we effectively replicate an act of the Lord's. In a sense the original question about walking after the Lord is answered both positively and negatively. We cannot *walk* as God walks; instead we choose to plant as God has planted. But by reading "walking" in a nonliteral fashion, as a metaphor for imitating God's ways, we see that we *can* imitate God. By making planting our first act in entering the land, we have imitated God's first act after Creation—planting the Garden of Eden.

Lurking behind the entire sermon, it seems, has been another question, a question typical of Midrash. What is the unifying principle, the Midrash asks, within the sermon-verse in Leviticus? That is, what is the connection between the first and second half of the verse: Why should planting be the first act of a people in possessing its land? Why not, say, building or worshiping? The answer, according to Midrash, is that we plant because we are acting in *imitatio dei:* we are imitating what God Himself had accomplished following the Creation of the world. Perhaps we are to understand taking possession of the land as a kind of new creation. The history of biblical Israel is restarted after the forty years of wandering by the entrance into the land. Surely it is appropriate at the crucial moment to replicate God's own original first act of possession— the planting of trees.

Although the term Midrash may be unfamiliar to many readers, one of the most important collections of midrashic literature is undoubtedly found in almost every Jewish home. I am speaking of the Passover Haggadah, the key liturgical text of the annual Passover Seder. The Haggadah is a multifaceted work—in its few pages one finds prayers, instructions for the Passover rituals and selections from the Bible. But one of the most important sections of Haggadah is devoted almost entirely to Midrash. The *maggid* (telling) section of the Haggadah, introduced by the "Four Questions," comprises the major portion of the seder prior to the festival meal, and its basic content is pure Midrash.

Many people are brought up with the idea of the Haggadah as a kind of prayer book; one recalls one's grandfather reading it out in the characteristic undertone of Jewish prayer. In fact, the Haggadah is more appropriately understood as a study compendium and the seder as a learning experience rather than a "service." Since midrashic literature is unfamiliar to most readers, the Haggadah may often appear arcane or incomprehensible. But these are texts to be discussed, pondered, and explored, and once one recognizes their midrashic structure, they become a good deal more understandable.

Take, for example, the story told at the beginning of the Haggadah of five rabbis in the town of Bene Barak discussing the Exodus from Egypt. The story, taken from the Mishnah, has been placed early in the Haggadah to offer us a kind of model for our own behavior: if these learned sages could spend the entire night studying the Exodus from Egypt, certainly we can engage in a similar kind of discourse.

Eventually, disciples enter to tell the rabbis that the night has passed and it is time to recite the Shema. We then read:

> Rabbi Eleazar ben Azariah said: "Behold, I am like a man of seventy years, yet I never understood why the story concerning the departure from Egypt should be recited at night until Ben Zoma interpreted it: The Torah says, 'That you should remember the day when you came out of the land of Egypt all the days of your life.' (Deut. 16.3) Had it been written 'the days of your life,' it would have meant the days only, but '*all* the days of your life' means the nights as well."

We have here a typical midrashic examination of a biblical verse. Rabbi Eleazar ben Azariah quotes a teaching that he learned from his colleague, Ben Zoma. By examining a biblical citation from Deuteronomy, Ben Zoma elucidates why the Passover seder should take place at night. The logic of Ben Zoma's reading is typical of texts we have examined before in this chapter. Every word of the Torah must have significance, Ben Zoma assumes. There can be no superfluity in the holy text. Thus the existence of the word "all" in the biblical verse telling of the departure from Egypt must be there to teach us something. Since we commonly use the word "day" to refer to both the dark and light parts of a twenty-four-hour period, in saying *all* the days the Torah, Ben Zoma suggests, must have wanted us to retell the Exodus in the *night* part of a day. Had it only said "days of your life" it would then have been referring to the non-night hours!

Obviously, the "logic" of the reading is in Ben Zoma's fertile imagination. To a casual contemporary reader this text seems peculiar indeed. But once we recognize the particular style of close reading and the typical playfulness of the midrashic mind, the Haggadah text makes perfect sense. Ben Zoma is simply applying good midrashic interpretation to adduce his case.

And yet, even in this small excerpt, we find that Ben Zoma's interpretation does not go unanswered. As if to join in a friendly competition, the sages offer their own reading of the verse from Deuteronomy:

> The other sages explain the verse differently: "Had it been written 'the days of your life,' it would have meant this world only; 'all the days of your life' means that the Messianic time is included as well."

For Ben Zoma "days" is read literally; his question is to which part of the day are we referring. But for the sages "days" takes on a different cast entirely. They see this verse metaphorically, as applying to the contrast between our lives today and our lives in the future time of the Messiah. Even then, the other sages argue, even in the messianic age, we will still tell the story of the Exodus from Egypt.

Throughout the entire *maggid* section of the Haggadah, midrashic texts such as the one above abound. Some have argued that one can find within the Passover Haggadah all the basic variations of midrashic exegesis. Thus the careful explication of the ten plagues, the dialogue of the "four sons," as well as the long examination of Deuteronomy 26.5–8, exhibit a stunning array of midrashic style. To the reader who understands that it is Midrash one is confronting in the Haggadah, this mysterious and often puzzling little book begins to make a great deal more sense.

Before we conclude we should mention another genre of classic literature text that, though not technically Midrash, is related or associated with it. There are in rabbinic writings a large number of legends and tales that are not directly related to interpreting any particular verse (and therefore not Midrash *per se*), but which also serve to express many of the same values of rabbinic Judaism. These tales, sprinkled throughout rabbinic literature, are sometimes parables or fables told to illustrate a point, and more often than not, they are legends told about the rabbis themselves.

Most of these stories about the rabbis, tales which for the sake of simplicity can be called free-floating *aggadot,* are found in the Talmud, though the classic midrashic works also contain many such stories. These *aggadot,* though ostensibly "biographical," should not be seen as historical in our sense of the word. Although they may tell us something about the actual rabbi who is being described, the more important point is to note the ideas that the stories are trying to convey. The Introduction to this book began with one of those *aggadot*—the story of Shammai, Hillel and the heathen who wishes to learn all the Torah while standing on one foot.

Other *aggadot,* often found in narrative Midrashim, are about magical events, biblical characters, or pseudo-biblical personages, such as the legendary Lilith. Sometimes they are almost like fairy tales. *Aggadah* in that sense easily crosses the line into folk literature. Some of these tales lived on, no doubt, in the popular consciousness of the people, never making it into the midrashic collections. Many years later folk tales began to be collected into books—sometimes books that *purported* to be midrashic collections—and they have remained as a popular Jewish literary form down to our time.

It should be quite obvious by now that distinctions among terms such as Midrash, *aggadah* and folk literature are extremely tenuous. The classic writers were a good deal less concerned about such matters than we are, and although this kind of labeling can be useful, we should remember that there is a kind of artificiality about any such endeavor.

WHERE TO GO FROM HERE

Background. An understanding of the historical background of the rabbinic period is a useful tool in approaching Midrash and the Talmud as well.★ A good place to begin a study of the history of rabbinic Judaism is with Judah Goldin's essay, "The Period of the Talmud" in Louis Finkelstein's *The Jews: Their History* (New York: Schocken [paper], 1970). Goldin gives an excellent historical survey of the rabbinic era, giving names, dates, and important events. Even more stimulating is Gerson Cohen's "The Talmudic Age" in *Great Ages and Ideas of the Jewish People,* edited by Leo Schwartz (New York: Modern Library, 1956). In that chapter Cohen gives a wonderful overview of the intellectual signif-

★ At the end of the last chapter there were suggestions for further exploring the Talmud.

icance of rabbinic thinking, emphasizing the notion of interpretation and its centrality to the mind of the rabbis. As mentioned in Chapter Two, the leading contemporary scholar of the rabbinic period is Jacob Neusner. Of his many works three are of particular relevance here: *The Study of Ancient Judaism* (New York: Ktav, 1981), *There We Sat Down* (New York: Ktav, 1978) and *The Glory of God Is Intelligence* (Brigham Young University, 1978). Neusner is particularly interested in the structure of rabbinic culture and its relationship to the religious consciousness of the founders of Judaism. His work has been essential in its concern for the questions of religion as they relate to the great rabbinic texts. Nahum N. Glatzer's *Hillel the Elder* (New York: Schocken, 1966) is also an excellent short introduction to the world of rabbinic Jewry. Glatzer does a fine job of outlining the context and turmoil of the Hellenistic world as he traces "the emergence of classical Judaism." Marcel Simon's *Jewish Sects at the Time of Jesus* (Philadelphia: Fortress Press, 1967) is also a useful book on these issues.

On Midrash itself the reader should look at Shalom Spiegel's poetic Introduction to Louis Ginzberg's *Legends of the Bible* (Philadelphia: Jewish Publication Society, 1956; see below for more on the Ginzberg work) which has been anthologized in Judah Goldin's collection *The Jewish Expression,* originally published by Bantam Books in 1970. Look also at James Kugel's "Two Introductions to the Midrash" which appeared in the journal, *Prooftexts,* vol. 3, no. 2 (May 1983).

Earlier in this chapter I mentioned Erich Auerbach's classic account of the contrast between biblical and Greek literature. It is in the "laconic style" of the Bible—as described by Auerbach—that we see at least one of the motivating causes behind Midrash. This essay can be found in Auerbach's *Mimesis* (Princeton: Princeton University Press, 1971), a seminal work of modern literary criticism.

Another and lesser-known book is A. G. Wright's *The Literary Genre Midrash* (New York: Alba House, 1956), a book, written primarily for the Christian audience, that is particularly good on the *method* of rabbinic exegesis.

A more obscure work, but important nonetheless, is Birger Gerhardson's *Memory and Manuscript* (Copenhagen: E. Munksgaard, 1964). Here Gerhardson tries to explore the process by which oral literature becomes written, both in rabbinic and early Christian texts.

Max Kadushin was a scholar who devoted his life to exploring the underlying ideas of rabbinic thought. Unlike much academic analysis of Midrash—which is concerned primarily with issues of textual transmission and variant readings—Kadushin's work tries to uncover the "value-concepts" (to use his term) embedded in rabbinic literature by exploring halakhic, aggadic and liturgical texts. Kadushin was a systematizer and an exceedingly original thinker. Because of that his writing cannot be said to be easy going, but anyone interested in Midrash will be well served by looking at sections IV, V, VI of *The Rabbinic Mind* and much of *Worship and Ethics* (both published in paperback by Bloch Publishing Company in New York).

The significance of Midrash is explored from another direction in the writing of the theologian Abraham Joshua Heschel, who sought to reaffirm the importance of the "aggadic" side of Judaism. Judaism, he believed, was too easily reduced to "religious behaviorism," *halakhah* without a true religious and spiritual content. Aggadic Judaism, Heschel argued, was equally important. Heschel presented his case poetically and at times movingly—chapters 32 and 33 of his masterpiece, *God in Search of Man* (New York: Harper and Row, 1955), represent a distillation of his views.

Finally, a poetic and highly influential essay by the great Hebrew poet, Hayyim Nahman Bialik (1837–1934)—"*Halakhah* and *Aggadah*." In this essay Bialik explores the two terms as essential polarities for a modern human consciousness. The essay has been abridged and translated in Nahum N. Glatzer's anthology, *Modern Jewish Thought* (New York: Schocken, 1977).

Texts. Many of the great midrashic works have been translated into English, although merely having the English does not by any means guarantee access to this literature! The Soncino Press translation of *The Midrash* is a multivolume presentation of Midrash Rabbah. As mentioned previously, Midrash Rabbah itself is not, in fact, a unified work, containing, as it does, both homiletical and exegetical Midrash from different places and times. But despite its problems, the Soncino *Midrash* is a monumental and exceedingly important accomplishment.

But what to do with it? The translation is by no means lilting and the notes, though useful, are sparse indeed. Understanding the wordplay and hidden dimensions of Midrash often requires some explication, and this we find only in small doses in the Soncino *Midrash*. Still, having the use of the work is undeniably important, and it gives one the opportunity to dive right into the midrashic sea. I would suggest beginning with the exegetical Genesis Rabbah, reading the texts carefully and slowly, more like poems than essays. Taking it in small doses and using the kind of reading we have tried to show earlier in this chapter, the Soncino

Midrash can give the English reader access to the world of "aggadic Judaism."

The homiletical Midrash par excellence is Leviticus Rabbah (volume 4 of the Soncino *Midrash*), but I would recommend another starting point for exploring this type of Midrash in English. *Pesikta de Rab Kahanna* (Philadelphia: Jewish Publication Society, 1975) or *Pesikta Rabbati* (New Haven: Yale University Press, 1968), both translated by William Braude, are somewhat more readable and probably easier to follow than jumping into Leviticus Rabbah. The two Pesiktas are very similar homiletical Midrashim (in fact five chapters are the same in both) organized around the Torah readings for holidays and special Sabbaths. Seeing these "sermons" we can get an insight into the rabbinic vision of the festival cycle. Braude provides overviews, summaries, and helpful notes that make the reader's task a good deal easier.

For narrative Midrash two texts are particularly apt. *Pirkei de Rebbe Eliezar,* probably the best known of the narrative works, is available in an older English translation (1916) by Friedlander from Sepher-Hermon Press (paperback) in New York. The translation sounds heavy-handed to a contemporary ear, but the text with its tales and legends has a unique and compensatory charm. William Braude and Israel Kapstein have translated *Tanna Debe Eliyyahu* (Philadelphia: Jewish Publication Society, 1981), another narrative text. The notes are useful as are the summaries.

A few other individual works also exist in English. Braude has translated *The Midrash on Psalms* for Yale University Press (1959), and an older English version of *The Mekhilta* by Lauterbach has recently been reissued in paperback by the Jewish Publication Society in Philadelphia.

The best introduction, however, to Mekhilta, the classic "Tannaitic Midrash," is to read Judah Goldin's lovely *The Song at the Sea* (New Haven: Yale University Press, 1971). Goldin has translated one self-contained section of Mekhilta called "Shirta," the commentary on Exodus 15, the song sung by the Israelites at the sea, with notes, explanations and a fine introduction. The translation is beautiful, and the book is an excellent way into this important midrashic work.

Collections. The greatest single anthology of midrashic texts in English is Louis Ginzberg's monumental *Legends of the Jews* (Philadelphia: Jewish Publication Society, 1909–39; not to be confused with the one volume abridgment, *Legends of the Bible*). In seven volumes Ginzberg used his enormous erudition to try to find some order in the vast variety of aggadic sources dealing with biblical themes. Collecting the texts, Ginzberg organized the materials according to the biblical chronology, retelling and sometimes conflating variants. Two volumes of notes give numerous cross references; an index volume categorizes the entire corpus.

Legends of the Jews is one of the great achievements of modern Jewish scholarship; the notes in particular are invaluable since they allow researchers to find parallel versions of individual stories and trace, as it were, the lineage of an individual Midrash.

The texts themselves are somewhat more problematic. In the main, Ginzberg wrote *Legends* in German, and Henrietta Szold (later the founder of Hadassah) did most of the translation into English. To a contemporary reader the English sounds rather dated, and it inhibits our appreciation of the beauty of the texts. Moreover, Ginzberg's editing and rewriting of the materials makes the patchwork quilt of Midrash into a much too seamless and unified whole. Often what is missing is the context of the original source, and one is forced to track it down to get the full flavor and meaning of the text.

But setting all that aside, Ginzberg's *Legends* is unsurpassed as a general collection of the *aggadot* of the tradition. Some of these are classic Midrashim; some are random tales. The notes are without parallel, and if one wishes to get a rapid and broad overview of the aggadic traditions about, say, Queen Esther or Moses, *the* essential source is Ginzberg.

Another anthology, of a more traditional sort, is the medieval collection called Ein Yaakov which exists in various English translations. Ein Yaakov is an inspired idea—basically it reproduces the Babylonian Talmud without all its legal components! (Since the halakhic sections of the Talmud are by far in the majority, Ein Yaakov is not anywhere near the size of the Talmud.) What we have left is a vast array of marvelous imaginative literature. Ein Yaakov is not Midrash per se—that is, interpretation of the Bible—but it includes aggadic materials, such as parables and stories about the sages themselves. Through these tales we are looking not so much at rabbinic history but at stories elucidating the values, conflicts, and concerns of the ancient rabbis.

For a compact and very satisfying anthology of Midrash, one can turn to Nahum N. Glatzer's lovely little *Hammer on the Rock* (New York: Schocken, 1962). Glatzer has put together evocative *aggadot* and Midrashim, beautifully translated, into a tightly organized format. This book is an absolute (and inexpensive) must. Another fine short anthology, thematically arranged, is *Our Masters Taught,* edited by Jakob J. Petuchowski (New York: Crossroad, 1982).

Another anthology containing important Midrashim is *The Literature of the Synagogue* by Joseph Heinemann and Jakob J. Petuchowski
(New York: Behrman House, 1975). Part two of this volume is particularly oriented toward the homiletical Midrashim—those midrashic
works that most resemble the sermons preached in the rabbinic synagogue. This is a good place to start looking at this very important type
of Midrash, since the authors have provided notes and introductions for
the texts they have translated.

Two other works deserve mention alongside of *Legends of the Jews.*
First is *Sefer Aggadah* (in Hebrew; an English translation from William
Braude has long been rumored!), edited by Bialik and Ravnitsky. In this
very popular work the editors arranged texts about biblical characters,
about major themes, motifs, and ideas of the tradition (such as "Torah,"
"God and Man," "Language"), and about the sages of rabbinic times
into a monumental and very useful anthology. This book has long been
used in Jewish schools, but a word of warning is in order. The editors
did not hesitate to cut and paste together the tales from various ancient
sources, thus we should be aware that "pure" Midrash is not to be found
here. Moreover, in their concern for language the editors took liberties
in rewriting and "beautifying" the language of the original sources.
Sometimes this works well, but at other times we lose a good deal by
the "improvement." The other important anthology is *Mimekor Yisrael*
by M. J. Bin Gorion (Berdichevsky). *Mimekor Yisrael* now exists in an
excellent English translation by I. M. Lask (Bloomington, Ind.: Indiana
University Press, 1976), with a fine introduction by Dan Ben-Amos.
Ben-Amos points out that each of the three great Midrash anthologies
used a different approach to the task: Ginzberg's concern for the ideas of
rabbinic thought led him in *Legends of the Jews* to overlook the necessity
of reproducing the texts with language intact; in *Sefer Aggadah* Bialik
and Ravnitsky's interest in language led them to "dress up" the words
of the ancient texts and to organize the materials along their own aesthetic principles. But Bin Gorion had a different idea in mind. He collected the folk traditions that he believed represented the "true" Jewish
imagination; and unlike the other two authors, he would often present
differing versions of the same story alongside one another. In that way,
he believed, the reader would see the full range of possibilities that the
Jewish mind could adduce from the same basic, inspiring motif.

Bin Gorion believed that by and large we do best to look at late
versions of tales rather than the earliest version accessible. Thus *Mimekor
Yisrael* is primarily gathered from sources of the early Middle Ages and
after. Unlike most scholars, Bin Gorion, it seems, believed that the folk

tradition was *more* reliable and less "censored" than the "official" texts whose editing was overseen by rabbinic authorities. Thus, where scholars in general tend to seek out the earliest version of a piece of literature as the most authentic, Bin Gorion felt that the later versions represented a freer and less restricted outpouring of imagination. *Mimekor Yisrael* is, therefore, a wonderful source of legends and tales, but by and large it does not deal with the literature of the rabbinic period per se.

Analyses of Midrash. Literary analyses of Midrash that explore the religious or intellectual significance of the texts are rare but invaluable aids for the English reader. A sensitive reading of a midrashic work can often unlock levels of meaning we did not begin to appreciate before. Perhaps the best-known example of such an approach is Shalom Spiegel's *The Last Trial* (New York: Behrman House [paper], 1979). Here Spiegel retells, organizes, and explicates many of the Midrashim that deal with Akedat Yitzhak, the biblical story of the binding of Isaac (Gen. 22). *The Last Trial* is a remarkable and moving work, as Spiegel explores the way that these Midrashim functioned in response to catastrophic occurrences throughout Jewish history.

Another work of midrashic explication is Elie Wiesel's *Messengers of God* (New York: Random House, 1976). Wiesel analyzes the characters of key biblical figures, weaving Midrashim in with his own personal and imaginative perspective. This is an unusual book—since it both explores Midrash and creates its own Midrashim. Although I disagree with some of Wiesel's readings of biblical characters, his retelling of Midrashim is marvelous and his own personal vision is well worth examining.

For an examination of one midrashic text nothing surpasses Joseph Heinemann's "Profile of a Midrash," *Journal of the American Academy of Religion,* June 1971. Heinemann's subject is Leviticus Rabbah, and this article, exploring both the content and the form of that great homiletical work, is an essential prerequisite before turning to the Midrash itself.

Jacob Neusner's essay "Story and Tradition in Judaism," appearing in his *Judaism: The Evidence of the Mishnah* (Chicago: University of Chicago Press, 1981), explores *aggadot* about the ancient rabbis and suggests an approach as to how we should view these stories. Neusner makes a strong and very convincing case for seeing this literature, not as history in the ordinary sense of the word, but as something that expresses the values and religious perspective of rabbinic culture. Interestingly, Neusner has used his scholarly perspective on *aggadah* to create an excellent textbook for children, which can be read fruitfully by adults as well, *Meet Our Sages* (New York: Behrman House, 1980).

An excellent model of a way to discuss the content of Midrash is

Arthur Green's "The Children in Egypt and the Theophany at the Sea," in the magazine _Judaism,_ Fall 1975. Green explores basic issues of theology and belief in a remarkable exposition of classical Midrashim about the children at the sea and shows how these works still speak to us today.

Finally, we should note that in recent times there has been a renewed interest in Midrash as a living Jewish literary form. Wiesel's _Messengers of God_ mentioned above represents a kind of midrashic exploration. Howard Schwartz has collected a number of new experiments in Midrash and organized them according to themes for an anthology _Gates to the New City_ (New York: Avon, 1983). It will be interesting to see if the old art of Midrash begins once again to find form in new compositions. This possibility, and the problems it raises, has been discussed in a challenging essay by Cynthia Ozick in _Commentary_ magazine, March 1983.

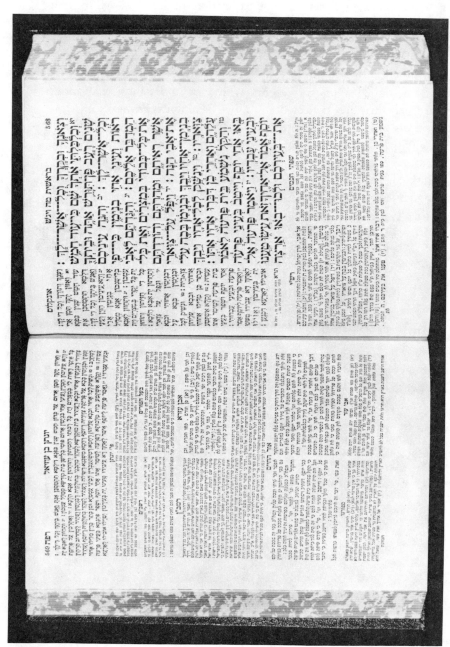

From Genesis 45, in standard edition of Mikra'ot Gedolot, the Bible with its classic commentaries.

CHAPTER FOUR

Medieval Bible Commentaries

EDWARD L. GREENSTEIN

Until recently, and here and there even today, Jewish literature has developed as some sort of interpretation of Scripture. The ancient, medieval, and modern legal codes build upon the foundation of the Torah. *Aggadah* warps its tales through the woof of the biblical narrative. The intricate poetry of the Middle Ages sets jewels of biblical words and motifs into the frames of contemporary meters. Even modern Hebrew literature tends to orient itself to the Bible's mythology and recycle biblical idioms.

But although the bulk of classical Jewish literature forms an explicit interpretation of the Bible, it is only in the Middle Ages that the genre of the running, direct commentary on the biblical text comes into its own as a major phenomenon. The great medieval commentaries continue to serve as the major companions to the Bible for those who study the text in the original Hebrew. The most distinctive personalities among the medieval commentators virtually sit in the room and share their opinions with the serious student. One encounters something odd or perplexing, and one turns to Rashi, to Ibn Ezra, to see what this or that one has to say about it. One becomes familiar with them, allowing for their idiosyncrasies and obsessions, learning when to consult this one and when to consult the other. Even when one understands, or thinks one understands the text, one often doesn't wish to proceed too far without checking in on the sensibilities of one or another of the medievals. Even where we may differ from them in our philosophical orientation, their commentaries function on the one hand as lenses through which we can see the facets of the text more sharply, and on the other as windows on some of the most interesting minds of medieval Jewry.

The label "medieval" often connotes the cloistered and reactionary, but in Jewish literature, for which there is no "Dark Ages," the Middle Ages symbolize a peak of scholarship, creativity, philosophy, and writing. Sectarian schisms within the Jewish fold and external pressure, mainly Christian persecution, upon the Jews had the effect of stimulating, not repressing, Jewish expression. The traditional Jewish edition of the Bible, *Mikra'ot Gedolot,* "Great Readings," or "Big Scriptures," known as the Rabbinic Bible in English, is essentially a medieval product. It presents the standard Hebrew text of the Bible, an ancient rabbinic translation into Aramaic—the *targum*—and a number of medieval commentaries in Hebrew. The number of commentaries included depends on the size of the printed edition. This is what a typical page looks like:

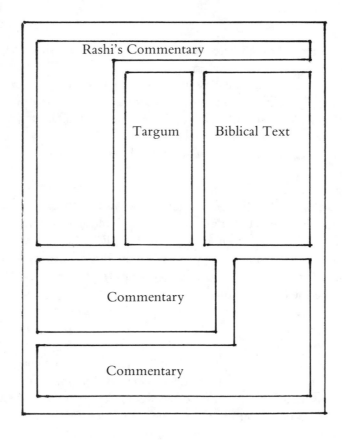

In ancient times the Bible was declaimed in the synagogue "two parts Scripture, one part *targum*." The approach of the commentaries is similar. A passage from the biblical text is read, then explanations from a commentary, back to the text, return to the commentary, and so on. The major commentaries must be read in this way—even those that allude to earlier ones. There are also commentaries on commentaries, or supercommentaries, but even large editions of *Mikra'ot Gedolot* will include few of them. Until the later medieval works of the fourteenth century, all the major commentaries operated by themselves and were composed as separate books in themselves. Each commentary in *Mikra'ot Gedolot* should be read, at least at first, as though it were the only one on the page.

The method by which the commentaries were written follows the structure of the classic Midrash collections (see Chapter Three) and the ancient commentaries found among the Dead Sea Scrolls, too. The text is disintegrated into units of sentence, phrase, or even word length. The unit of Scripture provokes a question or suggests a platform for a statement, which the commentary discusses, providing an explanation, drawing an implication, or expositing a general issue. Upon reaching the end of a unit, the commentary will cite a succeeding unit in the text, not necessarily the next one, and repeat the process. Of course, the nature of the question to address will change from unit to unit, and so, often, will the nature of the commentary. If one wishes to consult another commentary in *Mikra'ot Gedolot,* the reading of the text is arrested and the focus shifts from the text per se to an intriguing problem. Although most extant works of the major commentators are available in separate editions and can be read in isolation from the others, the arrangement in *Mikra'ot Gedolot* encourages dialectic among the distinguished voices on the page, confirming the well-known witticism that where there are two Jews, there are three opinions.

The Derash, or Homiletical, Approach

Pluralistic interpretation of Scripture has deep roots in classical Midrash. The most widely studied medieval commentator, Rashi, cites a famous prooftext from the Book of Jeremiah. Here is the more extensive version of this Midrash from the collection *Yalkut Shimoni,* a source from which Rashi often drew. It begins with a verse from Psalms (62.12):

One spoke God, two have I heard . . . [This means:] One verse
has several meanings, but one meaning cannot emerge from
two verses . . .

That is, if two verses seem to say the same thing, there must in fact be
some difference between them, because the Bible packs its significance
economically without wasting any words. The Midrash continues:

It was taught: *(Like a) hammer shattering a rock.* (Jer. 23.29) Just
as the hammer splinters into several sparks, so does one verse
have several meanings.

Jeremiah had been speaking of prophetic revelation, which he likened to
fire and the blow of a hammer. The rabbis transfer the verse's contextual
reference from the *experience* of revelation to the *substance* of revelation.
That which is revealed, the sacred text, has many meanings. In the
medieval period it was acknowledged that multiplicity in the Bible's
signification not only inheres in the nature of the text, but also results
from divergent methods or dimensions of reading it.

The rabbinic method from ancient times through the Talmudic period was basically Midrash or *derash*. The term *derash* derives from the
biblical verb *darash,* literally "to seek," but used technically for inquiring
of a divine oracle, primarily via a prophet.* The rabbis inquired of the
text that which the Israelites inquired of their prophets: revelation. It
was held that the text encodes crucial knowledge in its wording and
arrangement, not only in its explicit contents. The mode of *derash* endeavors to decipher and spell out the latent meanings of the text. The
techniques of midrashic interpretation were adapted from ancient procedures of dream interpretation. Sacred texts, like dreams, are symbolic.
Their meaning stems not only from their gist but from peculiarities of
their style, vocabulary, and spelling as well. In order to draw out the
full richness of the Bible, each element of the text must be "juiced" for
significance by means of very close analysis.

Watch the eleventh-century French exegete, Rashi, in a typical midrashic maneuver. In Genesis 41 Pharaoh wakes disturbed by dreams and
can find no one to interpret them. His steward recalls that Joseph, a
Hebrew incarcerated in Pharaoh's jail, possesses an uncanny knack at
dream interpretation and recommends him to the king. The steward
describes Joseph by three terms, which for all intents and purposes seem
matter-of-fact: "A-young-man, a-Hebrew, a-slave," in other words, a
young Hebrew slave (verse 12). Reacting to the curious tripartite detail

* E.g., Jer. 21.1–2; Ezek. 14.1–2.

of the steward's wording, Rashi induces distinct significance from each of the three Hebrew terms, adding up to a cynical message of caution regarding the ostensible kindness of gentiles.

> Cursed be the wicked whose kindness is not total. [The steward] refers to [Joseph] in derogatory language. *A-young-man:* [He means:] A fool, unsuitable for greatness. *A-Hebrew:* He doesn't even know our language. *A-slave:* It is written in the protocols of Egypt that a slave may not govern and may not dress in the garments of courtiers.

In customary homiletic fashion Rashi reads his own suspicion of gentiles into the text, or discovers his own contemporary lesson in it. It was by means of midrashic procedures, too, that the classical rabbis had generated the *aggadah* and the laws of the Talmud, the *halakhah,* and had grounded them in the biblical text.

The Peshat, or Context, Approach

After the rise of Islam in the seventh century, another mode of interpreting Scripture emerged and for several centuries overshadowed *derash* in biblical exegesis. This approach, that of *peshat,* sought to understand the biblical text within the parameters of its historical, literary, and linguistic context. Historical context requires that interpretation must read the text in terms of the world of ancient Israel and the biblical story as a whole. To see these two modes in contrast, we turn to the commentaries on the poem comprising Jacob's last will and testament. The patriarch says that he will "divide" his sons Simon and Levi within the people of Israel (Gen. 49.7). Rashi interprets *homiletically:*

> I shall separate this one from that one so that Levi will not be in the number of tribes—and they are indeed dispersed [literally, divided] among the tribes.

For Rashi, there is a moral here: Simon and Levi had gotten into shameful mischief by having banded together (see Gen. 34). Like a grade school teacher imposing discipline, the father separates them. But Rashi's grandson, Rashbam, sees this verse only *contextually,* in the scope of subsequent biblical history:

> For Levi was dispersed among the twelve tribes, as it is written in Joshua (chap. 21).

In Rashbam's reading Jacob's words anticipate the later history of the tribes, no more.

Literary context entails a recognition of the rhetorical features of the biblical text and the importance of reading a verse or a word within the frame of reference that the surrounding passage establishes. Consider another part of Jacob's rebuke of Simon and Levi (Gen. 49.6):

> Into their circle may my life not enter,
> In their assembly may my self not join.

Rashi cites a Midrash in which each part of the verse refers to a different future event. The first line foresees the obnoxious behavior of the tribe of Simon in Numbers 25, the second half foresees the rebellion of certain Levites in Numbers 16. Jacob prophetically wants nothing to do with either travesty. Another leading medieval exegete, Rabbi Abraham Ibn Ezra of Spain, reads the verse much differently. He understands the two lines as a single statement which is expressed in two parts for rhetorical, stylistic reasons. For him, *Into their circle* and *In their assembly* are synonymous; so are *my life* and *my self* and *not enter* and *not join.* "The meaning is doubled," he says, "as is the way of prophecies," that is, prophetic or poetic style. The sense of the verse for him is controlled by its literary form—what we today generally call parallelism—that is, its literary context.

Linguistic context compels the commentator to determine the meaning of a word or grammatical form from the way it is used in the Bible and according to the rules of biblical Hebrew. The most intense midrashic interpreter of the classical rabbinic period, Rabbi Akiba, read significant nuances into words in which the other rabbis saw nary a shade of semantic difference.* They compared the opening lines of oracles by Moses and Isaiah, respectively:

> Moses: Give-ear, O heaven, that I may speak,
>   Let the land hear the sayings of my mouth.
>   —DEUT. 32.1
> Isaiah: Hear, O heaven,
>   and give-ear, O land,
>   for the Lord speaks.
>   —ISA. 1.2

The rabbis ask:

> What did Isaiah mean by saying *Hear, O heaven* etcetera? None other than to teach you that all the words of the prophets are

* Deuteronomy Rabbah, *Ha'azinu.*

equal. Moses said *Give-ear, O heaven,* Isaiah said *Hear, O heaven.*

For the rabbis quoted here, the wording of an oracle is a matter of the prophet's predilections and style. The particular words that Moses and Isaiah select carry equivalent meanings. Rabbi Akiba rejects such a position in principle; different words *must* indicate distinct messages.

> Rabbi Akiba said: This teaches that when Moses spoke the Torah he was in heaven, and he would speak with the heaven as a man speaks with his fellow; for it says *Give-ear, O heaven.* And when he saw the land afar from him, he said *And let the land hear.* But Isaiah, who was on the land, began by saying *Hear, O heaven* as it was far from him; afterward [he said] *Give-ear, O land* as it was near to him, *For the Lord speaks.*

Rabbi Akiba insists that "to give ear" denotes listening up close and "to hear" denotes listening at a distance. From this he derives a distinction between the higher prophetic status of Moses vis-à-vis Isaiah and the other prophets, and by extension the higher status of the Torah vis-à-vis the prophetic writings. The Torah comes directly from heaven, the prophets' oracles were formulated on earth. Rabbi Abraham Ibn Ezra, the great medieval commentator, denies that "to give ear" and "to hear" refer to divergent types of listening:

> Now there is no distinction between *Hear* and *Give-ear* according to the *peshat* method. (commentary to ISAIAH 1.2)

The *peshat* method bases itself on context, and as far as Ibn Ezra can tell, biblical Hebrew does not assume a semantic difference between hearing and giving-ear.

Most secondary literature on Jewish exegesis defines *peshat* as the "simple," "plain," or "literal" approach, but these terms are misleading. The historical meaning of the biblical text may actually be complex and figurative, neither simple nor straightforward. Consider the following example. After delineating the laws of eating matzah as a symbol of the Exodus from Egypt, Exodus 13.9 says of that event:

> It shall be as a sign on your arm and a remembrance between your eyes so that the instruction of the Lord will be in your mouth . . .

In this case the *sign on your arm and remembrance between your eyes* is a figurative expression in its context, according to the *peshat* method of interpretation. This is the way Rashbam, Rashi's grandson and a *peshat* practitioner par excellence, explains it:

> *As a sign on your arm:* According to the actual *peshat* sense [of the verse, this means] it shall be a constant remembrance to you as though it were written on your arm. It is like [the verse in Song of Songs 8.6:] *Place me like a seal upon your heart.*

Here the *peshat* approach perceives the text's metaphor and interprets figuratively. It is the *derash* interpretation of the rabbis in the Talmud, reflected also in Rashi, that reads the verse literally. The *sign* and *remembrance* refer to the two boxes of tefillin, one strapped on the arm and the other onto the forehead, and the import of this verse is that the passages relating the laws of Passover should be included inside the boxes. The *peshat* method, therefore, should perhaps be glossed in English as the direct, *contextual* mode of exegesis, not "plain" or "literal," which it often is not. The *derash* method is the acontextual approach because it disregards the constrictions of the historical, literary, and linguistic conditions in which the text first came to us.

As we said above, the *peshat* method did not burgeon until after the rise of Islam. We may hold several factors responsible. Some are explained in the fine essay on "The Judeo-Islamic Age" by Abraham S. Halkin.* One thing that Islam brought with it was an emphasis on its scriptures, the Koran—*Kur'an,* a close Arabic cognate to Hebrew *Mikra',* "Scripture"—as the fundamental object of pious study and recitation. Especially in the Islamic lands of the Middle East, North Africa, and Spain, Arabic-speaking Jews began to regard the Bible as a corpus worthy of direct study in its own right, and not only as the basis of the rabbis' midrashically derived *aggadah* and *halakhah.*

By the seventh century most of the material collected in the Palestinian and Babylonian Talmudim had already taken editorial shape, and the *derash* method had made its crucial contribution to the formulation of Jewish law and saga. In the Islamic period of the early Middle Ages further refinements and adaptations of Jewish law took the form of legal arguments based directly on the Talmuds and Talmudic commentaries. No longer did the rabbis need to press the midrashic interpretation of the Bible into service as a primary means of learning God's will. This development opened the way for another method, that of *peshat.*

Jewish scholars in Arab lands for the first time in history acquired

* In Leo W. Schwarz, ed., *Great Ages and Ideas of the Jewish People* (New York: Modern Library, 1956), pp. 215–63.

the tools for proper contextual study of Scripture. Islam had spread the tenets of rationalism, mediating in part the philosophical teachings of classical Greece. Rational modes of thought lent the Jewish commentators historical perspective, an appreciation of rhetoric, and a conviction that the Bible must make sense. Some, like Maimonides, felt such a strong need to harmonize the Torah and Aristotle that they reverted to the methods of *derash* to force the Bible into the procrustean bed of Aristotelian logic. But in general, rationalism led to a commonsense approach to interpretation, of which the following example may serve as an illustration. When King David was about to die, two of his sons, Adonijah and Solomon, vied for the throne. The important officials of David's court sided with one or the other of the two. When it became clear that Solomon was going to succeed, David's general, Joab, attempted to flee. The text of 1 Kings 2.28, however, confuses the matter:

> When a report came to Joab that Joab was bent after Adonijah and after Absalom he did not bend, Joab fled to the Tent of the Lord and grasped the horns of the altar.

Joab was in danger because he was a political opponent of Solomon, not Absalom. What does Absalom, a son of David who had rebelled against David and in fact had been killed by Joab sometime before, have to do with the case? Today, critical Bible scholars will emend the Hebrew text and read *Solomon* instead of *Absalom,* a reading that many ancient versions of the Bible also had. In the medieval period, however, to emend the text was unthinkable.

Nevertheless, in a determined quest for sense here, the greatest of the medieval Jewish philologists, a Spanish Arab-speaking scholar of the eleventh century, Abulwalid Merwan Ibn Janah, also known as Rabbi Jonah, saw that the text must mean for us to understand *Solomon* and not *Absalom* in 1 Kings 2.28. So then why does the text say *Absalom?* Ibn Janah explains this case and others like it by recourse to an assumed rhetorical technique by which the Bible substitutes one word for another because it sounds better or suits the rhythm better. He compares a contemporary Hebrew poem which was composed in a typical Arabic meter. The poem praises a handsome man, saying he was:

> Just like Joseph in his form,
> And Adonijah in his hair.

Anyone familiar with the Second Book of Samuel knows that it was Absalom, not Adonijah, who was famed for his glorious locks. The poet used *Adonijah* in place of *Absalom* so that the meter did not fall flat. Ibn

Janah concludes that something similar must lie behind the Bible's own substitutions. Without such assumptions the Bible would not make sense.

A second prerequisite to the *peshat* method is a scientific approach to language. Jews in Arab lands had the potential to become comparative Semitic linguists. A learned Jew would know his native Arabic, biblical Hebrew, the Hebrew of rabbinic literature, and Aramaic, four Semitic languages. Jewish scholars applied their knowledge of Semitic languages to elucidate difficult words, idioms, and grammatical forms in the Hebrew Bible. In addition, Arab grammarians had developed a systematic method for analyzing the style and structure of classical Arabic, the language of the Koran. This enabled them not only to interpret the Koran but also to compose new works in the strict standards of the classical idiom.

Jews who studied Arabic language and literature, as well as other academic disciplines, learned the new linguistic science and desired to exploit it in their exegesis of the Bible and the analysis of Hebrew grammar. Only those who knew Arabic grammar developed the proper understanding of the Hebrew verb as a stem built upon three consonants. Hebrew verb stems in which the letters *alef, vav,* and *yod* appear, for example, do not display these weak consonants in all forms. These weak consonants do appear in the various forms of the Arabic verb, however. Jewish scholars with linguistic sophistication realized that the weak consonants were part of the Hebrew verb even where they were not evident. Jewish exegetes, such as those in France, who did not read Arabic, failed to comprehend the triconsonantal basis of the Hebrew verb-stem and, as a result, confused certain stems and misinterpreted them. *Ç'est la vie.* Characteristic of the Spanish Jewish scholars was their superior interest and training in linguistic analysis, a benefit of having grown up in an Arabic milieu.

The first great Jewish scholar with training in the sciences who began to develop a masterly philological approach to biblical study was the North African rabbi Saadiah, who completed his career as the Gaon, or Dean, of the Babylonian academy at Sura. This giant of tenth-century Judaism, also an important philosopher (see Chapter Five), composed a grammar and lexicon of biblical Hebrew, but they have survived only in fragments. His Arabic translation of the Bible, however, continues in use as the official version of Jews from Arab lands. It is also a mine of original insight into the meaning of difficult Hebrew words and phrases in the Bible, of which modern scholars have barely taken advantage. Students of the Gaon were the first to produce linguistic studies of biblical Hebrew in Hebrew rather than Arabic, and for this reason their books were for three centuries the primary texts for European Jewish scholars who knew no Arabic. Students of Saadiah's students became the teachers of the great philologist, Ibn Janah, to whom we referred above, whose two-volume analysis of biblical vocabulary, grammar, and style remains the most brilliant and valuable contribution of all time to the study of biblical language. The two volumes, *The Book of Roots* and *The Book of Embroidery* (his figure for grammar) exist only in the original Arabic and a medieval Hebrew translation.

It would seem that most Jewish contemporaries of Ibn Janah did not share his enthusiasm for the linguistic method in biblical exegesis. In his introduction to *The Book of Embroidery,* Ibn Janah upbraids the Jews for their laxness in grammar and failure to esteem its importance. Most Jews, he says, viewed grammar as an occult art, a heresy. Ibn Janah gets even by defaming those who stubbornly oppose the new science, calling them "rejected by God and debased by men." It is not hard to appreciate the suspicion that a pious Jew might harbor against the philological approach to biblical interpretation. Such a method relies on worldly knowledge, not the traditional teachings of the rabbis. In order to make a linguistic or philosophical argument, one had to flex the muscles of secular learning. It is hardly a coincidence that the new breed of Jewish scholar was often a mathematician, astronomer, or physician, as were Saadiah, Ibn Janah, Maimonides, Nahmanides, and others. The study of language and independent interpretation of the Bible might well have been carried out as secular pursuits and were surely perceived as such by many medieval Jews.

Ironically, it was precisely on account of its worldliness that the way of *peshat* fulfilled a vital need for medieval Jewry. The contextual method, resting as it does on academic disciplines more than on particular ideologies, formed the common ground of the various, conflicting religious traditions that base themselves on Hebrew scripture. In the arena of debate and dispute concerning the true meaning of the biblical text, the rabbanite Jews, their Jewish sectarian opponents—the Karaites —the Muslims, and the Christians had to forsake the weapons of their own partisan interpretations, which the others would not accept, and take up the arsenal of *peshat* methodologies, which everyone could respect.

Peshat as a Rabbinic Bulwark

A major impetus for the evolution of the *peshat* approach with Saadiah Gaon and his students was a zeal to combat the growth of the so-called Karaite heresy among the Jews of Babylonia and the rest of the Islamic world. In the eighth century one Anan ben David openly broke with rabbinic Judaism by rejecting the Oral Torah, the rabbinic interpretations of the Written Torah. Rabbinic law, it is true, often directly contradicts the plain meaning of Scripture and relies upon circuitous argumentation to establish its claims. This was necessary to imbue the biblical precepts with later Jewish values and adapt them to later social circumstances, as was discussed in Chapter Three. Anan advocated a rejection of rabbinic tradition and a return to the text of the Bible itself as the authoritative expression of God's will. In the ninth century, Anan's posture attracted many Jews, who, living among Muslims for whom the Koran, their Scripture, was central, found it only proper that Jews should seek the truth in their own Scripture, the text of the Bible. The antirabbinic schismatics came to be called Karaites, "Scripturalists," because they interpreted the Bible, the *Mikra'*, directly, independent of rabbinic tradition. In order to bolster their readings and argue linguistically, they had to master philology and grammar, the staples of the *peshat* approach. The rabbis, following the lead of Saadiah Gaon, had to respond in kind, by *peshat*.

Construing the meaning of the Torah narrowly often led the Karaites to unhappy results. While the rabbis helped develop the Sabbath into a day of rest and refreshment, the Karaites made it bleak. The Torah prohibits the igniting of fire on the Sabbath:

> You shall not ignite fire in all your dwellings on the Sabbath day. (Exod. 35.3)

The Karaites took this to mean that one must dwell in darkness, but the rabbis had permitted and promoted the lighting of lamps prior to the Sabbath which could continue to burn on the Sabbath. The twelfth-century Spanish commentator, Rabbi Abraham Ibn Ezra, derided Karaite exegesis on many occasions. On this verse he cites a book written by Saadiah Gaon to answer the challenges of "those who take issue with our predecessors concerning the Sabbath lamp." Similarly on Exodus 34.21:

> Six days shall you work, and on the seventh day you shall desist, in your plowing and in your harvesting you shall desist.

Ibn Ezra ridicules the Karaite interpretation, which finds in desisting from plowing a reference to sexual abstinence:

> Said Anan ["Cloud"]—may his name vanish like a cloud—that this refers to sexual intercourse, but shame should cover him, of course! For we say this means no more than to plow. The word *harvest* should silence him now!

Our translation of this particular comment departs from literalism in an attempt to reproduce the rhymes and puns in the taunting verse in which Ibn Ezra formulated his critique. He may have been a bit nasty, but he is correct: context makes it clear that the Torah is forbidding agriculture on the Sabbath, not sexual intercourse, which rabbinic Judaism has found to be most fitting on this joyous day.

The most famous example in which the Karaites read the biblical text without interpretation is their acceptance at face value of the law of retaliating for physical damages to persons:

> . . . a life in place of a life, an eye in place of an eye, a tooth in place of a tooth, a hand in place of a hand, a foot in place of a foot, a burn in place of a burn, a wound in place of a wound, an injury in place of an injury. (Exod. 21.23–25)

Rabbinic interpretation had always assumed that compensation for injuries would be monetary, not physical, but Anan adopted the literal sense of the text. Ibn Ezra reports a debate on the correct interpretation of this law between Saadiah Gaon and a contemporary Karaite exegete, Ben Zita, in his commentary to Exodus 21.24:

> *An eye [in place of an eye].* Said Rav Saadiah: We cannot interpret this verse in its literal sense. For if, say, a man injured the eye of his fellow, removing only one third of his eyesight, how can you be sure you duplicate precisely this injury, without an addition or subtraction? He might lose the entire sight of his eye! Even more difficult are a burn, a wound, and an injury, because if they had been in a dangerous place, [the perpetrator] might die! Reason cannot bear this. Said to him Ben Zita: But isn't it written elsewhere, *As he gives a damage to a man so may it be given to him?* (Lev. 24.20)
> But the Gaon answered him: We have [in the verse you cite] *to* in lieu of *upon.* You see, it means "So may a fine be given *upon* him."

Saadiah contends that Ben Zita is misreading the nuance of the Hebrew preposition *b,* which literally means *in. In* here stands for *upon.* Ben

Zita realizes that Saadiah's philology is forced and continues the argument.

> But Ben Zita answered him: [It means:] "As he did, so may it be done to him."
> But the Gaon answered: Look, Samson said *As they have done to me, so shall I do to them* [a paraphrase of JUDGES 15.11]. Now Samson did not take their wives and give them to other men [which is what the Philistines did to him]; he just requited what they had done.

Saadiah scores a point in this round; tit for tat need not be literal. Ben Zita considers a different line of reasoning.

> But Ben Zita answered: If the perpetrator were a poor man, how could he be fined?
> But the Gaon answered: If a blind man blinds a seeing man, what can be done to him? At least a poor man can acquire wealth and pay, but [in your method] the blind man could never pay!

For Ibn Ezra, Saadiah has dealt the *coup de grace* to Karaite logic, leaving Ben Zita speechless. To Ibn Ezra it is clear that philology and grammar do not by themselves suffice to establish the correct understanding of the Torah. One must also apply reason. The Bible must make sense and accord with what we know to be true. For this reason, he adds, "We cannot give the Torah's laws a full interpretation unless we rely on the words of the Sages. For just as we have received the [Written] Torah from our fathers, so have we received the Oral Torah. There is no dichotomy between them." Confidence in the partisan interpretations of the rabbis fortified the medieval Jewish commentators, who, nearly to a one, engaged—or were made to engage—in sectarian and interfaith polemics.

THE SPREAD OF PESHAT

The twin disciplines of rational exegesis and linguistic analysis spread among Jewish scholars from Babylonia, the land of Israel, and North Africa to Spain, where Ibn Janah and other Arabic-speaking grammarians elevated it to its heights. Having little linguistic or scientific training, it is remarkable that the Jewish scholars of France, beginning in the eleventh century, inaugurated an era of biblical interpretation and commentary according to the contextual, *peshat* method. They saw this approach as a supplement to the traditional rabbinic mode of *derash*. The relationship between *derash* and the newer method of *peshat* is clarified most explicitly in the commentary of Rashbam, a great French interpreter of the early twelfth century whom we mentioned above. At the very beginning of his Torah commentary he senses a need to explain the somewhat novel approach:

> Enlightened people will understand that all the statements of the rabbis and their homilies are valid and true. And so is it said in Tractate Shabbat [of the Babylonian Talmud]: I was eighteen years old and I still didn't know [the principle] that "A verse's interpretation should not neglect its direct meaning."

In other words, one could study the rabbinic method without even encountering the contextual approach in exegesis. Rashbam continues:

> The essence of the laws and homilies are inferred from superfluous wording or from variations in language. The direct sense of Scripture is written in such language that one can learn from it the essence of a homily. For example, *These are the generations of the heaven and the land in their being-created* (Gen. 2.4). The rabbis interpreted this homiletically to indicate *through Abraham* because of the excessive language, it being unnecessary to write *in their being-created*.

The Midrash that Rashbam quotes regards the last Hebrew word of Genesis 2.4 as redundant and therefore superfluous. Its Hebrew letters are B-H-B-R-'-M.★ In order to discover additional meaning in these letters, the rabbis interchange H and ' and read B-'-B-R-H-M, "with Abraham," instead of "in their being-created," which adds nothing to the sense. The purpose of creation will be fulfilled only by the works of Abraham and his descendants. Rashbam then goes on to explain why he chooses to explicate the biblical text by a different means. The method he adopts—*peshat*—is sensitive to context, style, and grammar. In his commentary to Genesis 37.2 Rashbam emphasizes the superior importance of *derash* for the derivation of law and homily; he, nevertheless, will expose the level of meaning that can be determined by the contextual approach. We shall return to Rashbam's contributions later, but we must first introduce the work of his grandfather and the "father" of the French school of *peshat,* Rashi.

★ The apostrophe (') is used to designate the Hebrew letter *alef.*

RASHI

Rashi is Rabbi Shlomo Yitzhaki, that is, Solomon ben Isaac, whose Hebrew initials spell Rashi (1040–1105). Like many Jews in northern France, he made his living growing grapes. Somehow he managed to find the time to study all the classic Jewish texts thoroughly and write commentaries on them. His most monumental achievement was his running commentary to the Babylonian Talmud, noted in Chapter Two, a masterpiece of *peshat* and an indispensable aid for interpreting that complex body of legal dialectics. Many of the didactic techniques that he utilized in composing the Talmud commentary, he also applied in his biblical commentaries: disambiguations of language and references, translation of technical terms and realia into contemporary French, and line drawings as illustrations. (Unfortunately, printers often omitted these graphic aids from their editions.) Thus, although Rashi was a scholar of astounding breadth, he saw his role chiefly as a teacher. He wrote textbooks rather than treatises. With pious soul and gentle humility he wished to share the learning of the ages with the Jewish community of his time. His work has received much attention in English, too.

It should be stated, however, that he was not, as is often claimed, writing for the "masses." He writes with a concise, though elegant, learned Hebrew style, which generally presupposes the reader's sensitivity to the problem that sparks his explanations. He alludes to sources that only an advanced student would recognize. Nonetheless, Rashi has been by far the most widely read Jewish Bible commentator; his Torah commentary was the very first Hebrew book to be printed mechanically, even before the Bible itself.

The sparest edition of *Mikra'ot Gedolot,* the Rabbinic Bible, will include his commentary, and students in traditional Jewish schools, *yeshivot,* usually begin to learn Rashi's interpretations as soon as they begin to learn the Torah. In traditional circles, Rashi's is the key version of what the Torah means. While very little of medieval commentary exists in any English edition, Rashi's commentary on the Torah may be found in two English editions. The main reason for Rashi's far-reaching success is that more than presenting innovative insights into the meaning of the Bible, he encapsulates traditional rabbinic understandings. His commentary to a great extent comprises a digest of rabbinic law and teaching. By virtue of his lack of originality, he is the most representative rabbi among the medieval commentators.

Rashi's anthological mode of commentary encourages the typical view in *yeshivot* that what the Written Torah means is what the Oral Torah (the Talmud and Midrash) explains; and what the Oral Torah explains is selectively distilled by Rashi. Thus the most essential or relevant meaning of the Torah, in the traditional view, is that which is found in Rashi's commentary. A modern, critical student of the Bible, however, will maintain a historical distance between what the Bible meant in its own period and what it came to mean to later generations. We read Rashi's commentary, not as the historical meaning of the biblical text but rather as an acute testimony to what rabbinic Jews of the classical and medieval periods found the text to mean. We read Rashi's commentary, in other words, as a text unto itself, and one with a spiritual significance and suggestiveness to us, too.

Much has been made of the difficulty in classifying Rashi's exegetical procedure. Here he gives *derash,* there he gives *peshat.* Rashi himself does not appear to have been quite so method-conscious as his critics. He does not distinguish between what we have called *peshat* and *derash,* but rather between what the text says without interpretation and what the text conveys once its full significance has been homiletically drawn out. He explains himself most clearly in his comment on Genesis 3.8, the verse that relates how the man and the woman in the Garden of Eden *heard* the Lord moving about on the premises.

> There are many aggadic homilies [on this verse], and our rabbis have already arranged them in their place in Genesis Rabbah and the other Midrash collections. I come only to present what the text says directly and such *aggadah* that sets the wording of the text on its proper bearings.

What he means, and what he in fact obeys in his practice, is that he will restrict the *aggadah* that he adduces to that which responds to some peculiarity or outstanding feature of the language of the text.

An example from his commentary to Exodus 1.7: The Torah says that in Egypt the Israelites grew very numerous, from seventy to 600,000 able-bodied men plus women, children, and the elderly. How did they do it? One of the verbs that the Hebrew employs to denote the multiplying of the Israelites is *vayishretzu,* "they swarmed," a word that connotes reptiles and other swarming creatures. In response to this peculiar wording, Rashi sees fit to present a midrashic interpretation from Exodus Rabbah:

> *They swarmed.* [This means] that the women would give birth to six in each womb.

Or take his comment on Genesis 37.3:

> Now Israel loved Joseph more than any of his sons because he
> was a son-of-old-age to him . . .

Rashi sees in the phrase *son-of-old-age* three levels of meaning: the direct
sense, the implied sense, and a sense drawn out by permutating the
Hebrew sounds into a like-sounding Aramaic idiom.

> *A son-of-old-age.* [This means] that he was born to him in the
> period of his aging. Onkelos [the official Aramaic *targum*] trans-
> lates, "a wise son is he to him"; all that he learned from Shem
> [the founder of the first academy in rabbinic lore] and Eber [his
> son, the namesake of the Hebrews] he handed down to him.
> Another interpretation [a clear signal of a Midrash]: his facial
> features *[ziv ikonin]* were similar to him.

The Hebrew phrase *ben zekunim* suggested the Aramaic *ziv ikonin*. Israel
(that is, Jacob) favored Joseph for three reasons: Joseph studied with him
and resembled him as well as delighted him unexpectedly in his advanced
age. The biblical text, the words of God, were calculated to proliferate
interpretation.

In his commentaries to the Prophets and the Writings, the latter,
less sacred parts of the Hebrew Bible, Rashi tends to comment less and
present less midrashic material than he does on the Torah. One can
imagine at least two good reasons for this disparity. First, Rashi sought
to use the commentary as an instrument of religious education. The
Torah is studied most and is read over and over from year to year in the
synagogue. It would, accordingly, be most effective to attach one's
teachings to the most frequently encountered Jewish book, the Torah.
Second, most of the essence of God's revelations, the commandments or
mitzvot, are contained in the Torah. The Torah embodies more precepts
per square foot, so to speak, than the rest of the Bible. Since there is so
much more to be learned from the Torah, one's commentary should be
more extensive and multifaceted. This is certainly true of Rashi's.

That Rashi sees the core of the Torah in its laws stands out in the
introduction to his Torah commentary. If the primary objective of the
Torah is to instruct us in the *mitzvot,* why does it defer the *mitzvot* by
first setting out the story of Creation, of the early peoples, of the patriarchs and their families? He begins, as usual, by adducing a Midrash.

> Said Rabbi Isaac: It was unnecessary to begin the Torah except
> from *May this month be to you . . .* [Exodus 12, the first chapter
> in the Torah packed with *mitzvot,* in this case the laws of Pass-

over], which is the first *mitzvah* which the Israelites were commanded. So for what reason does it begin with Genesis? On account of: *The power of his acts has he* [God] *related to his people, to give them the territory of nations.* (Ps. 111.6) If the nations of the world say to Israel, "Robbers are you, for you have conquered the lands of the seven nations!"—Israel can say to them: "All the land is the Holy One blessed be He's. He created it, and he has given it to those who are right in his eyes. By his will he gave it to them, and by his will he took it back from them and gave it to us."

The Book of Genesis places seven peoples in the land of Canaan before Abraham came to possess it by the command of God. The Torah introduces in Genesis the notions of God's dominion over all that he created and of God's covenant with the ancestors of Israel. Rashi elucidates the logic underlying the topical arrangement of the Torah.

In order to best taste the flavor of Rashi's interpretive approach, we shall read a short biblical story together with his commentary. Rashi's commentary will be set out beside a translation of the story in two parallel columns. We shall add explanations and observations after most of the comments, running across the width of the page in italics. Although it is possible to read the commentary selectively and maintain the integrity of the biblical story, the full impact of Rashi can be felt only by reading the text and continually interrupting it with Rashi's commentary. In the end, the text will be perceived only through Rashi's eyes, which is probably what Rashi intended and the way that the text has often been read traditionally. The narrative is the story of Hannah, from 1 Sam. 1.

Bible	*Rashi*
There was a man . . .	Everything in its order.

That is, the Book of Samuel begins its story as a direct chronological continuation of the preceding books of the Bible.

	Moses handed down the [Oral] Torah to Joshua and Joshua to the elders and each judge to the [next] judge until it reached Eli and from him to Samuel, as we have learned [in Pirkei Avot 1.1]: "and the elders to the prophets."

The significance of this story is that it documents the passage of the oral tradition

Bible	*Rashi*

from the last of the elders, Eli the priest of Shiloh, to the first of the prophets, Samuel.

from Ramatayim-Tzofim . . .

Rashi will explain why the place was named Ramatayim-Tzofim, literally, "Two Heights-Lookouts."

> There were two heights looking out and seeing each other. And [Targum] Jonathan translated [into Aramaic] "from the pupils of the prophets."

"Lookout" is also a Hebrew term for "prophet." Samuel, then, comes from a breeding ground of prophets.

from the mountain of Ephraim, and his name was Elkanah . . .

> A Levite was he from the sons of Abiasaph son of Korah; so is he connected in [the book of First] Chronicles [6 and 12].

This gives Samuel a priestly pedigree and legitimates the fact that he will offer sacrifices later on, taking up a priestly prerogative.

son of Jeroham, son of Elihu, son of Tohu, son of Zuph, an Ephrathite.

> [Targum] Jonathan translated "on the mountain of Ephraim" [relating Ephrath to Ephraim]. Aggadic Midrash [interprets] Ephrathite as a courtier, a noble, an important personage, as in [the Talmudic phrase] "a triumphant procession [*Apiryon,* a sound-alike of Ephrathite] of Rabbi Simon," from a word meaning "beauty."

Midrash often associates words and their meanings on the basis of superficial resemblances. This association gives Samuel high breeding as well as a priestly pedigree.

Bible

Rashi

Now he had two wives, the name of the one is Hannah, and the name of the second is Peninah. Peninah had children, but Hannah had no children. Now that man would go up . . .

The language is [to be taken as] present tense [although in form the verb seems to be in the past tense]. He would go up to Shiloh from the time of one festival to another festival. Yet another interpretation is: by the route he would go up one year he would not go up the next year so that he could teach the Israelites [all over] to do the same as he.

The first interpretation is contextually sound. The second draws out a homily. The father of a man like Samuel is the religious sort who would take pains to travel a different itinerary each year in order to set an example for another community of Israelites.

from his town year by year to do homage and make an offering to the Lord of Hosts at Shiloh. There the two sons of Eli were, Hophni and Phineas, priests of the Lord. Now on the day . . .

Which day? The significance of this day will materialize later on.

It was the day of the festival.

Elkanah would make an offering and he would give to Peninah his wife and to all her sons and daughters portions. But to Hannah he would give one lovely portion . . .

One choice portion which ought to be received gladly.

Wait and see Hannah's reaction.

Bible	*Rashi*
for Hannah he loved, though the Lord had closed her womb. Now her rival . . .	
	The wife of her husband, Peninah.
vexed her even vexation . . .	
	Extraordinary vexation, constant vexation. That's why it says "even vexation." She would say, "Haven't you a coat for your older boy today, or a jacket for your younger boy?" [knowing that Hannah was grieved over having no children].
in order to rile her . . .	
	To get her to complain. But the rabbis said that "to rile her" [means] to get her to pray, that she [Peninah] had the highest intentions.
since the Lord had closed over her womb.	
	"Over her womb" [means] across her womb, so too with every usage of "over."
And so would he . . .	
	Elkanah.
do year by year . . .	
	He would give her a choice allocation to show her his affection for her, but her rival in proportion to the affection her husband would show her [Hannah] would even increase her vexing of her.
as soon as she would go up to the House of the Lord, she would vex her. So she cried and did not eat. Elkanah, her man, said to her, "Hannah, for what do you cry, and for what do you not eat, and for what is your heart sad? Am I not better to you . . .	
	Show affection to you.

Bible	Rashi
more than ten sons?"	
	[The ten sons] that Peninah has borne to me?

Note that Rashi reads the text hyperliterally and produces a Midrash, that Peninah had ten sons.

Hannah got up after eating in Shiloh . . .

The word "eating" seems ambiguous. Did Elkanah actually persuade Hannah to eat? Rashi did not excel in grammar, but he resolves the matter correctly, Hannah did not eat—"eating" means the eating of the group, not Hannah's.

There is no possessive suffix on "eating" and the short first vowel indicates an infinitive, as though it were written, "after the eating at Shiloh and after the drinking." The language is the same for masculine or feminine. "After eating" is the infinitive form as though it said "to eat."

and after drinking. Now Eli the priest was sitting on the chair . . .

Which chair? Why does it say "the chair?"

That day he was sitting on the great chair on which he was appointed judge over Israel.

on the doorpost . . .

As though it said "*next to* the doorpost."

of the palace of the Lord. As she was bitter in spirit, she prayed to the Lord and cried a crying. She vowed a vow and said, "O Lord of Hosts, . . .

Why is this name [of God] used here? She said before him, "O Master of the World! Two hosts have you created in your world, the upper ones who do not bear

Bible   *Rashi*

fruit, do not multiply, and do not
die. If I were among the lower
ones, I would bear fruit, multiply, and die. But if I were of the
upper ones I would not die."
This [interpretation] I found in
the Aggadah of Rabbi Yosi the
Galilean. But our rabbis interpreted in Tractate Berakhot [of
the Babylonian Talmud] what
they interpreted: Up to then
there was no person who called
the Holy One blessed be He
"[The Lord of] Hosts." However, she [Hannah] said this before him: "Master of the World!
Of all the hosts that you have created in your world, would it be
too hard to give me just one
son?" (And from then on God
was known as the Lord of
Hosts.)

If you would only look, look
upon . . .

Our rabbis interpreted in Tractate Berakhot what they interpreted.

*Rashi does not approve of the somewhat wild Midrash there in which Hannah
threatens to go out alone with other men, which would arouse her husband's
suspicions and force him to invoke the Torah's trial by ordeal. The Book of
Numbers 5.11–31 prescribes a horrible ritual to determine if a wife suspected of
unfaithfulness is guilty. Since God knows Hannah is innocent, the ordeal will
be invoked under false pretenses. Hannah, according to this Midrash, seeks to
blackmail God into avoiding the misuse of the Torah. This conduct and its
ascription to Hannah offends Rashi.*

the affliction of your maidservant
. . .

The word "maidservant" is said
three times in this verse, corresponding to the three things that
a woman is commanded [exclu-
sively: lighting holy day candles,

Bible	*Rashi*
	preparing holy day bread—*hallah,* and attending to her periodic ritual impurity].
and pay mind to me, and do not neglect your maidservant, but give your maidservant seed of men . . .	
	Righteous men, just as you say [in 1 Kings 2.32] "two men, righteous men." "Men" [also means] important men, as you say [in Deut. 1.31] "men, wise men, and famous men."
then I will give him to the Lord . . .	
	May he be fit to be given to the Lord.
all the days of his life. A razor . . .	

Rashi cites a midrashic wordplay on the Hebrew word for "razor," morah.

	[Targum] Jonathan translated [into Aramaic]: "The domination *[marvat]* of man will not be upon him."
will not go up upon his head." Now it was, as she prayed more and more before the Lord, Eli was watching her mouth.	
	He was waiting until she stopped. Thus did [Targum] Jonathan translate it: "Now Eli waited for her until she stopped." "Watching" has the sense of deferring, as in "[Jacob] watched the matter" [Gen. 37.11; Jacob made no sense of Joseph's dreams at first, but he kept them in mind]; [or:] "You [God] do not watch my sin" [Job 14.16; that is, you hound me for my sins immediately].

Bible

Rashi

And Hannah, she was speaking on her heart, only her lips were moving, and her voice could not be heard, so Eli reckoned her a drunk.

Since people were not wont to pray in a hush.

So he said to her, did Eli, "How long would you be drunk? Turn away the wine from upon you!" Then Hannah spoke up and said, "No, my lord.

You are not my lord in this matter. You yourself have revealed that there is no holy spirit residing in you, for [if there were] you would know that I am not drunk with wine.

A woman of hard spirit am I. Wine and strong drink I have not drunk; I was pouring out my breath before the Lord. Do not treat your maidservant . . .

Since she said a harsh thing to him, she reverted to placating him so that he would not treat her as worthless and debased in the presence of her rival, a woman of no-good.

Rashi reads the syntax hyperliterally, not idiomatically, taking Hannah to mean: Do not treat your maidservant in front of a woman of no-good. In Hebrew the idiom "like a woman of no-good" has the literal sense: "in front of a woman of no-good," which woman Rashi identifies as Peninah.

like a woman of no-good. Rather from much anguish . . .

Did I speak harshly to you. "Anguish": There are places where it has the sense of anguish of the heart [although it is better known in the sense of uttering]. Another interpretation: "from much anguish" [means] what the *targum*

Bible	*Rashi*
	has: "from much wailing and stirring I held my prayer until now."
and vexation."	
	Which my rival vexes me. [Rashi now goes back to:] "Do not treat . . .": It [literally, " to give"] has the sense of giving over, as in "Do not give me over to my adversaries" (Ps. 27.12).

It will be noted that Rashi is reading the story as he would a legal document. Each word and phrase must have some specific basis and reference. He hardly allows for a more impressionistic reading.

Eli spoke up and said, "Go in peace. The God of Israel will grant the request . . .	
	[The word "request"] is missing the letter *alef,* in which we may interpret the sense of sons, as in [Deut. 28.57, where the word] "goes out" [is likewise written without the *alef*].

The missing letter symbolizes the missing son.

	"He will grant the request" [means that] he [Eli] broke the good news to her that her prayer was accepted.

After all, can a man promise that God will do this or that?

which you requested from him." She said, "May your bondwoman find favor in your eyes."	
	So that you will seek compassion for her.
Then the woman went her way and she ate, and her face . . .	
	A face of rage.
was no more with her. They arose early in the morning, they did homage before the Lord, and they returned and came into their	

Bible   *Rashi*

house at Ramah; then Elkanah
knew Hannah his wife . . .

From this we learn that it is forbidden to a wayfarer to have sexual intercourse.

Elkanah and Hannah made love only after they returned home. Rashi under-
stands that what Elkanah and Hannah do is not simply their choice but the
performance of the appropriate Jewish law. Midrash in general attributes strict
Jewish observances to exemplary figures in the biblical narrative.

and the Lord paid mind to her. It
was at the periods of the days
. . .

The minimum number of pe-
riods [of the year] is two, the
minimum number of days is
two. [Since the year has four periods, or seasons, two periods
and two days amounts] to six
months and two days. From this
we learn that she who gives birth
in seven months gives birth
early.

that Hannah conceived and bore
a son. She called his name Samuel
. . .

For God's name [El] and for the
fact [of what led to his birth] was
he named, for [Hannah reck-
oned], "I requested him from
him [God]."

because from the Lord have I requested him [*she'iltiv*, a play on
Shemu'el, Samuel]." When the
man Elkanah and his household
went up to offer to the Lord the
offering of the days . . .

[[Targum] Jonathan translated
into Aramaic:] the offerings of
the festivals.

and his vow, . . .

Vowed offerings that one would
vow between pilgrimages one

Bible	Rashi
	would bring near ["sacrifice"] on the pilgrimage.
Hannah did not go up, for she said to her man, "Once the boy is weaned . . .	
	At the end of twenty-two months, for that is the time a suckling suckles.
I shall take him, and we shall see the face of the Lord [i.e., worship], and he will stay there forever."	
	"Forever" for Levites is only fifty years, as it is said [in Num. 8.25]: "from fifty years old [the Levite] will turn from the duty of service [and will serve no more]."

You will recall from Rashi's comment above that Samuel is from the priestly tribe of Levites.

And indeed the days of Samuel's [service] were fifty-two [years]. You see, Eli judged Israel forty years. [Eli] was appointed to judge on the day that Hannah prayed.

You will recall that when he first noticed Hannah, Eli was, in Rashi's interpretation, sitting in a special chair for his installation as judge. The present comment shows how this amazing coincidence—Midrash abounds in amazing coincidences—must be assumed in order to calculate the chronology of Samuel's service.

Take off the year when Samuel was gestating, so thirty-nine years remained. Now Samuel maintained Israel after Eli's death thirteen years. You see, on the day that Eli died, the ark was alienated and stayed in Philistine territory seven months [1 Sam. 6]; from there it came to Kiryat-Ye'arim, until David took it up [to Jerusalem] after he had ruled as king for seven years over

Bible	Rashi
	Judah in Hebron and all the Israelites made him king over them. Now it says [in 1 Sam. 7.2]: "From the day the ark stayed in Kiryat-Ye'arim the days multiplied and became twenty years." Take off from these the seven years that David ruled in Hebron, and it turns out there were thirteen years and seven months from the time the ark was alienated until Saul died. And Samuel died four months before Saul.

So Samuel served for thirty-nine of Eli's years of tenure and thirteen years more, making a total of fifty-two.

The last comment reflects Rashi's interest in reconciling the story of Samuel with the laws of the Torah, as well as a widespread medieval concern in reckoning the chronology of the Bible and all other history. We shall leave Rashi's commentary and the story of Hannah at this point. We have seen in it the kaleidoscope of Rashi's hermeneutics: sensitivity to the nuances, even the spelling, of the text's wording; midrashic analysis of words into their possible components and permutations; drawing out the lessons of the text for pious living; expanding the story by filling in background and dialogue; a constant consideration of rabbinic exegesis that is both deferential and critical; and above all, a pedagogical desire to make clear.

We turn now to the more single-minded *peshat* methodologies of the generation of Rashi's grandchildren in France.

OTHER PESHAT INTERPRETERS IN FRANCE

The contextual approach, *peshat,* grew into a distinctive, self-conscious mode in twelfth-century France. While many rabbinic scholars devoted their energies to penetrating, often hairsplitting discussion of the Talmud, a number of shrewd commentators set their minds to the Bible. Only one, Rashi's grandson Rashbam, Rabbi Samuel ben Meir, wrote a Torah commentary that was later included in standard editions of *Mikra'ot Gedolot.* But we shall look at three great *peshat* exegetes of this group: Rashbam, Rabbi Eliezer of Beaugency, and Rabbi Joseph Bekhor Shor, each of whom holds special interest for us.

Although Rashbam was an expert Talmudist who completed his grandfather Rashi's commentary to the Babylonian Talmud, he is best known as an arrogant, independent, and immensely clever and successful commentator on the Torah. In a famed comment on Genesis 37.2, Rashbam claims that:

> Our rabbi, Solomon [i.e., Rashi], the father of my mother, who enlightens the eyes of the Diaspora, who interpreted the Torah, the Prophets, and the Writings, also set his mind to explain the direct sense of Scripture. Yet I, Samuel, son of Rabbi Meir, his son-in-law, of blessed memory, debated with him in his presence, and he admitted to me that if he had the opportunity he would compose different commentaries according to the new *peshat* interpretations coming to light every day.

Rashbam suffered no doubts about the superiority of his method and of his interpretations to those that differed among his grandfather's. Yet, Rashi did not commit himself exclusively to the *peshat* approach, nor did Rashbam in any way deny the paramount importance of the *derash* approach for deriving Jewish law and values (see above). Nonetheless, Rashbam may be correct when he suspects that

> Earlier commentators out of their piety busied themselves by tending toward the homiletical *[derash]* interpretations, as they are the essential ones, and for this reason did not become trained in the actual *peshat* of Scripture. . . . (comment on Gen. 37.2)

Rashbam understands that the only way to elucidate the *peshat,* or contextual, meaning of the biblical text is to stick to this dimension of meaning and not clutter it by overlapping other dimensions. Even if other dimensions have greater significance, Rashbam would contend, the *peshat* interpretation deserves to be heard.

Rashbam did need to state this point expressly because many midrashic interpreters feel threatened by *peshat. Peshat* may differ from the interpretation in rabbinic law. We have a clear example of this in the following passage from Rashbam's commentary to Genesis 1.5. In Jewish tradition the day commences at sundown and ends after sundown the next day. Sabbath and festival observance assumes this definition of the day. Traditional rabbinic interpretation would naturally find support for this definition in the story of creation, when the day was defined for the very first time. Rashbam scrutinizes the language of the text there and reaches a conclusion that would unsettle many a rabbi for whom the midrashic exegesis is the only one. After describing what God created each day, the text concludes: "There was evening and there was morning," which closes the first, second, third, and so on day. Rashbam says:

> It is not written here *There was night and there was day* but rather *there was evening,* meaning that the first day reached evening when the light [there was not sun yet] set, and *there was morning,* meaning the breaking of the night when the dawn rose. With this one day of the six days spoken of in the Ten Commandments [see below] was completed and the second day begun—*God said: "Let there be a dome."* The text does not come to say that evening and morning comprise one day, for we have no need except that it explain what makes six days—when day breaks and night is finished, then one day is finished and a second day begins.

Rashbam tangles two issues here. The first, and simpler, is that of language and style. The repeating formula, *There was evening and there was morning,* refers by dint of language alone to two specific stages in the passing of a day, dusk and dawn, not to two halves of the day, the dark one and the light one. To demonstrate the correctness of his reading, he creates what some literary critics today call a countertext: What else could the text have said? If the text had intended to convey the notion that the day has two consecutive parts, night and day, the text would then have said "There was night and there was day."

It does not. Rather, the text describes the passing of a day. First, the day begins. Then it reaches a point about midway when the light dims —evening. Finally, it reaches a point when the light returns—daybreak. It is precisely this point that signals the end of one day and the beginning of the next. Day, therefore, begins at dawn, not according to the definition of the day for the purpose of observing Jewish festivals, at sunset.

The second issue concerns a matter of the Bible's style. (For more on this see Chapter One.) Rashbam indicates in a number of places in his Torah commentary what he perceives as a literary feature of biblical narrative: it introduces information that has no immediate import but which will be necessary or significant as the text continues to unfold. This technique of anticipation, or "prolepsis," is the subject of an entire essay by Nahum Sarna.* For example, in an episode we have referred to above, after Joseph relates his dreams to his brothers and his father, the text says, "And his father kept the matter in mind." (Gen. 37.11) Rashbam:

---

* "The Anticipatory Use of Information as a Literary Feature of the Genesis Narratives," in Richard E. Friedman, ed., *The Creation of Sacred Literature* (Berkeley: University of California Press, 1981), pp. 76–82.

What need is there for this phrase? None except that when [later on] the news comes to [Jacob that Joseph is alive and viceroy of Egypt] and he didn't believe his sons [who brought the news that Joseph] was living, and when Israel saw the wagons that Pharaoh had sent—for they could not have been sent except by order of the king as it is written there, *wagons at the order of Pharaoh*—then [Jacob/Israel] believed on the basis of the dreams, which predicted that [Joseph's] future was to be a ruler, and these wagons come by dint of royalty and rulership. For this reason [Jacob] said *It is great that Joseph my son still lives* (Gen. 45.28). Isn't it surprising that [Jacob] would believe [this message] after he had seen his tunic full of blood? [He must have reacted] like Isaac did to Jacob [when Jacob convinced his father that he was Esau by wearing furry skins] by trembling, since he had found fur [like Esau's] on the area of [Jacob's] neck.

In other words, in a wordy style quite unlike his grandfather's, Rashbam explains that the only reason that Jacob could believe that Joseph was alive many years after he had thought that Joseph was killed by a wild animal was that he remembered the dreams; the dreams had come true. Only in order to establish the premise for this astonishing newsbreak did the text tell us earlier, "and his father kept the matter in mind."

Thus, in the Creation story of Genesis 1 the limit of the day must be defined, in Rashbam's view, in order that the fourth of the Ten Commandments can be readily comprehended:

> Pay mind to the Sabbath day, to hallow it. Six days you shall work and do your labor; but the seventh day is the Lord your God's. . . .
>
> —EXOD. 20.8–10

Genesis 1 instructs us how to count out six days. We wait until six evenings have passed and six new mornings have broken.

One unmitigated drawback of the sort of straightforward, commonsensical exegesis that we find in Rashbam is that it lacks the spiritual and ethical dimension that a commentator like Rashi tends to provide. A final contrast of Rashbam and Rashi will exemplify this. In Exodus 3 God appears to Moses in the burning bush and commissions him to return to Egypt, confront Pharaoh, and liberate the Hebrews. Moses shares his diffidence with God and says:

> "Who am I that I may go to Pharaoh and that I may take the Israelites out of Egypt?"

Rashbam reads the statement pragmatically:

> *Moses said, "Who am I?"* Whoever wishes to understand the actual direct sense of these words will become enlightened by my interpretation here, for the commentators before me did not understand a thing of it. Moses is responding to two matters that the Holy One had told him: to go to Pharaoh, and to take the Israelites out by the command of Pharaoh. Moses responded to each matter in turn. *Who am I that I may go to Pharaoh?* Even if I brought him tribute and gifts [could I get in to see Pharaoh]? Can a foreign man like me be suitable to enter the king's court? *And that I may take the Israelites out of Egypt?* That is to say, even if I were suitable to enter before Pharaoh, fool as I am in other matters, what could I say to Pharaoh that would be acceptable to him? Is Pharaoh a fool that he would listen to me and send a large nation of his own slaves free from his land? And what could I say that would be acceptable to him by which saying I would take them out of Egypt with the permission of Pharaoh?

Rashi prefers to see in Moses, a man the Torah calls more humble than any other, a model of humility:

> *Who am I?* What importance have I to speak with kings? *That I may take the Israelites out.* And even if I have the importance, what merit has Israel that a miracle should be done for them by my taking them out of Egypt?

Thus the grandson finds Moses to be ordinary, a man absorbed in his own predicament; the grandfather holds up Moses as a model of pious conduct.

Rabbi Joseph Bekhor Shor (twelfth century) was a younger contemporary of Rashbam's and, like him, a practitioner of *peshat*. His work is distinguished, however, by a more profound rationalism and an openness to appropriate sermonizing here and there. Like Rashbam, his commentary to the Torah does not flinch from exposing the contextual sense of biblical law, even where it contradicts the Talmudic interpretations. But more than Rashbam, and somewhat akin to Maimonides, the great Spanish philosopher, Bekhor Shor probed for the reasons underlying the particular commandments. Perhaps his most extraordinary venture in this region is his explanation of the Torah's taboo on hybrids, a theory that closely anticipates that of some recent anthropologists (see Chapter One, "Biblical Law"). The Torah forbids the Israelites to breed two species of animal together, to mix two types of seed, and to interweave two kinds of fabric (see especially Lev. 19.19). The Torah assumes that each mixture would produce, or at least smack of, hybridization. This law has generally been taken as illogical, mystical. But Bekhor Shor elucidates its rationale:

> *Your animals do not breed together two species.* If you would breed a horse and an ass, it would produce a mule, which I [God] did not create; you see, you would have altered the act of creation. This applies to any two species, such as a sheep and a goat, for [by breeding them together] you would be making yourself into the creator! . . . You would be creating a creature which is not natural in the world, you would be altering the order of the world, and it is forbidden. . . . (commentary to Lev. 19.19)

God created the world in divisions of species; it is a violation of the created order, and God's will, to blur those divisions. Bekhor Shor's penchant for the rational also informs his attitude toward miracles in the Bible. Lot's wife, he says, did not really turn into a pillar of salt (Gen. 19.26); she was simply coated with lime and sulphur and appeared to have turned into a pillar of salt.

Nor does the Torah, according to Bekhor Shor, mean to stretch our beliefs with respect to its literary arrangement. The Torah contains two very similar stories about the Israelites lacking water in the wilderness and Moses extracting water by smiting a rock. (Exod. 17; Num. 20.8–13) In the first story the location was named Massah and Meribah ("Trial and Contention"), and in the second the water was called the Water of Meribah. Aren't these two episodes actually two versions of the same event? Are we supposed to believe that the same hardship happened twice, with similar results, in the same spot? No, according to Bekhor Shor:

> It seems to me that this episode (in Num. 20) is the event in Exodus 17. . . . Only there the narrative tells of how the Holy One provided Israel with manna, quail, and water in the wilderness; afterwards, the narrative writes each episode in its own place.

The passage in Numbers presents the story in its sequential position in the wilderness narrative; the passage in Exodus joins that episode to thematically related ones. It is a stylistic technique:

> And such is the way of many passages, where it speaks concisely in one place but elaborates in another place.

Such interpretations run directly against the grain of Midrash, in which there can be no insignificant duplication, but *peshat* allows for a component of literary style in the formation of Scripture.

Nowhere is this more explicit in medieval Jewish exegesis than in the commentaries to the prophets by Rabbi Eliezer of Beaugency, another great French exegete of the twelfth century. It is most regrettable that Rabbi Eliezer's commentaries to the Torah and other books besides the prophets have not survived, because his keen sense of style, his eclectic interests, and his lucid writing make him as fine a Bible commentator as there has been. See how he explains a word that tradition had regarded as unknowable. When the prophet Ezekiel first caught a glimpse of the Lord descending on his heavenly chariot, he described the image as *hashmal*. What does *hashmal* look like? What is it? In modern Hebrew the word denotes electricity, but the Talmud cautions against any attempt to define it.* Rashi incorporates the Talmudic approach:

> *Like the appearance of HASHMAL.* Hashmal is an angel bearing that name. And like the color of the appearance of [that angel] [Ezekiel] saw from within the fire. Thus said our rabbis: There once was a boy who was studying the episode of the heavenly chariot and was deliberating on the *hashmal*. A flame came out of the *hashmal* and burned him up.

Rabbi Eliezer uses the language of the larger context as his guide. He observes that everything to which Ezekiel compares his vision is part of our everyday reality:

> *Like the appearance of the HASHMAL.* We are compelled [to interpret]: The prophet makes comparison to things that are visible to us: *like the appearance of Tarshish stone, like the look of torches, like the appearance of the awesome icecap, like the look of lightning, like the appearance of burnished bronze, like the look of a rainbow*— all of these are visible in the world. So, too, *like the appearance of the HASHMAL,* a thing that is in the world, but we just aren't proficient enough in the language of Scripture in many things, and we only have the context [to go by]. But the context instructs us that it is a very very lucid and bright radiance, like the radiance of the sun's rays, when it appears to ebb and flow like waves of water.

Recent philological study, benefiting from our knowledge of Babylonian language, suggests that *hashmal* is a jet-bluish mythical stone, but Rabbi Eliezer's explanation is a noble effort and a lovely image nonetheless.

* Babylonian Talmud, Tractate Hagigah, 13a.

There is, though, a radical side to his interpretation of Ezekiel: he doesn't think the prophet composed the book as we have it. He, like earlier commentators, notices how the beginning of the Book of Ezekiel wavers between first person narrative and third person description. The third person passages had been attributed by Rashi to "the holy spirit." But Rabbi Eliezer infers that the third person descriptions are the work of an editor who compiled the book and summarized statements made by Ezekiel elsewhere at the beginning of the book.

The French school of biblical exegesis had by the end of the twelfth century run its brief but energetic course, leaving a permanent legacy of unsurpassed Jewish commentaries in its wake. The Spanish scholars, and those of Provence in the border area between France and Spain, continued the process of Bible interpretation for another century or two, but we turn now to the preeminent exegete of the Spanish school, a contemporary of the early twelfth-century commentators, Rabbi Abraham Ibn Ezra.

RABBI ABRAHAM IBN EZRA

Ibn Ezra embodies in his eccentric but learned commentaries on the Bible the best of what the Spanish scholars had developed: linguistic savvy and a philosophical and critical bent. His rationalism and technical explanations of grammar and language crowd out spiritual insight, but his wit and intelligence sparkle on every page of his work. Since we have dealt above, at least cursorily, with some of his literary and philological observations, we shall here examine a lengthy passage in which he delves into the relation between divine revelation and human mediation in accounting for the words of the Torah. Ibn Ezra's criticism is most celebrated for his having pointed out several verses in the Torah which, contrary to ancient tradition, were not written down by Moses. His comments provide the springboard for Spinoza's famed eighth chapter of the *Theologico-Political Treatise,* where Spinoza argues that the Torah did not receive its final editorial shape until after the Babylonian Exile, that is, the fifth century B.C.E.

It is in his analysis of the differences between the two versions of the Ten Commandments in the Torah, in Exodus 20 and in Deuteronomy 5, that Ibn Ezra expresses himself directly on the nature of revelation. Did God speak all the words of the Torah? Does the Torah speak human language? What role, if any, does human perception play in mediating the mind of God? Applying an unblinded eye and a sure sense of reason to these two series of the Ten Commandments, Ibn Ezra noted all the variations, raised the most critical questions, and resolved the perplexities to his own satisfaction. In doing so, he adduced matters of style and linguistics as well as philosophy. This is from his commentary to Exodus 20.1:

> There are difficult questions with respect to this passage. Many have said that only the first two commandments did the Lord himself say. Their evidence is that in the first commandment is written *I am the Lord your God* and in the second *for I the Lord your God am a zealous God,* but in the third is written *[Do not swear by] the name of the Lord your God [falsely],* as well as *whoever swears by his name falsely.* It does not say *my name.* [Similarly] in the fourth [is written] *For in six days did the Lord make . . . for this did the Lord bless,* and in the fifth it says *which the Lord your God gives to you.*

Some critics, says Ibn Ezra, infer from the shift from first to third person that the Lord only spoke the first two commandments. Ibn Ezra himself uses this as one criterion by which he argues that the last chapter of the Torah, Deuteronomy 34, and other verses were not written by Moses.

> One may [also] ask: How can the commandment *I am the Lord your God* be counted among the Ten Commandments when he is the commander? This is neither a do-command nor a don't-command. There are even questions more difficult than these. Now we call this passage, which is from the Torah-portion [entitled] "Jethro heard" (Exod. 20) the first one, and [the other version in] the Torah-portion "I supplicated" (Deut. 5) the second one. We have seen that from the beginning of *I am the Lord your God* to *who swears by his name falsely* there is no variation between the two passages. And from the beginning of *Remember the Sabbath day* to the end of the Ten Commandments, there is variation all over. In the first [version is written] *Remember the Sabbath day* but in the second *Keep the Sabbath day.* Also in the latter is the addition *just as the Lord your God has commanded you.*
>
> But the most difficult of these is that in the first [version] the reason behind the Sabbath is written *For in six days did the Lord make the heaven and the land,* saying further *for this did the Lord bless the Sabbath day.* These statements are not written in the second [version]; rather a different reason [is written]: *Remember that you were a slave in the Land of Egypt,* saying later *for this did the Lord your God command you to make the Sabbath day.* In the first [version] the reward for respecting father and

mother is *so that you may live long;* it is the same in the second [version], but it adds *and so that you may fare well.* It also adds concerning respect for father and mother: *as the Lord your God has commanded you.*

In the first [version] is written *Do not murder, do not commit adultery, do not steal, do not testify [against your neighbor as a false witness],* and in the second [version] is written *Do not murder, and do not commit adultery, and do not steal, and do not testify [against your neighbor as a false witness].* In the first [version of the ninth commandment] is written *lying witness,* but in the second version is written *false witness.* In the first [version] is written *Do not covet the house of your neighbor, do not covet the wife of your neighbor,* but in the second [version] is written *Do not covet the wife of your neighbor, and do not crave the house of your neighbor.* In the first *his field* is not written, but in the second *his field* is written . . .

In the first [version] is written [at the conclusion] *God spoke all these commandments, saying,* but in the second [version is written]: *the commandments which the Lord has spoken to all your congregation.*

To summarize, Ibn Ezra has raised three basic questions, each fraught with theological import. If God dictated all ten pronouncements, why does the text begin with *I* and switch to *he?* Second, can God's assertion of existence and identification, *I am the Lord your God,* be reckoned as a commandment? Third, if God stated the Ten Commandments as they are written in the Torah, how can there be two divergent texts? By implication, there is even a fourth question: what function do the variations between Exodus 20 and Deuteronomy 5 serve? Such obvious differences between the two versions hardly went unnoticed until Ibn Ezra. The ancient rabbis, in the early halakhic Midrash on Exodus, Mekhilta, resolved the problem enigmatically. It is to their explanation that Ibn Ezra next turns:

When we explore the words of the sages for what they had to say on this we find they say: "*Remember* [the Sabbath day] and *Keep* [the Sabbath day] in one utterance were said." Now this utterance [of the sages] is more difficult than all the other difficulties we have, as I shall explain. Heaven forbid that I would say that they did not speak correctly, for our understanding is of little weight beside their understanding. It's just that people of our generation think that [the sages'] words are to be taken at their face value, which is not so, as I shall explain at the end after I have mentioned [all the] difficulties. At the end I shall explain the correct way to remove all the difficulties and questions in this passage.

Now it is unlikely that *Remember* and *Keep* could be said at the same time except through a miracle. We must admit that even so, we can ask: Why wasn't it written first *Remember and Keep* and then again [in the second version—that is, if both words were said simultaneously, why weren't they written together], and what would have happened in those verses if they were said at the same time, like *Remember and Keep,* and why didn't the sages mention this [if this is what they meant]? And there is even more reason for surprise: how could many verses have been said miraculously at the same time when their meaning is not even equivalent—as when two words with one, equivalent meaning are said at the same time? And why should God himself say, *as the Lord your God has commanded?* And more: Did [God] at any time before the revelation [at Sinai] command [the Israelites] concerning respect for father and mother?

In other words, the simple interpretation of the rabbis' solution only scratches the surface of the problem. Ibn Ezra then goes on to delineate the parallel commandments in the two sets that have different meanings. They certainly could not have been said at the same time, in the same utterance. Then he continues:

The mind cannot bear all these things. And the most difficult of all those things I have mentioned is that every wonder that was performed by Moses has at least some semblance to reality which an enlightened person can understand, but this notion of God saying *Remember* and *Keep* at the same time is most wondrous of all, and [if so] should have been written explicitly in the Torah more than the signs and wonders that were written. And if we say that God's speech is not like human speech, then how could Israel have understood the speech of God, for if a human hears *Remember* and *Keep* at the same time, he will understand neither this nor that. Even if one word were spoken at an instant, like *Remember,* a person could not make out the speech of the speaker unless the letters were presented in their proper sequence.

Ibn Ezra expands this comment into an elaborate discussion of acoustic perception and the impossibility of claiming that the rabbis would have us believe that God spoke different words simultaneously.

Then how does one explain the differences between the two versions? First, Ibn Ezra explains that words are only labels for concepts, like bodies covering souls. Different words may label the same concept. Thus there is no substantial difference between the versions in those places where the only difference is diction. He also shows that the presence or absence of the word *and* is insignificant. This strikes a heavy blow to typical midrashic interpretation, where an entire law could be derived from the presence or absence of so small a word as *and*. As for the first two commandments being in the first person and the following ones in the third, Ibn Ezra provides this solution: At first, God must address the Israelites as "I," as he commands them to recognize and worship him alone. But once that is clear and God is known to the Israelites, God may refer to himself in the third person. The Lord is identified already, he doesn't have to keep associating himself explicitly with the voice that is speaking. Ibn Ezra bolsters his interpretation by finding other instances in biblical Hebrew where a shift from first to third person is evidenced.

And as for the differences between the substance of Exodus 20 and the substance of Deuteronomy 5, they are due to the fact that Moses formulated the second set himself in a manner that would further clarify them to the Israelites:

> . . . the Ten Commandments written in this passage [Exodus 20] are the words of God without addition or subtraction, and they alone are written on the two [stone] tablets. It is not as the Gaon [Saadiah] said, that *Remember* was written on one set of tablets (which were smashed by Moses) and *Keep* on the second set of tablets. Rather, the Ten Commandments written in [Deut. 5] are the words of Moses. And the decisive proof is that there it is written twice *as the Lord your God has commanded you.*

Ibn Ezra has still more to say on this, but we take our leave at this point.

David Kimhi, Nahmanides, and Gersonides

Of the remaining important medieval commentators, we may mention here only three. In the thirteenth century a Provençal scholar, a scion of scholars, Rabbi David Kimhi (known by the acronym Radak), achieved a remarkable synthesis of the French traditionalism and Spanish philology in his Bible commentaries and grammatical works. His commentary, which does appear in scattered English versions, combines acute stylistic analysis, historical interest, theology, and anti-Christian polemic in a fascinating reflection of the concerns of Diaspora Jewry. In his comment on Psalm 97.11, for example, he reassures himself and his readers that the pious of Israel will ultimately find their reward for remaining steadfast in observing the covenant in Exile; the wicked, their tormenters, will ultimately be humiliated. He reads the Psalms on two levels, the historical-contextual and the contemporary, or mid-rashic. Two entire Psalms, 129 and 146, he interprets as allegories of the Exile.

Another thirteenth-century commentator, Rabbi Moses ben Nahman, Ramban or Nahmanides, turned to Biblical exegesis per se only after a long career as a leading Talmudist and spiritual leader of Spanish Jewry. Most of his great commentary to the Torah, which has been translated into English by Charles Chavel, he composed in the land of Israel, after he had been expelled from Spain by Christian authorities who were insulted by his polemics. His Torah commentary is distinguished by a number of features. It is the first major Bible commentary to introduce the new mystical teachings of Kabbalah. He also cites the works of Rashi and Ibn Ezra regularly, often to refute them. Ramban shows a marked preference for Rashi, who was more spiritual than his colder, more rational counterpart, Ibn Ezra. Ramban will criticize Ibn Ezra, for example, for providing a correct grammatical analysis, but stopping short of interpreting a deeper significance than the surface meaning of the text. Ramban characteristically reads the text on several levels, engaging extensively in allegory, too, something that had been rarely done since the Roman period with Philo of Alexandria and Rabbi Akiba.

Finally, we should mention the man who broke with the style of the typical Jewish commentary and supplanted the logic of the rabbis, Rabbi Levi ben Gershon, Ralbag or Gersonides. Ralbag is known best as a fourteenth-century southern French philosopher in the tradition of Maimonides (discussed at length in Chapter Five), except that he wrote in Hebrew, attempting to wrest an Aristotelian idiom out of the holy tongue. His commentaries on many of the later parts of the Bible are included in *Mikra'ot Gedolot,* but his maverick Torah commentary rarely is. In that work Ralbag introduced two major innovations. First, instead of writing a running commentary on the text, piece by piece, by which even the *peshat* commentaries hew to the pattern of the midrashim, he developed a more topical style. He divided the text into units of about a chapter or two. First, he would clarify the meaning of difficult words and idioms. Then he would present an interpretive paraphrase of the passage. Last, but certainly not least, he would list all the lessons that emerge from the passage in the areas of *mitzvot,* metaphysical truths, and ethics.

His other innovation is that, while he accepted the rabbinic laws and doctrines implicitly, he rejected the contemporary validity of the rabbis' methods of exegesis. He endeavored to derive all that the rabbis derived using more credible—to him—interpretive procedures based on logic. Some laws, for example, could be deduced from others because they all fit into the same legal paradigm. Ralbag's interest in the narratives of the Torah is didactic. The Biblical characters present us with models of good and bad behavior, and we are to learn the proper way of living by assessing those characters. This approach to the stories of heroes was a common one in medieval literature, where great figures were studied for the example of their behavior.

To sum up: After the extensive development of *aggadah* and *halakhah* through the interpretive method of Midrash, Jewish scholars in Arabic-speaking lands devoted more and more attention to the contextual, or *peshat,* method of interpretation. This approach required historical perspective, rationalism, and linguistic and literary sophistication. By dint of its fairly secular orientation, this method allowed Jewish interpreters to argue the meaning of Scripture on common ground with partisans of other faiths. We saw how the *peshat* approach emerged in the Orient and spread to Spain, where grammarians, such as Ibn Janah, and synthetic commentators , like Ibn Ezra, defined its decisive application to biblical studies. Simultaneous with Ibn Ezra, *peshat* surfaced as a major force in Bible commentary in France, where style and plain sense guided interpretation more than ever before. Later commentators, such as David Kimhi, Nahmanides, and Gersonides, assimilated the same overall method but each introduced special elements of his own interest. The following chart will summarize the various commentators we have discussed.

EARLY KARAITES	EARLY RABBANITE
Anan ben David (8th C.)	
Ben Zita (10th C.–Jerusalem?)	Saadiah Gaon (882–942)

SPAIN
Ibn Janah (early 11th C.)
Ibn Ezra (1089–1164)

FRANCE
Rashi (1040–1105)
Rashbam (1085?–1174?)

Eliezer of Beaugency (12th C.)
Joseph Bekhor Shor (12th C.)

SYNTHESIS
David Kimhi (1160?–1235?–Provence)
Nahmanides (1194–1270–Spain)
Gersonides (1288–1344–France)

Of the several commentators we have met in this chapter, though, only Rashi, Rashbam, Ibn Ezra, and Nahmanides will be found together in a standard edition of *Mikra'ot Gedolot* to the Torah. Positioned over against one another on the page, their voices generate a cacophony of difference and controversy. Let us imagine them discussing, for example, an enigma in Genesis 37.15. Jacob had sent Joseph, his younger, favored son, to find his brothers as they herded their flocks in the hills. Joseph was to locate them and bring back a report to their father. Dutifully, and perhaps naively, Joseph embarks on this mission, even though his brothers hate him and could conceivably take advantage of the opportunity to do him in. When Joseph doesn't find the brothers in Shechem, as his father had predicted, he began to meander. Suddenly, the text says, *A man found him. We might say:* A man? Where did he come from? Who is he?

RASHI: He is the angel Gabriel.

IBN EZRA: What? Where'd you get that from?

RASHI: From Midrash Tanhuma. This is the tradition that our sages have handed down to us.

IBN EZRA: Wait a second. Where does the text say anything about angels?

RASHI: You see, the verse says, *A man found him,* and, as everyone knows, in the Book of Daniel Gabriel is referred to as "the man." Same word.

IBN EZRA: You go to the Book of Daniel to explain this verse in Genesis? The *peshat* meaning is clearly: he was just an ordinary wayfarer, just what the text says, a man.

RASHBAM: I'm afraid you gentlemen are getting bogged down in the wrong, or at least a trivial, question. The interesting angle is: why does the text divert us from Joseph's inevitable confrontation with his brothers by introducing this episode about the man giving directions?

WE: Yeah, we were wondering the same thing. It creates suspense, doesn't it?

RASHBAM: You moderns are too obsessed with technique. The episode teaches us of the magnitude of Joseph's filial responsibility. Don't you think Joseph knew his brothers hated him?

WE: Well . . .

RASHBAM: Of course he knew. Yet, even after Joseph failed to find his brothers in Shechem, he made use of the wayfarer and asked him of his brothers' whereabouts. He persisted in fulfilling his father's request.

NAHMANIDES: Quite right, Rashbam. Joseph had good reason to give up the search, but he went out of his way to honor his father's wish. I don't think we should so glibly abandon the idea of the angel, however.

WE: You're a philosopher, and you take angels seriously?

NAHMANIDES: Don't be simpleminded. Angels aren't fairies with wings. They are human agents of God, "messengers" of God, as the Hebrew puts it. By elaborating on this episode of the strange wayfarer the Torah calls attention to this fellow. Obviously God has provided him to guide Joseph on his journey. The episode shows how human affairs are orchestrated behind the scenes by God.

WE: Oh. That does make sense. That guy couldn't have just flown out of the blue. So why didn't Rashi say all that?

NAHMANIDES: Rashi is very concise. You often have to reflect on what he's saying. It may sound simple, even silly, at first, but don't be deceived. I assure you there's usually something profound behind our teacher's remarks.

As the Middle Ages see the Jews become more cloistered and insecure, they return more and more to Midrash as a way of reading. One reason is surely spiritual: Midrash satisfies the soul, while *peshat* may tantalize the intellect. But there is at least one other reason that *peshat* lay dormant until the nineteenth century. Just as *peshat* needed the worldly disciplines of philosophy and linguistics in order to emerge in the first place, it needs those disciplines in order to proceed. Criticism and grammar demand learning and rigor that Midrash does not. When Jews turned inward to reinforce their collective ego, they devoted themselves more to the method that draws on the old heritage of Judaica, Midrash. Since the Enlightenment about a century or more ago, *peshat* has resurfaced as a major current in liberal Jewish learning. A few notable Jewish scholars began the historical-critical study of Bible during the nineteenth century, and by the middle of the twentieth century universities and Jewish seminaries were utilizing the fruits of archaeology, Semitic philology, and other academic disciplines to train a new generation of Jews in the practice of *peshat*.

WHERE TO GO FROM HERE

There is not a great deal of literature in English on Jewish Bible commentary of the Middle Ages, but two useful introductions are Bernard Casper's *Introduction to Jewish Bible Commentary* (New York: Thomas Yoseloff, 1960) and Louis Jacobs' *Jewish Biblical Exegesis* (New York: Behrman House, 1973), the latter of which provides extended passages from the sources in translation. For more information on the various commentators in brief, one may also consult articles in the *Jewish Encyclopedia* of 1905 and the *Encyclopaedia Judaica* of 1971. The article on "Bible Exegesis" by W. Bacher in the *Jewish Encyclopedia* is especially good.

The history of Spanish-Jewish Bible interpretation is surveyed in detail in the fine essay by Nahum Sarna, "Hebrew and Bible Studies in Medieval Spain," in Richard D. Barnett, ed., *The Sephardi Heritage,* vol. 1 (New York: Ktav Publishing House, 1971), pp. 323–66. For the development of medieval Hebrew linguistics in particular, one may consult Hartwig Hirschfeld's *Literary History of Hebrew Grammarians and Lexicographers* (London: Oxford University Press, 1926); also Salo W. Baron, *A Social and Religious History of the Jews,* vol. 6 (New York: Columbia University Press, 1958), pp. 235–313. A fine book on Saadiah Gaon is Henry Malter, *Saadia Gaon: His Life and Works* (New York: Hermon Press reprint, 1969). The polemical aspect of medieval Jewish Bible interpretation is particularly stressed in Erwin I. J. Rosenthal, "Medieval Jewish Exegesis: Its Character and Significance," *Journal of Jewish Studies* 9 (1964), pp. 265–81; and "The Study of the Bible in Medieval Judaism," in G. W. H. Lampe, ed., *The Cambridge History of the Bible,* vol. 2 (Cambridge: Cambridge University Press, 1969), pp. 252–79. The medieval rabbinic efforts at reconciling Scripture and truth is discussed in Marc Saperstein, *Decoding the Rabbis* (Cambridge, Mass.: Harvard University Press, 1982), especially pp. 1–20.

For Rashi, the best introduction is still Maurice Liber, *Rashi,* trans. Adele Szold (New York: Hermon Press reprint, 1970). A briefer presentation is Alexander Marx, "The Life and Work of Rashi," in H. L. Ginsberg, ed., *Texts and Studies,* vol. 1 (New York: Jewish Theological Seminary, 1941), pp. 9–30. A more comprehensive, albeit pedantic, volume is Esra Shereshevsky, *Rashi: The Man and His World* (New York: Sepher-Hermon Press, 1982). The nature of Rashi's methodology is analyzed in Sarah Kamin, "Rashi's Exegetical Categorization with Respect to the Distinction between *Peshat* and *Derash*," *Immanuel* 11 (Fall

1980), pp. 16–32; and in Benjamin Gelles, *Peshat and Derash in the Exegesis of Rashi* (Leiden: E. J. Brill, 1981). Rashi's Torah commentary can be found in two five-volume editions, an interlinear one edited by Abraham Ben Isaiah and Benjamin Sharfman, and a denser one with more explanation by M. Rosenbaum and A. M. Silbermann. The latter have also edited an edition of *Mikra'ot Gedolot* for later books of the Bible with Rashi's commentary in an English version.

The best way for the novice to study Rashi's commentary is to use a book such as Pinchas Doron's *The Mystery of Creation according to Rashi: A New Translation and Interpretation of Rashi on Genesis I–VI* (New York/Jerusalem, 1982), which gives the Hebrew, a translation, and an explanation in small sections. See also Chaim Pearl's collection, *Rashi: Commentary on the Pentateuch* (New York: Norton, 1970). Or find a teacher.

A fine overview of Abraham Ibn Ezra, in some detail, is presented in the Introduction to Etan Levine, ed., *Abraham Ibn Ezra's Commentary to the Pentateuch: Vatican Manuscript Vat. Ebr. 38* (Jerusalem: Makor Publishing, 1974), pp. 4–21. For essays on aspects of Ibn Ezra's Bible interpretation and philosophy, as well as Hebrew and English editions of his Isaiah commentary, see M. Friedlander, *Ibn Ezra Literature,* 4 vols. (London: The Society of Hebrew Literature, 1873–1877).

Those interested in Rabbi David Kimhi are served well by Frank E. Talmage, *David Kimhi: The Man and the Commentaries* (Cambridge, Mass.: Harvard University Press, 1975). For English editions of Kimhi's commentaries, see the references in Talmage, pp. 190–91. Nahmanides is treated in the popular book by Charles B. Chavel, *Ramban: His Life and Teachings* (New York: Philip Feldheim, 1960). Chavel has also produced a five-volume translation of Ramban's commentary on the Torah.

In connection with the study of medieval Jewish Bible interpretation, one may wish to read I. Husik's *A History of Mediaeval Jewish Philosophy* (New York: Meridian Books, 1958) and Beryl Smalley, *The Study of the Bible in the Middle Ages,* 2nd ed. (Notre Dame: University of Notre Dame Press, 1970), which deals with Christian interpretation primarily. Another useful backdrop on the trends of medieval literature is Ernst R. Curtius, *European Literature and the Latin Middle Ages* (New York: Bollingen Foundation, 1953).

If one wishes to study the Bible by way of the perspectives of various medieval commentators, one will be interested in the studies of Nehama Leibowitz: *Studies in Bereshit (Genesis), Studies in Shemot (The Book of Exodus), Studies in Vayikra (Leviticus), Studies in Bamidbar (Numbers),* and *Studies in Devarim (Deuteronomy),* all trans. by A. Newman (Jerusalem: World Zionist Organization, 1974–1980).

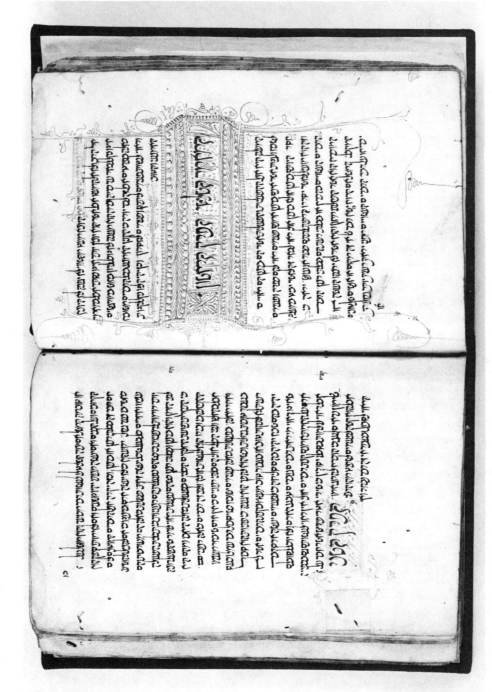

From Maimonides' *Guide for the Perplexed*, Spanish manuscript, 14th century.

CHAPTER FIVE

Medieval Jewish Philosophy

NORBERT M. SAMUELSON

WHAT IS JEWISH PHILOSOPHY?

The word "theology" is formed from two Greek words—*theos,* which means God, and *logos,* which means speech and/or an account. Hence, the original sense of the term "theology" was rational speech or thought about God.

As Aristotle used the term, theology was synonymous with what was subsequently called "metaphysics." More accurately, in Greek the term *metaphysica* means "after physics," which is the title given to that book of Aristotle that comes after his book, *Physics.* Aristotle himself called the topic of this book "theology."

Some works of medieval Muslim, Jewish, and Christian theology are simply instances of what we would call "metaphysics." But most theological works at this time were not merely metaphysics, and few, if any, presented complete metaphysical systems. Most works of medieval theology dealt with those problems in metaphysics in which there seemed to be a *conflict between what the author regarded as the dictates of reason and what he accepted as the dogmas of his religion,* which included more topics than questions about God. In this sense of the term, "theology" means the attempt to reconcile conflicts between philosophy and religion. I say "philosophy" rather than "metaphysics" because while most of the issues considered were topics in Aristotle's *Metaphysics,* the issues were not exclusively these. Problems in logic, physics, psychology, astronomy, and ethics also were discussed under the title "theology."

261

In modern times the term "philosophy" has come to denote a rather limited set of topics and approaches to these topics. For the Greeks as well as for medieval scholars the term "philosophy" had a broader meaning. What I here call "philosophy" in the medieval sense of the term was most often called *'iyyun* in medieval Hebrew, *nathar* in medieval Arabic, and *scientia* in medieval Latin. All three medieval terms signify human or rational (as opposed to divine or revealed) knowledge in general, rather than any specific kind of such knowledge. In other words, most courses that are offered in modern universities would qualify prima facie as instances of what medieval scholars called "philosophy."

All medieval theology presupposed multiple purported sources of truth—one of which was religious—and an apparent conflict between them. For the medieval Jewish philosophers the presupposed candidates as sources of authority for truth statements were called "Torah" and "philosophic thought." By "Torah" they meant the entire tradition of rabbinic and biblical literature. By "philosophic thought" they meant a tradition of philosophy that was either Neoplatonic or atomistic★ or Aristotelian in origin. The goal of the theologian was to examine those areas in which Torah and philosophic thought seemed to be in conflict, in order to show that either the conflict was apparent or, if the conflict was real, that a particular understanding of the Torah should be followed. On the surface there were undeniable conflicts between the teachings of philosophy and the teachings of rabbinic Judaism. Greek philosophy seemed to speak of an eternal universe; rabbinic Judaism seemed to speak of Creation *ex nihilo*. Greek philosophy seemed to affirm a God whose sole activity was self-contemplation; biblical and rabbinic Judaism seemed to posit a God who stopped the sun, spoke through a bush, and even wrote on tablets of stone. Certainly, both could not be right, and the cultured Jew of the Islamic world knew it. The Muslim faced a similar problem. It is this conflict between religion and philosophy that was the central theme of both Islamic and Jewish philosophy in the Middle Ages.

Since the general topic of Jewish philosophy was how to cope with the apparent conflict between what Jewish faith and what science claimed

★ Throughout this chapter we will have occasion to refer to atomism. Atomism is a general kind of scientific-philosophic position that claims that everything in the universe is a composite of ultimate, indivisible substances called "atoms," that these atoms are in every respect, except location in time and space, identical, and that all differences between composite entities are reducible to differences in the number and configuration of their constituent atoms. What passes as science in most American high schools is a version of atomism. Most science-philosophy in the Muslim world before the twelfth century also was atomist.

to be true, the specific subject matter of Jewish philosophy varied as the science varied. Furthermore, the science tended to be different in different cultures at different times. Hence, Jewish philosophy is different in different cultures at different times. Below is a chart that lists the major works in medieval Jewish philosophy divided according to time, place, and primary philosophic/scientific influence.

MAJOR FIGURES AND BOOKS IN MEDIEVAL JEWISH PHILOSOPHY

CENTURY	LOCATION	PHILOSOPHIC BACKGROUND	PHILOSOPHER	MAJOR WORK IN PHILOSOPHY
10th	Eastern Muslim Empire	Kalam	Isaac Israeli	The Book of Elements
			David Ben Merwan Al-Mukammas	The Twenty Chapters
			Saadia Ben Joseph Al-Fayyumi	The Book of Beliefs and Opinions
11th	Western Muslim Empire	Neoplatonism	Solomon Ibn Gabirol	The Fountain of Life
12th			Bahya Ibn Pakudah	The Duties of the Heart
			Abraham Bar Hiyya	The Logic of the Soul
			Joseph Ibn Zaddik	The Microcosm
			Judah Halevi	The Kuzari
		Aristotle	Abraham Ibn Daud	The Exalted Faith
			Moses Maimonides	The Guide of the Perplexed
13th	Christian Europe		Hillel Ben Samuel	The Rewards of the Soul
14th			Levi Gersonides	The Wars of the Lord
			Hasdai Ben Abraham Crescas	The Light of the Lord

MUSLIM SOURCES FOR JEWISH THEOLOGY

The Roman Emperor Justinian closed the Greek schools of philosophy in Athens in 529 C.E. By that time, however, the centers for Greek philosophy had moved from Greece to the Near East, with major schools in Alexandria, Egypt, and Antioch, Syria, and the most influential writings in Hellenistic philosophy and medicine were being translated from Greek or Latin into Syriac. Under the Abbasid Muslim dynasty, between 750 and 850 C.E., these works were again translated, this time into Arabic. In the realm of medicine the leading authorities were Hippocrates and Galen. Euclid, Archimedes and Ptolemy dominated mathematics and astronomy, while Aristotle, as understood through the commentaries of Theophrastus and Alexander of Aphrodisias, dominated the other branches of Muslim philosophy or science. The most important Muslim commentators on Aristotle's works were Al-Farabi and Ibn Sina (Avicenna), and at a later time in the western Muslim Empire, Ibn Bajja and Ibn Rushd (Averroës).

The first major theologians of Islam were the Kadariya and the Jabariya schools. Out of the school of the Kadariya in 723 C.E. developed first a group known as the Mutazila, centered in the city of Basra, and then other groups of theologians, all of whom are commonly referred to as "Mutakallimun." All of these groups shared in common the material atomism of Democritus, together with elements of Stoicism. They all viewed Aristotelian philosophy as a threat to religious faith and considered the defense of the true faith to be the primary function of theology. The Mutakallimun dominated all Jewish and Muslim thought in the eastern part of the Muslim Empire, and their influence, at least among Jewish philosophers, can be found as late as the fifteenth century. However, in the tenth century, in the eastern Muslim Empire, major opposition arose to the Mutakallimun based on the earlier teachings of Al-Ashari (born 873 C.E.). The name of this new sect of Muslim theologians was the Ashariya. The most notable example of the Ashariya was Ghazali (born in the middle of the eleventh century). Basically, these Muslim philosophers were less optimistic about the value of philosophy, more hostile to Aristotle, and more influenced by Stoicism than were the Mutakallimun.

It should be noted that the lines between all of these theologians, although significant, were not as great as this outline might suggest to the modern reader. None of these theologians was totally against philosophy, and all were committed Muslims. Similarly, the lines between

Muslim atomists, Aristotelians, and Neoplatonists were less sharp than would be assumed by a reader familiar only with the Greek sources. This was particularly the case with the views of the Muslim and Jewish Aristotelians and Neoplatonists.

Through the impact of the Muslim philosophers just noted, rabbinic Judaism developed its first philosophic theologians. It is convenient to categorize them by the philosophic tradition out of which they emerged. First is the group that was most strongly influenced by the Kalam, which is the name given to the philosophy of the Mutakallimun. Here we find three notable Jewish philosophers arising in the tenth century in the eastern Muslim Empire: Isaac Israeli, David Ben Merwan Al-Mukammas, and Saadia Ben Joseph Al-Fayyumi. Of the three the most influential was Saadia. Second, in the eleventh and twelfth centuries in the western Muslim Empire there arose a number of notable Jewish philosophers who were Neoplatonists. These theologians include Solomon Ibn Gabirol, Bahya Ibn Pakuda, Abraham Bar Hiyya, Joseph Ibn Zaddik, Judah Halevi, and Moses and Abraham Ibn Ezra. Although all of these thinkers had a great deal of impact on subsequent Jewish thought in any number of areas (most notably poetry, prayer, and biblical commentaries), philosophically, the most influential of these Neoplatonists was Judah Halevi. Finally, in the twelfth century in the western Muslim Empire, the Aristotelians won dominance over the Mutakallimun of the eastern Muslim Empire and in consequence, Aristotelian philosophy gained ascendency among cultured Jews as well. The first Aristotelian Jewish philosopher was Abraham Ibn Daud. The most influential Aristotelian was Moses Ben Maimon (Maimonides).

In Christian Europe, because of the influence of Maimonides, to the extent that Jews were concerned with philosophy they were concerned with Aristotelian philosophy. The most notable of the Jewish philosophers in Christian Europe were Hillel Ben Samuel in Italy in the thirteenth century, Levi Ben Gerson (Gersonides) in Provence in the fourteenth century, and Hasdai Ben Abraham Crescas and his pupil, Joseph Albo, in Spain in the last half of the fourteenth and the first half of the fifteenth centuries. Of these Jewish theologians the most influential were Gersonides and Crescas. We shall now look in some detail at the individual philosophers and their work.

PHILOSOPHY IN THE TENTH-CENTURY EASTERN EMPIRE

Although the first notable exponent of rabbinic Judaism who was a philosopher was Isaac Ibn Solomon Israeli (c. 855–c. 955), the first theologian of rabbinic Judaism to have an impact on the thought of the Jewish people was *Saadia Ibn Joseph Al-Fayyumi* (892–942). Originally, what had brought this Egyptian rabbinic scholar prominence was *The Book of the Seasons,* a work about a legal dispute that arose over the determination of the Jewish calendar. However, his most important work was *The Book of Beliefs and Opinions (Sefer Emunot Vedeot),* which was written as a philosophic, theological polemic against the Karaites.

By the tenth century the Karaite movement had grown sufficiently in numbers and strength to represent a serious threat to rabbinic Judaism. The leaders of rabbinic Judaism excommunicated the Karaites, and Saadia in particular led a conceptual battle against them. As noted above, it was for this reason he wrote his *Book of Beliefs and Opinions.*

Saadia begins *The Book of Beliefs and Opinions* with the following words:

> Blessed be the Lord, the God of Israel, who properly is regarded as the clear truth, who affirms as clear truth for thinking people the existence of their minds through which their senses find what clearly exists, by means of which their views are known to be correct. (Introduction, Introductory Treatise, I)

Note that this prayer is more than an invocation; implicitly it begins Saadia's argument for the legitimacy of Jewish philosophy. God is praised as the ultimate standard of truth; as such He guarantees truth in two ways. First, as *the* truth He is the standard to which all truth claims can be compared. Second, He is the creator of the tools by which human beings can discover truth. Our senses give us impressions of what is in the world, and our reason enables us to form judgments from these impressions of what is true. Since God is the creator of the senses and of human reason, tools whose natural function is to direct human beings to natural knowledge, if these tools were not reliable—if their proper use led people to error and not to truth—then God Himself would not be true. Hence, that God Himself is true entails the fundamental reliability of human thought. Furthermore, those who seem to defend Jewish faith by denying the reliability of reason in fact do the opposite; in their ignorance they deny God's truth.

Further on in his introduction, Saadia adds the following prayer and comment:

> O you who study this book, may God set you straight. Know that we are investigating and speculating about subjects presented in our Torah with two intentions. One is to make clear to us what we actually know from God's prophets. Two is for us to reply to what has been argued against us concerning any of the subjects in our Torah. (Introduction, Introductory Treatise, VI)

God is invoked to direct the intended readers—Jewish students of philosophy who will speculate about the positions presented in this book and the arguments supporting them—to understand both the arguments and their conclusions, so that they may attain true scientific knowledge and correct faith, which are for Saadia and those who followed him in Jewish philosophy the same thing. Then Saadia tells us that his study of Jewish belief has two purposes. The second is apologetic, viz., to defend the claims of Jewish faith against those who deny them (Karaites, Muslims, Christians, skeptics, and so on). The first and primary goal is to clarify Jewish faith for the faithful. Because revealed dogma is directed at a wide spectrum of people who differ radically in their intellectual abilities and scientific background, the way in which the prophets recorded their revelation in the Hebrew Scriptures necessarily and intentionally is vague. Saadia's primary intention, shared by all subsequent Jewish philosophers, is to clarify what those dogmas mean for those committed Jews who have the ability and the background to understand revelation with a higher degree of clarity than is possible for most Jews.

ELEVENTH- AND TWELFTH-CENTURY
WESTERN EMPIRE JEWISH NEOPLATONISTS

In the eleventh century, Muslim Spain broke off from the Abbasid dynasty and established its own independent caliphate under the purported Ummayad descendant, Abd Al-Rahman III. As the central Muslim Empire declined, Andalusian Muslim Spain flourished. Under the patronage of Hasdai Ibn Shaprut, who was an advisor to Abd Al-Rahman III, Menahem Ben Saruk wrote on Hebrew Grammar, Dunash Ben Labrat wrote poetry, and *Solomon Ibn Gabirol* (1021–1058) wrote Jewish philosophy. His major philosophical work was the *Fountain of Life,* which has survived only in Latin translation *(Fons Vitae).* This work is a Neoplatonic text that deals with the theory of the overflow *(hashefa),* the nature of the soul, and the theory of knowledge as it relates to knowledge of matter and form, the "Active Word or Will," and God designated as "the First Essence."

Ibn Gabirol was followed by *Bahya Ibn Joseph Ibn Pakudah,* who lived some time between 1090 and 1156. His major theological work, *Duties of the Heart (Hovot Halevavot),* closely paralleled the thought of Ghazali. Although Bahya was not himself a mystic, this work had a great deal of influence on subsequent Jewish mystics in their thought about morality. Also under the influence of Muslim sufis, *The Duties of the Heart* lists and analyses ten fundamental principles of Judaism intended to lead the individual Jew to a pure religion in service to God. The ten topics that Bahya lists are God's unity, Creation, the service of God, trust in God, God as the ultimate end of all human action, submission to God, repentance, self-examination, asceticism or the rejection of worldly pleasures, and the love of God. In this discussion of God's unity he emphasizes the attributes of power, wisdom, and life as the basic and minimal positive predications of God. However, like Al-Mukammas before him, he tends to emphasize the negative attributes of God similar to the way in which Maimonides would argue in his discussion of divine predicates.

Abraham Bar Hiyya, Joseph Ibn Zaddik, Judah Halevi, and Moses and Abraham Ibn Ezra all lived in Spain at approximately the same time as Bahya, and like Bahya they were strongly influenced by Neoplatonism. The single most important and influential Jewish theologian of this group was *Judah Halevi.* He was born in Toledo in the last quarter of the eleventh century at the time that the Christian king of Castile, Alphonso VI, captured Toledo from the Muslims. Halevi moved to Lucena where he studied Jewish law under Alfasi and later lived in Cordova where he was employed as a physician. Some time after 1140 he set out on a pilgrimage to "the Holy Land." His journey is recorded as far as Cairo and then Tyre and Damascus, but after he left Damascus for Jerusalem no more is known of him. According to legend, an Arab horseman killed him with a spear as he was singing his "Ode to Zion" at the gates of "the Holy City."

Halevi wrote one work in philosophical theology entitled *The Kuzari.* Influenced by Ghazali, as well as Neoplatonism, Halevi intended this work to be a defense of traditional rabbinic Judaism against the implied threat of both Islam and Christianity, and even more seriously, against the threat of what he called "Philosophy." In its external form *The Kuzari* is an account of how in the eighth or ninth century a king dreamed an angel told him that while his religious intentions were acceptable to God, his religious practice was not. In order to find a proper form of religious practice, the king consulted first with a philosopher, then with a Christian sage, and then with a Muslim doctor. Finding satisfaction from none of them, he turned to a "Jewish *haver,*" in whose religion the king finally found a practice acceptable to God. The body of the book is an account of the basic "truths" of Judaism in opposition to the purported truths of Islam, Christianity, and Philosophy.

Among the topics discussed in *The Kuzari* are the contention that the God of Israel known as YHWH is not the god of whom philosophers speak; the nature of divine attributes; the authenticity of the Torah and rabbinic Jewish tradition over all claims of revelation and religious traditions; the superiority of the land of Israel, the Hebrew language, and the Jewish people over all other lands, languages, and peoples; the nature of prophecy; ethics and human choice; and scattered discussions of physics, astronomy, and psychology. In any number of respects Halevi's *Kuzari* is the most original of all the works of medieval Jewish philosophical theologians. Perhaps what is most unusual in his writing is his emphasis on arguments based on purportedly authentic and ancient traditions rather than on syllogisms or mathematical reasoning, and his view that the land, language, and people of Israel are naturally superior to all other lands, languages, and peoples. According to Halevi, not only are species of creatures and spheres related in a hierarchy such that one is better than another, but that within the sphere of the Active Intellect★ there is a hierarchy of perfect places on Earth, and within the human species there is a hierarchy of perfect subspecies or races or families. Furthermore, languages are structured in a hierarchy of relative degrees of perfection. Just as what makes a human superior to other animals is that all humans have the possibility of reasoning even if they do not reason, and no other animal can rise beyond sense information, so Jews are superior to all other kinds of human beings in that Jews and only Jews have the possibility of being prophets. As the potentiality to prophecy places the Jews in a higher category than other humans, so prophecy marks off the land of Israel and the Hebrew language from other lands

---

★ In medieval astronomy the universe was divided into a series of spheres, each contained within the other. Each sphere was supposed to be governed by an intellect in the same way that a human body is governed by its soul. The intellect of the lowest or most central sphere, the one that contains the planet Earth, was called the "Active Intellect."

and languages, since, according to Halevi, prophecy is given only to Jews who speak Hebrew in the land of Israel.

Let us look in more detail at one part of Halevi's discussion of the prophecy in *The Kuzari*.

> The *haver* said: The conceptual characteristic *(ha'inyan hasikh-liy)* is what singles out the rational animal above all other animals. Necessarily there follows from it the improvement of individual character, home and state, which govern the rest of conduct and laws. (Bk. I, par. 35)

The ability to reason is what distinguishes human beings from lower species of creatures. The primary purpose of this function is to enable human beings to improve themselves, their families, and their homes by good conduct (moral theory) and their political state by good law (political theory). The ability to reason is a gift from God to the human species, which enables its members to have greater control over their lives and their world than is possible for any lower level of creature.

> If there exists a man (1) who goes through fire and is not harmed by it and/or who (2) endures without eating and is not hungry, and/or (3) there is a radiance *(zohar)* about his face at which the eye is not able to gaze, and/or (4) he becomes neither ill nor weak, and/or (5) when he reaches the end of his days he dies by his own will, just as someone will decide to go to bed to go to sleep and he will sleep at a certain time and a certain hour, (6) while at the same time he has knowledge of past and future, [viz.,] what was and will be, would not this separate [him] essentially from the virtue of human beings? (Bk. I, par. 41)

All six "wonders" mentioned are events attributed to Moses by Scripture and/or rabbinic tradition. According to Scripture, at Sinai Moses (1) passed through fire as he ascended the mountain, (2) went for forty days and nights without food or drink during the theophany, and (3) his face was radiant when he returned from the mountain. Furthermore, at the end of the Torah we are told that (4) even though he was 120 years old he had not aged at all (Deut. 34.7). Finally, since the Torah itself states what Moses knew, it follows that Moses knew the history of the world from the time of Creation at least through what would happen to Israel when it would conquer Canaan, i.e., (6) he had knowledge of both past and future beyond what a man could know by means of human reason. Furthermore, rabbinic tradition (viz., Midrash) tells us that Moses did not die like other human beings, where death is involuntary.

In Moses' case, (5) death was as much an act of choice as sleep is a choice given to ordinary human beings.

All of these wonders are taken to be facts, but they are not merely assumed to be facts. Instead, Halevi attempts to offer rational demonstrations that the words of the Torah are true because they are the revealed word of God, and the words of the rabbis are true because they constitute an accurate transmission of God's elaboration of the words of the Torah through Moses at Sinai. Given the truth of these reports, Halevi argues that a prophet like Moses must belong to a higher species of creature than does a human being. Just as a human belongs to a higher species than that of any other animal, because he can perform naturally acts that would be "wondrous" for animals to perform (i.e., beyond their possible talents), so for the same reason a prophet belongs to a higher species than that of any other human being. In other words, what prophets do seems to be wondrous because prophets seem to be humans, but in fact these are natural events performed by "superhuman" individuals. The following passage makes this understanding of the nature of prophecy more explicit:

> All of the prophets see things about which they testify to each other in the same way we do with our percepts. . . . These are states of affairs that we may not establish through logical thought. Hence, the philosophers of Greece refuted [the claims of the prophets] because logical thought rejects that the like of which it has not seen. But the prophets affirmed [these claims] because they were not able to deny what they saw with the spiritual eye, which is a superiority which [God] gave to them. . . . If the philosophers of Greece had seen the prophets in their state of prophecy and with their demonstrations, the philosophers would admit [the veracity of the visions of the prophets] and would seek some ways by which logical thought would confirm how man realizes this grade. (Bk. V, par. 3)

By means of prophecy we know claims that go beyond anything that can be either affirmed or denied by the limited powers of human reason (e.g., by reason we could not know the history of the human race prior to the age of Noah). Because pagan philosophers come from nations that lack prophets, they have no experience of either prophecy or of prophets. Hence, because of their limited opportunities, by means of an invalid generalization they reject the truth of these superhuman prophetic claims. In other words, in their ignorance they reason that since they have never had such experiences, no one else could. But if they had been blessed, as Israel had, with prophets, they would not misuse their rational talents to reject the claims of prophecy. Instead, they would use their intellects to attempt to understand how what otherwise is beyond them is nonetheless rationally and naturally possible. What prophecy claims cannot be known through reason but is nonetheless logically possible. In other cases, where we experience natural events that are unusual, the role of reason is to understand how what was experienced by the Jewish people is possible.

Halevi has been accused of being antirational, but the above passages should make it clear that this charge is a misreading of his words. To be sure, Halevi believes that there are limitations on what human reason can achieve. But within its range of applicability, Halevi is as committed to the validity of reason as was Saadia. Furthermore, for Halevi, reason is a vital tool by which mere mortals can approximate an understanding of what prophets have pointed to beyond human comprehension. Even in Halevi's case, intellect is a divine gift through which human beings can gain some glimpse of divine truth.

Halevi has been called the first "Zionist," but this is a misnomer. Halevi's emphasis on the Hebrew language and a return to the land of Israel was based on a notion of an inherent superiority of this land and language over all other places and speech. While the modern Zionists share with Halevi the special love as Jews for Israel's land and language, they do not share either his racial theories about the Jewish people or his judgment that this land and this language are inherently superior to other lands and languages. However, there is no question that the writing of Halevi had profound influence upon the conceptual development of the different forms of contemporary Zionism.

TWELFTH-CENTURY WESTERN EMPIRE JEWISH ARISTOTELIANS

The first Jewish Aristotelian philosopher was *Abraham Ibn Daud* (1110–1180), who was born slightly later than Halevi in Toledo, also Halevi's birthplace. Ibn Daud's major work in philosophy was *The Exalted Faith(Ha-emunah Haramah)*. He also wrote a historical work entitled *The Book of Tradition (Sefer Hakabbalah)* and a manuscript on astronomy which has been lost. *The Exalted Faith* is a study in Aristotelian philosophy understood through a tradition of commentators that culminates in Al-Farabi and Ibn Sina (Avicenna). Ibn Daud divided this work on Jewish theology into two main divisions. The first deals with scientific or purely philosophic issues. The kinds of questions discussed belong to the disciplines of physics, psychology, and astronomy. This section, the first part of *The Exalted Faith,* deals only with philosophic or scientific principles that Ibn Daud thought were necessary preconditions for correct Jewish belief. In the second section, which consists of the last two parts of this work, Ibn Daud turned to what he judged to be the correct Jewish beliefs. The list of fundamental or root doctrines *(ikkarim)* of rabbinic Judaism with which Ibn Daud dealt may be summarized as follows: While we know something about what God does and that God is one and incorporeal, we do not know what these or any other predicates affirmed of God mean literally. In addition, Ibn Daud identified Aristotelian intelligences with biblical angels, constructed a proof of the existence of angels based on this identification, and offered a defense of rabbinic tradition and law, which involved Ibn Daud in an account of the nature of prophecy, dreams, human choice, and ethics.

Ibn Daud introduced the Aristotelian language that was used and taken for granted in all Jewish philosophy, but *Moses Ibn Maimon,* known by his acronym Rambam or *Maimonides* (1135–1204), is perhaps the most influential Jewish philosophical theologian who has yet arisen, because of his impact on subsequent generations of both Jewish and gentile religious thought. He was born in Cordova, but as a result of the conflict in that area between the Almoravids and the Almohades, Maimonides and his family emigrated from Andalusia to Fez, Morocco, and from Fez to Old Cairo or Fostat in Egypt. Until the death of Moses' younger brother David in the Indian Ocean on a business trip, the family occupation was trading precious stones. After his brother's death Maimonides gave up this business and practiced medicine. His original fame was based on the fact that he was appointed physician to Alfadhil, the grand vizier of Saladin, in the Ayyubid Egyptian Muslim dynasty centered in Fostat. In consequence of his high position with the non-Jewish government of Egypt, he also was appointed by the Egyptian Jewish community to be their head under the title *nagid.*

As *nagid,* Maimonides gained his reputation as one of the great masters of Jewish law *(halakhah).* His major halakhic works included a collection of responsa or letters dealing with specific issues in Jewish law, the most famous of which is his letter to the Yemenite scholar, Jacob Al-Fayyumi, on Jewish persecution. Maimonides also wrote a commentary on the Mishnah and a code of Jewish law entitled *Mishneh Torah* or *Yad Hahazakah.* Until this day his code is one of the three most important compilations of rabbinic law and unquestionably had more influence on subsequent Jewish life than any other work produced either by Maimonides himself or by any other medieval Jew. (See the discussion in Chapter Two, "Talmud.") Of particular interest for our purposes is the commentary on the tractate *Avot,* in which Maimonides applied Aristotelian ethical concepts to explain the miscellaneous moral statements of the Tannaim, and his commentary on the tenth chapter of the tractate Sanhedrin in which Maimonides listed what he regarded to be the thirteen root beliefs of rabbinic Judaism.

Maimonides' specifically philosophical-theological writings include a treatise on logic (entitled *Millot Hahiggayon,* "Words of Logic" in English) and *The Guide of the Perplexed* (henceforth referred to simply as "the Guide"). The Guide itself was first translated into Hebrew by Judah Al-Harizi (after 1190) and then by Samuel Ibn Tibbon under the title *Moreh Nevuchim* (1204). Of the two translations, that of Ibn Tibbon is the more important. The Arabic original was published with a French translation and notes by Solomon Munk (1856–66). As was the custom of Maimonides' time the Arabic was written in characters of the Hebrew alphabet. Although transliterations into Arabic letters probably were made, Maimonides himself opposed this activity since he did not desire the Muslims to become familiar with the content of the Guide. There are also two modern English translations, one by M. Friedlander and the other by S. Pines.

At least in its external form the Guide was not written as a treatise on theology. Rather, it is a very long letter to his friend and student, Rabbi Joseph Ibn Aknin, of Ceuta in the Maghreb. Rabbi Joseph had spent time in study with Maimonides in Fostat. In the course of their work together Joseph had become perplexed over theological matters. As these perplexities arose, Maimonides would resolve them for his student. However, business matters forced Joseph to return home, and many of his questions remained unanswered. The primary stated purpose of the Guide was to answer specific perplexities of Rabbi Joseph. The Guide is first and foremost a letter, but a letter of a very special kind. When a rabbi in a distant place had a difficult legal question that he could not answer, he raised his question with a leading rabbi and the legal master sent an answer or responsum. The answer became not only a particular answer to a particular rabbi, but had the standing of a major legal judgment for all of the Jewish community. Inevitably, this legal responsa by a single rabbi was published for all subsequent rabbis to consider in their own legal deliberations. Similarly, Maimonides was not only a leading rabbi in legal matters, but also a master of theology. Hence it was inevitable that the particular answer or responsum that Maimonides wrote to a particular Rabbi Joseph Ibn Aknin would achieve the status of a major theological judgment for all of the Jewish community and eventually would be published, as it was in 1190. Maimonides recognized that this would happen, and so he addressed his letter not only to Ibn Aknin but to all those like him.

What it meant to be "like" Ibn Aknin is the following: You are a rabbi, which is to say that you have professional knowledge of and personal commitment to rabbinic Judaism. At the same time you have some smattering of knowledge of general theology and philosophy. In other words you are a reasonably well-informed amateur scientist in the medieval sense of that term. You are somewhat familiar with the corpus of works by Aristotle as interpreted by Alexander of Aphrodisias, Themistius, and Averroës. Also you are familiar with Al-Farabi's work on logic and the work of Ibn Sina and Ibn Bajja. Furthermore, you might be familiar with the works of Abu Bark Al-Razi, Isaac Israeli, and Joseph Ibn Zaddik (Maimonides called him "Joseph the Hasid"). However, the writings of these latter three thinkers were not highly regarded by Maimonides since either he had read them and did not like them, or he might have heard good things about them but was not sufficiently moved to read them.*

It is important to note that Ibn Aknin's knowledge of general philosophy or science is not comparable to his rabbinic knowledge, and in Maimonides' judgment it is his lack of knowledge that is a major reason for Rabbi Joseph's perplexity. However, we do not know how lacking Ibn Aknin was in this regard.

A second major reason for Rabbi Joseph's perplexity is that he did not know how to distinguish between those terms and sections in the Torah that are to be understood literally and those that must be interpreted in order to grasp the intended meaning of revelation. Hence, the first topic of the Guide which occupies most of its chapters is Maimonides' discussion of the meaning of individual terms and sections of the Torah as to whether or not they should be understood literally, and where they are not to be taken literally, how they are to be understood. The other general topics discussed in the Guide include: how to understand predicates affirmed of God; the meaning of the various names of God as distinct from His predications; proofs that God exists, is one, and is incorporeal; the nature of angels as separate intellects and of astronomy and cosmology in general; various purported demonstrations that the universe is eternal or was created out of nothing (ex nihilo, yesh meayin); the nature and degrees of non-Mosaic prophecy; various related ethical issues, such as the nature of divine knowledge and providence;

* See Maimonides' letter to Samuel Ibn Tibbon, edited by Alexander Marx, in the Jewish Quarterly Review, n.s. 25, pp. 378–80.

the origin of human error and ignorance; and the existence and extent of human choice. The final topic considered in the Guide is the general nature of the designated six hundred and thirteen laws of the Torah, in terms of a classification of the different kinds of laws, and a general account of why the Torah contains such laws.

Except for the meaning of biblical terms and the classification of laws, Maimonides' discussion of these topics in the Guide was not altogether straightforward in the way that it was in those works of medieval rabbinic philosophy that both preceded and succeeded the Guide. The legalist Maimonides was aware of and concerned about the rabbinic dictum that "Whoever considers four things does not deserve to come into the world [namely], what is above, what is below, what is in front, and what is behind" (Babylonian Talmud, Hagigah 11b). All medieval rabbis understood these four things to be metaphysics, demonology, speculation about when the Messiah will come and the nature of the messianic age, and cosmology or the nature of the universe at and/or before the creation of this world. In other words Maimonides did not want to violate any rabbinic law—he was writing a manuscript that dealt with metaphysics and cosmology among other matters, and it seemed that the law prohibited this enterprise. As Maimonides understood this law the rabbis had prohibited public teaching of these four topics. However these topics *could* be taught if, and only if, it were carried out privately on a one-to-one basis where the student could grasp what was being taught, the teacher said not more than the student asked, and in giving answers the teacher spoke only in "hints" and "flashes." Maimonides based his permission to write his philosophical manuscript in this way on the parallel rabbinic dictum, "Do not inquire about things that are too marvellous for you; do not investigate what is hidden from you; inquire into things that are permitted to you; you have no business with marvels" (B.T., Hagigah 13a; also see the Guide I, 32).

According to Maimonides' reading of this latter imperative you may not study what is beyond you. However, with care in the way suggested above, you may study what is not too difficult for you. In this way Maimonides maintained that his Guide did not violate the *halakhah*. The rabbis wanted to prevent people who were not able to understand philosophic matters from reading them, for if they did read what was beyond them, then one of two equally disastrous consequences would follow. Either the unqualified reader would believe what he misread and by so doing become an idolater, or he would continue in his true belief but would mistakenly attribute heresy to the author of the book that he had misread. In one case the reader would suffer and in the latter case the author, for example, Jeremiah (Guide II, 37) would suffer. Maimonides agreed with these rabbis, and in order to comply with the spirit as well as the letter of their dicta, he addressed the Guide to, and only to, people who knew as much as Ibn Aknin. In order to prevent anyone less qualified from reading his theological responsum, Maimonides took the following preventive measures: No hidden "secrets of the Torah" are discussed at length. Rather all discussions are given in mere subject headings *(rashei perakim)*, i.e., in outline form. In this way the Guide merely "hints" at its subject matter. Furthermore, he did not deal with his "hidden things" in any topical order. Instead, the important topics were dispersed throughout the text. In this way the topics were dealt with only in what Maimonides called "flashes." This technique was based on the assumption that the person qualified to read the Guide would have a good memory, whereas the unqualified person would not. Since the meaning of a given point is only hinted at, the unqualified reader would not understand a "secret" when it appeared. However, even if occasionally he would understand what was being said, he would not remember it by the time the next occurrence of the same topic arose.

Furthermore, Maimonides placed his important discussions of hidden matters only in the middle of the body of the text. Maimonides apparently assumed that the unqualified reader might read the beginning of the book and then, once he was sufficiently bored, would put it away, or he might glance at the end of the book before he put it down. However, in the case of the qualified reader who not only had the proper background, but the natural virtues and good fortune to be able to sit for long periods of time and read the text word by word without skipping, he, and he alone, would read the Guide in the middle sections where the subject matter is philosophic and the "secrets" are revealed. Finally, Maimonides tells us (Guide I, Introduction) that he would intentionally contradict himself in such a way that where these contradictions appear, only the qualified reader would know the intention of the author:

> The seventh cause [of the contradictions that can be found in the book is the following]: Concerning statements about very deep subjects it is necessary to hide some [parts] of their meaning and to uncover other [parts]. At times it will be necessary for one statement to follow from statements about [the deep subject] on the basis of assuming one premise, while in another place it is necessary that statements about [the subject] follow on the basis of assuming a premise that contradicts the first premise. And it is necessary [in these cases] that the masses [*al-*

jumhur in Arabic, *he-hamon* in Ibn Tibbon's Hebrew translation] in no way should sense the contradiction between them. Thus, it is necessary that the author should do something to hide it [Ibn Tibbon's translation reads that the author should use a *tahbulah*—a stratagem, trick or clever device to hide it; the Arabic says *fi akhba dhaliki,* which implies but does not explicitly state the use of a *tahbulah* in every respect]. (Guide I, Introduction)

This paragraph occurs near the end of the introduction where Maimonides enumerates seven causes for contradiction in any book, but later in the introduction he mentions this seventh cause as one of two reasons for contradictions that intelligent, qualified readers will discover in the Guide. Hence, Maimonides tells us that he will present arguments in some places based on one premise and arguments in other places based on a different premise that contradicts the first premise, and he will do everything he can to prevent anyone who is not qualified to read his book from catching the contradiction. Maimonides was so skillful in his obedience to the rabbinic prohibition against publicly making known the secrets of the Torah that to this day, while it is not difficult to say what Maimonides said on any given topic, it is at best extremely difficult to say what Maimonides *meant* to say on any given topic! In fact, the next three centuries of Jewish philosophical theology were occupied by the interpretation of Maimonides' meaning and the reactions that these interpretations aroused.

Part of the discussion of what Maimonides meant to say in the Guide involves a debate over the relationship between the Guide and the Mishneh Torah, his great law code. Everyone agrees that the former was intended exclusively for Jewish philosophers and the latter for all Jews. The question is whether or not Maimonides intended to say the same thing to both audiences, and if he did not, which work reflects Maimonides' true beliefs. Among those scholars who believe that Maimonides' two masterpieces make different claims, some have said that in the Guide Maimonides is a committed, rabbinic Jew pretending to be an Aristotelian (i.e., the Mishneh Torah exhibits his true beliefs) in order to sustain the faith of Jewish philosophers, while the others have said that in the Mishneh Torah Maimonides is an Aristotelian pretending to be a committed rabbinic Jew (i.e., the Guide exhibits his true beliefs) in order to uplift the minds of ordinary Jews. A few scholars have hinted at the possibility that he was neither an Aristotelian nor an orthodox rabbinic Jew but was a kabbalist (following in the tradition of Ibn Sina), and he tried in *both* works to uplift the spirits of the Jews. However, the current dominant view among scholars is that there is no real conflict between what Maimonides says in both works, and that Maimonides honestly believed that true philosophy and authentic rabbinic Judaism are in total agreement with each other.

Thirteenth- through Fifteenth-Century Christian Europe

In general, the unifying theme of all works of medieval Jewish philosophy after Maimonides is Maimonides' Guide. All of these works presuppose that the reader is familiar with the Guide and on the basis of this familiarity the author discusses either issues with the Guide itself or questions touched upon but not explained in Maimonides' great theological responsum.

Of those Jewish theologians who defended Aristotelian science the greatest was *Levi Ben Gerson* who was known to Jews as Ralbag, the acronym of his Hebrew name, and to the Christians as *Gersonides*. As a highly technical and creative thinker, Gersonides ranks among the greatest figures in the history of Jewish philosophy. He was born at Bagnols in 1288 and died April 20, 1344. Most of his life was spent at the papal cultural centers in Orange and Avignon. He wrote sixteen major works in rabbinic, philosophic, mathematical, and medical fields in addition to various responsa, two of which have been preserved. His major work in philosophy was *The Wars of the Lord (Milhamot Adonai)*. In addition, (see Chapter Four), he wrote commentaries on the Pentateuch, the earlier Prophets, Job, Daniel, Song of Songs, Esther, Ecclesiastes, and Ruth (of standard rabbinic commentators on the Bible, only the Italian Seforno rivals his level of intellectual sophistication), a treatise on direct syllogisms, algebra, and astronomy; super-commentaries on the Middle Commentaries and Resumes of Ibn Rushd (Averroës); and an introduction to books i, iii, iv, and v of Euclid; an astrological note on the seven constellations; and a remedy for the gout. In the rabbinic field Ralbag wrote a commentary on the thirteen hermeneutic rules of Ishmael Ben Elisha and a commentary on the tractate Berakhot of the Babylonian Talmud.

By Christians, Gersonides was regarded as one of the major astronomer-astrologers of his time. To the Jews, Ralbag was the author of *The Wars of the Lord,* which was the most precise, thorough, and consistent of all pro-Aristotelian works in rabbinic philosophical theology. Gersonides ruled that "the Law cannot prevent us from considering to be true that which our reason urges us to believe" (*The Wars of the Lord,* p. 6,

Leipzig edition). It was his uncompromising adherence to this principle that led him to his particular conclusions on the questions of God's omniscience in opposition to Maimonides, and that was responsible for the subsequent condemnations of his works by certain Jewish scholars, such as Shem Tov Ibn Shem Tov, who changed the title of *Milhamot Adonai* (The Wars of the Lord) to *milhamot im adonai* (the wars with or against the Lord)! Among the more controversial theses of Gersonides is the following:

> [God] knows [contingent particulars] in one way and in another way He does not know them. . . . It is clear that the respect in which He knows them is the respect in which they are ordered and defined . . . and the respect in which He does not know them is the respect in which they are not ordered, which is the respect in which they are contingents. . . . In this respect it is impossible that they should be known.
> —THE WARS, treatise 3, chap. 4

If you ask what any particular thing is, then the answer will contain two parts, viz., a conjunction of general terms preceded by a term such as "that" or "this." For example, the definition of Socrates could be, "That hemlock-drinking Greek philosopher who was Plato's teacher." In the language of medieval philosophy, the general term, "hemlock-drinking Greek . . .," expresses the essence, nature, and definition of Socrates. But as such it is not identical with Socrates, since the essence expresses something universal or general while Socrates is a concrete particular. Socrates is not just "hemlock-drinking Greek . . ." Rather, he is *this* particular one. Now the essence of Socrates expresses *what* Socrates is, but it cannot express the essence concretized in matter, in time and space, as the existent individual, Socrates. Gersonides' claim is that both revelation and reason dictate that God knows every individual insofar as they have an essence, but insofar as there is more to their identity than their essence they cannot be known by anyone, including God. Among the many considerations that led Gersonides to this conclusion is the following:

> The following dilemma is unavoidable. Either [God] knows the alternative from a set of possibilities which He knew would be generated has been generated, or He knows that the actualized alternative from a set of possibilities has been generated, even though it is different from that alternative which He knew would be generated prior to the generation of this actualized alternative. If we say that he knows the alternative from the set

of possibilities which He knew would be generated, then it necessarily follows from this that much of His knowledge of these things belongs to the class of what we call "error." . . . Anyone who thinks that what has not been actualized has been actualized without a doubt errs. . . . One may not reply that the particular which God knew would be actualized before the generation of the thing subject to generation is without a doubt the alternative which was actualized, since if the case were so posited then everything would be necessary and there would be no contingency in this world at all.

—THE WARS, treatise 3, chap. 2

Because God is perfect, if He knows anything of a certain type then He must know everything of that type. Now consider whether or not God knows future events. Again, because God is perfect, if He knows them after they occur, then He must have known them before they occurred. Now these events are either contingent or necessary. If they are contingent, then they need not have occurred, in which case God believed that they would occur, but He was in error because they need not have occurred. If, on the other hand, they are necessary, then God could have known them but they would not be contingent. Hence, either there are contingent events, in which case God has no knowledge whatsoever of them, or God knows all particulars, in which case everything is determined. To affirm the former entails denying God's perfection, and to affirm the latter entails denying the validity of human choice!

This dilemma is religious as well as philosophic:

The basic tenet of the Torah and the axis upon which it revolves is that in this world there exist contingents. Therefore the Torah can command [us] to do certain actions and to refrain from doing certain [other] actions. [At the same time] the basic tenet of the words of the prophets in general is that God made known to the prophets these contingents prior to their coming to be. As [Scripture] says, "Surely the Lord God does nothing without revealing His secret to His servants the prophets." (Amos 3.7) But it does not follow necessarily from their testifying to a certain evil that it will be actualized. As [Joel] said, "For the Lord is gracious . . . and repents of evil." (Joel 2.13) Thus a combination of these two tenets is possible only if it is posited that these contingents are ordered in one respect, namely the respect in which knowledge of them occurs, and that they are not ordered in another respect, namely the respect in which they are contingent.

—THE WARS, treatise 3, chap. 6

The Torah is first and foremost a book of divine commands. But it makes no sense for God to command human beings to do anything if everything is determined. However, it is equally clear from Scripture that God makes known to prophets what will happen before it happens, which seems to imply that God has determined the events. Yet, if events are determined, how could God "repent," i.e., how could God alter what He knew He was going to do?

In both cases, Gersonides argues that his distinction between the two respects in which an individual can be said to be known is the key to solving both the philosophical and the religious dilemmas. There is a respect in which God knows individuals and it is in this respect that the future is revealed to prophets. But there is another respect in which no one, including God, can be said to know a particular, and it is in this respect that human beings have the choice to obey or disobey God's commandments and thus what God has foreseen can be altered.

In *The Wars of the Lord* Gersonides dealt only with those questions that Maimonides either resolved in direct opposition to Aristotelian principles or explained so vaguely that the reader is left in the dark as to what was Maimonides' real opinion on the subject. Gersonides organized these questions into six topics, each of which constitutes one of the six books of *The Wars of the Lord*. The topics are the immortality of the soul; the nature of prophecy; the nature and extent of God's knowledge of His world; the nature of the extent of Divine Providence; the nature of the celestial spheres which Gersonides judged to be the instruments of Divine Providence, and the eternity of matter. The method that Ralbag followed in discussing each of these topics was the following: he begins by presenting the various views of his Muslim and Jewish (but not Christian) predecessors on the given topic. Then he gives a critical analysis of the differing views, attempting to show what is valid or invalid in the arguments for each view. Finally, he presents his own view on the topic, trying to show that none of the arguments that he investigated raises any valid objections to his own position, and furthermore, that his position and the proper interpretation of the Torah are in agreement.

The only Jewish philosopher comparable to Gersonides in technical ability as a philosopher was *Hasdai Ben Abraham Crescas* (1340–1410) of Barcelona. His chief work in philosophical theology was *The Light of the Lord (Or Adonai)*.

In the Guide (II, Introduction) Maimonides listed twenty-six propositions that he took as premises in his attempt to demonstrate that given

Aristotelian physics and metaphysics, God exists, is one, and is incorporeal. Subsequent generations of Jewish philosophers came to regard this list of propositions as the axioms, or fundamental assumptions, on which Aristotelian science or philosophy was based. Crescas' contention was that the apparent conflicts between rabbinic Judaism, or "Torah," and philosophy were real conflicts but that revelation was a more reliable source of truth than human reason. Considering Aristotelianism to be the best expression of human thought, and accepting Maimonides' twenty-six propositions as the pillars upon which Aristotelian philosophy stood, in *The Light of the Lord* Crescas examined each of these propositions in terms of what possible grounds there are for accepting them, and what, if anything, is wrong with the proposed supportive arguments. Crescas' assumption was that by showing any of these propositions to be either unfounded assumptions or even false, Crescas had discredited all philosophy, and in so doing, vindicated reliance on Torah and rabbinic traditional authority.

The first Aristotelian premise listed by Maimonides in the Guide (II, Introduction), is "it is false (to claim that there can be) an infinite existent entity that has magnitude." Crescas collects Aristotle's arguments for this claim in his various books, generalizes them into four classes of arguments, and proceeds to refute each argument for each part of the claims made in each class of general arguments. The third class of arguments consists of three specific arguments to prove that an infinite object cannot have rectilinear motion and six distinct arguments to prove that an infinite body cannot have circular motion. The fifth argument reads as follows:

> If an infinite body could be moved in a circle, then a line that extended from the center [of the circle] could be moved in a circle that would intersect the two ends of an infinite line, if an infinite perpendicular [line] upon the diameter [of the circle] were posited. But [this] is impossible, since the perpendicular line [is posited as] infinite, and it is impossible to intersect an infinite line in a finite [amount of] time. Consequently, it is impossible for an infinite body to be moved in a circle.
> —*The Light of the Lord* Bk. I, prop. 1, pt. 2

Consider a circle (page 284) in which AB is a line that extends from the center of the circle, A, to some point, B, CD is the diameter of the circle, and EF is a perpendicular line to the diameter, CD. Aristotle says that it is impossible for EF and/or the radius AB, and/or the diameter CD to be infinite. Hence, it is impossible for the circle itself to be infinite.

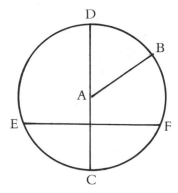

Against this and a similar argument Crescas says the following:

If there were an infinite line, it need not follow that there exists an infinite distance between the two ends. The reason for this is that it is certain that we could not possibly mark at a point the line that extended infinitely from the center of the circle such that the line between the center and the point would not be finite. . . . In general, when we say that a line is infinite, we say that it has no limit or end. But if there were an infinite distance properly it would have to be [measured] at an end. Hence, there cannot exist an infinite distance between lines. So even if the whole infinite body were moved, every part of it would be moved on a finite line. (Ibid.)

Crescas' objection is that the argument confuses what it means to claim that a circular body is infinite with what it means to say that the distance measurement of a line from one end to the other is infinite. Necessarily the circle pictured above is finite. But an infinite circle could not be pictured in this way. Instead, we could draw the following diagram:

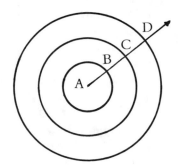

Pictured here is an infinite circle that contains within itself an unending number of finite circles. The ray that begins at the center of the Circle, A, extends endlessly through points B, C, and D. This ray is the radius of the infinite circle. The line segment AB is the radius of a second, larger, finite circle, and line segment AD is the radius of a third, yet larger finite circle. But there is no line segment AZ, where Z is a point at the surface of the infinite circle, which constitutes the radius of the infinite circle. That is not what an infinite circle is. Rather, an infinite circle is such that whatever radius is drawn from the center, rotating that line segment 360 degrees around A forms a circle, the circle actually drawn is always finite, the radius of that circle is finite, that radius is less than the radius of the infinite circle, and the area of that finite circle is less than the area of the infinite circle. Hence, since Aristotle's argument misconceives what it would mean for a circle to be infinite, that argument fails to refute the possibility that an infinite body could have circular motion.

The model for Crescas' attack on the Aristotelian philosophy of Maimonides was Ghazali's attack on the Muslim Aristotelianism of Al-Farabi (d. 950) and Ibn Sina (Avicenna 980–1037) in his *Incoherence (Tahafut)*. Like Ghazali, Crescas' goal was to discredit the reliability of human science as such. Instead, again like Ghazali, what Crescas produced was one of the most profound philosophical critiques of Aristotelianism in the Middle Ages, which set the ground for a return to the material atomism of the Mutakallimun in the Christian Renaissance. The key weaknesses in Aristotelian philosophy upon which Crescas concentrated his attack were Aristotle's arguments against an actual infinity and a vacuum, and Aristotle's definitions of motion, time, matter, and form.

Jewish philosophy did not end with Gersonides and Crescas. Several rabbinic Jewish philosophers in the fifteenth century could be mentioned, the most notable of whom was Crescas' disciple, Joseph Albo (1380–1444) of Monreal in Aragon. Albo's major work was *The Book of Root Beliefs (Sefer Ikkarim)*. However, no subsequent works in the tradition of medieval Jewish philosophy are comparable to the writings of the Aristotelian Gersonides and the anti-Aristotelian Crescas. The next giant of Jewish philosophy would be Spinoza, with whom the study of modern Jewish religious thought begins.

An Example of Medieval Jewish Philosophy: Proving God's Existence

At this point it should be clear that the major issues of Jewish philosophy are no more limited to the usual questions that modern American and European Jews associate with religious belief than Jewish law is limited to questions of ritual. Just as questions about damages and property rights are as much a part of Jewish law as are questions about religious festivals, so questions about science are as much a part of Jewish philosophy as are questions about God and morality. Eventually, if readers become serious about learning Jewish philosophy, they will want to know what Judaism has taught about topics like infinity, logic, motion, and the origins of the universe. In fact much of the discussion of familiar religious questions presupposes this knowledge, in the same way that discussions in Jewish law about marriage, for example, are not inseparable from discussions in Jewish law about different categories of property and contracts. It would be inappropriate in a chapter of this sort to summarize all of the issues in medieval Jewish philosophy, but I will give one example so that the reader may have some idea about the way questions are approached in the field. The question chosen is, can God's existence be demonstrated?

With the possible exception of Philo there were no formal attempts to demonstrate the existence of God in Jewish religious thought before Saadia. There are many biblical and classic rabbinic texts that may be read as arguments for belief in God, but none of them is a formal proof.

Isaiah 40.21–26 exemplifies a sort of argument for the existence of the God of Israel found in Scripture:

> Do you not know
> Have you not heard?
> Have you not been told
> From the very first?
> Have you not discerned
> How the earth was founded?

> It is He who is enthroned above the vault of the earth,
> So that its inhabitants seem as grasshoppers;
> Who spread out the skies like gauze,
> Stretched them out like a tent to dwell in.

> He brings potentates to naught,
> Makes rulers of the earth as nothing

Hardly are they planted,
Hardly are they sown,
Hardly has their stem
Taken root in earth,
When He blows upon them and they dry up,
And the storm bears them off like straw

To whom, then, can you liken Me,
To whom can I be compared?
— Says the Holy One.

Lift high your eyes and see:
Who created these?
He who sends out their host by count,
Who calls them each by name:
Because of His great might and vast power,
Not one fails to appear.

In effect Isaiah presents a crude form of the argument from design. He asserts that anyone who carefully observes the activities of nature and who studies human political history and who tries to understand them can reach only one conclusion, namely, there is a God of Israel who is their ultimate cause. But again, this is not presented as a formal argument, and this is only one possible way of reading the text.

Generally, in biblical texts the existence of God is taken for granted, because it purportedly is known directly through experience in true prophetic visions and indirectly through the reports of these prophets. Usually, proofs are called for only in cases where there is some reasonable doubt, and where there is no such doubt there are no proofs. In the biblical context, where many Israelites are purported to have had frequent direct contact with their deity, no proof that this entity exists was required. However, in the rabbinic period there is a strong sense that the God of Israel is the God of the world. Israelites may have direct contact with their deity insofar as He is their deity, but no individual in the world can have direct contact with the God of the world insofar as He rules the world in general. That the God of Israel exists was affirmed daily through the Jews' contact with their deity in sacrifice and prayer, but that Israel's God also is the ruler of the *world* could not be verified in any direct experience of this kind. Hence, in the rabbinic period some Jews began to present indirect proofs that the God of the world, whom Jews identify with the God of Israel, exists. Such rabbinic statements tend more to resemble a formal expression of the argument than do any biblical texts, such as the Isaiah passage noted above.

According to one Midrash, an unnamed unbeliever *(min)* came to

Rabbi Akiba and asked him who created this world. Rabbi Akiba answered, "The Holy One blessed be He." Then the unbeliever said to Akiba, "Show me a clear thing" *(harayni davar barur)*. (Usually this expression is translated "give me proof," but it is not exactly a proof in any formal sense that seems to be demanded here. Akiba's answer does not involve stated premises with conclusions drawn in any formal way from those premises. Instead, the unbeliever is asking Akiba to show him something that will make Akiba's answer clear or evident to the unbeliever.) Akiba told the unbeliever to return on the next day. When the unbeliever came back he asked what the rabbi was wearing. Akiba answered, "A garment." Then Akiba asked the unbeliever, "Who made the garment?" and the unbeliever responded, "A weaver." Then Akiba said, "I don't believe you; show me something clear." And the unbeliever replied, "What can I show you? Do you not know that the weaver made it?" to which Akiba retorted, "And do you not know that the Holy One blessed be He created this world?" Presumably this "demonstration" satisfied the unbeliever. But Akiba's students still were confused, and they asked their rabbi to explain what he had done. To them Akiba said the following: "My children, just as a house makes known the builder and a garment makes known the weaver and a door makes known a carpenter, so the world makes known the Holy One blessed be He who created it."

Akiba's "demonstration" has difficulties only if the demonstration is taken to be a proof in some strict sense of the term. Logically, Akiba's demonstration is an analogy, and no analogy can settle an issue. But Akiba did not intend his demonstration to be an argument for the existence of God. Akiba showed something to the unbeliever (a garment) in order to help the unbeliever see what was obvious to Akiba. The problem was not to prove God's existence; the problem was to teach something self-evident to a slow student. In the Midrash quoted above, Akiba used his garment in order to illustrate a statement that he considered to be self-evident. Akiba's assumption was that if someone questions that God created the world, it could only be that he does not understand what it means to say that God created the world. Akiba attempted by means of an "audio-visual aid" to help his student over his intellectual difficulty.

Saadia Ben Joseph Al-Fayyumi (892–942)

Not until Saadia's *Book of Beliefs and Opinions* is Akiba's teaching lesson transformed into a formal version of the argument from design.

As in the case of Akiba, Saadia's argument is ultimately based on Creation. The major argumentation of the proof is to show that the world was created, and given that it was created, then it is easily concluded that necessarily there exists a creator. Again, there is no doubt that if it was created there exists a creator, but what is different in Saadia's case is that there is reasonable doubt that the world was created. Also, as in the case of Akiba, no one in Saadia's world seriously doubted that God exists. The primary intent of Saadia's proofs is not to show that God exists, but rather to demonstrate that reason, independent of prophetic vision, can show that God exists. While God's existence was universally accepted, the claim that theology falls within the range of rational argument was not, and it was the latter rather than the former claim that was at stake in Saadia's attempt to demonstrate the existence of God by rational argumentation.

Saadia attempted proofs of God's existence in several works including his commentary on Genesis and his *Sefer Yetsirah,* but the fullest and most systematic statement of his proof is found in the first Treatise of his *Book of Beliefs and Opinions.* The main steps of his argument are (A) that the universe was created, and (B) that the universe was not self-created, from which it follows (C) that the universe was created by someone other than itself and that someone is God. Saadia offered no argument for the conclusion (C); it is simply taken for granted as an immediate and obvious consequence of statements (A) and (B). In the first chapter Saadia offered four demonstrations *(ra'ayot)* of the first claim (A), and in the second chapter he presents three perspectives *(panim,* which Rosenblatt erroneously translates as "reasons") from which the reader should see the truth of (B). In the interest of brevity we will limit ourselves here to an examination of only the four demonstrations of claim (A).

Saadia's first demonstration that the world was created may be summarized as follows: (premise 1) If the Earth is at the center of the universe and the heavens revolve around the Earth (as was claimed by the astronomers of Saadia's time), then the universe is finite. (p2) An infinite force cannot reside within a finite body. Therefore, (1) (from p1, p2) if the universe is finite, then the force that maintains the universe must be finite. Now (p3) what is finite has beginning and end. Therefore, (2) (from 1, p3) the universe has beginning and end, from which it follows that (3) the universe was created.

Without asking any questions about the astronomy that underlies Saadia's proof, there are obvious objections that can be raised. First, a line may be infinite in one direction and finite in the other. In general, something that is infinite in one respect need not be infinite in all respects. Hence, against (p3) it can be argued that given that the universe is finite in time it need not follow that it has a beginning. It may have an end without a beginning. Similarly, against (p1) it may be argued that from the claim that the universe is a sphere whose center is the Earth it need not follow that the universe is finite, for while it has a definite center, it need not have a definite radius, i.e., the extent of the universe from its center may be infinite. Saadia himself considers this objection and replies as follows: The critical factor in astronomy is not just that the universe is a sphere whose center is the Earth. Astronomy also asserts that the heavens complete a full circuit around the Earth. Now that would not be possible if the radius of the sphere were infinite, since it would entail some objects in the universe traversing an infinite distance around the center.

But again there is an obvious objection to Saadia's reply. We need not claim that any object in the universe is infinitely far from the Earth. Every heavenly object is a finite distance from the Earth and its circuit is a finite distance. But it is not the case that there is some object which is more distant from the center than every other object, and whose circuit is longer than that of any other object. It may in fact be the case that no matter how distant any object is and no matter how great is its circuit, there is another heavenly object more distant with a greater circuit. It is this claim that is what it means to say that the universe is infinite, and nothing in Saadia's argument shows that this claim is not possible. What lies at the heart of the weakness of Saadia's argument is confusion about what infinity is. This problem in particular will become a central focus in the writings of Gersonides and Crescas in the fourteenth century.

Saadia's second demonstration is that since every body in the universe consists of a combination or composite of parts, therefore the world was created. The hidden assumptions in this stated demonstration are (1) that the universe itself is a body (i.e., a tridimensional, extended object) composed of parts, (2) what is composed of parts depends on its parts for its existence, and (3) if something x depends on something else y to exist, then something must cause x to exist which is not x. The first assumption is taken from the astronomy of Saadia's contemporaries. But even granting Saadia's presupposed science, the last two assumptions need not follow. According to the atomic theory that was commonly accepted by the scientists of Saadia's time, the universe consists ultimately of indivisible entities called atoms, and it is not obvious at all that the atoms need depend on anything other than themselves to exist. Saadia exhibits no awareness of these two difficulties, but they would come into prominence in the twelfth century when Aristotelian science gained prominence in the western Muslim Empire. More specifically, Abraham Ibn Daud would argue at length for the claim that no material entity, including a simple one, namely, an atom, can exist by itself or can be the sufficient reason for the existence of any material object. But Ibn Daud, like Saadia, would assume uncritically that as the entities within the universe are composite bodies, so the universe itself is a composite body. Maimonides would be the first Jewish philosopher to challenge this claim on the grounds that there is no justifiable basis for assuming that what is true of what is within the universe need be true of the universe as such.

Saadia's third demonstration is that every body contains "accidents" (i.e., nonessential characteristics), and whatever cannot exist without accidents must be caused to exist by something other than itself, from which it follows that every body is caused to exist by something other than itself. Again, Saadia's argument rests on an assumed analogy between the universe as such and its parts, so that what is claimed to be true of what is within the universe is said to be true of the universe, that is, a composite body that contains accidents. The claim that the universe contains accidents is essential in order that Saadia may later defend his claim that there is human choice. If nothing occurs accidentally, then nothing can be other than the way it is, i.e., it would seem that there is no consistent way to claim both that the universe is completely determined and that there is some kind of human freedom. All Jewish philosophers until Spinoza would share this logical presupposition, and Spinoza in his *Ethics* would give considerable attention to its refutation.

Saadia's final demonstration of the claim that the universe was created is based on his conception of time. (p1) Time consists of units called "moments" *(atot)*. (p2) While it is possible in thought to divide a particular time set into an infinite number of such moments, this division could not occur in actuality. In general there are composite entities that may be conceptually divided infinitely, but nothing in reality can be so divided since there cannot exist an actual infinity of material entities. Therefore, (1) (from p1, p2) it follows that nothing could in reality traverse an infinite number of moments. Therefore, (2) (from 1) existence *(havayah)* could not have traversed an infinite number of past moments in order to reach the present. Therefore, (3) (from 2) if existence extended infinitely into the past, existence could not have reached the present, in which case nothing would now exist, which is self-evidently false. Therefore, (4) (from 3) existence reached the present by traversing a finite number of past moments, i.e., there was a beginning to existence, from which it follows (4) that the world was created.

Note that the objections raised about Saadia's concept of infinity apply with equal force to this fourth demonstration. But that is not the critical problem with this argument. Clearly, "existence" is not an entity; it is a concept. And on Saadia's own terms, while there may be an objection to an actual infinity there is no objection to a conceptual infinity. Prima facie there is no reason why, given Saadia's stated beliefs, existence could not traverse an infinite number of moments. The most obvious example of such a claim is that there has been an infinite series of finite existent entities in the past. Maimonides would argue against this possibility and Crescas, believing that the existence of God cannot be demonstrated by human reason, would argue for its possibility.

In general, Saadia was the first Jewish philosopher to present systematic, formal proofs of the existence of God. Their primary weakness is that they presuppose the atomistic universe of the early Muslim philosophers. Now the goal of a formal proof of the existence of God is to show that necessarily God exists, and to show this means that there can be (to use language subsequently introduced by Leibniz) no possible world in which there is not God. For Saadia, any world that is not atomist is not possible. Hence, while Saadia's claim may be reasonable in an atomist universe, it is not in any sense shown to hold in a different kind of universe. Therefore the argument fails to show what it was intended to show.

The first Jewish philosopher to attempt to demonstrate the existence of God in all possible Aristotelian universes was Abraham Ibn Daud. Then Maimonides would combine both forms of demonstrations into a claim that God exists in all possible worlds. To make the same point somewhat differently, Saadia demonstrates that in any atomist universe God creates the world; Abraham Ibn Daud demonstrates that in any Aristotelian universe God necessitates the world; and Maimonides attempts to free these claims about God from any particular theory of the physical universe.

ABRAHAM IBN DAUD (1110–1180)

In the twelfth century a change took place in philosophy, a change that led to a new form of demonstration of the existence of God. The new philosophy was Aristotelian, and the first Jewish philosopher to use an Aristotelian world view to demonstrate the existence of God was Abraham Ibn Daud in his *Exalted Faith (Ha-emunah Haramah)*.

Ibn Daud's demonstration that God exists consists of two claims. First is a demonstration that no ordered infinite corporeal entity can actually exist (Bk. I, chap. 4), and second is a demonstration that everything that is moved has a mover and there is a first mover (Bk. I, chap. 5). His proof of the first claim has three major steps. Step one is an argument for the claim that no actual line can be infinite. Step two is an argument for the claim that since no actual line can be infinite, no actual surface and no actual body can be infinite. Bodies are composed of surfaces and surfaces are composed of lines. Since actual lines are finite, the parts of actual surfaces are finite and the whole cannot be greater than its parts. Therefore, all actual surfaces are finite and for the same reason all actual bodies are finite. Step three concludes that no ordered, actual number is infinite. The conclusion of Ibn Daud's three steps is that no quantity can be ordered, actual, and infinite. All quantities are either lines, surfaces, bodies, or numbers; no actual, ordered line, surface, body, or number can be infinite; therefore, no quantity can be infinite. Next, Ibn Daud supplements this argument with two demonstrations, (which we will not give in detail here) that no body can be infinite, leading him to the conclusion that since God is infinite, God cannot be a body, and since God is not a body, He is not divisible.

Ibn Daud offered two arguments for the second claim, that every motion originates from a mover. First, if something moved itself then it would be both what moves and what is moved in a single respect; every mover is greater than what it moves; therefore, if something could be what moves and what is moved in the same respect, it would be greater than itself, which is not possible. Second, if something moved itself, then it would be both what moves and what is moved in a single respect; there exists something that actually belongs to a mover and potentially belongs to what is moved; therefore, if something could be what moves and what is moved in the same respect, it would possess something that is both actually and potentially existent in a single respect, which is not possible. The key expression in the major premise of these two arguments is "in a single respect" (mitsad ehad). The claim is not that something cannot both be moved and be a mover. Ibn Daud acknowledged that composite entities can both be movers and what is moved, but he stated that they are not in both roles in the same respect. In such cases one part is moving another part, but no part moves itself. Hence, Ibn Daud's claim is that something cannot be both the moved and the mover of the same motion. An immediate consequence of this argument is that there can be no circular chain of causes such that *a* moves *b* that moves

. . . that moves *a*. This claim is central to the third claim of Ibn Daud's demonstration that a first mover cannot itself be moved.

Ibn Daud's argument for the final claim—that every motion ends at a first mover—works as follows: Everything that is moved has a mover; there are not actual, ordered infinite existent entities; therefore, all motion ends at one or more first movers. Ibn Daud's argument for the claim that a first mover is a mover that is not itself moved reads as follows: If the first mover were moved it would either be moved by some other entity or its motion would be part of a circular causal chain; given that the mover is a first mover, by definition it cannot be moved by another entity; it is not possible for a first mover to be a part of a circular causal chain; therefore, a first mover has no mover. We have already noted that the denial of the possibility of a circular causal chain was an immediate consequence of the major premise of Ibn Daud's arguments for the first part of his main demonstration in this chapter. At this place he offered the following argument in support of this claim: A mover is "stronger" than what is moved; in any circular causal chain everything would be both what is moved and the mover of the same motion; hence, everything would be stronger (as cause) and weaker (as effect) than anything else in the circular causal chain, which is impossible.

It is interesting to note that the claim that God exists falls under the topics of Book One of *The Exalted Faith* and not Book Two. Book One deals with claims in science that are relevant to Jewish faith, while Book Two deals with the basic principles *(ikkarim)* of that faith. For Ibn Daud the claim that God exists is a doctrine of science and not religion. In opposition to Saadia and the early Muslim philosophers, Ibn Daud's Judaism affirms that God is an incorporeal necessary being and that God is one, but not that God exists. To be sure, the two basic principles of Jewish faith about God presuppose that He exists, but His existence is not in itself a faith claim. Rather, it is a universal truth that will be affirmed by all rational beings through sound science, and as such it has no special place on the list of fundamental beliefs of Judaism. It is also of interest to note that not only is Ibn Daud's demonstration of the existence of God independent of the claim that the universe was created, but Creation is mentioned nowhere in *The Exalted Faith* and certainly is not listed by Ibn Daud as one of the basic principles of Judaism. Saadia gave us the most complete statement of a demonstration of the existence of God in any created universe whose laws of nature are atomistic; Ibn Daud in turn provided us with the most complete statement of a demonstration of the existence of God in an eternal universe whose laws of nature are Aristotelian. Next, Maimonides would combine these two sets of arguments into a demonstration of God's existence as a claim of universal rational religion, purportedly independent of any specific system of natural science.

MOSES BEN MAIMON (1135–1204)

In the Guide Maimonides argued as follows: The basic difference between the Mutakallimun and the Aristotelian philosophers is that the former posit that the world is created and the latter assume that the world is eternal, and that neither can give a valid demonstration of their respective presuppositions concerning the creation or eternity of the world. Hence what is wrong with the proofs of the early Muslim philosophers is that they rest on the doctrine that the world is created, which cannot be demonstrated. Similarly, the Aristotelian proofs suffer from resting on the dogma of the eternity of the world, which also is subject to doubt. Maimonides concluded that in this case we ought to follow Scripture literally and accept the doctrine of creation out of nothing, but at no time did he say that either doctrine can be demonstrated. Thus, since neither the Mutakallimun arguments (employed by Saadia) nor the Aristotelian arguments (employed by Ibn Daud) alone are certain, we can base a certain proof of God's existence only on a disjunction of the two arguments. In other words, Maimonides joined two sets of arguments into a single argument of the following form: either the world was created or it is eternal. While neither horn of the disjunction is demonstrable, the disjunction itself is necessarily true. If the world was created, then God exists. (This proposition is the topic of the Guide, I, chapters 73–76.) If the world is eternal, then God exists. (This proposition is the topic of the Guide, II, chap. 1.) Therefore, whether the world is created or is eternal, God exists.

In the introduction to the Guide, Book II, Maimonides lists twenty-six propositions that he would employ in chapter one where he presents four proofs for the existence of God. All twenty-six are taken from Aristotle's science, the last of which is the claim that the universe is eternal. Maimonides' first and fourth proofs are examples of what is known in Western philosophy as the cosmological argument. Stated generally it goes as follows: For everything that exists there must be a cause or a mover. If every cause or mover of a thing were external to the thing caused or moved, then the causal chain would be infinite. But there cannot be an infinite chain of causes. Hence, there must exist a cause or mover which has only itself as its cause or mover, and this entity is called God.

There is one, but only one, sense in which this argument can be said to be valid. Although multiple variants are possible, this form of argument presupposes that in some sense Aristotle's view of the world is true. In other words, while some of Aristotle's assumptions about the world can be denied, other assumptions can be added in their place and the cosmological argument will still validly establish that God exists. What this argument establishes is that if the world is to be viewed in Aristotelian terms, then God exists; but the world need not be viewed in these terms. This is all that Maimonides claimed that his Aristotelian arguments demonstrated.

Maimonides' second proof goes as follows: Assume an entity that is composed of two parts. Aristotle asserted as a premise that if one of those parts exists independent of the composite, then the other part also must exist independent of the composite. Thus, for example, oxymel consists of honey and vinegar, and since honey exists independent of oxymel, vinegar also exists independent of honey. Similarly, since there exist entities that both are moved and are movers and there exist entities that are only moved, so there must exist at least one entity that is only a mover.

The question could be asked why the major premise of this second argument was not listed by Maimonides together with the other twenty-six premises employed in Maimonides' other arguments. One answer might be that as this premise was applied to Maimonides' proofs of God's existence, it is invalid in a far more obvious way than are any of the other premises. The sense in which vinegar and honey make oxymel composite is entirely different from the way that being moved and being a mover makes a single object composite. At best there is only an analogy between what the premise of the argument states and the application of the premise to movers. In other words, the most that Maimonides could claim is that just as in the case of things composed of two parts, if one of those parts has an independent existence so the other has an independent existence, so in the case of things subject to two principles, if there exist entities subject only to one of those principles then there exist entities subject only to the other principle. This is just an analogy, however, as Maimonides himself recognized in the purported Aristotelian arguments for the eternal existence of the universe, and arguments from analogy are not proofs. Hence, while the first and the fourth demonstrations can be rejected only if questions are raised about Aristotle's view of the universe, this second argument can be rejected independent of any skepticism concerning Aristotelian science.

Maimonides' third demonstration goes as follows: Either (A) nothing is subject to generation and corruption or (B) everything is subject to generation and corruption or (C) some things are subject to generation and corruption and other things are not subject to generation and corruption. By experience we know that A is false. Hence either B or C is the case. But B also is false for the following reasons: If everything is subject to generation and corruption, then everything undergoes corruption, i.e., ceases to exist. Since everything can undergo corruption, it is also possible that there is a time at which everything is undergoing corruption. But if everything should undergo corruption at one time, then after that time nothing could be generated, i.e., come into existence, since after the time of universal corruption there would exist nothing to bring anything else into existence. Hence, if B is correct, then there was a time at which everything was subject to corruption and nothing has existed since that time. We are taught by experience, however, that this conclusion is false. Consequently B is false. Therefore, the only remaining alternative is that while some things are subject to generation and corruption there are other things that are not subject to generation and corruption. In other words, there exists at least one thing that is a necessary being, since only necessary beings can exist without being subject to generation and corruption, and that entity is called God.

The critical step in this argument is the move from the possibility of a time at which everything undergoes corruption to the assertion that given this possibility nothing ought to exist now. In order to make this move Maimonides needed two assumptions that he did not explicitly state. One assumption is a variant on the twenty-sixth premise, which states that the universe is eternal. If the universe is eternal, then from the definition of time that Maimonides' noted in his premise fifteen, time also is eternal. For the purpose of this argument, Maimonides had to assume that time is not only eternal with respect to the future but that it is also eternal with respect to the past.

A second necessary assumption for the demonstration is a variant on Maimonides' twenty-third premise, which states that anything that is in fact possible must at some time be actual. For the purpose of this argument Maimonides had to assume that if anything is in fact possible, then given an infinite duration of time, even where that duration is entirely in the past, that possibility would have been realized. In other words, in order to infer from the possibility of everything being corrupted that there was a time at which everything ceased to exist, Maimonides had to assume that time is endless in the direction of the past, and that if anything is in fact a possibility, then it would have been realized during an infinite or endless duration of time. Without either premise Maimonides' third argument collapses. In this connection it can be noted that the assumption of infinite duration in time need not be endless in all directions. Just as a line can be endless at one, but only one, end, so time can be open at one end, either in the past or in the future. In other words, Maimonides continued the confusion about the conception of infinity exhibited by every Jewish philosopher before him.

Hasdai Ben Abraham Crescas (1340–1410)

Between the time of Maimonides and Spinoza no new demonstrations of God's existence were offered. In Gersonides' *The Wars of the Lord (Milhamot Adonai),* for example, the existence, oneness and incorporeality of God were not even topics for discussion, since it was assumed that Maimonides settled these questions. Only in the case of Hasdai Crescas' *Light of the Lord (Or Adonai)* were Maimonides' proofs based on eternity reconsidered. When Maimonides listed his twenty-six propositions from Aristotelian philosophy, he did so to isolate those principles in Aristotle to be employed in his demonstrations of God's existence. His intent was not to provide a complete list of axioms for a geometrically conceived Aristotelian science. However, by the time of Crescas, Maimonides' list was understood in these terms. Crescas presented an analysis of these premises in order to show the inadequacy of rational theology.

For his Jewish predecessors in philosophy, reason rooted in sense experience as well as authentic tradition based on revelation were sources of knowledge. Crescas argued that Aristotelian science is the best expression of rational knowledge; that science rests on the foundation of Maimonides' twenty-six propositions; many of those propositions are dubious; therefore, reason as a source of knowledge is dubious and only revealed tradition is reliable. In so arguing, Crescas convinced many Jews that philosophy in general is a misdirected route toward truth and persuaded other Jews that there may be better science than Aristotelian philosophy. In fact, Crescas himself continued to accept the validity of Maimonides' third argument, but the seeds were sown for questioning the entire enterprise of extending reason to demonstrate the existence of God.

In summary, most Western philosophers today, including Jewish theologians, do not believe that it is possible to state a valid, formal demonstration of the existence of God. Some non-Jewish philosophers, such as Norman Malcolm, have argued that at least some forms of demonstration are possible. (See N. Samuelson, "On Proving God's Existence," *Judaism* [Winter 1967].) But for the most part this current discussion in philosophy has had minimal impact on contemporary Jewish thought. In any case, what has been and continues to be at stake for Jewish theology in this dispute is not whether God exists; the dispute concerns the range of human reason in dealing with matters of Jewish belief. Whereas Ibn Daud believed that the claim that God exists is a scientific and not a religious claim, Maimonides, Gersonides, and Spinoza believed that the claim is common to both realms, and most Jewish theologians today believe, like Crescas, that the claim lies beyond the range of what can be demonstrated by philosophers and scientists.

WHERE TO GO FROM HERE

General Overview. Before beginning to study medieval Jewish philosophy it is helpful first to see where this area of study is in relationship to other aspects of Jewish history and culture. Hence the first books to read are a general intellectual history of Judaism and an introduction to medieval Jewish philosophy. There is a problem with such books of which the reader ought to be aware: the more general the history, the more blurred are the individual works in that history. But at this stage of study such inaccuracies ought not to concern the reader. The details of Jewish philosophy are always blurred and sometimes even inaccurate in general overview works, but for the purpose they serve, these errors are unavoidable and need not concern the reader. Inaccuracies at this level will be corrected as the reader goes on to more advanced, specific studies. In my judgment the best general intellectual history of Judaism is Robert M. Seltzer's *Jewish People, Jewish Thought* (New York: Macmillan, 1980) and the best history of medieval Jewish philosophy remains Isaac Husik's *A History of Medieval Jewish Philosophy* (New York: Jewish Publication Society, 1930). The Husik book begins with a general introduction to the relevant positions in Aristotelian and atomist philosophy and then proceeds to give a detailed plot summary of each classic of medieval Jewish philosophy with a minimum of interpretation. Having read Husik, readers will have a good knowledge of what every major figure in medieval Jewish philosophy says, although readers will have little idea of what these philosophers meant by what they say.

The more background that readers have in general Western philosophy the more they will profit from what they read in medieval Jewish philosophy. Of particular value is knowledge of Aristotle and then Plato, in that order of priority. Readers who have no familiarity with either of these major figures in classical philosophy may want to turn to a general history of philosophy. Bertrand Russell's *A History of Western Philosophy* (New York: Simon and Schuster, 1945) is the best-written general history of philosophy in the field. Its limitation is that it is strongly interpretative and Russell's interpretations of premodern philosophers are not the best. But because it is so well written it is, in my judgment, the best first book in philosophy. A more accurate but less well-written general history of philosophy is Frederic Copleston's *A History of Philosophy* (Westminster, Md: Newman, 1946). After reading the chapters on Plato and Aristotle in Russell's book, the reader may want to turn to the same chapters in Copleston's book. At the next level, for books specifically about Aristotle and Plato, I would recommend Werner Jaeger's *Aristotle* (Oxford: Clarendon, 1934) and A. E. Taylor's *Plato* (New York: Meridian, 1956).

Reading Primary Sources. At this stage readers already have sufficient general ideas about what the Jewish philosophers are saying to begin to read primary texts. There are detailed introductions to many of these books, but I would recommend that readers first expose themselves to the texts. Readers may give wrong interpretations to what they read, but the more advanced interpretations of these books may also yield wrong interpretations. The book to start with is the Hirschfield translation of Judah Halevi's *Kuzari* (New York: Schocken, 1964). Whatever else are its virtues it is clearly the best-written, aesthetic work in medieval Jewish philosophy. It is the only work in the field that has a plot and is written in the style of a dialogue. For these reasons novices are more likely to feel that they understand what they are reading than will be the case with any other work in medieval Jewish philosophy. The relative simplicity of the language suggests to the reader clarity of thought. With greater exposure to the field and greater sophistication, works that initially seemed confusing will appear to be clearer and works that initially seemed clear will appear to be more confused. In fact, this change in feeling about writing is one sign of progress in the field.

The Kuzari at this stage of study should be read for two reasons— enjoyment and a sense of satisfaction in being able to read a book of Jewish philosophy with minimal background. But Halevi's thought is unique and therefore not representative of medieval Jewish philosophy. What the reader ought to turn to now is Abraham Ibn Daud's *The Exalted Faith* (East Brunswick, N.J.: Littman Library, Fairleigh Dickinson Press, forthcoming).

The main body and development of works in Jewish philosophy

presuppose Aristotle's view of the universe. For this reason the study of medieval Jewish philosophy should begin by mastering the Aristotelians rather than concentrating on Neoplatonists like Ibn Gabirol or atomists like Saadia. For this purpose *The Exalted Faith* is the best introduction. Ibn Daud wrote for people who were in the same situation as the readers of this book: that is, intelligent Jews who are interested in Jewish philosophy but have no background in the field. In contrast, Maimonides, as has been discussed above, wrote in such a way as to *prevent* uninformed readers from understanding what he said; Gersonides wrote for readers who knew what Maimonides said; and Crescas wrote for an audience who knew what Maimonides and Gersonides both said. The first part of *The Exalted Faith* is a general introduction to Aristotle's philosophy, and as such, it is the best introduction to how Jewish philosophers, including Maimonides, Gersonides, and Crescas, understood Aristotle. Furthermore, the topics dealt with by Ibn Daud in the last two parts of *The Exalted Faith* are more detailed and comprehensive than the topics dealt with by any other Jewish philosopher. As such this book has the advantage of giving the reader an excellent overall general introduction to the field while at the same time being itself a major primary work in medieval Jewish philosophy.

Having read Halevi and Ibn Daud, the reader is now prepared to turn to the most influential of all works in Jewish philosophy, Maimonides' Guide. There are two English translations available. I would recommend the S. Pines translation (Chicago: University of Chicago Press, 1963). See also *A Maimonides Reader,* edited by I. Twersky (New York: Behrman House, 1972).

Next one should read Saadia's *Book of Beliefs and Opinions* (New York: Yale University Press, 1948). As in *The Exalted Faith,* the author covers a wide range of topics, and the book is intended for an audience that has little background in philosophy, which makes the meaning of the book at a certain level accessible to the beginner. The book is worth reading in its own right, the Samuel Rosenblatt translation is reliable, and it serves to acquaint the student with Jewish philosophy based on the Kalam rather than on the Aristotelians.

Readers who are used to reading novels and literary prose, but not mathematics and science or philosophy, need a word of caution on how to read any philosophical text. Expect to read at a slower rate. One's rate of speed will be more or less one-tenth of what it normally is. The way to read philosophy is word by word and sentence by sentence and not paragraph by paragraph. After each sentence and paragraph ask yourself if you understand what you have read; does it agree with what has been said before; do you agree with it; and if you do not agree, then why do you not? In other words, take seriously what the author says and in your imagination enter into a discussion with him about it. Rarely is it sufficient to read a philosophy book only once, and rarely on first reading will one discover everything that there is to be discovered. In all likelihood each subsequent work of philosophy that you read will itself add to your insight into the philosophy that you had formerly read. In other words, read philosophy the way commentators read Scripture, with two notable exceptions. You ought not assume that necessarily anything an author says is consistent with anything else he or she says, and you ought not to assume that just because the author is an author (even the author of a Jewish classic) that what the writer says is true.

More Advanced Studies. The best Jewish philosophy is the thought of Gersonides and Crescas. (By "best" I mean technically the best. I am not making a judgment about the truth of what is being said. Rather, I am saying that the thought of these two giants in the field excels beyond the work of earlier Jewish philosophers in subtlety, complexity, conceptual clarity, and precise use of language.) But their works are least accessible to the novice because these philosophers assumed that their audience at least knew the writings of Maimonides and probably much more, notably the works of Aristotle as interpreted by the Muslim commentator, Ibn Rushd (Averroës). Now I think that it is possible to read the major books of Gersonides and Crescas profitably without having read Ibn Rushd, but it is not possible to do so without having the general overview of the Aristotelian tradition spoken of above and without having some familiarity with Maimonides' Guide.

At this stage the reader may wish to read some secondary material about the thought of Maimonides before tackling Gersonides and Crescas, but it is not necessary to do so. The modern commentaries on the Guide may have a correct interpretation of what Maimonides intended to say, but what Maimonides intended to say may not be how Gersonides and Crescas interpreted him, in which case the reader may be confused in reading Gersonides and Crescas, because what they thought that Maimonides said may not be what the informed modern reader thinks that he said. In any case if readers do choose to turn now to commentaries on Maimonides, they should keep this point in mind when they read Gersonides and Crescas: To understand these later Jewish philosophers it is important to determine what they think Maimonides said—which need not be what Maimonides in fact said. To begin the study of Maimonides criticism I would recommend two books. The first is David

Hartman's *Maimonides: Torah and Philosophic Quest* (Philadelphia: Jewish Publication Society, 1976) and the second is Isadore Twersky's *Introduction to the Code of Maimonides (Mishneh Torah)* (New Haven: Yale University Press, 1980). My recommendation in no way rests on my agreement with what these authors say. Rather, both books have the virtues of dealing with Maimonides' thought in general and proposing interesting ways of integrating what Maimonides says in the Guide with the philosophic content found in Maimonides' halakhic writings. I suggest reading Hartman's book first only because the style in which it is written makes the book appear to be easier to understand than Twersky's study.

The major work of Gersonides is *The Wars of the Lord*. The whole work has not as yet been translated into English. However, Book IV on Divine Providence has been translated by J. David Bleich, *Providence in the Philosophy of Gersonides* (New York: Yeshiva University, 1973); the selection from Book VI that deals with the creation of the world has been translated by Jacob J. Staub, *The Creation of the World According to Gersonides* (Chico, Calif.: Scholar's Press, 1982); and Book III on divine attributes and God's knowledge has been translated by Norbert Samuelson, *Gersonides on God's Knowledge* (Toronto: Pontifical Institute, 1977). Of these three books the work that requires the least philosophical background to understand is Bleich's and the work that requires the most is Samuelson's. If this is a concern to the reader, then the order of reading about Gersonides should be Bleich, Staub, and Samuelson. But if this is not a concern then the reader would benefit by reading about these topics in *The Wars of the Lord* in their logical order as Gersonides wrote them, since the discussion of Creation presupposes the subject of Divine Providence, which in turn presupposes what Gersonides had to say about God's knowledge. In this case the order of reading about Gersonides should be Samuelson, Bleich, and Staub.

Only the first part of Crescas' *Light of the Lord* has been translated into English. It is the section in which Crescas carefully criticizes Maimonides' list of central claims or premises in Aristotelian science. The translation is by Harry A. Wolfson, *Crescas' Critique of Aristotle* (Cambridge, Mass.: Harvard University Press, 1929). No serious student of medieval Jewish philosophy can study this field without confronting this superb example of intellectual history. Wolfson's work on Crescas continues to be the standard of excellence for all historical studies in the field. Other important works by Wolfson include: *Philo* (1962), *The Philosophy of the Church Fathers* (1970), and *The Philosophy of Kalam* (1976).

זה השער לי"י

ספר הזהר
על התורה מהקדום האלהי
ר'שמעון בן יוחאי זלעם סתרי
תורה ומדרש הנעלם ותוספתא
על קצת פרשיות עם מור מקום
מהפסוקים' ופי' המלות בסוף
הספר' הודפם והוגה עם רב
העיון ש' הנעירים עימנו ככמ'
גבריאל יב' מקורלופלי מתאספקת
הנאליקי' ואברהם יב' ככמ'ר
מטלם זנל ממדינא.

פה מנטובה
תחת ממשלת מעלת אדוניני סלוכום
גוליאלמו גונואנט ירס וסדרו
פי סטומפוס ה'ה הספר כזר עאיר יב'
בכמ'ר אפרים וכל מפדובה
וייעקב בכמ'ר כפתל'יסבחן וכל מג'אוולי

Title page of the first printed Zohar, Mantua, Italy, 1558–60.

CHAPTER SIX

Kabbalistic Texts

LAWRENCE FINE

The Reapers of the Field are the Comrades, masters of this wisdom, because *Malkhut* is called the Apple Field, and She grows sprouts of secrets and new meanings of Torah. Those who constantly create new interpretations of Torah are the ones who reap Her.
—Moses Cordovero, OR HA-HAMMAH on Zohar III, 106a

INTRODUCTION: A CHARACTERIZATION OF MYSTICAL RELIGION

There are few aspects of religion that have been subject to more misunderstanding than the topic of mysticism. Mysticism has been identified at one time or another with magic, superstition, the occult, and just about anything else regarded as mysterious or cryptic. While it has not been completely devoid of such elements, the fact is, that on the whole, mystical religion constitutes a highly subtle and sophisticated way of being religious. More often than not mystical practice has found adherents among the spiritual elite rather than the folk at large.

Before suggesting some of the specific traits of mystical religion, we want to indicate the fundamental methodological point of view that underlies our approach to the study of mysticism. Mysticism ought to be thought of as an *historical* phenomenon that develops within particular traditions. By that we mean it is impossible to speak meaningfully of mysticism in the abstract, as if there were a set of ideas or practices "out there" that characterize it wherever and whenever it has expressed itself. Mystical systems grow out of historical religions and thus reflect and draw upon the symbols, rites, ideas, and ethics of one tradition or another. As such, mystical religion is shaped and largely determined by the tradition that nurtures it. While there can be no doubt that mystics tend to be innovative in their outlooks, bringing a whole new level of meaning to their tradition, or seeing their tradition in a genuinely fresh way, they are, to begin with, to be situated *within* that tradition.

Not only is Jewish mysticism different from Islamic or Christian mysticism, not to mention Hinduism, Buddhism, or Taoism, but one finds a significant variety of mystical systems within Judaism itself. Thus, mystics of the Talmudic period conceived of and experienced God in ways that were very different from the kabbalists of the Middle Ages. We have, in other words, to explore the particular historical situation, the unique imaginative world in which a literature and way of life developed, in order to understand it adequately. We cannot assume, as have many students of mysticism, that mystics the world over, across time and space, have thought the same thoughts and had the same experiences.

Having argued in this way, are there any things we can say about mysticism in general? We believe so, but they are broad generalizations that point to certain tendencies without narrowly defining mysticism. Let us suggest five such tendencies.

a. Generally speaking, mystics seek intimate knowledge of the divine that goes beyond intellectualization and rational thinking. Mystics are not necessarily anti or nonintellectual—something kabbalism itself amply demonstrates—but they *are* interested in the *experience* of the sacred in a way that is *intuitive, direct,* and *intense.* The deep and unmediated experience of the divine in which one's total self is caught up is, more often than not, part of the mystical goal.

b. Mystics tend to find in *themselves* something in common with the divine. They frequently turn inward in order to discover that an aspect of their being, or the totality of their being, corresponds to or is akin to God. It is this very kinship that serves as the basis for the mystic's longing to establish some sort of bond with the sacred beyond his or herself. Mysticism, in other words, is typically associated with the development of self-awareness, not as an end in itself, but as an attempt to discover an identity between the self and the Other.

c. Just as mystics tend to locate some aspect of the divine in themselves, they likewise tend to look upon the world of nature as a whole, as an opportunity for discovering the sacred. God is often construed as being *immanent* in all of nature—although this does not necessarily take the form of pantheism, a theological perspective according to which nature is identified in its totality with the divine.

d. Mystical religion almost always involves a specially *disciplined* way of life. While conventional religion also entails submission to some form of discipline, mystics go further, either by way of more intense practice or by developing new practices. Rites and modes of ethical behavior are *practiced* with the goal of perfecting the self, achieving special levels of awareness, or attaining certain types of experiences.

e. This special discipline involves using various kinds of techniques of meditation or prayer. These may be for the purpose of increasing one's knowledge and awareness of the divine, or to promote communion of one sort or another between an individual and the divine.

It will be useful to keep these observations in mind as we explore the nature of Kabbalah; they should provide some orientation in our effort to understand the ways in which Kabbalah distinguishes itself from other forms of spirituality, particularly rabbinic or classical Judaism.

The Development of Early Kabbalah: From the Sefer ha-Bahir to the Zohar

During the last half-century, research into the mystical tradition has served to revise substantially our understanding of Jewish religious history. For one of the most important consequences of the groundbreaking work of Gershom Scholem (1897–1982), the great historian of Jewish mysticism, has been to demonstrate the enormously important role of mystical creativity within Jewish tradition. The first modern scholars of Judaism, the German-Jewish school of the "Science of Judaism" which emerged in the nineteenth century, sought to relegate mysticism to a minor role, and even worse, to belittle it. They did so out of a profound embarrassment with an aspect of Judaism that they regarded as irrational, superstitious, and spiritually impoverished. In a time when many European Jews were seeking to prove the liberal, rational, and humanistic character of Judaism, these historians had little tolerance for "narrowmindedness" and "primitive superstition." Scholem and others, however, have shown that from the Talmudic period forward, Jews cultivated profoundly rich and highly diverse forms of mysticism which, far from being merely fringe movements, played central roles in Judaism.

We find, for example, that the rabbinic period produced not only the Talmuds and the midrashic literature, but a fascinating esoteric literature, that of the *Hekhalot* (Palaces) or *Merkavah* (Chariot), mentioned briefly on page 171. The heart of this mysticism was the attempt of adepts to ascend contemplatively through the seven heavens and the palaces of which they are comprised, in order to merit an ecstatic vision of the divine throne of glory. This extraordinary literature, which has preserved wondrous descriptions of these contemplative journeys, was not the work of a fringe heretical group opposed to the religion of the rabbinic sages. Instead, it involved some of the most important Talmudic figures. We now know that any well-rounded picture of the rabbinic period calls for study of this literature, both on its own terms and in terms of the way it alters our thinking about "normative" rabbinic Judaism.

The same observation may be made with respect to Kabbalah. The Hebrew term Kabbalah refers to tradition that has been received or passed down. In this sense it was in use before it came to be associated with Jewish esotericism. Popularly, it has been used to denote the broad range of Jewish mystical literature and speculation from the rabbinic period to the present. More technically, and the meaning with which it will be used here, Kabbalah refers to a specific historical movement which originated in the second half of the twelfth century in that area of southern France known as Provence, and in northern Spain in the thirteenth.

The very earliest kabbalistic work was *Sefer ha-Bahir*. It was written in pseudepigraphic style, that is, it was deliberately attributed to a false author. *Sefer ha-Bahir* appeared in Provence sometime between 1150 and 1200, although it was actually composed elsewhere. The *Bahir* is a rather brief, poorly organized, often obscure collection of speculations about God in the form of commentaries on scriptural passages. Its literary quality notwithstanding, the *Bahir* is a remarkable book insofar as it represented the emergence of a striking set of Gnostic motifs within the heart of rabbinic Judaism.* In colorful mythic symbolism it describes ten *Sefirot,* attributes or "lights" which comprise the life of God. (The notion of the *Sefirot,* as we shall see later on in this chapter, becomes the

---

* The Gnostics were members of various sects in the early centuries of the Common Era who believed there were two gods, an evil deity who was responsible for the creation of the world, and a transcendent deity, the source of the human soul. The Gnostic element in *Sefer ha-Bahir* does not refer to this kind of theological dualism, but to the mythic notion of many powers or dimensions within God.

foundation of kabbalistic thinking.) The *Bahir* speaks, for example, of the divine realm as "the secret tree," the mythical structure of God's creative powers from which souls blossom forth. The precise circumstances of the book's composition are still unclear, although it is known that at least part of the *Bahir* is an adaptation of a far older work, *Raza Rabba,* only fragments of which are extant. Among the Spanish kabbalists of the thirteenth century, this book was regarded as an ancient and authoritative work, believed to have been "composed by the mystic sages of the Talmud."

The Provençal kabbalists included prominent rabbinic figures: Abraham ben Isaac, president of the rabbinical court at Narbonne, his son-in-law, Abraham ben David, and the latter's son, Isaac the Blind (c. 1160–1235). Of these men, only Isaac deserves to be considered a full-fledged kabbalist who devoted all of his literary efforts to mystical speculation. Isaac was primarily influenced by the philosophical tradition known as Neoplatonism, according to which all reality is described as resulting from a process of divine unfolding or emanation. In Isaac's writings one finds a systematic description of the *Sefirot* which are said to emanate from the realm of divine "Thought." Isaac liked to describe this process as a linguistic development; from divine "Thought" there emerged the divine utterances, the "words" through which Creation came about.

Influenced by these early kabbalists, the Kabbalah spread from Provence to Spain by the beginning of the thirteenth century. In particular, the rabbinic circle in Gerona became an important center of mystical writing. It included Moses ben Nahman, the outstanding Spanish Talmudist of his day, Ezra ben Solomon and his younger contemporary, Azriel, Jacob ben Sheshet, and the poet Meshullam ben Solomon Da Piera. Among these men Azriel's contribution stands out owing to the systematic and profound nature of his thinking. In his writings, the Gnostic and Neoplatonic traditions which preceded him are synthesized.

The chief representatives of yet a third important circle, the so-called "Gnostics" of Castile, were Jacob and Isaac ha-Kohen, Todros Abulafia, and Moses of Burgos. The prominent feature of their thinking was the development of an elaborate theory of a demonic emanation of ten *Sefirot* paralleling the ten holy *Sefirot*. Various elements of these three different schools of kabbalistic speculation crystallized in the imagination of a certain Spanish Jew by the name of Moses ben Shemtov de Leon. The result was the writing of the Zohar *(Book of Splendor),* a work of extraordinary quality which was to exert profound influence upon virtually all subsequent Jewish mystical creativity. The Zohar is one of the seminal pieces of Jewish literature, a genuinely unique book without parallel in the whole history of Judaism.

As befits an esoteric work such as the Zohar, questions of its authorship and origin have been surrounded by a certain degree of intrigue ever since its appearance in the second half of the thirteenth century. The intrigue has to do with the fact that Moses, who was born in about 1240 in the town of Leon, near Castile, began circulating manuscripts in the 1280s and 1290s which he had written, but which he claimed were ancient Midrashim, interpretive and homiletical comments on Scripture. Moses pretended merely to be copying from a manuscript which, he argued, originated in the circle of the second-century Palestinian rabbi, Shimon bar Yohai, but had only recently made its way to Spain. In all likelihood, de Leon opted to write in this pseudepigraphic way out of the conviction that a work of antiquity would be more readily considered to be authoritative truth. In the introduction to his translation of Zohar texts (see the bibliographical suggestions), Daniel Matt suggests, moreover, that Moses de Leon was able to set loose his imagination by attributing these teachings to someone other than himself:

> By surrendering his identity to Rabbi Shimon and company, by adopting a talmudic alter ego, Moses de Leon has been liberated. Relieved of the burden of self-consciousness, he is free to plumb the depths of his soul and soar to timeless dimensions. Released from the constraints of acknowledged authorship, he can record his own ecstasy and pathos. The personality of Rabbi Shimon makes him immune from criticism and enables him to publish all secrets. He expounds mythology and mysticism; revels in anthropomorphic and erotic imagery. (p. 27)

In any case, this pretense might have gone unchallenged had it not been for the appearance of a certain Isaac of Acre who traveled from Palestine to Spain where he settled in the year 1305. With his curiosity aroused by reports of a recently discovered manuscript purported to have been composed by Rabbi Shimon bar Yohai, Isaac sought out Moses in the city of Valladolid. De Leon agreed to show Isaac the manuscript in Moses' home in Avila. This meeting never took place, however, as Moses died while on his way home from Valladolid. Isaac eventually went to Avila where he was astonished to hear a report according to which Moses' wife denied that her husband had ever possessed such a book. She is said to have announced that her husband actually composed the work by himself!

While it is unclear what Isaac made of all this, we do know that early on at least—and to a certain extent down through the centuries—some skepticism accompanied the Zohar's claim to have originated in Talmudic times. A kabbalist by the name of Joseph ibn Wakkar of Toledo, as late as 1340, cautioned his readers to take care in using the Zohar as it contained many errors.

Despite Isaac's investigative activities, and other occasional challenges to the antiquity of the Zohar, Moses de Leon's attempt to portray the Zohar as a text from rabbinic times succeeded. The memory of de Leon himself eventually retreated into the background as the Zohar established itself as an authoritative work of mystical wisdom, written by none other than the great sage, Shimon bar Yohai. It was this literary ploy on Moses' part, along with the inherent fascination with which the Zohar was greeted, which ultimately assured the Zohar's near-canonical status by the sixteenth century. Alongside the Bible and Talmud, the Zohar was studied with reverence, awe, and intensity by Jews in the most diverse communities throughout the world. And as with the Bible and Talmud, the Zohar spawned an entire literature consisting of commentaries, guides to its study, translations and imitations.

Two imitations in particular, written by a single anonymous author near the end of the thirteenth or beginning of the fourteenth century, actually became an integral part of the corpus of Zoharic literature. These are known as *Tikkunei Zohar* and the *Raaya Meheimna*. While the *Raaya Meheimna* was incorporated into the three printed volumes of the original Zohar, *Tikkunei Zohar* was printed as a separate volume. Yet a fifth volume, *Zohar Hadash,* contains Zoharic texts found in manuscripts from sixteenth century Safed, but which had not been included in the original printing of the Zohar. In addition to all this, the Zohar served as the inspiration for centuries worth of independent kabbalistic treatises of diverse sorts. It must thus be regarded as the chief cornerstone of all kabbalistic literature. Indeed, it is difficult to imagine the history of Jewish literature and Judaism without the Zohar.

The work produced by Moses de Leon is actually made up of two basic strata composed over a number of years. The oldest stratum, which he entitled *Midrash ha-Neelam (Hidden Midrash),* was written sometime between 1275 and 1280. Composed in a mixture of Hebrew and Aramaic, de Leon had not yet settled on Shimon bar Yohai as his protagonist. Instead, he introduces a range of rabbinic authorities, emphasizing especially the supposed mystical teachings of another sage, Eliezer ben Hyrcanus. Between 1280 and 1286 de Leon wrote the main body of the Zohar, which itself consists of a variety of literary styles and a wide range of subjects. The largest portion of this material is arranged according to the weekly Torah portions into which the Five Books of Moses are traditionally divided. It is not, however, anything like a systematic commentary. De Leon chooses selected verses from each portion of the Torah that appeal to him and that he utilizes for his own creative purposes. Whereas the *Midrash he-Neelam* is characterized by short homilies, the main body of the Zohar tends toward much lengthier interpretations which frequently give way to various kinds of stories, monologues, and novelistic-like dialogues.

Shimon bar Yohai and his son Eleazar, along with a small group of disciples or companions, are the primary actors here. They are portrayed as traveling about the land of Israel using every possible opportunity to pause and converse about hidden mysteries of the Torah. The Zohar describes an almost idyllic situation in which the companions appear to have little else to do but sit down by a tree, a stream, or in a cave in order to indulge in mystical discourse. The following example is typical:

> Rabbi Shimon set out one time for Tiberias, and with him were Rabbi Yose, Rabbi Judah, and Rabbi Hiyya. On the road coming toward them they met Rabbi Phineas. All dismounted and sat down on the mountainside, under a tree. Rabbi Phineas spoke: While we sit, I should like to hear some of those wondrous ideas which figure in your discourse daily.
> —ZOHAR I, 49b

These discourses frequently end with an expression of delight and gratitude on the part of those present for having had the privilege of listening to such marvelous teachings. This gratitude is so intense, so palpable, that the reader almost feels invited to share in their pleasure:

> Rabbi Eleazar and the companions then approached him (i.e., Rabbi Shimon after he had finished speaking) and kissed his hands. Rabbi Abba was also present. Said he: "Had I come into this world only to hear these words, it would have been worthwhile." Then he wept, and said: "Woe unto us, Master, when thou shalt depart from the world! Who will then light up for us the greater radiances of the Torah? This subject was hidden in darkness until now, but at last it has emerged and shines even unto the highest heavens."
> (II, 193b)

There is, in the Zohar, a very strong quality of drama, a sense of the importance of the present, of every word spoken. Every moment is an opportune one for mystical conversation, each word is spoken and listened to as if the fate of the universe depended on it. Unlikely individ-

uals—a young child or a humble donkey driver—turn out to be repositories of the most recondite wisdom. Rabbi Shimon and his disciples are
portrayed as divulging secret mysteries which have incalculable potential
to transform themselves, the Jewish people, and even God.

The language they speak is Aramaic, the language in which the
Talmud is written. While the Aramaic was no doubt used by de Leon to
help establish the antiquity of his work, it also had the effect of bestowing upon the Zohar an aura of mystery. The Aramaic is contrived,
replete with medieval usages in grammar, syntax, vocabulary, and ideas;
de Leon derived all his knowledge of it from the rabbinic texts composed
in this language.

The Zohar's literary sources covered a wide range. In addition to
the Talmuds, he drew generously upon many of the classic Midrashim.
From the literature of the medieval period, he utilized biblical commentators such as Rashi, Abraham ibn Ezra, David Kimhi, and Moses ben
Nahman. His earlier flirtation with philosophy is reflected in his use of
Maimonides' *Commentary to the Mishnah, Guide of the Perplexed* and *Mishneh Torah.* Finally, and most significantly, de Leon was influenced by a
variety of kabbalistic writings. These include the *Sefer ha-Bahir,* the
works of Ezra and Azriel of Gerona, and the books of the Castilian
"Gnostics" with whom he had close contact. In addition to these
sources, Moses' playfulness and fancifulness is evidenced by his frequent
allusion to or "quotation" from an entirely fictitious set of books, including the Book of King Solomon, the Book of Adam, and the Book
of Rav Hamnuna the Elder.

To what may we attribute the power of the Zohar and the strong
appeal that it has held for readers over the centuries? The answer to this
question is not to be found in the book's mystical ideas per se, remarkable though they surely are. Similar themes may be found in many other
kabbalistic works, written before and after the Zohar. Yet of all the
kabbalistic books composed up until the sixteenth century, the Zohar
alone stimulated a particular kind of enthusiasm. It is not that the structure of the author's midrashic homilies are so exquisite, but rather that
we are confronted by a mind that possesses remarkable imaginative
resourcefulness. It is the depth of his insight, the vivid character of his
imagination, which alternately charms, disarms, mystifies, and arouses
the reader. No ordinary writer, de Leon had to have composed out of
the wellsprings of his own contemplative experience. The Zohar stands
in sharp contrast to that other awesome monument of medieval Jewish
faith, Maimonides' *Guide of the Perplexed,* with its architectonic structure, restrained rhetoric and austere logic (see Chapter Five). With the

Zohar it is the flashes of insight and intuition, and the seemingly limitless images with which God is described, which one finds so compelling. It is the flights of fantasy, the ability of the author's mind to grasp and articulate in symbols the inexhaustible dimensions of divine life, which so indelibly impress themselves upon the reader.

We close this section with a brief passage from the Zohar which we hope will illustrate something of what we have in mind. Later in this chapter we will analyze a section from the Zohar in some detail. The passage below describes how, from the depths of God's hiddenness, the process of divine self-revelation took place. Even without analyzing its symbolic details, it provides us with a glimpse into the Zohar's appeal to the imagination.

THE CREATION OF *ELOHIM*
ZOHAR I, 15a★

In the Beginning

When the King conceived ordaining
He engraved engravings in the luster on high.
A blinding spark flashed
within the Concealed of the Concealed
from the mystery of the Infinite,
a cluster of vapor in formlessness,
set in a ring,
not white, not black, not red, not green,
no color at all.
When a band spanned, it yielded radiant colors.
Deep within the spark gushed a flow
imbuing colors below,
concealed within the concealed of the mystery of the Infinite.
The flow broke through and did not break through its aura.
It was not known at all
until, under the impact of breaking through,
one high and hidden point shone.
Beyond that point, nothing is known.
So it is called Beginning,
the first command of all.

★ This translation is drawn from Daniel Matt, *Zohar, The Book of Enlightenment* (New York: Paulist Press, 1983) p. 49. We acknowledge the Paulist Press for its permission to use this material.

KABBALISTIC THEOLOGY AND SYMBOLISM

Having considered the historical and literary setting of early Kabbalah, we now turn our attention to a discussion of kabbalistic theology
and symbolism. One useful way of thinking about the distinctive character of kabbalistic thought is to compare it with other forms of Jewish
spirituality. Rabbinic Judaism—as formulated in the literature of the
Talmud and Midrashim—and medieval Jewish philosophy constitute the
two most prominent theological systems prior to the emergence of Kabbalah. What is the basic conception of God and the nature of His relationship to the world from the point of view of these two traditions?
What kind of knowledge can human beings have of God, and in what
ways do they enter into relationships with Him? By asking these questions of rabbinic Judaism and medieval philosophy we will be able to
discover the distinctive religious point of view expressed in the literature
of Kabbalah. In the present essay we can, of course, do little more than
briefly characterize the views of the rabbis and philosophical rationalists.

If it is possible to ask "where" God resides, the response of rabbinic
Judaism is that He is simultaneously far and near, or to use more theological language, transcendent and immanent. The question of God's
location is, of course, not really one about where God "lives" as much
as it is about the nature of His relationship to the world. God is said to
be transcendent in the sense that as *Creator* of all nature, He stands *apart*
from that which He has brought into being. Whereas various ancient
mythological systems located the gods in the very forces of nature, going
so far as to identify divine beings with nature, rabbinic Judaism insisted
on the radical separation of Creator and creation. Unlike everything else
that exists, God is neither subject to the laws of nature nor limited in
any way whatsoever. From the point of view of human experience, God
is exalted above all else. He is the awe-inspiring mystery behind creation.
In the words of the historian of religion, Rudolf Otto, He is the *myster-
ium tremendum;* or, as Abraham Joshua Heschel expressed it, He is the
One who evokes in us wonder and radical amazement.

Do the rabbis leave us, then, with a God who is utterly distant from
creation and humankind, who is indifferent and uninvolved with history? This view—known in the philosophy of religion as deism—is
altogether rejected by the sages. On the contrary, God is near to humanity, He is called *Shekhinah,* the "close presence" which is everywhere
accessible. Thus, for example, the rabbis taught that the reason why God

appeared to Moses out of a thorn bush was to demonstrate that no place is devoid of His presence. God heeds the human cry, He listens to the prayer of worshipers, He protects and preserves His people Israel. If the concept of transcendence did not translate into deism, so too the conception of immanence did not translate into pantheism, the notion that God and nature are identical. To say that God is near to creation is not to say that He and the world are one and the same thing.

In the place of pantheism and deism, rabbinic Judaism posits theism —the conviction that God is other than creation, but concerned with it. The different names by which deity is called in rabbinic literature capture these two poles of God's relationship to the world. As the transcendent Creator, He is called Almighty, the One on High, Master of the Universe, or King. In his nearness, He is known by such expressions as Father, the Place, the Merciful, and as we have seen, the Divine Presence.

God is known in a variety of ways. His greatness is testified by the wonders of nature. He is known through His work in history, discernible in microcosmic as well as macrocosmic events. Thus He revealed Himself at Sinai when He gave Israel the Torah. In prayer and devotion, individuals respond to God by praising Him, entreating Him, and expressing their love for Him. None of these ways of knowing God provide human beings with insight into the inner workings of God's "life" or "personality." Nor do they constitute communion in the mystical sense. As we shall see, on both of these accounts, rabbinic Judaism and Kabbalah part company.

When we turn to the philosophical systems of the medieval period, from the ninth century forward, we see that Jewish thinkers such as Saadia Gaon and Moses Maimonides confronted similar questions—although they dealt with them in far more systematic ways than did the rabbis of late antiquity. To the philosophers, the most important task was to preserve the absolute integrity of God's *transcendence* vis à vis the world. While they did not deny the rabbinic conviction that God is providentially concerned with the world, the philosophers placed the greatest emphasis upon the otherness and uniqueness of God. To them God was utterly beyond comparison to anything in nature. He is incorporeal, without body; unlike human beings, He is not subject to change or limitation. It is fair to say that the philosophical rationalists took up the theme of transcendence that rabbinic Judaism posited and drove it to extreme conclusions, making it the cornerstone of their theological vision.

These assumptions led to serious problems for the philosophers with regard to speaking about God. What can we possibly say about God without violating these convictions? The issue was most seriously joined in the effort to interpret Scripture which does, of course, describe God in *human* terms, that is, in anthropomorphic language. They employed various interpretive methods to show how to read the Bible properly. In the first place, the philosophers claim that we cannot say anything *positive* about God; we can only speak of God's attributes in *negative* terms. We can only say what God is *not*, rather than what He is. In addition, they used what is known as the doctrine of effects. According to this we can recognize the *effect* of God's actions in the world without actually claiming to know about God's Self. These techniques are not mere semantic games; they are the most earnest attempts to safeguard the pure idea of God against anything that would even *appear* to limit Him in any way. Finally, we should note the use of allegory, according to which biblical words or expressions that speak of God in human terms are to be understood as revealing some philosophical truth or idea. Thus when Scripture refers to God's "eye," it means to convey the notion of God's watchful, providential nature.

In the philosophical tradition, then, one's knowledge of God is actually determined by the individual's ability to recognize the extent of his or her ignorance. Understanding the Bible in the proper philosophical way, and learning what language may or may not be applied to God, are the means by which one refines the intellect and perfects oneself spiritually. One of the hallmarks of the philosophical enterprise is the extremely *conservative* way in which language is used to describe God. Because of God's incomparable nature there is ultimately very little that one can say about Him. As we shall see, it is precisely the question of what kind of language can be appropriately used to describe God that reveals the deep division between the medieval philosophers and kabbalists.

We are now in a position to examine the views of the kabbalists on these same religious questions. Although they inherited rabbinic theology, and although they were significantly influenced by the philosophical trends of their time, the kabbalists nevertheless developed a range of innovative and even daring conceptions. By spelling out the essential themes of kabbalistic theology, we ought to be able to assess some of the ways in which the medieval mystics departed from both the rabbinic and philosophical traditions.

1. THE DOCTRINE OF *EIN-SOF*

According to the kabbalists, the life of God may be said to comprise two parts, the first of which is known as *Ein-Sof.* Literally, *Ein-Sof* means "infinite" or "without end." In kabbalistic terms, it is that aspect of God which is utterly unknowable and unreachable, concealed beyond all human apprehension. The hidden and perfect root of all reality, *Ein-Sof* can be neither positively named nor imagined. At most it can be described as "that which thought cannot attain," "the concealed light," or "indistinguishable unity." Frequently, it is called the "root of all roots" or the "cause of causes." *Ein-Sof,* then, constitutes the dimension of the divine life that is absolutely transcendent, God as He is known only to Himself. The limitations of human cognition make it impossible for people to contemplate *Ein-Sof.* According to some kabbalists in fact, even Scripture makes no reference to God in His capacity as *Ein-Sof.*

This doctrine, with its radical insistence upon the inability of human beings to know God's inner essence, strongly resembles the "negative theology" of the medieval philosophers. If anything, the kabbalistic for-mulations are even more extreme than those of the rationalists. Were this the whole of the matter our description of Kabbalah might well have come to an abrupt halt. The kabbalists, however, go far beyond the philosophical point of view by means of the notion of the *Sefirot,* ten aspects of the divine that emerge from within the inner recesses of *Ein-Sof.*

2. THE DOCTRINE OF *SEFIROT*

With the conception of the *Sefirot* (singular, *Sefirah*) we arrive at the most prominent feature of the kabbalistic system, that which lends it its highly distinctive quality. As early as the first kabbalistic work, *Sefer ha-Bahir* (see above), the term *Sefirah* is related to the Hebrew word *sappir* (sapphire), suggesting the image of divine radiance or illumination. The ten *Sefirot,* or radiances of God, are *emanations* that flow out of the hidden wellsprings of *Ein-Sof.* It is as if the concealed dimension of God gives birth to other, more manifest parts of Itself. As we shall see, each of these *Sefirot* are known by different names and have highly distinctive characteristics.

We see immediately, then, that the kabbalists do not describe God in the conventional terms of the biblical or rabbinic tradition. In the Bible and rabbinic literature, God is one in number, not "divided" into component parts. It is true that He is described as having various attributes of personality, such as mercy, forbearance, and so forth. These, however, are personality traits in the way we speak of the personality of a friend. To the kabbalists, the *Sefirot* are not mere external traits, but symbols for the various essential elements of God's very life. That is, they should not be thought of as things we say *about* God, as if they were somehow separate from God's very being. Instead, they are the constituent elements, the organic parts of divine life. They are not mere metaphors, but symbols that point to *spiritual realities* comprising the life of deity.

One of the primary preoccupations of kabbalistic literature is the description of the way in which the *Sefirot* emanate from the hidden ground of all being, *Ein-Sof*. Whereas the rabbis of the Talmudic period simply assert God's existence, the kabbalists reflect, again and again, on the intricate process by which divine life moves from concealment to disclosure—a process that, in the first place, occurs entirely within God. The great difficulty they face at every turn is the paradoxical relationship between *Ein-Sof* and the *Sefirot*. While *Ein-Sof,* as we now know, is *beyond* the reach of human comprehension, the *Sefirot,* which derive from *Ein-Sof,* and which are ultimately bound up with it, are *accessible* to human imagining. Thus, the kabbalists are at pains to describe that subtle moment of transition in which the unknowable God becomes knowable in the guise of the *Sefirot*. A plethora of images are developed in kabbalistic literature to describe the relationship between *Ein-Sof* and the *Sefirot*. The latter are called "garments," "colors," "faces," "limbs," "crowns," and "names," among other things. All of these images have one thing in common: they seek to convey the idea that the *Sefirot* are outer layers of the hidden dimension of God to which they are intimately bound. They are ways of naming that which is ultimately beyond naming. They are, say the kabbalists, like the rays of the sun in relationship to the sun itself, or like the heat that radiates from a burning coal.

3. Sefirotic Symbolism

While *Ein-Sof* cannot be named, the *Sefirot* can be imagined using a tremendous variety of symbols. *Keter* (Crown) is the first and highest of the *Sefirot*. So closely united with *Ein-Sof* is *Keter* that many regarded it to be as much a part of the hidden God as it is an actual emanation from *Ein-Sof*. In this view, *Keter* has two sides to it, one that is bound to *Ein-*

THE SEFIROT

SEFIRAH	ENGLISH EQUIVALENT	NAME OF GOD	SOME ADDITIONAL NAMES AND SYMBOLIC ASSOCIATIONS
Keter	Crown	Ehyeh	Will, Nothingness, Primordial Ether, Hidden Upper Light, White, Black
Hokhmah	Wisdom	Yah	Beginning, Point, Beginning of Thought, Upper Father
Binah	Intelligence/ Understanding	YHVH (vocalized as Elohim)	Palace, Womb, Inner Voice, Upper Mother, Supernal Jubilee, Repentance
Hesed	Mercy/Love	El	Abraham, Water, Right Arm, White, South
Din (or Gevurah)	Judgment (or Power)	Elohim	Isaac, Left Arm, Red, North, Fire
Tiferet	Beauty	YHVH	Jacob, Torso, Holy One, Blessed Be He, King, Prince, Green, Son, Sun, Heaven, East, Wind, Written Torah, Tree of Life
Nezah	Lasting Endurance	YHVH Zevaot	Moses, Right Leg
Hod	Majesty	Elohim Zevaot	Aaron, Left Leg
Yesod	Foundation	El Hai or Shaddai	Joseph, Phallus, Righteous One
Malkhut (or Shekhinah)	Kingdom (or Presence)	Adonai	King David, Rachel, Lower Mother, Daughter, Bride, Princess, Queen, Speech, Blue, Black, Oral Torah, End of Thought, Apple Orchard, Tree of Knowledge, Seventh Year (Shemittah), Earth, Moon, Sabbath, Community of Israel, Great Sea, West

THE TEN SEFIROT

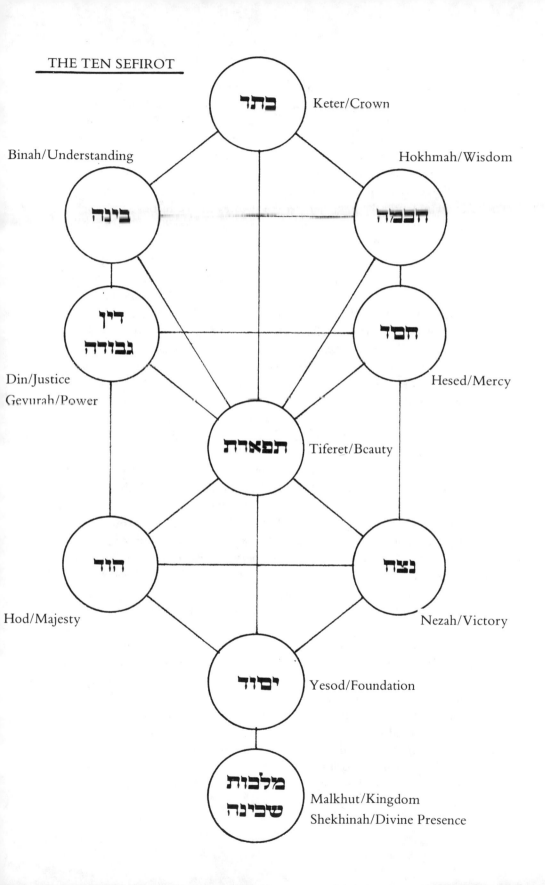

Keter/Crown

Binah/Understanding

Hokhmah/Wisdom

Din/Justice
Gevurah/Power

Hesed/Mercy

Tiferet/Beauty

Hod/Majesty

Nezah/Victory

Yesod/Foundation

Malkhut/Kingdom
Shekhinah/Divine Presence

Sof and one that turns outward toward that which is below it. The general opinion is that *Keter,* while intimately connected to *Ein-Sof,* does indeed constitute a distinct emanation. One of the favored names for *Keter* is primal Will, an appellation that expresses the conception that even the most subtle stirrings of volition can legitimately be applied only to that which is outside of *Ein-Sof.* Another image associated with *Keter* is divine Nothingness; from the subjective point of view of an individual contemplating the *Sefirot, Keter* constitutes the point beyond which the imagination cannot penetrate. It is the barrier between God's conceal-ment and manifestation.

It is only with the second *Sefirah, Hokhmah* (Wisdom), that we can speak of actual "thingness" or existence within the sefirotic structure. *Keter* looks downward, so to speak, and brings forth *Hokhmah,* a greater degree of divine willfulness. *Hokhmah* is called the "Beginning" or the primordial "Point," insofar as it constitutes the first truly discernible aspect of the Godhead. It represents the perfect idea of creation in the mind of the Creator. It is also imagined as an active masculine principle within God and is thus known as the "Upper Father." In an image suggesting the organic nature of divine existence, *Hokhmah* is said to impregnate the third *Sefirah, Binah* (Intelligence), thereby sowing the seeds of further unfolding of God. *Binah* is, then, the female coun-terpart to *Hokhmah,* the "Upper Mother," the "Womb" from which all the rest of life—divine and earthly—will emerge. It is, in other words, the union of the "parents" *Hokhmah* and *Binah* that results in the birth of their "children," the seven lower *Sefirot.* In Her capacity as divine Mother, She is called "Building" or "Palace," images suggest-ing the many "rooms" within *Binah* that contain the lower *Sefirot.* In another image, the relationship between *Hokhmah* and *Binah* is de-scribed as the flow of a stream of water from Eden *(Hokhmah)* into a river *(Binah).*

The fourth *Sefirah,* on the right side of the sefirotic diagram, is called *Hesed* (Mercy). It symbolizes that aspect of the divine that is wholly filled with God's "abundance" *(shefa)* and loving light. It is the vessel through which God's unrestrained love flows down into the lower regions, a source of the purest blessing and goodness. It is counterbal-anced on the left side by the fifth *Sefirah, Din* (Judgment). Were it not for the countervailing tendency of this *Sefirah,* the unbridled light of *Hesed,* would be too overwhelming for human beings to receive. Thus *Din* serves as a needed *restraint* upon the forces of *Hesed.*

While *Din* is absolutely necessary for all existence, it is at the same time regarded as the root of evil within the sefirotic structure! Here we

confront what is one of the truly remarkable features of kabbalistic mythology. The kabbalists do not hesitate to assert that the principle of evil
resides within God Itself. *Din* is capable of becoming full-fledged evil
when it fails to remain in harmonious balance with *Hesed*. This comes
about as a result of human sinfulness. The quality of divine limitation or
strictness becomes inflamed or aggravated and assumes the character of
actual evil. *Hesed* and *Din* reveal more than something about God's
moral nature. They express the intuition that love and strictness, flow
and restraint, are dialectical principles that are part of the very nature of
all existence.

Tiferet (Beauty), the sixth *Sefirah,* stands in the middle of the divine
structure. It is understood as a *harmonizing* principle which serves to
blend the forces of *Hesed* and *Din*. Through it, equilibrium is maintained
among the *Sefirot*. While all of the lower seven *Sefirot* are the offspring
of *Hokhmah* and *Binah, Tiferet* in particular is their "Son." Its most
common name is "The Holy One, blessed be He."

Nezah (Lasting Endurance) and *Hod* (Majesty), on the right and left
sides, respectively, are the seventh and eighth *Sefirot*. They symbolically
express two aspects of divine kingship. As *Nezah,* God is the compas-
sionate ruler, while as *Hod* God is a more regal king. *Yesod* (Foundation)
is the ninth *Sefirah* and is symbolized as phallus; it is the vehicle through
which the procreative vitality of the divine flows downward.

Malkhut is imagined as the receptive female, called also by the name
Shekhinah. She is receptive or passive in the sense that She possesses no
light of Her own, but is an empty vessel until She receives Her nourishment from the other *Sefirot*. She is filled with divine abundance from the
upper *Sefirot*. In rabbinic literature *Shekhinah* is not an independent entity, nor female in character. It is, as we saw earlier, merely the term
applied to God in His nearness to the world. In the Kabbalah, however,
we find an altogether different conception. Now the *Shekhinah* is *one* of
the ten manifestations of the Godhead, the "Daughter" of *Hokhmah* and
Binah. She goes by many other names, including "Lower Mother,"
"Princess," "Queen," "Bride," "Matrona," "Rachel," "Earth," and
"Moon." She is *Tiferet*'s lover. Unlike *Hokhmah* and *Binah* whose love
is described as harmonious and perfect, the relationship between *Tiferet*
and *Malkhut* is one of tension. Under the proper conditions they are in
perfect union while at other times this union is rent asunder. They
express the intuition that all life, patterned after the model of divine
being, is constituted of male and female. And they reveal the eternal
dialectic between male and female.

Thus far we have described some of the general associations of each of the *Sefirot*. But these are also part of various symbolic *systems*. One of the most important of these systems is the imagery that associates the *Sefirot* with the great personalities of the Bible. Thus Abraham, Isaac, and Jacob are symbols for the *Sefirot Hesed, Din,* and *Tiferet,* respectively. Moses and Aaron symbolize *Nezah* and *Hod,* while Joseph, exalted in the rabbinic Midrash for his virtuous sexual restraint, symbolizes the *Sefirah Yesod.* In its kingly role, *Malkhut* is symbolized by David. More commonly, though, it is symbolized by mother Rachel who weeps along with Her people in exile.

The *Sefirot* are also imagined as the various parts of the human anatomy. Indeed, one of the most important expressions for the sefirotic structure as a whole is Primal Man *(Adam Kadmon)*. In this symbolism, *Keter, Hokhmah,* and *Binah* correspond to the head and different parts of the intellect. *Hesed* and *Din* are God's right and left "arms," while *Nezah* and *Hod* are the right and left "legs." *Yesod,* as we have seen, is the phallus, while *Malkhut* represents the female genitalia.

The *Sefirot* are also imagined to be the various elements of divine speech. Whereas *Hokhmah* is divine thought which is too concealed to issue forth in speech, *Binah* is the *inner* voice which does not yet emit sound. *Tiferet* is the sound of the divine voice, but not yet fully articulated. *Shekhinah* is the locus of the actual speech *(dibbur)* of God, by reason of which it is generally associated with prophetic utterance, the fully articulate voice of God speaking through the medium of the prophets.

The many colors of nature are to the kabbalistic imagination symbols for the different colored lights within God. *Keter* is "the hidden upper light" which is pure white, or alternatively, pure black. *Hesed* and *Din* are frequently symbolized by the colors white and red, respectively, or alternatively, silver and gold. *Tiferet* is associated with green while *Malkhut* is symbolized by either blue, the color of the sea, or black. Still other images from nature form part of the vast symbolic world of the kabbalists. Thus, *Tiferet* and *Malkhut* are sun and moon, heaven and earth, light and darkness, East and West. *Hesed* is symbolized by water, *Din* by fire, and *Tiferet* by wind.

In sum, we have in the *Sefirot* a rich symbolic and mythic world. The possibilities of describing God through the imagery and symbolism of the *Sefirot* are plentiful. They may be understood as the symbols through which countless images from the natural world and human experience are used to convey the multiple dimensions of divine life. It should now be clear just how far beyond the rabbinic and philosophical conceptions of God the kabbalists go. The rabbis never dreamt of describing God in such intricately detailed and daring ways—endowing God with good *and* evil, or maleness and femaleness! Unlike the rabbis, the mystics boldly contemplate and describe the inner workings of deity. And as for the philosophers, few things could have been more offensive to their passionate effort to deny any plurality or multiplicity to God than the multilimbed divinity of the kabbalists. Despite the frequent attempts of the kabbalists to demonstrate that the *Sefirot* refer ultimately to the One, simple God, generally speaking the philosophical believer could not help but regard the kabbalistic conceptions with incredulity at best, and repugnance at worst.

4. THE LOWER WORLD

The sefirotic structure that we have thus far described comprises what the kabbalists refer to as the upper world, or the world of unity. Below the sefirotic realm is our world—the lower world or the world of separation. What is the relationship between these two levels of reality?

In the first place, the early kabbalists described the divine unfolding that takes place in the upper world and the creation of our world as two aspects of the very same process. Creation takes place on two levels simultaneously, the material world being a visible manifestation of a process that occurs in a concealed way in the sefirotic realm. One passage from the Zohar expresses it this way.

> The process of creation, too, has taken place on two planes, one above and one below, and for this reason the Torah begins with the letter "Bet," the numerical value of which is two. The lower occurrence corresponds to the higher; one produced the upper world, the other the lower world.
>
> —ZOHAR I, 240b

The primary difference between the two realms is that whereas the world of unity is one in which there is, ideally, perfect harmony and integration, the world of separation is characterized by materialization and flaw. Nevertheless, inasmuch as the lower world was created as a result of the emanation of divine life above, it *corresponds* to and *parallels* that world in its very structure. It constitutes a *mirror image* of the sefirotic realm. Everything in our world has a counterpart, a correspondence in the world above. The earth, moon, sun, stars, rivers, oceans, and all of the processes of nature of which they are a part, reveal to us the processes of dynamic life that take place on the level of the *Sefirot*. It is precisely because of this that the Kabbalah freely uses images from nature and the created world in order to express something about the inner workings of God's life. Gershom Scholem described this correspondence in these terms. "Everywhere there is the same rhythm, the same motion of the waves. The act which results beyond and above time in the transformation of the hidden into the manifest God, is paralleled in the time-bound reality of every other world. Creation is nothing but an external development of those forces which are active and alive in God Himself." *

Nothing in creation attests to this more than human beings themselves. As we have already seen, one of the ways in which the *Sefirot* are imagined is in the guise of the human form. Thus our own bodies reflect and thereby symbolize the constituent elements of the life of God.

To leave this subject at this point, however, would be to provide an incomplete picture of the kabbalistic view of the relationship between the two realms. For more than a relationship of correspondence is involved. Not only does everything in the material world *mirror* a spiritual reality above but everything in creation is *invested* with divine vitality *(hiyyut)* or abundance *(shefa)* from the *Sefirot*. There is a continuous flow of divine nourishment and blessing from one realm to the other, endowing all things in the lower world with life. God "fills everything" in the sense that all of nature pulsates with divine light. There is, in other words, a substantive continuity, an integral connection between the two levels of reality. In order to express this relationship the Kabbalah employs the image of a cosmic chain in which everything is *linked* to everything else. All the elements of existence—from the most hidden to the most visible—are intimately and inextricably bound to one another. All things trace their roots back to the inner recesses of the Source of all being, *Ein-Sof.*

While kabbalism's pantheistic tendencies are clear here, on the whole the kabbalists were not true pantheists. They resisted the impulse to completely identify God and the world, settling instead for a formulation in which all things in the created world are *enlivened* by virtue of the divine life within it. It was precisely their insistence on the radical concealment of *Ein-Sof* which made it possible for them to speak so freely about the manifold ways in which God infuses the material world. The notion of *Ein-Sof* establishes, in effect, that for all the symbols and images describing God's life and its integration into our world, the Root of all roots remains an inexhaustible mystery.

* *Major Trends in Jewish Mysticism,* p. 223.

5. The Role of the Individual

Where do human beings fit into this complex mythological scheme? Concerning this critical issue Kabbalah is as theologically daring as it is elsewhere. In traditional rabbinic terms, the biblical notion that woman and man are created in God's image means essentially that human beings alone are capable of imitating God. Endowed with speech, the ability to reason and to distinguish right from wrong, human beings are in a position to choose moral life. Nowhere, though, is the idea that humanity is created in God's image understood to mean that there is an actual *identification* with God. While we can find passages in rabbinic literature in which the soul is said to *resemble* God in that it is invisible, or that the soul sustains the body much in the way that God sustains the world, the soul is never identified as being divine in nature.

In the Kabbalah we find a fundamentally different approach. To the mystics, the human personality, as we have shown, represents the totality of the sefirotic structure and, even more, is imbued with divine life. This is most true of the highest part of the soul, the *Neshamah,* which is regarded as deriving directly from God. To the question concerning the precise source of the *Neshamah,* different answers are provided. For some kabbalists it is located in the *Sefirot Hokhmah* or *Binah,* while for others it derives from *Malkhut.* In any case, the important point is that the *Neshamah* is said to be made up of the same "stuff" as some aspect of God. Just as the Gnostics of an earlier age had taught that it was the *pneuma* or soul within a person that constitutes the divine portion, so the kabbalists taught that by virtue of the *Neshamah* there exists an intimate and immediate bond between human beings and God. The sixteenth-century kabbalist Elijah de Vidas expresses this notion that the soul derives from God in these words: "Souls are flaming threads drawn below from on high, their vitality stemming constantly from their Source."

While the lowest level of the three aspects of the human soul *(Nefesh)* is automatically present and active in every individual, the two more elevated levels, *Ruah* and *Neshamah,* are present only in the case of one who has become spiritually aroused, having striven to develop oneself through prayer, the study of Torah and religious observance. These activities assist in the development of the higher intuitive powers of cognition and represent the fullest maturation of the soul. It is the divine nature of the soul, and the fact that the individual constitutes a microcosm of the sefirotic world that serve as the basis for what is surely one of the most remarkable kabbalistic convictions. This is the idea that human deeds have an effect upon the upper world. Every action reverberates, so to speak, on the level of the *Sefirot.*

In order to understand this conception more clearly we need to discuss an aspect of kabbalistic mythology that we have thus far put aside. The kabbalists taught that prior to Adam's sin there was no material world whatsoever. Adam himself was of a purely spiritual nature. What is more, the *Sefirot* interacted with one another in a state of perfect harmony. With Adam's fall, however, this paradisical situation ended. Adam assumed bodily form and was no longer located in the upper world. The intrasefirotic relationship was no longer characterized by unceasing unity. Instead, a degree of disharmony was introduced, most frequently conceived as separation between *Tiferet* and *Malkhut,* male and female within God. The task of all human beings is to *restore* the original harmony through ritual and moral activity. Every proper deed contributes to the well-being of the life of God while every improper action serves to reinforce the disunity within divine life. Insofar as every individual possesses a spiritual essence that links them with the sefirotic world, each person has the inherent capacity to effect the life of God. No gesture, no utterance of speech, no thought is lacking in potential significance in the higher realms of reality. As the Zohar itself says: "The impulse from below calls forth that from above" (Zohar I, 64a).

Not only does proper action contribute to the reintegration of divine life, but the momentary reunification of God brought about by such an action enables divine light to flow downward into the material world. That is, earthly deeds stimulate or arouse the life of the *Sefirot* in such a way as to cause energy from the upper world to descend into the lower. Thus there is a *mutual* and *dynamic* relationship between human beings and the transcendent realm with which they are so essentially united. As a microcosm, a perfect paradigm of the upper world, and as one *link* in a cosmic chain of being, a person simultaneously reflects the world of deity and arouses it—only to be aroused and nourished in return.

To put this another way: proper earthly action serves to *reverse* the consequences of Adam's sin in two ways. In the first place, it reunites the life of God itself, chiefly by restoring the love between *Tiferet* and *Malkhut.* Second, it reestablishes the relationship between an individual and the *Sefirot.*

Prayer is one of the primary means by which people can accomplish these mystical goals. The words of the liturgy, according to the kabbalists, *symbolize* the various *Sefirot.* In the course of prayer the mystical adept is able to contemplatively focus on the *Sefirot* and their meaning. By doing so one can imaginatively reascend the ladder of the sefirotic realm and bind oneself to God. Prayer was thus transformed by the kabbalists into a vehicle for "repairing" divine life and enabling divine abundance to flow back into the lower realm. Here we see that the mystics did not discard traditional forms of observance in the pursuit of spiritual life; instead, they endowed conventional forms with new and deeper meaning. In addition, they devised altogether novel rituals and meditative techniques that set apart their practice from that of nonkabbalists.

I lere too we find a decisive break with both rabbinic and philosophical Judaism. For in Kabbalah not only has the *conception* of God so radically changed, but the *function* of religious observance has been redefined and invigorated with altogether new status. The cosmic repercussions of religious deeds is one of the most far-reaching and radical conceptions of Jewish mysticism. The effect of kabbalistic theology—although the mystics themselves never spell out such a conclusion—is to thoroughly revise the notion of God's autonomy. God is no longer conceived to be in control of all history in the older sense; rather, God's *own* well-being is determined by human action. While in rabbinic theology God may be said to mourn and suffer distress upon witnessing Israel's fate, He cannot be said to experience *injury,* let alone injury that can only be healed by virtuous human activity. As for the medieval philosophers, their conviction that God is not subject to change in any way whatsoever could not have been more antithetical to the conception of the kabbalists.

There can be little doubt that the appeal of Kabbalah had something to do with this new sense of opportunity and responsibility with which it endowed religious life. For it suggested that even if the external realities of history—and Israel's situation within that history—cannot be decisively shaped by individual action, the inner, spiritual realities can be. The popular success which Kabbalah eventually achieved must also be attributed to its willingness to take up with vigor the questions of evil and the demonic, as well as the issue of sexuality's role in the spiritual life. Matters such as these—which occupy so much attention in the literature of Kabbalah—were ones that rational philosophy did not address in ways that satisfied the average individual. Moreover, by its theology and its mythical symbolism, Kabbalah represented a means by which people could imagine and commune with a living God. It allowed them to discover in themselves, in Torah, and in the world of nature, signals of transcendence.

A Passage of Zohar

> *YHVH* spoke to Moses, saying:
> "Speak to the Children of Israel, saying:
> On the fifteenth day of this seventh month
> the Festival of *Sukkot,* seven days for *YHVH* . . .
> When you have gathered in the yield of the land
> celebrate the Festival of *YHVH* seven days:
> a complete rest on the first day
> and a complete rest on the eighth day.
> On the first day take fruit of lovely trees,
> branches of palm trees, boughs of leafy trees
> and willows of the brook.
> Rejoice in the presence of *YHVH* your God seven days.
> Celebrate it, a festival to *YHVH,* seven days a year.
> An eternal decree throughout the generations:
> celebrate it in the seventh month.
> Seven days dwell in *sukkot;*
> every citizen in Israel shall dwell in *sukkot,*
> so that your generations may know
> that I lodged the Children of Israel in *sukkot*
> when I brought them out of the land of Egypt,
> I, *YHVH* your God."
> —Lev. 23.33–34, 39–43 ★

GUESTS IN THE SUKKAH
Zohar III, 103b–104a †

Rabbi Eleazar opened
"Thus says *YHVH:*

★ Unlike the Zohar itself, which does not provide this full citation of biblical verses, we have provided the scriptural passages that serve as the basis for the Zohar's homily. The Zohar text immediately preceding ours does cite Leviticus 23.42 which, as we shall see, plays an important role in our passage. In general, it is a good idea when studying a text from the Zohar involving scriptural verses, to open a Bible and look at the context in which those verses are found. The Zohar may have in mind verses it does not quote at the beginning of the homily.

† As we indicated above, the main part of the Zohar is divided into three printed volumes. The first volume contains the Zohar's comments on the book of Genesis, the second volume comments on Exodus, while the third comments on verses from Leviticus, Numbers and Deuteronomy. Each volume is further divided into portions *(parashot)* based on the weekly Torah cycle of the Penta-

'I remember the devotion of your youth,
your love as a bride,
how you followed Me in the wilderness, in a land unsown.' "

—JER. 2.2

Zohar portion *Emor* contains, among other things, commentary having to do with the pilgrimage festival of *Sukkot*. In typical Zoharic fashion, first a verse from another part of the Bible is cited and interpreted for the purpose of shedding light on the meaning of the verse or verses under consideration. In our case, the author of the Zohar is interested in commenting on Leviticus 23.42–43: "Seven days dwell in *sukkot;* every citizen shall dwell in *sukkot,* so that your generations may know that I lodged the Children of Israel in *sukkot* when I brought them out of the land of Egypt. . . ." He does so by citing Jeremiah 2.2 because it bears an intimate connection to the verses in Leviticus. Jeremiah is recalling the wandering of the people Israel in the wilderness which is, of course, the period during which the Israelites built temporary booths in which to dwell. The interpretation given to Jeremiah 2.2 will serve to illumine or explain the original scriptural quotation from Leviticus. This technique of juxtaposing scriptural verses from different parts of the Bible is characteristic of rabbinic Midrash.

This verse refers to the Community of Israel
when She was walking in the wilderness along with Israel.

The Zohar begins by elucidating the kabbalistic meaning of Jeremiah's words. The Zohar's expression "Community of Israel" *(Knesset Yisrael)* refers *not* to the actual people Israel, but symbolically to the tenth and final *Sefirah, Malkhut* or *Shekhinah. YHVH,* which symbolizes the fifth *Sefirah, Tiferet,* is thus addressing His beloved, the *Shekhinah,* rather than the people Israel, when He says: "I remember the devotion of your youth . . ." The literal meaning of Scripture is completely transformed, in other words, as Rabbi Eleazar replaces the people Israel with the *Shekhinah* as the object of *YHVH'*s love.

---

teuch itself. The text under consideration is found in portion *Emor,* that is, that part of the Zohar which comments upon selected verses from *Emor* (Lev. 21–24). Zohar III, then, refers to the third volume of the three volumes of the Zohar, while 103b–104a refers to the folios on which our particular text is found. The letter *b* indicates the *recto* or righthand side of a page, while the letter *a* indicates the *verso* or lefthand side of a page. We want to acknowledge the Paulist Press for its permission to use the translation of this passage from Daniel Matt, *Zohar, The Book of Enlightenment* (1983), pp. 148–51.

'I REMEMBER THE DEVOTION'
This is the cloud of Aaron
which floated along with five others,
all bound to You, shining on You.

According to a passage from the Talmud (*Sukkah* 11b), Rabbi Eliezer teaches that the verse "I lodged the children of Israel in *sukkot*"
refers to "clouds of [God's] glory" rather than actual booths. These
clouds represented the Divine Presence which surrounded and protected
the people while they journeyed in the desert. According to another
rabbinic text, from the Midrash (Numbers Rabbah 1:2), Rabbi Hoshaya
says that there were *seven* such clouds. These two related rabbinic motifs
are now drawn upon in the Zohar for the purpose of explaining Jeremiah's words. The seven clouds of glory of which the Midrash speaks,
in which the children of Israel were "lodged," are now *kabbalistically*
understood to refer to the seven lower *Sefirot, Hesed* through *Malkhut.*
The scriptural word "devotion" *(Hesed)* corresponds to the first of these
seven; it represents the *Sefirah Hesed* inasmuch as Aaron was the high
priest, priest being a symbol for *Hesed* in the Zohar. Thus the cloud of
Aaron (i.e. *Hesed*), along with the five "clouds" or *Sefirot* below it, are
joined to the seventh "cloud" *Malkhut* or *Shekhinah* who escorted Israel
in the desert.

'YOUR LOVE AS A BRIDE'
They decorated, crowned, and arrayed You
like a bride bedecked with jewels.
Why all this?
Because 'YOU FOLLOWED ME IN THE WILDERNESS,
      IN A LAND UNSOWN'

The six "clouds" or *Sefirot* above *Shekhinah* decorated and adorned
Her as befits a bride. They dwelled with Her and filled Her with their
divine radiance. The reason for this is because the *Shekhinah* followed
YHVH in the wilderness, in a land unsown.

Come and See:
When one sits in this dwelling, the shade of faith,

Shekhinah spreads Her wings over him from above,
Abraham and five other righteous heroes come to dwell with
      him!

The Zohar now turns from Jeremiah to the meaning of the text
from Leviticus. We learn that when individuals fulfill the obligation of
dwelling in the *Sukkah*, then "the shade of faith," understood to mean
the *Shekhinah*, descends upon them. The *Shekhinah*, who contains the
light of the upper *Sefirot*, "spreads Her wings over him from above."
This same idea is conveyed in another way by reference to "Abraham
and five other righteous heroes." They symbolize the *Sefirot* of *Hesed*,
Din, *Tiferet*, *Nezah*, *Hod* and *Yesod*, respectively. These are Abraham,
Isaac, Jacob, Moses, Aaron and Joseph. Here we have one of the central
themes of our text. These patriarchs and biblical figures are *symbols* for
various *Sefirot*, different dimensions of God's being which, along with
the *Shekhinah*, dwell with a person as he or she fulfills the obligation of
celebrating in the *Sukkah*. The *Sukkah* becomes a truly sheltering environment when an individual is joined in it by the presence of the various
dimensions of divine life, the "patriarchs," that is, the lower *Sefirot*.
    Rabbi Abba adds a seventh figure, David, who is another symbol
of *Malkhut*.

      Rabbi Abba said
      "Abraham, five righteous heroes, and King David dwell with
            him!
      As it is written:
      'SEVEN DAYS, DWELL IN *SUKKOT*'
      'SEVEN DAYS' it says, not 'FOR SEVEN DAYS.'
      Similarly it is written:
      'SIX DAYS *YHVH* MADE HEAVEN . . .'
      (EXOD. 31.17)
      Day after day, one should rejoice with a radiant face
      along with these guests who abide with him."

The word "days," corresponding to the seven primordial days of
Creation, is a Zoharic symbol for the *Sefirot*. Thus, by means of Rabbi
Abba's syntactical reconstruction of the verse Leviticus 23.42, according
to which he reads the words "You shall live in booths for seven days"
as "Seven Days, dwell in *Sukkot*," the seven lower *Sefirot* are instructed
to dwell in the *Sukkah*. Words which in the plain meaning of the biblical
text are instructions to the Israelites to dwell in booths, are now trans-

formed into a *directive* to the *Sefirot* to join an individual in his or her celebration.

On the basis of these motifs, a kabbalistic ritual developed known as *Ushpizin,* the welcoming of guests, that is, the sefirotic guests, into one's *Sukkah.* On each of the seven nights of *Sukkot,* all the patriarchs are invited, although each night a different one of them is featured. Thus, on the first night, the following words are recited in the *Sukkah:* "O Abraham, my exalted guest, may it please you to have all the exalted guests dwell with us—Isaac, Jacob, Joseph, Moses, Aaron and David." The celebration of *Sukkot* was thus transformed into a mystical rite in which the celebrants contemplatively focused on the indwelling presence of the various qualities of God which visit as guests in the *Sukkah.* This ritual can be found in most sephardic prayerbooks, or any prayerbook that contains kabbalistic customs and liturgical variations.

It is worth pointing out that this is only one of a significant number of rituals that were introduced into Jewish practice by Kabbalah. Other such rites include the practice of studying specific sections of biblical, rabbinic, and kabbalistic literature throughout the evening of Shavuot *(Tikkun Leil Shavuot),* the midnight vigil for purposes of prayer and study known as *Tikkun Hazot,* the celebration of the day before the new moon as a "minor Day of Atonement" *(Yom Kippur Katan),* and best known of all, *Kabbalat Shabbat,* the special service that ushers in the Sabbath. (See Chapter Eight.) Similarly, the practice of reciting the Song of Songs on Sabbath eve, as well as Proverbs 31.10–31 at the festive Sabbath table, are customs that originated among the kabbalists. A number of these and other rituals are still practiced among Jews today; indeed, some, such as *Tikkun Leil Shavuot,* are enjoying renewed popularity. Taken together, they demonstrate that kabbalism exerted very great influence upon Jewish ritual and devotional life, as well as Jewish theology.

And Rabbi Abba said
"It is written: 'SEVEN DAYS, DWELL IN *SUKKOT';*
then, 'SHALL DWELL IN *SUKKOT.'*
First, 'DWELL'; then, 'SHALL DWELL.'
The first is for the guests;
the second, for human beings.

The two different references to dwelling in *Sukkot* found in Leviticus 23.42 are understood to indicate two different *kinds* of guests. The expression "Seven days, dwell in *Sukkot*" refers, as we have seen, to the sefirotic guests, while the slightly different expression "shall dwell in *Sukkot*" refers to human guests.

> The first is for the [sefirotic] guests:
> as Rav Hamnuna Sava, upon entering the *sukkah,*
> used to stand in joy inside the opening and say:
> 'Let us invite the guests!'
> He would set the table, stand erect, recite a blessing
> and then say:
> 'Seven Days, dwell in *sukkot!*
> Sit down, sublime guests, have a seat!
> Sit down, guests of faith, have a seat!'
> Raising his hands in joy, he would say:
> 'Happy is our portion!
> Happy is the portion of Israel!
> As it is written:
> "THE PORTION OF YHVH IS HIS PEOPLE" '
> (DEUT. 32.9).
> Then he would sit down.

The blessing that Rav Hamnuna Sava, a third-century Babylonian teacher, is said to have recited is the traditional blessing in the *Sukkah:* "Blessed are You, *YHVH* our God, King of the Universe, who has sanctified us by His commandments and commanded us to dwell in the *Sukkah.*" This blessing is recited directly following the festival *kiddush* or sanctification over wine.

> The second, for human beings:
> One who has a portion among the holy people and in the holy
>   land
> sits in the shade of faith to welcome the guests,
> to rejoice in this world and the world that is coming.
> Nevertheless, he must make the poor happy.
> Why?
> Because the portion of those guests whom he has invited
> belongs to the poor.
> One who sits in this shade of faith
> and invites these sublime guests, guests of faith,
> and does not give them their portion—

all of them rise to leave, saying:
'DO NOT EAT THE FOOD OF A STINGY PERSON . . .'
(PROV. 23.6).
It turns out that the table he set is his own, not divine . . .''

Not only must an individual invite the sefirotic guests to join in the celebration, but he must also invite earthly guests, the poor. The poor, we are informed, are "the portion of those guests (i.e., the *sefirot*) whom he has invited." The meaning of this is that Abraham and his compatriots are honored and served through the generosity shown to the needy. If there are no poor people present at the festive meal, the guests from the upper world "rise to leave" his table. A sacred table is one to which the poor are invited; one who seeks divine blessing, to establish a bond between oneself and the divine realm, must see to the needs of the poor.

We see here that the mystical and the ethical are not separate aspects of spirituality in the Zohar. In order for the divine guests to remain with a person, one must also see to the needs of fellow human beings. Ethical action itself serves a deeply mystical function.

> Rabbi Eleazar said
> "Torah does not demand of a person more than he can do,
> as it is written:
> 'EACH ACCORDING TO WHAT HE CAN GIVE . . .'
> (DEUT. 16.17).
> But a person should not say:
> 'First, I will fill myself with food and drink;
> what is left I will give to the poor.'
> No, the prime portion belongs to the guests.
> If he makes the guests happy and full,
> the Holy One, blessed be He rejoices with him!''

In a midrashic passage from Exodus Rabbah 34.1 we learn that "The Holy One, blessed be He does not come to His creatures with excessive demands: He comes to a person only according to his capacity."

FURTHER COMMENTS

Several additional comments ought to be made about the passage in question and the process of analyzing Zoharic texts in general. Insofar as the Zohar interprets biblical verses, it is critical for the reader to look for and recognize the midrashic pretext upon which an interpretation depends. The reader must find out precisely what in a given verse constitutes the Zohar's interpretive concern, or at least is used as an excuse to express that concern. (This is a process similar to that described in Chapter Three on Midrash.) Thus, for example, as we saw above, the two different references to dwelling in *Sukkot* in Leviticus 23.42 are used as an opportunity to describe the two different kinds of guests that an individual is supposed to invite into the *Sukkah*. One also wants to pay close attention to the way in which a biblical verse from another location is used to explain the meaning of the primary text under discussion.

Moreover, we have learned that the reader must become accustomed to regarding biblical language in a kabbalistically symbolic way. The kabbalists taught that the Torah is not only the speech or word of God, but it is also the many names of God or expressions of God's being. It is a vast body of symbols which refers to the various aspects of divine life, the *Sefirot,* and their complex interaction. The simple meaning of biblical language recedes into the background as symbolic discourse assumes control. The true meaning of Scripture becomes manifest only when it is read with the proper (sefirotic) code. Thus, the Torah must not be read on the simple or obvious level of meaning; it must be read with the knowledge of a kabbalist who possesses the hermeneutical keys with which to unlock its *inner* truths. The kabbalists did not deny the simple level of the Bible's meaning. They claimed, however, to have discovered or recovered the truest, deepest level of understanding. The Zohar itself expresses it this way in an often cited passage:

> Thus the tales related in the Torah are simply her outer garments, and woe to the person who regards that outer garb as the Torah itself! For such a person will be deprived of a portion in the world to come. Thus, David said: "Open Thou mine eyes, that I may behold wondrous things out of Thy Torah" (Ps. 119.18), that is to say, the things that are underneath. . . . Just as wine must be in a jar to keep, so the Torah must be contained in an outer garment. That garment is made up of tales and stories; but we, we are bound to penetrate beyond.
> —ZOHAR III, 152a

If we consider the beginning of our original text again, we can explore this symbolizing process a bit further. One of the main clusters or constellations of symbols in this passage has at its center the symbol of the *Shekhinah*. The *Shekhinah* is depicted as the female lover of *YHVH,* or *Tiferet.* She is the *Bride* who devoted Herself to *YHVH* in the wilderness. In addition, She is called *Community of Israel (Knesset Yisrael)*, the divine counterpart to the earthly people Israel and a common kabbalistic symbol for *Shekhinah*. Going beyond the Talmudic-midrashic association of *Knesset Yisrael* with the historical people of Israel, the medieval kabbalists identified *Knesset Yisrael* with the feminine aspect of deity, *Malkhut/Shekhinah*. In the process, all of the references in the Talmud and Midrash to the people of Israel as God's bride, lover or daughter—such as are found, for example, in the rabbinic reading of the Song of Songs—were transferred to the image of the *Shekhinah*. The older meaning does not altogether disappear, but it does become—at least on the conscious level—less important than the esoteric one.

Not only is the *Shekhinah YHVH*'s lover and bride in our text, She is also the protector of the people of Israel. Along with the other "clouds" of God's glory, that is, the other lower *Sefirot,* the *Shekhinah* "spreads Her wings over him from above," when an individual dwells in the *Sukkah*. The *Shekhinah* is thus a sort of *Sukkah* Herself, as the Zohar itself states explicitly elsewhere (II, 135a). The shelter of the *Sukkah* is, esoterically speaking, the protection and comfort provided by the seven lower *Sefirot* (mediated through the *Shekhinah*) in which a person "lodges." We thus see from this that the symbol of *Shekhinah* is part of a broader pattern of imaginative associations: Lover/Bride/Community of Israel/Protecting Cloud and *Sukkah*. By recognizing the network of symbolic associations present in this passage we begin to gain a clearer sense of the richness and meaning of the imagery involved.

As we have already seen, the conception of deity as being constituted of male and female aspects is a central feature of kabbalistic mythology. The kabbalists transcend conventional rabbinic theology according to which God is exclusively masculine in nature. In so doing, Kabbalah shares much in common with other religious traditions in which feminine deity plays such an important role. As Lower Mother, Daughter, Bride, Princess, Queen, Earth, Moon, Sabbath, Sea—to name but a few of the associations connected to *Shekhinah*—this symbol enables the kabbalists to express a far broader spectrum of human experiences than is the case with more traditional theology. While it is not clear precisely how the kabbalists arrived at such conceptions, it is evident that they were seeking to go beyond the confines of conventional religious language and to express something new: Not only is God Father, King, Judge, Shepherd. God is also revealed through and signified by women, the moon, the oceans, the earth; moreover, the processes within the life of God are paradigmatically expressed in and through the male-female relationship.

From all of this we learn that one of the crucial tasks in studying the literature of the Zohar is to familiarize oneself with the symbolic associations with which the Bible is read. Thus, it is a useful idea to keep a list of the *Sefirot* and their associations as one learns them. But beyond becoming familiar with individual symbolic associations, it is necessary to learn to recognize the *networks* and patterns of associations which characterize Zoharic thinking.

In addition, it should be clear that the Zohar is as much commentary on earlier rabbinic and midrashic motifs as it is on the Torah itself. Thus we saw that the Zohar interprets Jeremiah's words in such a way as to kabbalistically transfigure rabbinic motifs originally developed in relationship to a verse from Leviticus. The Midrash figuratively interprets the *Sukkot* in which God lodged Israel to mean clouds of Divine Presence or glory. The Zohar appropriates this motif and transforms it by regarding these clouds as mystical symbols for the varied dimensions of God's inner life. In other words, the Zohar—along with numerous other kabbalistic works—is midrashic in more than literary *style;* it is thematically connected to a great network of midrashic motifs which it reshapes for its own purposes. The reader of the Zohar, then, ought to try and detect the midrashic background of the Zohar's images and motifs inasmuch as these connections frequently provide important insight into the meaning of the text.

On a different level of familiarity, one must develop the ability to think a bit as the Zohar itself does. Just as the Zohar represents a freeing of the mind from literalism and surface meaning, we need to do the same in studying Zohar. The symbol systems and images which are at the heart of kabbalistic literature cannot be understood simply by memorizing certain associations. They require, like the study of poetry or any imaginative literature, a deeper, more reflective sort of attentiveness. In this sense the study of Kabbalah may be somewhat different from that of certain other kinds of Jewish literature. Learning to think in imaginative or poetic ways is not something that comes naturally to most of us, but it is not impossible either. It seems to us that being at home in the world of kabbalistic literature involves becoming at least something of a kabbalist. A person can certainly gain a degree of appreciation for a piece of music by understanding its formal characteristics; but to come close to that music calls for a more personal involvement.

What is it that *distinguishes* us from the kabbalists themselves? Surely, it is our inclination to position ourselves at a distance from the immediacy of the text, its symbolism and its assumptions. That is, our cultural and intellectual vantage point is *different* from theirs. We may—

as students of religion in general—want to compare the notion of *Binah/ Shekhinah* with that of the Great Mother in Taoism, or the goddesses of Hindu mythology. Or we may learn something about the conception of the dark side of deity by reference to the speculative systems of the Gnostics. As students of literature we may find it intellectually interesting and religiously suggestive to think about Zoharic language in terms of one or another contemporary theories of semiotics, hermeneutics, or literary criticism. Insofar as we are students of Judaism as a whole, we can find value, as we have done earlier in this chapter, in comparing kabbalism with other kinds of Jewish theology, in thinking about it as one form of spirituality among a range of possibilities. We are in a position to consider kabbalistic creativity against the historical backgrounds and cultural influences that helped shape it.

In such ways we establish ourselves as different kinds of readers from the kabbalists themselves. To recognize this does not, of course, mean that we do not take the text with the utmost seriousness, or that it does not speak to us in important ways. It simply acknowledges the fact that we find ourselves in a fundamentally different situation from the kabbalists. The kabbalists may have had a more "limited" point of view, but they also had an intimate relationship to the texts which we can scarcely hope to recover. We may have a less natural relationship to the texts, but we enjoy a complex and diverse perspective that gives excitement to our reading. It may be an intriguing—but ultimately moot—problem to conjecture whether we are "better off" or "worse off" than the kabbalists. What we can say is that the texts themselves are still compelling and they continue to provide a bond between us and earlier communities of readers.

The Kabbalah in Sixteenth-Century Safed

Following the appearance of the Zoharic literature at the end of the thirteenth and beginning of the fourteenth centuries, kabbalistic activity continued unabated. Besides spreading to many parts of Spain, kabbalistic writing took place in Germany, Turkey, Italy, and elsewhere. Italy in particular was the scene of considerable interest in Kabbalah from the fourteenth century forward. Menachem Recanati, for example, composed a widely read kabbalistic commentary on the Torah at the beginning of the fourteenth century. Judah Hayyat was the sixteenth century author of a lengthy and important commentary on an earlier kabbalistic book, *Maarekhet ha-Elohut,* itself a classic work from Spain. It was in the sixteenth century that Kabbalah achieved unprecedented popularity—a turn of events associated with a small town in the Galilee known as Safed.

It is well known that following centuries of flourishing political, social, and cultural life in Spain, the Jews of that country were expelled in the year 1492. In the wake of the Spanish Expulsion, tens of thousands of Jews seeking refuge migrated to the Muslim countries of North Africa, to Italy, and to various parts of the Ottoman Empire. It was the Ottomans who actively welcomed the Jews of Spain, resulting in the development of a large and prosperous Jewish community.

An event of decisive importance for Jewry took place in the years 1516–17 when the Turks succeeded in extending their territory in the East by overpowering the Mamlukes, thus gaining control over Egypt, Syria, Palestine, and the Arabian Peninsula. As a result of these events Jews were able to settle in the land of Israel under highly favorable and secure conditions. The ensuing immigration, which reached into the end of the sixteenth century, brought to Palestine former exiles and their descendants who were already living under Ottoman rule, as well as Jews from North Africa, Italy, and the Germanic states. Many of these were individuals who had been forcibly converted to Christianity and were interested in openly returning to Judaism, and in doing penance for their sins. These immigrants joined Arabic-speaking Jews who had lived in the land even before the Arab conquest in the seventh century. It is estimated that by the middle of the sixteenth century there were approximately 10,000 Jews in the land of Israel.

For a variety of reasons Safed, located high in the Galilean hills, experienced the largest increase in population. Safed was the choice of many, in part, on account of the far greater economic opportunities there as compared to Jerusalem. Safed became especially known as a textile center of which the Jews were an important part, although they also occupied themselves with various crafts, agriculture, shopkeeping, and peddling. Additionally, the region around Safed was the burial place of numerous sages from the Talmudic period, lending it an aura of importance. Of particular significance in this regard was the presence, just a short distance from Safed, of the grave of Rabbi Shimon bar Yohai, to whom, as we have seen, tradition ascribes authorship of the Zohar.

Under these relatively stable conditions, a rather extraordinary community began to develop from about 1530 forward. Safed attracted an unusual array of scholars and rabbis. Religious life took on a vitality that the Jewish community in the land of Israel had not experienced for centuries, as Safed emerged as a great spiritual center, not only for the

Jews of that country, but for Near Eastern Jewry as a whole. In the study houses, synagogues, and academies, piety and learning flourished. In several different fields of Jewish literature Safed scholars made contributions that were to exert great influence upon Judaism. It was in Safed, for example, that Joseph Karo (1488–1575) composed the *Shulhan Arukh* (mentioned toward the end of Chapter Two) which is to this day regarded as the authoritative code of rabbinic law for traditional Jewish practice. Religious poetry of high quality, much of which made its way into the prayerbook, was written by men such as Israel Najara, Eleazar Azikri, Solomon Alkabez and Isaac Luria. (See the discussion in Chapter Eight.) Influential and innovative homiletical writings were composed by Moses Alsheikh, Elisha Gallico and others.

It was in the sphere of Kabbalah, however, that Safed made its most distinctive contribution, influencing the course of Jewish history in fundamental ways. Building upon earlier kabbalistic tradition Safed became the scene of a mystical renaissance of considerable proportions. The Safed mystics promoted a radically innovative doctrine, according to which the practice of mystical devotion was no longer to be confined to small conventicles or groups of initiates as had been the case in the thirteenth century; instead, it was held to be the legitimate domain of each and every person. This attempt to democratize and popularize the mystical life proved to have unforeseen consequences, the impact of which were felt long after Safed itself began to decline toward the end of the sixteenth century. The widespread messianic movement of the seventeenth century, Sabbatianism, had its roots in Safed kabbalism. Further, it is difficult to imagine the rise of Hasidism in the eighteenth century without the contribution made by sixteenth-century Kabbalah.

Between approximately 1530 and 1590 the kabbalists of Safed developed a theological world view and a religious way of life that were highly distinctive, even while they appropriated much of earlier Kabbalah. At the center of this new religious outlook was a synthesis between mysticism and messianic aspirations. Not long after the Spanish Expulsion, efforts were made to impose some meaningful religious perspective upon the events that had recently taken place. In this pre-Safed period, one of the most outstanding and influential advocates of an emerging messianic response was Isaac Abrabanel (1437–1508). Abrabanel was the author of a number of books that expressed hopes for redemption and interpreted contemporary events as messianic tribulations. He sought to convince the exiled Jews that the tragedy that had befallen them was purposeful, that it was a prelude to the arrival of the messianic age which he calculated would start in 1503.

In this post-expulsion period, a Jerusalem kabbalist by the name of Abraham ben Eliezer ha-Levi (c. 1460–c. 1530) became well known as a zealous messianic propagandist and preacher of repentance. Through his writings and activities he sought to inspire Jews to engage in penitence in order to ready themselves for the inevitable messianic coming—which would begin in the year 1524 and lead to the Messiah's appearance in 1530–31. This intense eschatalogical fervor, which hinged all its hopes on the conviction that the Messiah was about to appear, eventually dissipated after 1530 when these hopes went unfulfilled. It gave way to a rather different mood which can be discerned in the writings of the Safed community. This new mood differed from the older one in at least two basic ways.

To begin with, the view of the apocalypticists and messianic calculators toward the expulsion was, paradoxically, a positive one. Inasmuch as it fit into God's overall plan to usher in the messianic time, the tragic suffering brought on by the exile was ultimately a good thing, an unfortunate but indispensable element within the broader eschatalogical scheme of things. The point of view that emerged among the Safed kabbalists differed in that for them the exile did not have such positive meaning. They came, instead, to regard it more as the catastrophe it actually was, as another powerful illustration of the reality of Israel's exile and the severe bitterness of unredeemed existence. The earlier apocalyptic tension now gave way to the search for a resolution to the problem of exile on a deeper level of spirituality.

A second and intimately related departure from the earlier outlook was the appropriation of kabbalism on the part of the Safed mystics. While Abraham ben Eliezer ha-Levi may have utilized kabbalistic sources for the purpose of building a case for the imminence of redemption, he did not synthesize Kabbalah with messianic ideas in any fundamental way. In Safed, on the other hand, messianic views were, from the beginning, bound up with the deepest kabbalistic themes.

The strong sense of exile to which we have referred expressed itself in the preoccupation of the Safed mystics with the fate of the *Shekhinah*. As a feminine principle within God, the last of the ten *Sefirot* who possesses no divine light of Her own, but who only reflects the light of the upper *Sefirot,* the *Shekhinah* was regarded as having been cut off from the source of Her nourishment. The external realities of history, most recently the tragedy of the expulsion, were viewed as having their *parallel* in the life of God. Just as the people Israel had been dealt a severe blow, sent once again into exile, so too God Himself had suffered a rending. Even though the earlier Kabbalah of the Spanish period had already spoken of the *Shekhinah*'s exile, it was the mystics of Safed, now consumed by the horrors of historical exile, who took up this theme and pushed it to extremes.

A perfect illustration of this may be seen in a practice by Moses Cordovero and Solomon Alkabez, two of the leading figures of Safed. In a small book called *Tomer Devorah,* Cordovero described how he and Alkabez used to wander among the grave sites of rabbinic sages believed to be buried in the environs of Safed, in *imitation* of the wandering of the *Shekhinah*. In this practice—which resulted in their experiencing a form of automatic speech in which they uttered kabbalistic interpretations of biblical verses—we see how these individuals identified so intensely with the *Shekhinah*.

Whereas at an earlier time men such as Abraham ha-Levi had believed that the redemption would come of its own accord, the Safed kabbalists taught that it would *only* come if the people Israel worked for it. Mystical devotion of every sort—prayer and fulfillment of the commandments, rigorous ascetic behavior, ethical deeds—would lift the *Shekhinah* out of Her exile and restore Her to *Tiferet*. Every gesture, every rite now took on new importance. The reunification of male and female within God had messianic implications, thus imbuing religious life with the greatest of responsibilities. What is more, the Safed pietists, following a tradition found in the Zohar itself, which promised redemption if even one Jewish community would achieve perfect repentance, regarded themselves as standing at the very center of the messianic drama. In this drama, every single individual had a role to play and no action was without national and messianic significance. It is this more than anything else that defines the special nature of Safed spirituality.

Safed appropriated a theme that is axiomatic to Kabbalah as a whole, namely, the efficacious nature of human deeds, and made it the foundation of the religious life. It did so by heightening the stakes, so to speak. The Spanish kabbalists discussed earlier were, generally speaking, concerned more with their own individual spiritual condition than they were with history or the messianic end. The Safed pietists, by contrast, were motivated by a sense of responsibility for the cosmos as a whole. They believed that the collective efforts of this intensely single-minded community could reverse the flow of history, bringing about physical and spiritual redemption. The true redemption would occur, not when Israel had sunk to the lowest possible depths, but when it had succeeded in restoring all things to their flawless primordial condition.

While kabbalism permeated the air of sixteenth-century Safed in general, and few could have been left untouched by the powerful currents around them, there can be no doubt that some regarded themselves as especially devoted to the kabbalistic life. This resulted in the development of a number of *havurot* or intentional brotherhoods. These devout fellowships brought together individuals interested in a greater degree of specialization when it came to the life of piety. Persons of like mind could organize to pursue a particular course that served their needs. These *havurot* served to institutionalize kabbalistic life to a certain degree. They helped to define the proper direction piety ought to take and to channel religious energy in a disciplined way. Most of the individuals whose names appear with any frequency in the mystical literature are likely to have been associated with one or another of the several groups we know about. Some of the *havurot* were under the spiritual guidance of particular personalities, such as Moses Cordovero, Eleazar Azikri, Isaac Luria and, following Luria's death, Hayyim Vital. Other groups appear to have been devoted to highly specialized goals, such as rejoicing at the conclusion of every Sabbath.

Another noteworthy feature of the religious life of Safed was its asceticism. While the Safed kabbalists were by no means the first medieval Jewish community to be attracted to the ascetic life, the scale on which it took place and the motives underlying it, serve to mark Safed as an unusual case. Ascetic practices in which the Safed pietists engaged were of several types. We find frequent reference to the value of avoiding meat and wine. Abraham Berukhim, for example, reports that "there are certain especially pious scholars of Torah who neither eat meat nor drink wine during the entire week." Joseph Karo's mentor-angel, a *maggid* or voice which spoke to him on a regular basis, exhorts him to "take care not to enjoy your eating and drinking and marital relations. It should be as if demons were compelling you to eat that food."

Fasting was another type of ascetic practice that was widespread. Cordovero, for example, instructs his disciples to fast for three consecutive days during each of the four seasons, though it is preferable to increase this amount. One authority instructs individuals to "fast on Thursdays and pray the afternoon service with a quorum of ten people who are likewise fasting." Even more extreme regimens of fasting involving long periods of abstinence were enjoined by Isaac Luria in order that his disciples might atone for specific transgressions. Other kinds of self-mortification exercises were practiced as well, including flagellation and the donning of sackcloth and ashes. For his disciples Isaac Luria prescribed ritual immersions in the winter, sleeping upon the ground, as well as rolling naked in the snow and upon thorns for especially egregious sins.

Such asceticism can be explained in several ways. The Safed mystics shared the generalized sense of deep guilt concerning the state of exile under which the Jewish people continued to live. Such traditionally motivated guilt was enhanced by the responsibility felt for the fate of the *Shekhinah*. Every sin was believed to exacerbate the exiled condition of the *Shekhinah*, whereas every proper devotional act contributed to the reunification of the Holy One, blessed be He *(Tiferet)*, and the *Shekhinah*. Safed asceticism was also bound up with the related notion that perfect purity was required of a person who wished to achieve the mystical state of *devekut* (cleaving to God), or to attain various other kinds of mystical inspiration. Finally, we should take notice in this connection of the particular needs of Marranos living in Safed. Having accepted baptism against their will, these penitents sought to atone for their sins by recourse to especially severe acts of self-mortification. Surely the presence of these individuals only contributed to the climate of penitence in this community.

It should not be thought, however, that the austerity portrayed here was unalleviated. Certainly, the requirements of Jewish law served to temper what might have otherwise been even more extreme ascetic behavior. Thus, for example, Jewish law prevented a man from renouncing marriage even if he might otherwise have been inclined toward celibacy. In a similar way, no rabbinic Jew could, in good conscience, ignore the obligation to celebrate the Sabbath and the other holidays with the appropriate joyfulness. More generally, the traditionally social character of Jewish life with its insistence on involvement with the larger community, made it unthinkable for ascetically oriented kabbalists to go off on their own to form truly private communities along the lines of a monastic sect.

Besides these factors, joyfulness in the service of God was actually a spiritual *ideal* among the Safed pietists. Thus Isaac Luria, for example, is reported to have discouraged sadness, calling it an impediment to the acquisition of mystical inspiration. Finally, we should point out that the burden of responsibility which they felt did not lead to resignation and despair. The mystics of this community were *activists* who were convinced that they held in their hands the power to alter history and heal the cosmos. There were, then, two foci to the Safed world view: the bitterness of the *Shekhinah*'s exile and the dread of sin on the one hand, the anticipated redemption and the enthusiasm for serving God on the other. It is precisely this tension between death and rebirth, between exile and redemption, that stood at the center of the creative forces at work in sixteenth-century Safed.

As an illustration of Safed literature we now turn to the work of one of the foremost authors of this community, Elijah de Vidas (d. c.1593). De Vidas wrote a book called *Reshit Hokhmah (Beginning of Wisdom)* which he completed in 1575, and which was published for the first time in Venice in 1579. It is the most important example of a new type of literature that developed in Safed, in which kabbalistic ideas were fully synthesized with ritual and ethics. As part of their attempt to disseminate the knowledge and practice of Kabbalah, the Safed mystics set out to demonstrate systematically how each and every ethical and religious deed exerted an effect on the sefirotic world, as well as on the relationship between the world below and the world above.

In the introduction to his book, de Vidas writes that he wishes to enable individuals to develop their ethical and spiritual life so as to *prepare* themselves for the study of Kabbalah. Thus, he says, he has called his work the *beginning* of wisdom, insofar as it constitutes the gateway to the study of inner wisdom. In particular, it appears that de Vidas thought of his own work as a primer which would lead a student to the study of his teacher's *Pardes Rimmonim,* Moses Cordovero's systematic treatment of kabbalistic theology. In fact, the *Beginning of Wisdom* is far more than a primer. It is an encyclopedic work which is divided into five large parts: "The Gate of Fear," "The Gate of Love," "The Gate of Repentance," "The Gate of Holiness," and "The Gate of Humility." It turned out to be, not just an important work of kabbalistic ethics, but one of the several greatest and most influential books of Jewish spirituality ever written.

THE *BEGINNING OF WISDOM:*
A PASSAGE FROM THE "GATE OF LOVE," CHAPTER FOUR

"Cleaving" to God consists in a person's attaching himself with his soul to the *Shekhinah* and concentrating all his attention upon Her unification, as well as upon separating all the evil shells from Her. Similarly, a person ought to remove from his mind all impure thoughts, as Rabbi Shimon bar Yohai, may he rest in peace, explained. For at the moment of unification he must contemplatively unite the *Shekhinah* without allowing any extraneous thoughts to distract him.★

In this chapter Elijah de Vidas discusses three aspects of the love of God: "cleaving," "longing," and "desiring" God. Cleaving involves, among other things, divesting the *Shekhinah* of the evil that adheres to Her as a consequence of Her fallen state, Her exile from *Tiferet,* the Holy One, blessed be He. The term "shells" *(kelipot)* refers to the realm of materiality in which the *Shekhinah* finds Herself quagmired.

The situation of every individual is compared to that of the *Shekhinah.* Just as the latter must be rendered pure by removing all evil from Her, so too must a person divest *himself* of all evil thoughts. Impure thoughts that interfere with one's concentration on the *Shekhinah* prevent an individual from cleaving to Her, as well as from unifying Her.

> This is what our Sages, of blessed memory, meant when they taught: "One may not drink out of one goblet and think of another" (Babylonian Talmud, Nedarim, 20b). This is also what is known as a child born of "a woman mistaken for another" (Nedarim, 20b). A person must concentrate exclusively on the *Shekhinah* and recognize that his impure thoughts are distractions from without which can separate him from Her, God forbid. Instead, one should cleave to the *Shekhinah* in the proper manner, and divest Her of all evil.
>
> Further, in the case of an individual who loves two women, we find that their love for him is not whole inasmuch as they are envious of one another. In order for a wife's love for her husband to be perfect, it is important that she see that he loves no other woman in the world besides her. She will then bind herself to him in a covenant of unrestricted love. In the same way, the *Shekhinah* will not bind Her love to a man who is devoted to worldly matters. Hence, the essential element in love consists in his not loving anything whatsoever in this world more than he does God, may He be blessed. His love for God ought to be greater than that which he bears for his wife and children and all other worldly things. For a man becomes separated from the love of the Holy One, blessed be He, while praying or studying the Torah, due to the evil, distracting thoughts which intrude upon his awareness. This happens because he is not totally immersed in the love of the Holy One, blessed be He. Instead, his love is greater for matters of

★ This translation is drawn from my forthcoming book *Safed Spirituality, Rules of Mystical Piety and Elijah de Vidas' Beginning of Wisdom* (New York: Paulist Press).

this world, for this or for that thing. If only he would not love worldly things more than he loves the Holy One, blessed be He! When God sees that a person's love for Him is deficient, and that he abandons Him, He likewise departs and separates Himself from that individual . . .

The key to cleaving to God is for a person to feel greater love for God than for anything else in the world—even his own family. Only then will he have the proper concentration with which to immerse himself totally in the love of God. It is interesting to notice that de Vidas has no trouble moving from speaking of the *Shekhinah* as the object of love to *Tiferet*. This passage makes vividly clear something that characterizes kabbalistic literature as a whole: the kabbalists write from the *male* point of view.

As in the case of cleaving to God, there are two aspects to one's "longing" for Him. First, a person should cleave to the *Shekhinah* with his soul by means of each and every commandment that he performs; he must carry them out with longing, heartfelt enthusiasm and very great love. This is what is intended by the quality of "desire of the heart" of which the Zohar frequently speaks. It is not possible to attain such desire of the heart—which is what this longing is—unless a person initially sets his mind on God, may He be blessed, and upon the love which he feels for Him. This longing derives from the realm of love, as explained by Rabbi Shimon bar Yohai in the Zohar (II, 198b). He also comments (Zohar II, 128a–b) that the means by which an individual draws upon himself the *Shekhinah* is primarily desire of the heart. We read there that the evil powers rest upon a man "for free," provoking him to act foolishly so that they might abide with him. Following this the Zohar comments:

But the Holy Spirit is not like the evil powers. It demands a full price and great effort, purification of one's self and one's dwelling, desire of the heart and soul; and even so one will be fortunate to succeed in having it take up its abode with him.

Therefore, a person needs to gain control over his evil inclination and not be deflected from his goal by worldly considerations. Instead, his soul should continuously yearn for the *Shekhinah* whose name is "heart." This is what is meant by "desire of the heart."

The second dimension of one's love of God, "longing," depends upon the depth of "heartfelt enthusiasm" with which a person performs the commandments. We also see here that as far as the Safed kabbalists were concerned, every person was engaged in a continuous battle against the powers of evil. The way to combat them was to constantly guard against falling prey to the temptations of the material world. An individual has to labor at all times to arouse his love for God and to sustain it at the highest level of intensity.

> . . . With respect to "desire" for God, an individual must turn away from all worldly concerns and thoughts. This is in order for his soul's desire to gain in strength and to enable his soul to cleave to God. Thus, he will become so impassioned while carrying out the commandments that even if he were to be given all of the money in the world, he would still not stop performing them.
>
> In reality, a man would not delay making love to his wife when he feels passion for her, even if he were given all the money in the world. In a similar manner, it is proper that he feel passionate about carrying out the commandments since, through their performance, he makes love to the King's Daughter, that is, the *Shekhinah,* the Daughter of Jacob; for every wife is her husband's daughter. Rather, he must perform the commandments unhesitatingly and with intense zeal. In this way, he will cleave to the upper life and his soul will be illuminated by the upper light which shines upon a person when he performs a precept.

"Desire" for God appears to be similar to "longing" for Him. It involves bringing passionate zeal to the performance of the commandments. De Vidas goes so far as to compare this passion to that which a man feels for his wife. The analogy is taken dramatically further when he writes that the passionate performance of religious acts constitutes "making love" to the *Shekhinah!* While the older Spanish Kabbalah was prepared to describe the relationship *within* the sefirotic realm in sexual terms, it was on the whole more reluctant to depict the relationship between an individual and God in erotic terms. As we see here, de Vidas does not shy away from conceiving of the divine-human encounter in openly erotic ways.

> Just as "desire" may be found in connection with the performance of the commandments, so too when it comes to the study of Torah. Study will strengthen his soul's desire for God, causing all physical sensations to fade away. His soul will cleave to God in the course of the intensive study of Torah until he

feels absolutely no worldly sensation. For just as an individual who longs for the one whom he loves eliminates all other thoughts from his mind because of his preoccupation with his lover, and a fire of love burns in his heart even while he eats, drinks and sleeps, so should a person's love for God be likewise.

We learn this from a story told by Rabbi Isaac of Acre. Among the stories having to do with ascetics which this sage reported, he wrote that a person who has never experienced longing for a woman is like a donkey—even worse. The reason for this is that as a result of the feeling of longing for a woman, one learns to cultivate longing for God. We can learn from this that the man who loves the Torah with such great passion that he thinks of no worldly matters whatsoever, neither by day nor by night, will assuredly attain to a most wonderful grade of soul. He will have no need for mortification of the body or for fasts, for cleaving to God depends upon nothing but the longing for and loving of the Torah. He should love the Torah with as great passion as he loves his wife. One expresses this love for God by rising regularly at midnight out of his great desire.

Isaac of Acre is the same individual mentioned earlier in connection with the appearance of the Zohar. Isaac himself became one of the leading kabbalists of the fourteenth century. He combined kabbalism with elements of the meditative practices of Abraham Abulafia, an important thirteenth-century mystic known for his unique approach to contemplation.

Once again de Vidas compares the love that men have for women with that which they should have for God, as well as for the study of Torah. Study of Torah is transformed here into an opportunity for contemplatively focusing on the love of God. More than mere intellectual activity, study is regarded as having mystical value. The love of women is important, if for no other reason than that it endows a man with knowledge of what genuine passion is! While intellectualism played as considerable a role in sixteenth-century Kabbalah as it did in Spanish Kabbalah, the emphasis in the text before us is clearly on the critical importance of *emotion* in the love of God. Over the course of his long book, Elijah de Vidas provides a wide range of rationales and justifications for devoting oneself—above all else—to God. Ultimately, however, what matters in the religious life for him is a person's capacity to arouse the strongest and purest passion for God. In this respect Safed Kabbalah serves as an important antecedent for Hasidic piety. Hasidism is, of course, well known for its emphasis on the emotional and ecstatic aspect of religious experience. One of the differences between the two, however, is that the Safed mystics regarded cleaving to God *(devekut)* as the *end product* of a drawn-out process, whereas in Hasidism *devekut* is thought of as a point of *departure*.

The practice of rising at midnight for the purpose of praying, studying and devoting oneself to God is a very common theme in the *Beginning of Wisdom,* as it is in Safed literature in general. Under the influence of Isaac Luria, the preeminent kabbalist of the sixteenth century, an elaborate ritual known as *Tikkun Hazot* developed. This rite was practiced for centuries among Jews who followed kabbalistic customs.

WHERE TO GO FROM HERE

Introduction. While some valuable scholarship was written in the nineteenth century, the study of Kabbalah really begins in a serious way with the work of Gershom Scholem in the 1920s. Critical research into Jewish mysticism has now became a mature field of study, although there are still relatively few individuals who make it a full-time specialty. In sheer quantitative terms it lags behind other areas of Judaica research which have been the object of attention for a much longer period of time. For example, a great many of the classic texts of medieval Jewish philosophy have been translated into English, whereas precious few translations of kabbalistic texts exist. The following bibliographical suggestions are limited to works that are available in English and that treat Kabbalah. We have not sought to cover the entire range of Jewish mysticism.

Bibliographies and General Introductions to Kabbalah. The best bibliographical essay available in English devoted to secondary sources is Jochanan Wijnhoven's "Medieval Jewish Mysticism" in *Bibliographical Essays in Medieval Jewish Studies* (New York: Anti-Defamation League of B'nai Brith, 1976). The section on Kabbalah provides a useful overview of materials on the several phases of kabbalistic literature from its beginnings in the twelfth and thirteenth centuries through Sabbatianism and Frankism in the seventeenth and eighteenth centuries. The essay as a whole gives a good sense of the wide scope of Jewish esotericism.

The sixteen-volume *Encyclopaedia Judaica,* published by Keter Press in 1972, is a treasure of information on all aspects of mysticism and Kabbalah. The entries were written by some of the most important scholars of Kabbalah, including Alexander Altmann, Joseph Dan, Ephraim Gottlieb, Rivka Schatz, Gershom Scholem, Isaiah Tishby, and

Georges Vajda. Each entry provides bibliography at the end, although these vary widely in quality. Volume ten contains the nearly book-length entry entitled "Kabbalah" by Scholem. This superb essay is divided into sections on the historical development of Kabbalah, the basic ideas of Kabbalah, and "the wider influences of and research on Kabbalah." This piece, along with many of Scholem's other *Encyclopaedia* entries are conveniently collected in a separate book called *Kabbalah* (Jerusalem: Keter, 1974). It is an indispensable volume for the student of this literature.

Scholem's *Major Trends in Jewish Mysticism* (New York: Schocken, 1941) is based on a series of lectures that he originally gave in 1938 at the Jewish Institute of Religion in New York City. The book is one of the great classics of twentieth-century Jewish scholarship, and is credited with bringing the study of Jewish mysticism to worldwide attention. The fifth lecture deals with the problem of the Zohar as a literary document, while the sixth lecture discusses the doctrines of the Zohar. Lectures seven and eight discuss sixteenth-century Kabbalah and Sabbatianism, respectively. While some find the style of *Major Trends* rough going, it is well worth tackling. It is also a book that can be reread with profit as one's knowledge increases. Yet another book by Scholem, *On the Kabbalah and Its Symbolism* (New York: Schocken, 1965), introduces the reader to a number of significant problems in the study of Kabbalah, such as "Religious Authority and Mysticism," and "Kabbalah and Myth."

A brief but lovely essay on the basic ideas of the Zohar by Abraham Joshua Heschel, "The Mystical Element in Judaism," is found in L. Finkelstein's *The Jews—Their History, Culture, and Religion* (Philadelphia: Jewish Publication Society, 1949). A work of a more popular type is *9 1/2 Mystics—The Kabbala Today* by Herbert Weiner (New York: Collier, 1969). It represents the author's personal journey into the world of Jewish mysticism. As such, it is an interesting, highly readable means by which to think about the possible significance of Kabbalah in our own time.

Specialized Studies on Early Kabbalah and the Zohar. Regrettably, there is not an abundance of secondary work in English on the kabbalists of the early period, though there are some studies to which we can point. A short discussion of the *Bahir* by O. H. Lehmann, "The Theology of the Mystical Book Bahir and Its Sources," can be found in *Studia Patristica* I (Akademie Verlag, 1957). Alexander Altmann's "The Motif of the 'Shells' in Azriel of Gerona" in his *Studies in Religious Philosophy and Mysticism* (Ithaca: Cornell University Press, 1969), is one of the few articles in English dealing with this exceedingly influential figure. Several other essays in this book make substantial reference to the conceptions of the older Kabbalah. While these are not especially easy essays to read, they are immensely erudite pieces by one of the most eminent historians of Jewish philosophy and mysticism. They will reward the reader who wishes to see how the various medieval traditions—philosophical, mystical, exegetical—can be studied together for the purpose of analyzing the development of religious motifs. Valuable essays on the kabbalistic views of Azriel and Moses ben Nahman by Moshe Idel and Bezalel Safran are found in *Rabbi Moses Nahmanides: Explorations in His Religious and Literary Virtuosity,* edited by Isadore Twersky (Cambridge, Mass.: Harvard University Press, 1983).

An important study by Joseph Dan of one of the Castilian kabbalists, Isaac ha-Kohen, is "Samael, Lilith, and the Concept of Evil," *AJSreview,* 5 (1980). A thirteenth-century Spanish kabbalist, whose distinction rests in the fact that he synthesized philosophy and Kabbalah, was Isaac ibn Latif. He is studied in Sara Heller Wilensky's "Isaac ibn Latif—Philosopher or Kabbalist," in A. Altmann, *Jewish Medieval and Renaissance Studies* (Cambridge, Mass.: Harvard University Press, 1967).

On the Zohar itself we have already mentioned the two chapters in *Major Trends in Jewish Mysticism.* An informative discussion of Moses de Leon and the Zohar is found in the introduction to Daniel Matt's translation of Zohar texts entitled *Zohar, The Book of Enlightenment* (New York: Paulist Press, 1983).

David ben Judah he-Hasid was another Spanish kabbalist who produced the *Book of Mirrors,* a fourteenth-century anthology of older Kabbalah and an original commentary on the Torah. It also contains the first lengthy translations of Zohar from Aramaic into Hebrew. This work has been analyzed by Daniel Matt in "David ben Yehudah Hehasid and His Book of Mirrors," *Hebrew Union College Annual* 51 (1980). The kabbalistic conception of man is described in Louis Jacobs' "The Doctrine of the 'Divine Spark' in Man in Jewish Sources," R. Loewe, *Studies in Rationalism, Judaism and Universalism* (London: Routledge and Kegan Paul, 1966). This same subject is taken up by A. Altmann in his article "God and the Self in Jewish Mysticism," *Judaism* Vol. 3, no. 2 (1954). Essays bearing upon the relationship between Kabbalah and messianism are found in Scholem's collection *The Messianic Idea in Judaism* (New York: Schocken, 1971).

Sixteenth-Century Kabbalah. The historical setting of sixteenth-century Kabbalah is described nicely in Yizhak ben Zvi, "Eretz Yisrael Under Ottoman Rule, 1517–1917," Louis Finkelstein, *The Jews.* A classic essay by Solomon Schechter "Safed in the Sixteenth Century" is still well worth reading, although it is somewhat dated. Still in print it appears in Schechter's *Studies in Judaism,* second series (Philadelphia: Jewish Publication Society, 1908).

A full length study of Joseph Karo's unusual mystical experiences by R. J. Z. Werblowsky is *Joseph Karo—Lawyer and Mystic* (Oxford: Oxford University Press, 1962). It serves at the same time as a penetrating treatment of the spiritual life of the Safed community in general. This book offers the unique insights of a comparative religionist who is also a scholar of Kabbalah. A wonderful essay by Scholem, "Tradition and New Creation in the Ritual of the Kabbalists," describes the innovative practices of the Safed pietists. It is part of Scholem's aforementioned *On the Kabbalah and Its Symbolism.*

A valuable essay concerning a central Safed figure, Moses Cordovero, is Kalman Bland's "Neoplatonic and Gnostic Themes in R. Moses Cordovero's Doctrine of Evil," *Bulletin of the Institute of Jewish Studies,* 3 (1975). In this connection, see also Joseph Dan, " 'No Evil Descends From Heaven'—Sixteenth Century Concepts of Evil," in *Jewish Thought in the Sixteenth Century,* edited by Bernard Cooperman (Cambridge, Mass.: Harvard University Press, 1983). The Gnostic elements of Safed kabbalism are discussed briefly in Isaiah Tishby, "Gnostic Doctrines in Sixteenth-Century Jewish Mysticism," *Journal of Jewish Studies,* 6 (1955). The development of techniques of mystical experience played a primary role in the religious life of this community. One such technique having to do with the attainment of maggidic revelations is described in my own "Maggidic Revelation in the Teachings of Isaac Luria," in *Mystics, Philosophers, and Politicians—Essays in Jewish Intellectual History in Honor of Alexander Altmann,* edited by J. Reinharz and D. Swetschinski (Durham, N.C.: Duke University Press, 1982). Hayyim Vital's mystical experiences are analyzed in my "Recitation of Mishnah as a Vehicle for Mystical Inspiration: A Contemplative Technique Taught by Hayyim Vital," *Revue des Ètudes Juives* 141 (1982). This author also discusses the character of Safed spirituality in the introduction to his *Safed Spirituality, Rules of Mystical Piety and Elijah de Vidas' Beginning of Wisdom* (New York: Paulist Press, 1984).

Isaac Luria (1534–72) was the preeminent kabbalist of Safed in the sixteenth century. Luria's influence upon Jewish mysticism ranks with that of Moses de Leon. Luria's original mythological doctrines and ritual practices were of fundamental importance to virtually all Jewish mystical creativity after him. It has been observed that Lurianism was the last theological system to enjoy nearly universal acceptance within Judaism.

Scholem describes Lurianic mysticism in the seventh lecture of *Major Trends,* "Isaac Luria and His School." A more detailed discussion of Lurianic teachings, which deals extensively with the spread of Lurianism and its impact upon seventeenth-century Jewry, is given by Scholem in part 1 of his *Sabbatai Sevi,* a book described below.

The messianically oriented kabbalistic movement that developed around the fascinating personality of Sabbatai Sevi in the seventeenth century has been written about in many places. But the indispensable study of Sabbatianism is the monumental work by Gershom Scholem entitled *Sabbatai Sevi—The Mystical Messiah,* 1626–1676, (Princeton, N.J.: Princeton University Press, 1973). This voluminous book—translated from the earlier Hebrew version by R. J. Z. Werblowsky—is a stunning contribution to Jewish scholarship. In it Scholem draws upon a range of different kinds of documents to tell the dramatic story of Sabbatai's career and the movement it inspired.

English Translations of Kabbalistic Texts. Worthwhile translations of the classical literature of Kabbalah are few and far between. This obviously represents one of the most serious obstacles to the student of Kabbalah who is restricted to English. Nevertheless, a number of works have appeared in the recent past and there is reason to hope that this development will continue.

The Zohar was translated into English by Harry Sperling and Maurice Simon with an introduction by J. Abelson. It was published in five volumes under the title *The Zohar* by the Soncino Press in London and appeared between 1931–34. The translation is not complete, as Sperling and Simon translated only part of the main section of the Zohar, leaving out the *Midrash ha-Neelam, Raaya Meheimna, Tikkunei Zohar,* and *Zohar Hadash,* among other things. This work is also limited by the fact that the authors do not always translate the text accurately because of misunderstandings of the kabbalistic meaning. Nevertheless, the Soncino Zohar is still a very useful translation which can serve the beginning student well. Several important sections of Zohar, not translated in the Soncino version, have been translated in a volume entitled *The Anatomy of God* (New York: Ktav, 1973) by Roy A. Rosenberg. It contains "The Book of Concealment," "The Great Holy Assembly," and "The Lesser Holy Assembly." A very slim selection of Zohar texts was published by Scholem as *Zohar: The Book of Splendor* (New York: Schocken, 1963). Its usefulness is somewhat limited insofar as it contains just a few exceedingly brief notes. In explaining the virtual absence of notes Scholem writes the following in the book's introduction. ". . . I ventured to assume that the interested reader would himself desire to reflect on the profuse symbols and images as they appear herein. It was in such manner that the Zohar did appeal to wider circles of readers through the ages. It matters little whether this or that symbolic connotation is properly recognized, or not." It is hard to read the last sentence of this quotation without being pleasantly taken aback, coming as it does from Scholem, the scholar's scholar.

A fresh translation of Zohar texts is now available in Daniel Matt's *Zohar, The Book of Enlightenment,* mentioned above. This book translates a significant number of excerpts from various parts of Zoharic literature. The translation is lively and compelling; it succeeds nicely in capturing some of the special literary qualities discussed earlier in this essay. Importantly, the texts are accompanied by extensive and learned notes which go a long way toward assisting the reader. This is a highly recommended volume. It was published by Paulist Press (1983) as part of its series "Classics of Western Spirituality."

While we have so far avoided mention of works in any language other than English, perhaps one exception may be permitted. This is a two-volume Hebrew work entitled *Mishnat ha-Zohar.* The first volume (Mossad Bialik, 1949) was prepared by Isaiah Tishby and Fishel Lachover, while the second volume (1961) was done by Tishby alone. *Mishnat ha-Zohar* contains clear and systematic essays on the ideas and motifs of the Zoharic literature that are illustrated by generous selections from the Zohar. The excerpts are beautifully translated into Hebrew from the original Aramaic and are accompanied by accurate, lucid, and informative notes. The notes indicate the sefirotic symbolism and briefly explicate the text. This book can be read and studied by individuals who know a fair degree of Hebrew. It is a superb tool for the person who is prepared to move beyond English translations, but who is not quite ready to jump into the Aramaic text. It can be used, as well, as an introduction to the Aramaic text by comparing the *Mishnat ha-Zohar* passages with the original. David J. Goldstein has prepared an English translation of *Mishnat ha-Zohar* which is to appear as part of the Littman Library of Jewish Civilization, Fairleigh Dickinson University.

A fine collection of materials having to do with mystical *experience* is brought together by Louis Jacobs in *Jewish Mystical Testimonies* (New York: Schocken, 1977). The kabbalists were generally reluctant to record accounts of their personal experiences, or even to record descriptions of how to go about achieving such experiences. This collection is valuable insofar as it makes available in English some of the texts that represent exceptions to this pattern of reluctance.

The present author has translated a volume of texts from sixteenth-century Safed mentioned above, *Safed Spirituality, Rules of Mystical Piety and Elijah de Vidas' Beginning of Wisdom.* The translations are of two kinds. First, there are *hanhagot,* lists of customs, rituals and ethical behaviors that were practiced in Safed. Some of these were composed for specific fellowships such as that of Moses Cordovero. The second part consists in extended excerpts from Jacob Poyetto's influential condensation of Elijah de Vidas' *Beginning of Wisdom.* Another Safed text, Moses Cordovero's *Tomer Devorah (The Palm Tree of Deborah)* was translated in full by Louis Jacobs (London: Valentine and Mitchell, 1960). This little book is an excellent introduction to the ethical Kabbalah of Safed.

Anthologies of kabbalistic texts in English translation that the reader may want to consult include *Understanding Jewish Mysticism* by David Blumenthal (New York: Ktav, 1978) and *The Jewish Mystical Tradition* by Ben Zion Bokser (New York: Pilgrim Press, 1981). An interesting collection of texts may be found in Aryeh Kaplan's *Meditation and Kabbalah* (New York: Samuel Weiser, 1982).

CONCLUDING REMARKS

Though the subject is beyond the scope of this essay, it should at least be pointed out that Kabbalah has had a very significant impact upon contemporary Jewish thought and culture. One has only to think of the work of Abraham Isaac Kook, A. D. Gordon, Martin Buber, Abraham Joshua Heschel, Richard Rubenstein, Adin Steinsaltz—and such younger contemporary writers as Arthur Green and Lawrence Kushner—to recognize the pervasive influence of kabbalistic thinking. Within the field of fiction the names of Isaac Bashevis Singer, Elie Wiesel, Cynthia Ozick, and Chaim Potok come readily to mind as examples of authors whose short stories and novels are indebted to the kabbalistic tradition. Even the field of literary criticism has gravitated to discourse about Kabbalah, as no less a reader of texts than Harold Bloom, writing in his book *Kabbalah and Criticism,* finds in the stance of the kabbalists toward Jewish tradition "the classic paradigm upon which Western revisionism in all areas was to model itself . . ."

Toward the conclusion of *Major Trends in Jewish Mysticism,* Gershom Scholem wrote the following words: "The story [of Jewish mysticism] is not ended, it has not yet become history, and the secret life it holds can break out tomorrow in you or in me. Under what aspects this invisible stream of Jewish mysticism will again come to the surface we cannot tell." Almost half a century after this was written, perhaps we may say that Scholem's reflections were not mere wishful thinking. For though it is still not apparent where it will all lead, it is clear that the *nizozot kedoshot,* the "holy sparks" of which the kabbalists spoke, have not died.★

★ I wish to thank Professor Daniel Matt for reading this entire chapter and for his helpful suggestions.

Title page of *Kedushat Levi* by Levi Yizhak of Berdichev, Lemberg, 1858.

CHAPTER SEVEN

Teachings
of the Hasidic Masters

ARTHUR GREEN

The history of the Hasidic movement tells one of the great success stories in the history of religion. Within a period of fifty years following the death of the movement's first central figure, Israel Ba'al Shem Tov (1700–60), his little band of followers in the Ukraine had spread out to conquer the hearts of what was probably a majority of Jewry in the old Russo-Polish empire. We would search Jewish history in vain for another phenomenon of religious transformation that succeeded in so rapid and yet so long-lasting a manner. It took the rabbinic movement hundreds of years to win the allegiance of the Jewish people, while the Sabbatian movement of the seventeenth century, th[...] reading like wildfire, essentially petered out a few years after it [...] e into being. Other major currents in Jewish spiritual history, i[...] both medieval rationalism and early Kabbalah, were primarily literary and intellectual movements. Hasidism, in one or another of its forms, dominated Jewish religious life in Russia, Poland, and parts of neighboring Hungary and Romania throughout the nineteenth century. It continues to play a major role in Judaism today, both through the survival of the Hasidic communities themselves and through its influence, however transformed, on even the most thoroughly modern of Jewish religious thinkers.

The keys to an understanding of the movement's rapid spread lie in the profound vision and charismatic personalities of its leaders, on the one hand, and on the people's deeply felt need for such a revival on the other. The Ba'al Shem Tov and his followers told, in semi-

pantheistic fashion, of a God who was present and directly accessible throughout His universe, of a world in which even the seemingly
most irretrievable evil was capable of (indeed longing for) redemption,
and of an essential role that each Jew had to play in the joyous transformation of matter into spirit, of mundane into holy. It did so
while remaining entirely faithful to the deep-seated traditions of rabbinic Judaism, using the very texts and institutions of the normative
tradition to effect a revolutionary and yet inherently conservative
revival. The leaders of this delicately balanced transformation were, perforce, both men of authentic religious vision and masters of integration, able to interpret their own mystical and devotional experiences in
terms derived from the received body of traditional symbols. It was
largely because of this latter skill that the faithful Jewish masses recognized and accepted the wandering Hasidic preacher as their own,
hearing a message that was entirely familiar in language and form,
while still fresh and invigorating in content and in the person of its
bearer.

For a Jewry that had lived through a long period of political and
social decline, that faced new and feared oppression at the hands
of its recently acquired Russian masters, and that had of late suffered
its own inner spiritual turmoils as well, Hasidism was able to provide the answers it sought. If liberation in the political sense was impossible—and this included messianic adventurism—the vision of a
spiritualized reality would allow for an inner freedom, even while
the physical shackles remained unbroken. If the old social tensions
of the Jewish community added to the burden of oppression—the
oligarchy of the wealthy and learned poised against an increasingly
restive, though hardly politicized, mass of Jewry—Hasidism spoke for
a spiritual democratization of sorts, one in which the readily accessible
virtues of piety and enthusiasm surpassed those of classical erudition
and family status. To be sure, a new elite was proclaimed almost
from the movement's beginning: it was through the true *zaddik* (literally "righteous person," used in the Hasidic context to mean the spiritual leader, or *rebbe,* of a particular Hasidic group) and devotion to him,
as well as through following his teachings, that this inward redemption could be achieved. In this it may be said that Hasidism, like many a
revolution, bore within it the seeds of its own decline. But the Hasidic
holy man, with the mysterious yet kindly mien drawn for him by the
leading figures of the movement's early days, played a positive and
crucial role in the uplifting of spirits that lay at the very core of Hasidism's message.

THE LITERATURE OF HASIDISM

It was primarily orally rather than by the written work that Hasidism was first spread. The Maggid (Preacher) Dov Baer of Miedzyrzec (Mezritch), the Ba'al Shem Tov's successor, and most of his followers were *preachers,* some wandering from town to town and others appointed by a specific community to a regular preaching office. It was in lengthy homilies delivered in the synagogue or at the Sabbath table, in which strands of earlier tradition were skillfully rewoven to highlight elements of Hasidic teaching, that a theology of Hasidism began to develop. As the fame of these preachers, along with healers and other sorts of holy men (and occasionally women) associated with them, began to spread, wise sayings were attributed to them, snippets of their teachings were excerpted and retold in their names, and tales of their powers, often including elements of the miraculous, began to be told among the folk. *All* the later genres of Hasidic literature, including homilies (Hebrew: *derashot;* Yiddish: *droshes*), aphorisms *(peshatim; pshetlekh),* and tales *(sippurim; mayses),* had their origins in the spoken word.

Of these genres, it was the homilies that first made the transition from the spoken medium to that of print. Beginning in c[...]e *Toledot Ya'akov Yosef,* by a disciple of the Ba'al Shem Tov, in[...] bits[...]mes of collected teachings of individual Hasidic masters beg[...]ed t[...] published by often obscure printing houses that dotted [...] th[...]f Byelorussia and the Ukraine. By the turn of the n[...]e[...] works by Dov Baer and most of his disciples, in addition to several other leading figures of the movement, had already been compiled and published. This tradition of editing and printing originally oral homilies flourished especially in the early decades of that century, but continues within Hasidic circles right down to our own day.

In most cases it was the sons or disciples of the authors who prepared such works for publication, rather than the masters themselves. While the homilies were usually delivered without notes (spontaneity was considered a great virtue in such preaching) and on days when note taking by the hearers would have been forbidden by halakhic restrictions, faithful disciples went home after the Sabbath or festival on which the master had spoken and composed written synopses of the *derashot* their masters had preached. These notebooks formed the basis, sometimes in conjunction with the masters' own written notes, of the literary works of Hasidism. By their very nature, it should be realized, such literary recreations of oral homilies contain a degree of artifice: they are briefer and often much more formal than the rather chatty vernacular in which the masters spoke. Most important, they are *translations,* abbreviated Hebrew renditions of sermons preached in Yiddish. It was unthinkable in the East European milieu that the sacred tongue be used for any sort of oral performance other than liturgy, and the Hebrew preserved was of a purely literary character. When it came to recording the holy teachings of the masters, however, it was equally unthinkable that any vessel short of Hebrew, the classical and sacred language of Jewry, be employed. Since the masters generally wove their homilies around a series of quotations from the Bible and other classical sources, the first task in the literary reconstruction of the homily would be an outlining of the various sources quoted. Once these quotations had been listed, the writer would reestablish the link between them, highlighting the theological or devotional motifs that were brought out in the course of these associations. In some cases the resulting volume was a collection of rather short, almost aphoristic comments on individual biblical verses, while in others the homilies were preserved in a more complete form, resulting in long homiletical essays in which the verse at hand served merely as a point of departure.

The collected homilies of individual masters were joined late in the eighteenth century by several anonymous or misattributed volumes of assorted of Hasidic wisdom. Such works as *Zava'at Rivash* (the purp estament of the Ba'al Shem Tov), *Keter Shem Tov,* (The e Good Name) and *Likkutim Yekarim* (Precious Selections), t popularity and contributed much to the spread of Hasidic ideas. By means of brief comments on passages from the Bible or rabbinic literature, they tended to highlight the devotional focus which was so important to the Hasidic world view, and often offered practical advice on such matters as concentration in prayer, the uplifting of evil thoughts, and the maintaining of a devotional posture even while engaged in worldly pursuits. These collections are thematically related to the literature of *hanhagot,* lists of the personal practices of individual masters. Such lists also began to appear in print toward the turn of the nineteenth century, often as addenda to the published collections of the masters' homilies. A classic example of this type of list, frequently reprinted and widely revered in Hasidic circles, is the *Tsetl Katan* by Rabbi Elimelech of Lezajsk.

The genre of Hasidic literature best known in modern times, that of the tale, was in fact the last to appear in print. While *Shivhei ha-Besht,* the hagiographical life of the Ba'al Shem Tov, appeared in 1815, the heyday of publication for the tales was the period between 1864 and the

First World War, when hundreds of such collections were brought to light. The tales were in many cases printed in Yiddish rather than Hebrew, intended for a popular audience that did not have the degree of Hebrew education that was assumed among readers of the homilies and teachings. This audience included women as well as men, and (at least later) non-Hasidic as well as Hasidic Jews. Some of the tales' editors were in fact not *hasidim,* but publicists of a more modern sort who sought either literary fame or financial gain by collecting and publishing tales that were then widespread in oral form among the folk.

There has been much discussion in recent years as to the value of these tales for an authentic understanding of the Hasidic movement. Though the tales will not be the main object of our attention here, some discussion of their place in Hasidism is essential. The debate as to the tales' value was best expressed in a series of exchanges between Martin Buber and Gershom Scholem, certainly two of the most profound readers of this literature in the twentieth century. Buber, the philosopher/theologian, saw the tales as preserving the very essence of Hasidism. They reflected "life," actual moments of real human encounter in the life with God, rather than the mere disembodied "teachings" to be found in the theoretical literature. Never mind the fact that they were published late and in popular form; the true spirit of Hasidism could only have been recorded orally, and it is to these oral traditions of the masters' lives that one must first turn to encounter Hasidism. Scholem, ever the critical historian, was concerned not only with the lateness of the published tales, but with the fact that they portrayed a somewhat different picture of Hasidism than did the homilies, which were clearly early and authentic. The theoretical writings pointed to a more mystical theology, one that denied all reality other than the singular existence of God. The tales tended more toward a humanization of God, an anthropopathy, while the homilies veered closer to the edge of pantheism. While both genres glorified the virtues of simplicity, the homilies presented a Hasidism deeply rooted in the traditional sources and life patterns of Judaism, while the tales (especially as reread by Buber) offered an almost peasant-like life of religious exuberance in the presence of God in each moment. Scholem was suspicious of the portrayal offered in the tale literature as a latter-day romanticization of Hasidism, one that was conveniently well suited to Buber's own religious philosophy and relatively "appealing" to the Western audiences, both Jewish and Christian, for whom Buber was writing.

The fact is that a very wide range of materials is included in the literature of Hasidic tales; rather little work has yet been done in sorting out the various types of tale and in distinguishing the value, both historical and literary, of one collection over another. There are wonder tales of miraculous healings, the slaying of mythical beasts, and the battle between goodly sages and evil wizards, many of which had been current long before Hasidism and were simply adapted to the names and outer trappings of the new movement. At the other extreme are incidents from the lives of various masters, occasionally verifiable through the earlier sources, but often embellished in the telling. There are parables told *by* the early masters, along with events in their lives that were used by later generations as moral *exempla*. A special subgenre are the tales told by Rabbi Nahman of Bratslav, where well-known East European folk motifs are rewoven to create symbolic fictions around the theme of the longing for redemption. There is of course a moral or didactic point to many of the Hasidic tales, if only the general one of illustrating how the masters lived a life of holiness and religious awareness. This is not to deny that the tales also served as a form of literary entertainment in a small-town society not far removed from that world where storytelling in the tribe or clan was the chief form of entertainment, a way of passing on the group's tradition, and a repository of the collective wisdom and values that that tradition had to offer its adherents.

Many of the tale collections were published in cheaply printed chapbooks intended for reasonable sale and mostly local distribution; some of these, because of decaying paper, have now become great bibliographic rarities. Others were published with greater fanfare and in more substantial editions, including such later collections as *Zekhut Yisra'el* by David Berger of Bucharest and *Si'ah Sarfey Kodesh* by Yo'etz Kaddish Rakatz. These latter collections, edited by and for the *hasidim* themselves, are a far cry from the wonder tales of the 1860s; here the intended audience, even of the tales, is assumed to have a degree of education and traditional sophistication.

Our choice of the theoretical and homiletic writings over the tales for explication here does not indicate total agreement with Scholem in his devaluation of the Hasidic tales. The tales are quite widely available to the English reader, and in most cases, their meaning is rather readily comprehensible. The homilies, on the other hand, are almost unknown outside of Hasidic and scholarly circles. It is these that are in need of "rescue" and presentation to the broader reading public.

For the *hasidim* themselves, it has always been clear that the homiletic/theological sources are the pride of Hasidic literature. These are truly *sforim,* sacred volumes, distinguished by the nuance of Yiddish speech from the tale collections, which are merely *bikhelekh* (booklets).

In the more intellectual Hasidic circles, notably *HaBaD* (Lubavitch), but also those descending from such other schools as Zydachow, Sanz, and Bratslav, the writings of the early masters are avidly studied and discussed. Among the relatively few Polish *hasidim* (as distinct from the Russian, Galician, and Hungarian) who survived the holocaust, a similar status has been conferred upon a number of later Hasidic authors; there it is the writings of Yehudah Leib Alter of Ger *(Sefat Emet),* Yehudah Leib Eiger of Posen, and Zadok ha-Kohen of Lublin that are most revered. Once Hasidic leadership began to follow the pattern of dynastic succession, it became natural, of course, to give a place of primacy to the writings of one's own rebbe's ancestors. Thus *Sefat Emet* is chiefly studied by Gerer *hasidim, Tanya* by Lubavitchers, and so forth. Often neglected by latter-day Hasidic readers are those classics of the movement by authors whose lines did not survive, or who did not, even from the first, initiate a pattern of dynastic succession. Among these are the *Toledot Ya'akov Yosef* (though the neglect of this is surely in part due as well to its inherent difficulty), *Or ha-Me'ir* by Wolf of Zbarasz, the works of Benjamin of Zalozhtsy, and many others. *Hasidim* will still know of and want to *own* books like these (a rabbinic and Hasidic library is the pride of any true *hasid's* home), but there is not much evidence that they are widely read. Interestingly, it is precisely these otherwise neglected volumes that have been at the center of nearly all the academic research on the history and teachings of Hasidism.

What the Texts Assume

To introduce the reader to the theoretical literature of Hasidism, three selections are offered below. The passages selected have been chosen in order to display a range within Hasidic theological writings and differ widely from one another in style and tone. The first is from one of the homiletic classics, *Kedushat Levi* by Levi Yizhak of Berdichev. The second is a page—it can hardly be called a single passage—from the anonymous *Likkutim Yekarim,* demonstrating the aphoristic style of the more popular works. Third is a selection from the *Sefat Emet,* as an example of those later Hasidic writings that still maintain vibrancy of tone and originality of content.

Before we turn to the texts themselves, some questions on the assumptions that underlie these sources must be treated. Only by understanding and allowing ourselves, however temporarily, to identify with their authors' presuppositions, will the texts themselves be comprehensible. The task that lies before us as readers is a complex one, and it seems best to lay out the requirements in advance. In studying Hasidic sources as moderns, rather than as *hasidim,* we are engaged in a three- or four-step process, each portion of which must be kept quite distinct from the others if our reading is to be successful. First we must try to become *hasidim* or, if that sounds overly pretentious, to enter into the intellectual and religious world for which the authors of these texts were writing. Some of the specific literary assumptions of this world will be discussed below. But beyond the particulars, we should recall that hearing Torah from the master's lips is a religious act of great intensity; the rapt devotion and deeply personal involvement of the audience is as much a part of the Hasidic *derashah* as is the technique of biblical interpretation. If we cannot entirely *become* such an audience, we must at least be attentive to this aspect of the setting in which our homily was first spoken.

In this first stage of understanding, our reading of the text will be much like that offered within the Hasidic community. The *rebbe* is speaking about such-and-such a verse, he brings the following passages from Midrash or Gemara to bear on it, quotes further from here or there, and winds up with a new reading of the verse before him. It is important on this level to follow the text closely, seeing in its seemingly unrelated sections (we speak here of the longer homilies) the emergence of a thread of argument, one that can eventually be brought to bear upon the text at hand. It is always important to ask, as we reach the end of such a selection, how the author has read the original verse. Much of the Hasidic hearer or reader's joy in this genre is a pure appreciation of homiletic ingenuity. There is a love of the virtuoso performance to be felt here, not unlike that of the East European Jew in hearing a great *hazan* (cantor) render some favorite part of the liturgy. There is also a deeper sense, however, in which the living quality of Torah is renewed as the text shows itself capable of bearing yet a new rung of interpretation.

Returning to our own modern sensibilities, we are now ready to add a second level to our reading of the text. Here we confront the text as historians and as phenomenologists of religion, addressing to the text a series of questions that would not readily occur to the latter-day Hasidic reader. First, we seek to know all we can about the historical circumstances in which the teaching was offered. Homilies, after all, often seek to use the tradition to focus on an issue of current importance to the preacher and his congregation. Unlike modern sermons, however, the Hasidic homily never makes direct mention of such matters, and they must be surmised from circumstantial evidence. The original hearers, of course, knew full well what the preacher had in mind; it is only the later pious reader who tends to ignore such situating of the text. A homily preached in Poland in 1810, dealing with the theme of legitimate and illegitimate kingship, clearly has something to do with Napoléon and his meteoric rise to power. A text from the 1770s that speaks of evildoers and their wicked words must be seen against the background of the anti-Hasidic persecutions of that decade, even if a specific association cannot be proven. To offer a more contemporary example, a homily delivered by the Lubavitcher *rebbe* in New York in 1947, speaking of how the *yeshivot* established by Jacob's sons in Egypt allowed for Jewish survival until the redemption by Moses, clearly must be viewed as part of his campaign, just getting under way at that time, to establish Lubavitcher educational institutions in every corner of this new Egypt— though even so holy and upright a goal would not be mentioned openly in the context of a *derashah*.

It is only in a minority of cases that we are able to offer such concrete suggestions as to the historical setting of the Hasidic teaching. Homilies by their very nature are in part ephemera, and the situation to which they are addressed dies with the memory of their hearers. But where specific historical details are lost to us, the general setting of the Ukrainian shtetl, a sense of distinguishing one district from another, one decade from another, and most important, when possible, the personality and style of one preacher from another, are all part of the historian's task.

Following on the heels of historical questions are those of phenomenology. Once we have understood the text as best we can in its own terms and have clarified the historical setting in which it was born, we are ready to ask what sort of religious vision or understanding of the world is suggested by the preacher's words. We may ask in what sense his teaching may be considered mystical (immediately involving questions of definition and comparison), what notions of prayer proceed from his words, how he views the relationship between sacred and profane, and so forth. In a popular sense these may be called "philosophical" questions that emerge from the text; contemporary students of religion are especially interested in examining the ways these questions are treated in cross-cultural terms, and have developed certain categories helpful to such understanding.

Finally, the reader may wish to be addressed by the text in a personal way. This aspect of reading the Hasidic sources is entirely legitimate; indeed it is the most appropriate sort of reading, given the intentions of the authors. Since such an understanding is quite subjective and individual, we have avoided engaging in it here, except for the final paragraph of our essay. It should be emphasized, however, that such a contemporary personal reading must not be confused either with the first level of understanding (for we are surely not *hasidim* of the early nineteenth century) or with the attempt at phenomenological analysis.

Hasidism stands on the very border between the postmedieval and modern periods in Jewish history. Its dates give it the appearance of modernity; if we identify the heyday of Hasidism as the century beginning with 1760, it will be hard to deny that the movement flourished within that time frame generally seen as belonging to the modern era. There are also specific ways in which Hasidism as a social and religious phenomenon may be viewed as at least a harbinger of modernity. The fact that it emerged as a reaction to the breakdown of the long-standing sociopolitical order of East European Jewry has been noted, and there is no doubt that part of its success was as a new form of social organization, the charismatic community around the *zaddik* replacing the weakened normative *kehillah* (community organization). From a religious point of view, there is also something remarkably modern about the attention Hasidism gives to the inner life and unique spiritual tasks of each individual, a fact that has done much to make it attractive to Buber and other twentieth-century theologians. Hasidism's rejection, or at least neutralization, of the complex edifice of kabbalistic theosophy also has a certain ring of modernity about it, insofar as it renders the devotional core of its message accessible to the reader who approaches it without initiation into these obscurities.

All of this becomes secondary to us, however, as we approach the task of reading Hasidic literature. The fact is that here Hasidism is dressed in its most classical garb, and forms a late chapter in the ongoing literary creativity of medieval and postmedieval Jewry. The essential assumptions of Hasidic literature are those shared by Jewry throughout its classical period, stretching from Talmudic times down into the nineteenth century, but held by relatively few Jews, including those labeled as Orthodox, in our own day. First among these is the absolute and literal veracity of Scripture; that is, for the Hasidic author a point can be made in a final and authoritative way by reference to a biblical verse. Even more important are the principles of homiletic license in reading Scripture, as articulated by the early rabbis. Much of Hasidic literature is loosely midrashic in form (see Chapter Three), weaving together an array of verses from various books and sections of the Bible that seem, on the literal face of things, to have nothing to do with one another. The same approach is now applied to the rabbinic writings themselves, as well as to the basic interpretive and theological works of medieval Judaism. Thus, a single Hasidic homily may, after departing from a biblical verse as interpreted by Rashi (see Chapter Four), proceed to draw into its net one or several statements from rabbinic *aggadah,* a passage from Maimonides, a fragment from the liturgy, a comment by Tosafot on a Talmudic phrase, a text from the Zohar, and a passage from the writings attributed to Isaac Luria. All of these are interpreted harmonically, for all are assumed to point to the same single truth. They were, as Scripture itself is made to say, "all given by a single shepherd"; all of them derive ultimately from the revelation of God's word at Mount Sinai. The harmonization of such diverse sources is the very stuff of which Hasidic and other late Jewish homiletics is made. It is thus crucial for the reader to understand just why each reference is incorporated into the homily, how it is being read, and what place it has in the final tour de force by which the original verse at hand is to be interpreted.

The highly traditionalist form this literature takes should not serve to mask the true intention of such exercises. The fact is that Hasidism is engaged in a calculated creative *mis*reading or reinterpretation of the entire received and accepted body of previous Jewish tradition. From within the juxtaposition of prior sources there begins to emerge a pattern of distinctively Hasidic foci in its presentation of classical Judaism. Sometimes these take the form of specific ideas, such as the raising of wayward thoughts or the service of God through corporeal things. Elsewhere they are promulgated by subtleties of emphasis, by seemingly flippant plays of language, or by sometimes startling parables told apparently by way of illustrative example.

Coupled with this set of assumptions concerning the prior literary sources of Judaism goes a series of assumptions about the wording of those sources and the language in which they are written. Since the entire biblical corpus is the revealed word of God, it may be assumed that He in His infinite wisdom counted carefully each word, its spelling as preserved in the Masoretic text, its numerical equivalent (for each letter of the Hebrew alphabet also has a numerical value), and the possible implications of reversing or otherwise rearranging its letters. This attitude toward the text, inherited by the Hasidic authors from the midrashic and kabbalistic traditions, allows for a freedom and playfulness that in no way diminish the seriousness of their endeavor or their reverence for the text that becomes so seemingly malleable in their hands. On the contrary, such homiletic reinterpretation is seen as the fulfillment of religious duty; such readings are the primary form of Torah study as practiced in the early Hasidic world.

As might be predicted for a popular movement of mystical piety within postmedieval Jewry, the three elements of the literary tradition that served as chief objects for this effort of reinterpretation were the Pentateuch, the aggadic teachings of the early rabbis, and the Zohar. While the influence of many other texts and genres can be felt within Hasidic literature, none approaches the centrality of these three as a *recognized literary* source. A few words on each of these as they are treated in Hasidic circles, with special emphasis on the Zohar and the treatment of kabbalistic themes in early Hasidism, is essential to any understanding of the texts before us.

The written Torah stands at the base of that great inverted pyramid known as the Jewish exegetical tradition. Always the best-known book, along with the prayerbook, even among relatively unlettered Jews, the entirety of its text is kept freshly in mind through the annual cycle of synagogue reading. From earliest rabbinic times, the weekly reading formed the basis for most of Jewish homiletics. To this Hasidism is no exception; the vast majority of the published volumes of Hasidic teaching follow the weekly cycles of the public reading. As is natural for homiletic literature (as distinct from scriptural exegesis), it is most often the opening verses of a section that will serve as the basis for a preacher's thoughts. Only incidentally will the homily shed light on the meaning of the verse with which it opens. The purpose is rather the opposite: for the verse of Scripture to shed light on some other issue which is the chief object of the homilist's concern. In Hasidism this issue will frequently be a devotional one: the technique of "raising sparks," the problem of distracting thoughts during prayer, the transformation of inner (and cosmic) darkness into light, and so forth. The nature of the Hasidic authors' concerns, combined with the penchant for discussing them chiefly in this homiletical context, often leads them to an extreme spiritualization of the biblical text, one that some will be surprised to find within so traditionalist a Jewry. Thus the ark of Noah (thanks to a fortuitous play on words) becomes the word of prayer, the descent into Egypt becomes the exile of the soul, the tabernacle in the wilderness becomes the holy place within the heart, and all the rest. While this in no way sacrifices their belief in either the external authority or the historical accuracy of the biblical text, it is quite clear that the chief object of the Hasidic preachers' concern is an eternal message of the struggle for spiritual attainment, a Torah that applies "in every time and to every person," as their frequent admonitions would have it.

The basic store of rabbinic teachings to which most Hasidic works refer is a rather limited one. Bits of exegesis quoted in Rashi's universally known commentary to the Torah, aggadic statements collected in certain well-worn pages of the Babylonian Talmud, and the basic midrashic collections (Rabbah and Tanhuma) on the Torah cycle would supply the seeker with by far the larger part of them. Of course no homilist was perforce restricted to these, and the greater his knowledge the wider his range of potential sources of inspiration. The very first printed book of Hasidism, the *Toledot Ya'akov Yosef,* shows a particularly broad range of rabbinic erudition. Most of the authors, however, restricted themselves to those sources mentioned, perhaps not only out of their own limitations but out of those of their anticipated hearers. A homiletic point made by a new and forceful stringing together of sources familiar to the listener's ear is potentially of greater power than one that has to turn to prooftexts that the listener has never heard before. Since most of the homilies were intended, first orally and then in writing, to have a broad-based popular appeal, it was best to remain close to the Rashi passages that much of the audience was sure to remember from study in childhood.

Hasidism remained, throughout its history, deeply faithful to the authority of rabbinic law, *halakhah.* Whatever flirtations it may have had with radical spiritualization of the commandments, in fact its enemies could find only the most minuscule legal objections to Hasidic behavior when they sought to describe it in bans and letters of denunciation. But while the life-style of the Hasidic community remained totally within the law, halakhic sources provide but little of the inspiration for the movement's thought. Essentially there is no reason why an originally legal text of the Talmud could not provide a departure point for the spiritual homily just as well as could *aggadah.* Most of the early leaders seemed to eschew such a mixing of realms, however, perhaps out of deference to a certain disdain Hasidism had originally felt toward the ivory-tower legal learning of the contemporary rabbinic world. This lack is particularly noted when the writings of the Maggid's circle are compared with those of some of the late nineteenth-century figures we have mentioned; the later works are filled with typically Hasidic comments on those legal portions of the Talmud that form the bread and butter of a traditional rabbinic education.

The use of kabbalistic materials in Hasidism is particularly problematic. (See Chapter Six for more on Kabbalah itself.) Like any group of latter-day pious Jews inclined toward mysticism, the Hasidic authors greatly revere the Zohar, which they hold to be the second-century composition of Rabbi Shimon bar Yohai. Numerous phases of the Zohar's Aramaic had crept into the Hebrew sacred vocabulary by the time of Hasidism, and in many of the homilies one can see that the author had prepared his words by looking into the Zohar text (or at least the opening paragraphs of it) for the particular Sabbath on which he was speaking. It is said of Rabbi Pinhas of Korets that he thanked God for having created him in that era when the Zohar was already known to the world, "for the Zohar has kept me a Jew." Both the kabbalistic system of the Zohar, in its rudimentary outlines, and the religious *ethos* of the Zohar had a great influence on all of Hasidic theology.

The *content* of kabbalistic teaching, however, underwent drastic change as it entered into Hasidism. The Maggid and his school, despite their own intellectuality, had little use for the latter-day Lurianic Kabbalah as they had received it, with its baroque overgrowth of heavenly realms and meditative techniques of access to them. Their rejection of cold and distant rabbinic erudition as a value had its parallel in the rejection of an arcane and inaccessible kabbalism: both were equally alien to the simple nearness of God that the Ba'al Shem Tov and those around him had known. To a certain extent this rejection applied to the theoretical concerns of the Zohar as well; the emphasis that the work places on an esoteric theosophy and cosmogony could hardly find a comfortable home in a popular movement of religious enthusiasm. There is a single-mindedness about the devotional focus in which Hasidism views the religious life that does not permit such "idle" speculation. Where the constant striving for nearness to God is the only legitimate value, even extended discussion of His nature and deeds, when lacking that devotional focus, may be depicted as distraction.

We are now ready to allow the Hasidic authors to speak for themselves. Each text will be preceded by a brief discussion of the author and/or the volume from which it is drawn. The text will then be presented in sections, interrupted by our own explication, as though it were being taught in a classroom. Some readers may choose to read the text in its entirety before turning to the discussion, and the format in which the texts are printed will allow for that option. Particularly in the first and longest passage, however, since the argument is a complex one, we recommend following the section-by-section approach as we have presented it.

LEVI YIZHAK OF BERDICHEV: ON INTERPRETATION

Levi Yizhak of Berdichev (c. 1740–1810) is one of the best-known and most widely revered figures in the history of Hasidism. A favorite of later Jewish folklore, his personality and deeds (at least as recorded in legend) perhaps did more to create and popularize the image of the Hasidic master than those of any other single figure save the Ba'al Shem Tov himself. A powerful but gentle and loving leader, he was especially known for his concern for the lives of ordinary Jews and a habit, retold in many a later tale, of defending them before God. He served as rabbi (in the normative halakhic, as well as the Hasidic, sense) of Berdichev, an important town in the Ukraine, from 1785 until his death. In this position he was able to do much for the spread of Hasidic influence, and history records that he was an important political figure in the life of Ukrainian Jewry during that time.

Less widely known is Levi Yizhak's contribution to the spread and development of Hasidic ideas. A major disciple of the Miedzyrzec school, he was able to dress the Maggid's often difficult mystical thoughts in popular and accessible homiletic garb. His collected teachings, *Kedushat Levi,* first published in 1811, is regarded as a classic of Hasidic literature. Less an original work of theory than a popularization of his master's teachings, the work still contains a good deal of homiletic ingenuity and many a daring formulation of the radically spiritualized vision of Judaism that lay at the heart of Hasidic teaching. Its frequent reprinting and wide distribution, despite the fact that there was no later Berdichev "dynasty" to assure such publication, bear witness to the fact that the work served as a source of inspiration to many a reader, both within the Hasidic camp and beyond.

The passage we have chosen from *Kedushat Levi* deals with the question of interpretation itself, and the role of the Hasidic master in the ongoing revelation of God's word. As such, it is one of those passages that deals directly with the assumptions that underlie all Hasidic homilies. Though seeming at first to meander, the text presents a sustained argument for the participation of the *zaddik* in the revelatory process. Such texts have a legitimating role in Hasidism, seeking justification in traditional religious language for the rather daring innovations in their readings of the sources. In the course of his homily, Levi Yizhak will address various other issues of importance to Hasidic thought: the levels of religious consciousness, the nature of miracles, and so forth. These briefer discussions, while not always germane to the final point of the homily, are important in their own right, and here, as frequently, contain insights of great profundity.

We now turn to the text, taken from the *Kedushat Levi* on *Yitro,* the Torah portion that includes the revelation at Mount Sinai.

I AM THE LORD YOUR GOD WHO TOOK YOU OUT OF THE LAND OF EGYPT (Exod. 20.2). Nahmanides asks why the verse did not say: "I am the One who created heaven and earth." Here is the solution that appears to us.

A basic principle in the service of our blessed Creator is that we Israelites are obliged to have faith in two Torahs, the written and the oral. Both "were given by a single shepherd" (Eccles. 11.12). He handed the written Torah to us by Moses, His faithful servant, engraved on the tablets in black fire on white fire. The Oral Torah was given to Moses in the form of commentary, including "what every faithful student was ever to find anew" (Jer. Talmud Peah 2.6). This is to say that the oral Torah was so given that whatever the righteous (zaddikim) of a particular generation say would indeed come to pass. This was the great power that the blessed Creator gave to us, out of love for His chosen folk Israel. According to their will, as derived from Torah, all the worlds were to be conducted. Of this the sages said: "God issues a decree but the zaddik cancels it" (Mo'ed Qatan 16b). This refers to those who serve their Creator, blessed be His name, aware that He is master and ruler.

The homily opens, after stating an initial and well-known question, by articulating a basic and universally accepted tenet of Jewish faith, one that even the most cautious listener could not find objectionable. But within a line or two of deft interpretation, Levi Yizhak has given this idea a very characteristically Hasidic cast, one that in fact goes to the heart of many an objection to Hasidism. The Talmud's claim that Moses' revelation contained all that any faithful student was ever to discover is used here to justify the notion that the Torah *must* in fact be reinterpreted by each generation. Each generation has its own history and questions; it is these that must be found by the leaders of that generation as they study the Torah. Here the "Oral Torah" is no longer the classic collection of early interpretations and legal codes that comprise rabbinic literature, but rather a process that needs continual renewal, a constant reshaping of Torah so that it be appropriate to the issues facing each community in its own time.

The identity of those leaders who are given the task of making the Oral Torah is also here presented in specifically Hasidic fashion. Rather than the *scholars,* it is the *zaddikim* who are to declare the Torah's meaning in each time. It is by virtue of their personal righteousness and closeness to God that such leaders claim their authority, rather than by

their mastery of the traditional sources. Here Levi Yizhak ties the ongoing reinterpretation of the oral law to a rabbinic reference that is taken
entirely out of context and originally had nothing to do with oral tradition and its development. "God issues a decree but the *zaddik* cancels it"
is a fragment of *aggadah* usually associated with powers of intercession
and miraculous healings. Now it is taken much further; the "decree" is
the Torah itself, and indeed reality itself, which of necessity becomes
whatever the *zaddik* declares it to be! As the Torah mirrors the changing
cosmic situation, the cosmos itself is moved by the will of the *zaddikim*
as they interpret the Torah.

Aware of the dangers lurking in the misuse of such an approach,
Levi Yizhak quickly adds a line to define the sort of *zaddik* he has in
mind for such broad powers in the shaping of Torah. Such a person
must be one who operates with full awareness that God alone is master
and ruler. Only humility can protect the *zaddik* from degenerating into
a magician, one who worships his own powers rather than those of God.
The homily continues:

> The rabbis said that when the Torah was given God appeared
> to Israel as an old man, while at the Exodus He had the appear-
> ance of a youth (Mekhilta Shirta 4). The point is that there are
> two aspects to the service of the Creator. Some serve Him
> because He is master and ruler, paying no attention to the
> blessings or rewards that God may shower upon them. All such
> benefits and pleasures are as nought to them, compared with
> the true joy of serving their blessed Creator. Here I am serving
> the great and glorious King, who has myriads of servants and
> countless realms of glory. Such a one is said to be serving God
> with the "greater mind" or an expanded consciousness.
>
> Others serve the blessed Creator because of the great bounty
> that is bestowed upon them. This is called the "lesser mind," a
> service of God with a small degree of consciousness.
>
> At the Exodus, Israel beheld the great miracles and wonders
> that God had wrought for them, the ten plagues, the splitting
> of the Red Sea, and the destruction of the Egyptians. Then they
> served God with the lesser mind; this is the meaning of "He
> had the appearance of a youth," the consciousness of a child.
> But as they stood before Mount Sinai to receive the Torah,
> "the poison passed out of them" and they thought nothing of
> worldly pleasures, but only of God's service. Then they wor-
> shipped Him as Lord and Master, with the greater mind. And
> so at Sinai He appeared to them as an elder, signifying that
> mature consciousness.

This is also why the letter *tet* does not appear in the commandments as they were engraved on the first tablets. *Tet* stands for *tovot,* goodly rewards, and when those first tablets were given the souls of Israel were so clear and pure that they would have wholly disregarded any such *tovot,* thinking only of the joy of His service, may He be blessed and exalted for all eternity. That was a moment of greater mind.

Here again a well-known rabbinic motif is taken far from its original meaning. The two appearances of God, say the early rabbis, teach that though He may appear in multiple forms, a single deity underlies them all. The youth at the sea and the elder at Sinai demonstrate that God will choose a form of manifestation appropriate to the needs of those to whom He is revealed. Now the motifs of youth and elder are made to serve a Hasidic purpose: they stand for two devotional states that are commonly found among worshipers. This transference of earlier theological statements into categories of religious psychology is again quite typical of Hasidic writings. The focus in Hasidism is on practical matters of devotion, rather than on grand theological truths. Never mind how God appeared to Israel, says Levi Yizhak. Think rather of how you appear before Him.

The idea that true service of God should be offered without thought of reward has a long history in Jewish sources, going back to the maxim of Antiginos of Socho in the Talmudic Pirke Avot ("Do not be like a servant who serves the master in order to receive a reward . . ."). This notion is much emphasized in the theoretical literature of Hasidism, especially of the circle around the Maggid. Its specific address was probably within the community of Hasidic listeners, as a warning against those who came to the *zaddikim* in search of personal blessings or earthly rewards. The fact is that the Hasidic leaders did claim the power to affect this realm, but the most spiritual among them sought the sort of disciples who would not approach them with such thoughts in mind.

The reference to the "first tablets" is to those that were fashioned and given by God, but then broken by Moses as he came down the mountain ʼand was greeted by the worship of the Golden Calf. The Talmud claims (Shabbat 146a) that the poison put into Eve by the primordial snake was carried through all of her descendants until Sinai, but that Israel was purified of this original taint as its people prepared themselves to receive God's word. At the moment of that first revelation they were returned to the state of purity originally intended in God's creation. Immediately after the revelation, however—for such is the human condition—those same Israelites prevailed upon Aaron to fashion the

Golden Calf. Functionally it may be said that the sin of the calf, that of idolatry, takes on the role of "original sin" in Jewish moralistic literature. After the calf was destroyed, Moses returned to God and received a second set of tablets, these fashioned, however, by human hands. Later writers associate the version of the Ten Commandments presented in Exodus 20 with the first tablets, while that in Deuteronomy 5 is taken to be the revised text of the second version. It is to this tradition that Levi Yizhak makes reference; indeed the *tet* is absent from the Exodus version, but appears twice, as the wording is only slightly revised, in Deuteronomy.

The theme of "greater" and "lesser" states of mind in the service of God is an important one in Hasidic literature, not always associated with the question of reward. The terms *mohin de-gadlut* and *mohin de-katnut* are derived from Lurianic Kabbalah, where they serve to designate alternating modes in the ongoing life of the *sefirot* within God. These terms too are now psychologized, and in Hasidism they refer to a person's worship in an ordinary ("lesser") state of mind as opposed to true contemplative prayer and the state of either detachment or rapture it requires. Frequent use is made of these terms in the literature of prayer instruction, some of which we shall see in our next selection.

We should stop here to take note that our teaching thus far has two sections, one on the role of *zaddikim* in the making of Oral Torah, the other on the greater and lesser mind at the Exodus and at Sinai. The connection between these sections and the relevance of either of them to the initial question (Why did the revelation not begin with "I am the Lord who created heaven and earth?") have not been made clear. Levi Yizhak continues:

> We know that whoever serves God with the greater mind has no fear of events that may befall him. Seem as he may to be in trouble, in his mind and heart he remains unperturbed, trusting firmly that he will come to no harm. Only from without is his distress apparent. The one who serves with lesser mind, however, does indeed feel all the fears and stresses of those events that surround him; his mind and heart too dwell in fear. Since he is subject to external forces, they overpower him and he comes under their domain. This is what King David meant when he said in the Egyptian Hallel (Ps. 118.10– 11) "All the nations have surrounded me; by the name of the Lord I will cut them down. They beset me *(sabuni)*, they surround me *(sevavuni)*; by the name of the Lord I will cut them down." Why the repetition? And what does he add by *sevavuni*

in the second verse? The path we have set out should help us
to understand these verses. King David said "All the nations"
—this refers to those events brought about by the nations.
"Have surrounded me"—they encircled me only from without, but in my mind I had no fear, knowing that God would
destroy them and save me from their clutches. This is "by the
name of God I will cut them down." King David's constant
mode of service was that of the greater mind. He too, however,
would sometimes fall from his rung and worship in a lesser
state. When that happened, the events that passed really would
cause him fear. When that happened, he said, the doings of the
nations "beset me" and "surround me," they enter right into
me, since I have fallen from my rung. I felt their surrounding
in my very mind, as fear fell upon me. Even then, though, "by
the name of the Lord I will cut them down"—I still trust in
divine goodness to cut off all those who rise up against me,
delivering me from *ZaRaH,* trouble, to *RaZaH,* desire.

Continuing on his earlier theme, here Levi Yizhak underscores the
unperturbability of that religious consciousness designated as *gadlut.* The
one who serves in such a way not only has transcended thought of
reward, but has completely overcome any sense of vulnerability to the
tragedies of this life, including especially the persecution of Jews at the
hands of their oppressors, a situation never far from the daily experience
of those who heard this homily. The greater mind is so detached from
any investment in life in this world that he is able to put his unquestion-
ing trust in God, knowing that the One to whom he is so devoted will
never abandon him.

While emphasizing this value of detachment, it is no small part of
Levi Yizhak's intent here to remind the hearer that even so noble a soul
as King David, author of the Psalms, underwent moments when that
state of higher awareness seemed to depart from him. Much of Hasidism's success was due to its realistic understanding of the vicissitudes
of human spirituality, and its willingness to accept the "lesser mind" too
as a realm of legitimate service. It undoubtedly consoled many a hearer
to know that even the spiritual giants of old had experienced "falls" or
moments of fear and insecurity much like their own. Levi Yizhak and
most of his colleagues insisted that even the *zaddik* himself had such
moments, and the knowledge of how to maintain faith in the face of
them was an essential part of their practical counsel. That is the force of
the Psalm verse as read in this passage: even when David fell into the

lesser state he remained confident that "by the name of the Lord I will cut them down."

The "external forces" to which the person in a lesser state of mind may fall prey are deserving of some comment. The Hebrew term *hizonim* is a richly ambiguous one. It refers to those things "outside" the proper purview of the religious mindset, "distractions" might properly translate one aspect of the term. In kabbalistic literature, however, *hizonim* takes on the very specific meaning of *demonic* forces, those that dwell "outside" the realm of holiness, standing arrayed against God in the great cosmic struggle of good and evil. The people Israel, and especially the righteous among them, are aligned with God in this struggle, while the nations of the world are the agents of these demonic powers, doing their bidding most particularly in their persecution of God's chosen and beloved people. This mythic and dualistic picture of reality, both cosmic and political, was very much a part of the Hasidic world view, and of course seemed to be constantly reaffirmed by the behavior and attitudes of those East European Christians in whose midst the Hasidic communities were destined to live. Thus Levi Yizhak has no trouble here in identifying David's outcry against "the nations" *(goyim)* with the evils that befall his own flock as they are distracted from religious concentration in its most total form. We will see further discussion of Israel and the nations as we go on in this text.

> That is why the authorities decided that the Sabbath before Passover should be designated as *Shabbat ha-Gadol*, the "great" Sabbath. This refers to the great miracle that took place preceding that first Passover in Egypt. On the tenth of the month they set aside their lambs and tied them to the bedposts. When the Egyptians asked them what these lambs were for, they replied "to be slaughtered for the Passover, as God has commanded us." The Egyptians became enraged at this (literally: their teeth were set on edge) slaughter of what they considered to be a god.

> Now why should this be called the "great" miracle of Egypt? Were there no miracles greater than this one? How about the splitting of the Red Sea and all the others? Were not all those wonders, wrought by God for His people Israel, greater than this? But here we are taught that Israel at that time was serving God in the greater mind. Whoever serves Him in that state has no fears of whatever may befall him, as we have taught above. That is why they designated this as the "great" miracle, the

miracle of the "greater" mind. The miracle was that they had
no fear of the Egyptians, even though they were about to
slaughter their gods. Now too we understand that on the tenth
of the month they were able to take these lambs, tie them to
the beds, and tell the Egyptians that they were going to offer
sacrifices. Just a while earlier they had said: "Can we slaughter
that which is sacred to the Egyptians before their very eyes and
not be stoned by them?" (Exod. 8.22). Note that the text says
"before their eyes"; they were afraid of the Egyptians, who
were always keeping close watch on them. But now that they
entered the state of greater mind, as we have explained, they
no longer paid any attention to the Egyptians watching them.
They had no more fear of anything, and the rule and might of
Egypt were not considered. Perhaps this is why, in fact, God
commanded them to set aside the lambs on the tenth day, to
bring them into this state of greater mind.

Here we have a religious assertion of considerable profundity. What
is truly the great miracle of the Exodus from Egypt? The fact that God
can bring plagues, destroy enemies, or even split the sea should cause no
great wonder to the person of real faith. Knowing securely that He is
Creator and Ruler, the fact that He can, if need be, change the course of
nature will constitute no great surprise. But the change that took place
in the hearts and minds of Israel—that is truly miraculous. How did the
cowardly and fearful slave masses gain the courage to prepare for their
liberation, and to do so publicly at that? Herein lies the greater miracle,
and its approximate anniversary (Passover is on the fifteenth of Nisan,
so Shabbat ha-Gadol is the Sabbath closest to the tenth) is indeed worthy
of celebration!

Of course this miracle is so important to Levi Yizhak because of its
contemporary and twofold message. Do not sit about and wait for miracles, he says to the often wonder-seeking Hasidic public. The true
miracle is the turn to gadlut, the wholehearted dedication to God that
must take place within you; this is the miracle toward which your attention should be focused, rather than on the tricks that some masters can
perform for you. No less important here is the not-so-subtly promised
reward (despite his prior admonitions) for this gadlut: he who directs his
mind in this manner will no longer feel afraid of the nations. The message, delivered in Berdichev in the closing years of the eighteenth century, could not have been clearer.

Now we can understand why Scripture, in recounting the
words of Jethro to Moses, said "Blessed is the Lord who saved

you from the hand of Egypt and the hand of Pharaoh, who saved the people from under the hand of Egypt. Now I know that the Lord is great . . ." (Exod. 18.10–11). The language seems redundant; there were not two redemptions here, but only one. And why does he say "Now I know that the Lord is great"? It is as we have said: he who serves God with the greater mind no longer fears the events that befall him, and is no longer subject to the "other side." On the contrary, he overcomes these forces. This is what Jethro meant to say. "Blessed is the Lord who saved you from the hand of Egypt and the hand of Pharaoh" refers to the great miracle by which they were delivered from their troubles. But "who saved the people from *under* the hand of Egypt" shows that God, in powerful love for His devoted ones while they were yet in Egypt, granted to them a higher consciousness, so that they could serve Him with the "greater mind." This brought them forth from "under the hand of Egypt"; they no longer submitted to them and no longer feared them. Thus "now I know that the Lord is great" refers to their service in this greater mind.

Here the theme he has already developed is tied to another section of the day's Torah reading, the account of Jethro's conversion. Rather than expounding a new idea, he has clarified and enriched his claim that Israel, while yet in Egypt, attained an inner liberation that preceded its physical deliverance on Passover itself. Though he does not say so directly, the impression is clear that this inner transformation, carrying with it a new strength and willingness to defy the Egyptians, was a necessary precondition for the actual liberation. One does not have to stretch the imagination too far to hear in this ordering of priorities echoes of the discussions among Zionist thinkers, only a century later, about how an inner transformation of the Jewish people, including a new sense of pride in their identity, would have to precede their political liberation.

Now Levi Yizhak is ready to tie together the seemingly diverse themes that make up this homily, and he returns to his opening comments on the *zaddik*'s powers in the face of divine decree and the relationship of these powers to the ongoing revelation of Torah. At this point an identity of *zaddik* and "he who serves with greater mind" is assumed, showing that by *zaddik* Levi Yizhak here has in mind not only the institutionalized Hasidic leader, but in fact every Jew who attains that rung of service.

Now we have already explained that whoever serves God with the greater mind conducts all the world and brings the flow of blessing into them all. When God issues a decree, he has the power in his hands to nullify it, to "sweeten" the forces of judgement from *ZaRaH* to *RaZaH,* transforming trouble into the desired state. This was the sages' intent when they said that the word *'aNoKHiY* [the "I" of "I am the Lord your God"] is an abbreviation for *'ana Nafshai Katvit Yahavit,* "I Myself have written and given it." The soul *(nefesh)* is the will, as in "If it is with your soul" (Gen. 23.8). This is "I Myself have written" —referring to the written Torah. "And given" refers to the Oral Torah, for I have given My will to you. You have leave to interpret according to your will, and by your will all the worlds will be conducted. And do not think that God feels woe at this sense of being "defeated"; on the contrary, it is a source of pleasure and joy to Him. Thus the rabbis said: "What was God doing? Smiling and saying "My children have defeated me." (Baba Meziah 59b). They also said that "God's temperament is not like that of flesh and blood. A person, if you best him, is saddened, but God is happy when He is bested" (Pesahim 119a). Now the word *ne'imah* refers to sweetness, and the rabbis also interpreted *'aNoKHi Y* as *'amirah Ne'imah Ketivah Yahivah,* "sweet speech, written and given," as though to say: "It is sweet to Me that I have handed My will over to My people Israel, so that all the worlds be conducted by their will. I derive the same pleasure from this that a father finds when his son defeats him."

The interpretive function of the *zaddik,* it is now made fully clear, goes far beyond mere homiletic license. The Torah is a portrayal of reality, that of the upper divine cosmos as well as the lower world. As the *zaddik* interprets the Torah and changes God's "decree," he actually partakes of God's cosmic rule, bringing about the flow of that divine blessing that is the source of all life. This notion, deeply embedded in the kabbalistic ideas that are a central part of Hasidism's heritage from earlier generations, is here stated with unmitigated boldness. God is author of the Written Torah, but the Oral Torah, which is the actual rule by which the universe (cosmic as well as halakhic) is ruled, has been handed over to Israel.

There is something in this notion, as stated thus far, that could almost be reminiscent of deism, an ideology contemporary with early Hasidism, as it happens, but far removed in space and cultural context. God sets the world in motion, establishes the rule of natural law, and abandons it to the wisdom and folly of human conduct. Here God authors and delivers the "ground rules" of the Written Torah, allowing all further development to rest in the hands of His people and the righteous in their midst. Levi Yizhak seems to sense the problem in this diminution of divine power when he asks whether God Himself might not feel troubled by the lessening of control over His creation. His answer is again classically Hasidic: God loves and trusts the righteous; He feels toward them as a father toward his children, a love and pleasure undiminished by any tinge of jealousy or regret. The service of the *zaddikim* brings Him joy, a gift to which He responds, quite naturally as a parent, by bestowing something of His own upon them. The king can only rejoice as he sees his chosen child learn to take up the reins of his kingdom.

The Talmudic passages that Levi Yizhak quotes, while important in their own right, are here extended far beyond their original intention. The first and best known of these quotations ("What was God doing? Smiling and saying 'My children have defeated me' "), was written as a postscript to the Talmud's account of a famous debate among the early sages. Rabbi Eliezer seeks to prove his point in a halakhic argument by miraculous signs and finally by a voice from heaven. His opponent Rabbi Joshua, however, has the majority of the sages on his side in the debate. Finally it is made clear that "the Torah is not in heaven," and that the majority opinion is that which will rule. Of this God says, "My children have defeated Me." The other passages are of similar force, referring to the independence of the sages and their deliberative processes in determining the law. The cosmological implications here attributed to these sayings are the product of later kabbalistic thought. The Talmud sees God's authority as legislator handed over to the sages of Israel; the Hasidic master, reading the same sources, sees in them the giving of cosmic rule to Israel's righteous.

Now the question with which the homily began may finally be answered, as the whole is brought to an integrated conclusion. Levi Yizhak opened his talk, we will recall, by quoting Nahmanides' question as to why the Ten Commandments begin with "I am the Lord thy God who took thee out of the Land of Egypt" and not "who created heaven and earth."

> This is why God made mention of the Exodus from Egypt rather than the creation of heaven and earth. Mention of creation would only show that He is the First of all firsts, and that the world was created. But by saying "I am the Lord your God who brought you out of the Land of Egypt" He showed His

love for His people Israel and taught them to serve Him with fire in their hearts. He brought His chosen folk out of Egypt in love, giving them the power and ability to sweeten the judgement forces, to turn woe to desire, and to rule all the worlds. In this way they are truly the children of God, and this should bring them to true rapture in His service.

This is why He continues "You shall have no other god beside Me." "Beside Me" seems to have no meaning. But following our way it will make sense. "My love for you is so great that I have called you My children. This means that I dwell right in your midst, for My love cleaves to My children and I dwell chiefly among them. When you make an idol, then, God forbid, it is indeed, as it were, right beside Me."

The homily turns out to reveal Levi Yizhak at his most passionate, bearing testimony to the infinite love of God and the intimacy with Him that only those who know themselves to be God's children can conceive. God remains at your side always; He is with you no matter what you do. His commandment, then, turns into a heartfelt plea: since I am with you in any case, do not place idols at My side.

COUNSEL FOR THE RELIGIOUS LIFE

The homiletical literature of Hasidism was augmented, as we have said, by a number of anonymous aphoristic collections of teachings attributed to the masters, first published in the closing years of the eighteenth century. Here the reader did not have to follow a complex thread of homiletic argument to get the point. These collections spoke directly to the matter at hand; they taught how to pray, gave advice on concentration, and emphasized such basic Hasidic virtues as simplicity, humility, and wholeness.

Our selection is the opening page of *Likkutim Yekarim,* first published in Lvov in 1792. The title page claims that the teachings are those of four major figures in the early history of Hasidism: the Ba'al Shem Tov, the Maggid of Miedzyrzec, Menahem Mendel of Premyslany and Yehiel Michel of Zloczov. The latter two were important leaders of Hasidism in the Ukraine in the generation of and immediately following the Ba'al Shem Tov; neither was particularly associated with the Maggid's school. Menahem Mendel of Premyslany (b. 1728) migrated to the Holy Land in 1764 and founded the Hasidic community in Erez Israel, along with Nahman of Horodenka and a group of followers. Yehiel

Michel (1731–86), also a younger contemporary of the Ba'al Shem Tov, was a well-known preacher and the father of five sons, each of whom served as leader of a considerable Hasidic following in the next generation, and many of whose disciples were probably the original intended audience for this volume.

The fact is, however, that all the teachings in *Likkutim Yekarim* should be regarded as anonymous. With occasional exceptions the individual masters are not mentioned again in the volume, and many of the teachings found here have their parallels in other such collections composed about the same time. The ideology of the volume, underlying its devotional instructions, sometimes reflects the rather intellectual orientation of the Maggid, but much of it is so general as to be attributable to almost any of the early Hasidic teachers. The text begins:

> "The man Moses was more exceedingly humble than any person on the face of the earth." (Num.12.3)

> This refers to two levels, one in which a person's thought is entirely above, even [when involved] in lower matters, since he is entirely separated from the corporeal, and another in which he is not so fully separated from matter.

> This is the meaning of "Moses Moses" (Exod. 3.4), where the cantillation does not indicate a pause between them, while "Jacob, Jacob" (Gen. 46.2) is interrupted by a pause. There exist Moses above and Moses below, Jacob above and Jacob below. Moses has no pause, for he is all one, both above and below; he is so removed from matter that even when dealing with corporeal things (and certainly when dealing with matters of spirit!) he is entirely turned upward. Still he held fast to the quality of Humility, even when at his most spiritual, considering himself more lowly than "any person on the face of the earth," even than those whose thoughts were entirely directed toward earth.

The virtue of humility, though an important one in the moralistic thought of Judaism in every period, is particularly underscored in the literature of Hasidism. This probably has to do with the very special burden the Hasidic master faced with regard to questions of humility and pride. Surrounded by an adulating mass, reputed capable of doing wonders, and even, as we have seen, of changing the will of heaven and "conducting all the worlds," it was no easy task for the *rebbe* to maintain an honest perspective on his own powers and worth. The example of

Moses, the greatest master of all time and yet the most humble man on earth, is frequently and sharply called to mind.

The notion that each person has both an upper and lower self which are to be kept in tune with one another has a long kabbalistic history. Here it is used chiefly in a moral sense; even when engaged in "lower" pursuits, the spiritual self must remain dominant. The service of God is not to be interrupted when one engages in the earthly matters that are required for the sustenance of life in this world. Hasidism teaches that each moment and each object contain a unique spark of holiness that calls forth for redemption, and its popular message differs from most prior spiritual counsel in that it insists on the integration of the self and the unity of all being. Rather than turning away from the things of this world, the *hasid* is taught that the person of true spirit can live *in* the world while yet remaining "above" in the true focus of his attention. The text proceeds, without relation to what has come before:

> Know that each word is a complete form. You must say it with all your strength, or else it will be like one lacking a limb.

> It is an act of divine grace that a person remains alive after prayer. It would be natural to die because so much strength is lost, for the one who prays puts all his strength into the prayer, in the intensity of his concentration.

Here begins a series of brief instructions on concentration in prayer, the center of contemplative life as it is practiced in Hasidism. The whole self must be present in each word of prayer, and the intensity demanded of the one who prays is uncompromised, even to the point of would-be death. Here we see Hasidism at its most serious, a far cry from the popular and jolly face it is often given in modern portrayals.

> Rabbi Israel Ba'al Shem Tov said: A person who is reading the Torah and sees the lights in its letters, even though he does not chant the text according to its proper notations, shows such great love and rapture in his reading that God, blessed be He, is not strict with him about this matter. This is true even if he does not pronounce the words themselves properly. This may be compared to a child, greatly beloved by his father. He asks something of his father, and even though he does not speak properly, his father derives pleasure from his words. One who speaks words of Torah lovingly receives the love of God; He is not concerned with whether the words are properly recited. Thus the rabbis said on "His banner *(diglo)* over me is love"

(Cant. 2.4) "his stammering *(liglugo)* over me is love (Cant. Rabbah 2.13).

Seriousness of personal emotional demand is not to be confused with learned elitism. "The Merciful One demands the heart," as the Talmud says (and as the Hasidic masters were fond of quoting), not details of proper diction. It should be recalled, however, that this seemingly lax attitude with regard to precision in performance stopped short when it came to that which was required by the canon of *halakhah* itself. Whatever tendencies it may have had toward a total spiritualization of Judaism, Hasidism struggled hard—and successfully—at remaining within the normative traditions from which it emerged.

> Crying is very bad. It is in joy that a person is supposed to serve God. Only tears that flow from joy and attachment to God are beneficial.

> When a person performs the commandments by rote they are dry; you have to fulfill each precept with heart and desire.

> A person should train himself to recite even the hymns of prayer in a low voice, crying out in a whisper. Speak the words, whether in prayer or study, with all your strength, as Scripture says "All my bones shall say 'O Lord, who is like You' " (Ps. 35.10). But the shout that comes from true attachment should be a whisper.

The counsel to pray quietly, or to "shout in a whisper," may be a reaction to criticism that was leveled against Hasidism in its early days. The bans against the movement spoke of strange noises and wild animal-like shouts that could be heard in the first Hasidic prayer houses. This counsel of quiet prayer was not universally accepted among the *hasidim,* and even today there are groups (especially the Karlin-Stolin tradition, but others as well) that are marked by loud and seemingly boisterous styles of prayer.

> Every person can reach the rung of Moses in self-purification. Perhaps not precisely that of Moses, for "Moses went up to the Lord" (Exod. 19.3) in the world of *'azilut,* but a rung like Moses' can be attained. If your soul is from *malkhut* of *'asiyah,* the lowest rung in the lowest world, you might reach the rung of Moses by ascending to the highest *('azilut)* within *'asiyah,* and the same if your soul is of another world.

Here the editor returns to the example of Moses. You may long to emulate the greatest of men, he tells the reader. Indeed you can do so, but this does not mean that you will become Moses; each person can achieve high degrees of self-purification, but within the bounds of his own soul's nature. *'Asiyah* and *'azilut* (along with *beri'ah* in the following passage) refer to the kabbalistic doctrine of four worlds. Each human soul is rooted in one of those worlds, and it cannot reach higher than its origins will allow. A fully realized soul from *'asiyah,* the lowest world, may reach the highest rung within *'asiyah,* but no higher. Do not strive for that which is beyond your grasp, as a well-known Hasidic admonition would have it. We are here reminded of a famous quip attributed to Rabbi Zusya of Anipolye: "When I reach the true world," he said, "they will not ask me why I wasn't Moses. They will ask me why I wasn't Zusya."

> Sometimes a person feels that he has reached a certain level, and makes himself happy over this. He should rather humble himself, and think that perhaps he has only reached the bottom of *'asiyah,* or maybe *'azilut* of *'asiyah.* There are, however, some *zaddikim* who have attained to *beri'ah* and *'azilut.*

Be humble and do not rush to rejoice over your spiritual attainments. Know, however, that the highest rungs are not utterly beyond human grasp.

> You have to go step by step in prayer, not using up all your strength right at the beginning. Begin slowly, and when you reach the middle of the service attach yourself to God in a more intense way. Then you should be able to say all the words of prayer, even at a quickened pace.

> Even if you can not attain a sense of attachment to God as you begin your prayers, say the words with concentration and strengthen yourself bit by bit. Then God, blessed be He, will help you to pray with great attachment.

> A person cannot pray properly unless light surrounds him from all sides. He should be able to feel that light.

These three (originally separate) statements are almost a study in contrasts within the array of prayer instructions to be found in early Hasidic writings. The first two are practical guides, and reflect the realistic problems of the worshiper who strives to pray with intensity but cannot always achieve such prayer. One of the strengths of Hasidism was the ability of the masters to understand and react sympathetically to the simple but devoted folk, and to instruct them at their own level in the life of prayer. The final statement addresses *true* prayer, or inward devotion at its highest. Perhaps the speaker is trying to warn disciples who feel they have reached those heights, challenging them to feel the light of God's presence surrounding them as they pray.

> When you hand over all your thoughts to the blessed Creator, He will put into your mind that which you have to do. "Cast your burden upon the Lord" (Ps. 55.23). When you then long for some pious quality, surely it will be because you need that thing. It is God who has sent the thought to you.

> Rabbi Israel Ba'al Shem Tov said: When you are in a state of attachment to God and some thought comes into your mind, surely it will be a true one. This is a small measure of the Holy Spirit.

> He also said: If you have studied Torah on a certain day, and afterwards some matter comes up that requires a decision, the very matter you have been studying will teach you how to act. Only if you are constantly attached to God will He instruct you through your studies. If you walk crookedly with God, however, He will treat you in the same way. Then He will not bring your way those garments or foods containing sparks that need to be redeemed by the root of your soul.

The quality of trust or *bittahon* is a central value to the religious world view of the *hasid*. One who casts his burdens upon the Lord can be assured that He will provide, not only in the material sense, but in guiding the *hasid*'s footsteps as he goes along the devotional path. It is interesting that Torah study is here presented as the chief vehicle for such guidance. Contrary to popular opinion, Hasidism did not denigrate the study of Torah "for its own sake." Rather it sought to rescue the study of God's word from being a dry, academic pursuit, seeing it rather as an essentially charismatic activity. Since Torah, in its broadest sense, is the living word of God, what better channel could there be than study through which God might speak to us about those issues that affect our daily life?

But it is not only prayer and study, the essential acts of devotion, through which God calls out to the *hasid*. Each object that one encounters, even in the material world, is said to contain sparks of fallen divine light that cry out for redemption, bits of divinity that long to be restored to their source. An essential part of the *hasid*'s trust is that God will bring within his reach those particular things that can be redeemed by him alone, belonging as they do to the unique root of his own soul. This will happen, the speaker warns us, only if trust is total and the seeker acts in unmitigated good faith.

> When you want to be alone in prayer, at least one companion should be present. A person who is completely alone is in danger. The two should be in the same room, but then each can address himself to God in solitary prayer.

> Sometimes a person who has attained true attachment can be alone with God even in a house where other people are present.

Hitbodedut or "aloneness with God" has a long history in the devotional literature of Judaism. Sometimes it refers to silent meditation, at others to private prayer or outcry. The counsel offered here, to have another person present when engaged in such activity, is not universally held by the Hasidic masters—some explicitly call for complete self-isolation. The warning offered may have to do either with the dangers of distraction or with those of an overintensity that could threaten one's ability to return—or both.

> Sometimes you fall from your rung because of yourself; God knows that you are in need of such a fall. At other times it is the people around you who cause you to fall. Such descent is for the sake of ascent, to reach a still higher rung. Thus Scripture says: "He will lead us over death" (Ps. 48.15). "Abram went down into Egypt" (Gen. 12.10) and "Abram rose up from Egypt" (Gen. 13.1). Abraham here refers to the soul, and Egypt to the "shells."

Returning to a realistic psychology of devotion, we find the text dealing with those states of "fall" that periodically plague anyone who strives for higher spiritual attainment. Continue in your trust, the reader is told; God knows that you need this alternating rhythm of rise and fall in order to reach those rungs you seek. "Descent for the sake of ascent" is a major theme in the literature of Hasidism; the *zaddik* must go down in order to be further uplifted and in order to uplift those around him.

The allegorical reading of Abram's descent into Egypt, adopted from the Zohar (I, 122b) is taken as scriptural evidence of the need for such falls. In order to rise to the heights of devotion exemplified by his act at Mount Moriah, the patriarch first had to encounter the greatest depths. Similarly, as we are frequently told in Hasidic homilies, Israel had to endure Egyptian bondage, in that place of the thickest "shells" that hide God's light, before they could arrive at the heights of their encounter at Mount Sinai.

RETURNING TO GOD:
A PASSAGE FROM THE SEFAT EMET

Yehudah Leib Alter (1847–1905), the rabbi of Ger (Gora Kalwaria), was one of the leading figures in Polish Jewry during the latter decades of the nineteenth century. Heading a dynasty founded by his grandfather, Yizhak Meir of Ger, his followers numbered in the tens, perhaps even hundreds of thousands. The collection of his teachings, entitled *Sefat Emet*, is the best known work of later Polish Hasidism, and is still studied avidly by the Gerer *hasidim*, currently centered in Jerusalem.

The Hasidism of Ger is historically and ideologically rooted in the traditions of the Przysucha and especially the Kotsk schools. These were characterized by a renewed respect for Talmudic learning (both Yizhak Meir and Yehudah Leib were well-known halakhic scholars), a strong sense of political/social awareness, and a relentless search for truth. The *Sefat Emet*, while written in traditional homiletic style, is marked by a constant search for the essentials of Jewish spiritual teaching: the innermost core of what it means to be a Jew, the essence of Torah, the purpose of existence itself. Yehudah Leib had a profound understanding of sacred time and the meaning of religious life as a reenactment of mythical paradigms. While educated wholly from within the classics of the Jewish tradition, and speaking in a style deeply rooted in those sources, there is much that is strikingly modern in the content of his teachings.

The homily offered here was delivered on Shabbat Shuvah, the Sabbath of Repentance, in 1881 (*Sefat Emet* is one of the few Hasidic works in which the individual homilies are dated). The year 1881, it should be recalled, was a fateful one in the history of Russian Jewry. Alexander III had just acceded to the throne, and the spring of that year had been marked by the first large-scale pogroms against Jews in over a century. While the outrages had taken place in the Ukraine, some distance from the central Polish Gerer "kingdom," word had certainly traveled, and those who listened to Yizhak Meir during that holy-day season surely had the events of the year behind them in mind. It was those same pogroms, of course, that were an important factor in stimulating both large-scale emigration of Russian Jews to England and America and the proto-Zionist BILU movement, establishing the first new Jewish settlements in Erez Israel.

The teaching speaks of the nature of *teshuvah* (return, i.e., repentance) and the place of Israel's return to God in the cosmic scheme. Readers familiar with the thought of Abraham Isaac Kook may notice a certain similarity in the notion of *teshuvah,* though the styles of these two writers differ vastly from one another.

The preacher takes as his point of departure a well-known passage from Pirke Avot (5.1): "The world was created by ten utterances. What does this teach? Surely it could have been created by one! It was so done in order that the wicked be punished for destroying a world created by ten, and that the righteous be rewarded for preserving such a world." The ten utterances to which the text refers are the ten times when God says: "Let there be" in the course of Creation. The Talmud, commenting on this passage (Megillah 21b), notes that there are but nine such occurrences, not ten, in the text of Genesis, and suggests that "In the Beginning" itself is also an utterance of God. In midrashic literature a parallel is often cited between these ten utterances and the Ten Commandments, while in later kabbalistic writings it is widely understood that these utterances are the ten *Sefirot* (discussed in Chapter Six), and the passage is taken as a Talmudic source for the kabbalistic doctrine.

> The ten days of *teshuvah* are the ten utterances by which the world was created. Rosh Hashanah is parallel to "In the Beginning," as the Talmud says " 'In the Beginning' too is an utterance." This one includes them all, and that is why they asked if Creation could not have taken place through a single utterance. This is the statement of Oneness, that which entered God's mind before Creation. This also is the state of the future, after all has been redeemed.

The first of the ten utterances, according to the kabbalistic reading, is parallel to *Keter,* the highest of the ten emanations within God. Since all the lower *Sefirot,* detailing the process of divine flow and the aspects of God's self, are derived from *Keter,* this aspect of divinity may be said to include them all, an absolute state of Oneness that precedes the first movement toward Creation. In many kabbalistic writings *Keter* is identified with *ein sof* itself, the hidden Godhead that remains beyond all Creation. Thus "in the beginning" is separated from the conclusion of that first verse in Scripture; it is taken as a description of the state that existed *before* "God created heaven and earth."

The absolute unity of God is a state that is interrupted only temporarily by Creation and the events, including all of history, that follow. In the end, after Israel has completed the work of redemption, that unity will be restored, and the separate existence of the world will cease to be. This idea of an ultimate restoration of Oneness is an often unstated assumption of Jewish theology, most of which tends to concentrate on the this-worldly redemption associated with the Messiah. The reader will recognize this idea most readily from its statement in the well-known liturgical hymn *Adon 'Olam:* "Lord of the universe who ruled before any creature came to be. . . . And after all is finished, He shall rule in awe, alone . . ."

> This is also why the rabbis said that "At first it entered God's mind to create the world through the aspect of judgment. When He saw that the world would not survive, He added to it the aspect of compassion." (Genesis Rabbah 12.15) Until the sin of Adam He was ready to create the world by a single utterance. But due to the mixing [of good and evil], the quality of compassion was brought in and the world was created with ten utterances, in order to make for reward and punishment, as the Mishnah says. In fact it was the wicked who were to emerge from Adam who brought about the sin. The righteous, and the children of Israel who are called "Your people are all righteous" (Isa. 60.21), are the ones who arouse the power of Oneness. That is what the rabbis meant when they said that Israel too entered God's mind before He created the world (Gen. Rabbah 1.4).

Here the preacher expostules on a number of rabbinic dicta about Creation; it is especially clear in this passage that the teaching is preserved in extremely abbreviated form. Creation through *middat ha-din,* the aspect of judgment, was God's original intent. This is associated with Creation through a single utterance: the complexities of sin, evil, and the need for forgiveness were not part of the original divine plan. If all was to exist in a state of oneness, there could be no thought of alienation between God and His creature. The creation of man, with his freedom and ability to choose evil over good, caused a change in this plan. The force of divine compassion and forgiveness would have to exist if evil was to be overcome and the original harmony restored. Thus Israel, personifying the righteous power in the world, also needed to exist in God's mind before the Creation would be complete: it is they who arouse His mercies over all His creatures and allow the work of restoration to begin.

Of the situation after the sin it is said: "There is no righteous one in the earth who does not sin" (Eccles. 7.20), due to the mixing. This is especially true while we are in exile, among the wicked. The only counsel is *teshuvah;* it is this to which the *shofar* calls us. Each of us must seek to restore the world to what it was in the primal divine thought, or to what it was in the moment when we received the Torah, before the sin that followed.

Here the cosmic exile of humanity from Eden and the primal state of oneness is associated with the historical exile of Israel, dispersed among the wicked nations. Because Israel embodies the power of goodness, it is their return to God that makes for redemption. Following older tradition, the *Sefat Emet* notes that such redemption almost took place at the moment Israel received the Torah, had not the sin of the Golden Calf intervened and brought about the wandering in the wilderness. As we have seen in the homily of Levi Yizhak, this sin of idolatry serves to renew the original sin of Eden.

The Talmud says that all Creation took place consciously (Rosh Hashanah 11a). So it is that on each Rosh Hashanah the Creation is renewed, in accord with the consciousness and willingness of Israel to accept His blessed kingdom. They succeed in this renewal through their longing to return the world to that which it was before the sin. This is what the sages meant when they said that He "consulted the souls of the righteous" before Creation (Gen. Rabbah 8.7).

Adam repented of his sin on the same day; only afterwards does Scripture say: "God saw all that He had made, and it was very good" (Gen. 1.31). This grace was called forth by Adam's *teshuvah.* Of this the holy Sabbath was made, a return of Creation to Oneness, with no admixture of evil. Of this Scripture proclaims: "He blessed it and declared it holy" (Gen. 2.3). That is why there is no need to sound the *shofar* on the Sabbath: the Oneness is aroused of its own accord. The shofar sound is meant to arouse this Oneness, as Scripture says: "Make yourself two trumpets of silver . . . when the community is assembled, you shall sound them" (Num. 10.2,7). It is through *teshuvah* that the power of Oneness is awakened.

The consciousness with which all beings were created (Rashi says that each creature was asked if it wished to be created and responded

"Yes") is given over to Israel; it is their annual willingness to return to God that allows the world to be sustained. Creation can only continue to exist so long as there is hope for restoration of the primal unity. Israel's desire for *teshuvah* bears witness to that hope and it is this desire that arouses God's mercies and allows the world to be. The power of *teshuvah* is dramatically illustrated by the effect of Adam's return; only by the power aroused through his *teshuvah* could Creation have been declared "good" and could God's Sabbath have come into being. Since Sabbath is "a foretaste of the world to come," and a temporary state in which Creation is unified and evil banished, it testifies weekly that man's return to God has within it the power to restore His world.

> Of this it is said: "Take words with you and return to the Lord" (Hosea 14.3). God created everything through the power of Torah, which is also called "Beginning" (Gen. Rabbah 1.1), the root of all. By many contractions all was created from it, being out of nothingness. Israel has to return all of Creation, making Nothing out of being, including everything in the Torah. This is done through the commandments that apply to all of our actions. By the proper direction of their deeds the righteous join everything back to the power of Torah—this is the essence of *teshuvah*. *Teshuvah* exists in both deed and thought: "Let the wicked one leave his way" applies to the weekday world, in which evil deeds must be set aside, and "the sinful man his thoughts" (Isa. 55.7) applies to the Sabbath, a higher form of *teshuvah*. Such a one may not be considered evil in his actions, but on the Sabbath he is to repent for thoughts and reflections.

Here the specifically Jewish content of Yehudah Leib's teaching becomes clearest. Until this point it is only because Israel is identified in general with "the righteous" that it is central to the process of cosmic renewal. Now that claim is made more specific: since Creation took place through Torah (the cosmic, preverbal Torah, to be sure), it is by faithfulness to the commandments of that Torah that the transformation of "being into nothingness" (a favorite formulation of the Maggid of Miedzyrzec) can come about. The return of being to God takes place by means of the Torah, just as did the original Creation. The commandments that rule the daily life of the Jew bring all things back into the domain of God's word; it is through this channel that they are restored to God Himself.

It is written: "As the rain or snow drops from heaven and returns not there, but soaks the earth and makes it bring forth vegetation, yielding seed for sowing and bread for eating, so is the word that issues from My mouth: it does not come back to Me unfulfilled, but performs what I purpose, achieves what I sent it to do" (Isa. 55.10–11). This refers to the words of Torah that God has implanted in each one of Israel; "eternal life has He planted in our midst." This too is the meaning of: "Give ear, O heavens, and I shall speak; hear O earth, the words of my mouth. May my teaching flow forth like rain, my expression like the dew" (Deut. 32.1–2). Just as rain saturates the earth, arousing the power of growth so that earth gives forth vegetation, so does that oral Torah, planted in the hearts of Israel, its soil. But the help of heaven is still required; this is the written Torah. By struggling over the words of the written Torah, the power that lies within man is aroused; man was created wholly for the purpose of working at Torah. His raising up of the words to God is the fulfillment of his mission; he returns the words to the One who has sent him. But his uplifting can take place only by the repair of all one's deeds, as they follow the words. Then they will "perform what I purpose, achieve what I sent them to do." Then they return to their source; this is the essence of *teshuvah*.

Teshuvah here is finally taken in a dual sense: the return of man to God, and the fulfilled restoration to Him of that word which He has sent to man for his guidance.

The convictions of the *Sefat Emet* on the role of Israel's *teshuvah* in the survival and renewal of the cosmos come to him through a long history of prior rabbinic and kabbalistic thought. While there have been many voices in the history of Judaism that have insisted upon the absolute freedom of God from any dependence on humanity (a position most often identified with Maimonides), there is an equally strong current that claims that God Himself and His universe require the merits of Israel's good deeds for their very life. The kabbalists saw this primarily in terms of ritual performance: the fulfillment of the *mitzvot* gives strength to God and leads Him to triumph over the forces of evil. The tendency in Hasidism is to make such demands upon *all* of Israel's actions; the entirety of human life must be directed toward God.

Though the *Sefat Emet* lived to see the beginning of the twentieth century, it is hard to imagine (without ascribing to him powers of prophecy) that he could have foreseen just how true and appropriate his message would become for a generation only half a century removed from the end of his lifetime. Still, the present-day implication of his teaching should not be lost on the reader: the very survival of our universe depends on the collective will of humanity to accept the task of *teshuvah*.

WHERE TO GO FROM HERE

There is no comprehensive work on the history of Hasidism that can be recommended to the reader. The work of S. M. Dubnov (unavailable in English, in any case) is badly outdated, and nothing has yet been published to take its place. There are, however, books, articles, and sections of books on specific topics to which one could well turn for guidance.

Introductory histories of Hasidism are available in Bernard Weinryb's *The Jews of Poland* (Philadelphia: Jewish Publication Society, 1973); in Raphael Mahler's *A History of Modern Jewry* (London: Valentine, Mitchell, 1971; written from a Marxist point of view); and in an essay by S. Ettinger in H. H. Ben-Sasson's *Jewish Society Through the Ages* (London: Valentine, Mitchell, 1971; *Journal of World History,* vol. 11). The movement's religious roots are discussed by Gershom Scholem in the final chapter of *Major Trends in Jewish Mysticism* (New York: Schocken, 1941) and by Martin Buber in *The Origin and Meaning of Hasidism* (the most recent paperback edition is New York: Horizon, 1972).

Specific aspects of Hasidic thought are covered in an important series of essays by Joseph Weiss, published over several years in the London *Journal of Jewish Studies,* by Scholem in his *The Messianic Idea in Judaism* (New York: Schocken, 1971) and by Louis Jacobs in *Seeker of Unity* (New York: Basic Books, 1966) and *Hasidic Prayer* (paperback, New York: Schocken, 1973).

Individual figures in the history of Hasidism have been treated in monographs by Samuel Dresner, *The Zaddik* (paperback, New York: Schocken, 1974; on Jacob Joseph of Polonoy) and *Levi Yitzhak of Berditchev* (New York: Hartmore House, 1974) and by the present writer in *Tormented Master: A Life of Rabbi Nahman of Bratslav* (University of Alabama, 1979; also in Schocken paperback). An important series of essays by Abraham J. Heschel on various figures in the early history of the movement has been translated by Samuel Dresner and is soon to appear in English.

A vast critical and historical literature on Hasidism is extant in Hebrew, primarily by scholars at the Hebrew University, including the students of Gershom Scholem. The Hebrew reader is especially commended to the writings of B. Dinur, I. Tishby, R. Schatz, M. Piekarz and further studies by Scholem and Weiss. There is also an extensive quasi-critical scholarly literature on Hasidism written in Hebrew by latter-day *hasidim* and by others who are quite close to the movement. While such works are to be selected with care, much information is found there that cannot be gleaned from other sources.

As to the Hasidic sources themselves, almost none of the important homiletical or theological works of Hasidism has been translated into English. The great exception to this is the writings of the Lubavitch school, including the *Tanya* by Shne'ur Zalman of Liadi, an important systematic compendium of Hasidic ideas. HaBaD/Lubavitch works in translation, often with excellent annotation, are available through the Kehot Publishing Company in Brooklyn, associated with the Lubavitch movement.

Other Hasidic works in translation include *Upright Practices* and *The Light of the Eyes: Homilies to Genesis* by Menahem Nahum of Chernobyl, which I have recently published through the *Classics of Western Spirituality* series of the Paulist Press (New York, 1982). An earlier collection, undertaken with Barry W. Holtz, is *Your Word Is Fire: The Hasidic Masters on Contemplative Prayer* (New York: Paulist Press, 1977). On the difficulties attending the translation of such works, see my reflections "On Translating Hasidic Homilies" in a recent issue of *Prooftexts,* vol. 3, no. 1 (Winter 1983).

The Hasidic tales have fared much better in translation than have the homilies. Especially recommended from the scholarly point of view are Dan Ben-Amos' rendition of *In Praise of the Ba'al Shem Tov* (Bloomington Ind.; Indiana University Press, 1970) and Arnold J. Band's translation of *The Tales* of Rabbi Nahman of Bratslav, also in the *Classics of Western Spirituality* series (New York: Paulist Press, 1980). The tales as retold by Martin Buber are a classic in their own right; especially recommended is his major collection *Tales of the Hasidim* (New York: Schocken, 1948). Other collections available include Elie Wiesel's *Souls on Fire* (New York: Random House, 1972), and, a special favorite of this reader, Jiri Langer's *Nine Gates to the Chassidic Mysteries* (New York: Behrman, 1961). Critical research on the Hasidic tale is still in its early stages. The Hebrew reader would do well in this area to consult the studies by Joseph Dan, especially *Ha-Sippur Ha-Hasidi* (Jerusalem, 1975), and Gedalyahu Nigal. Again, for the Hebrew/Yiddish reader, the collected essays of Chaim Lieberman (*Ohel Rahel,* New York, 1980) are a great mine of information.

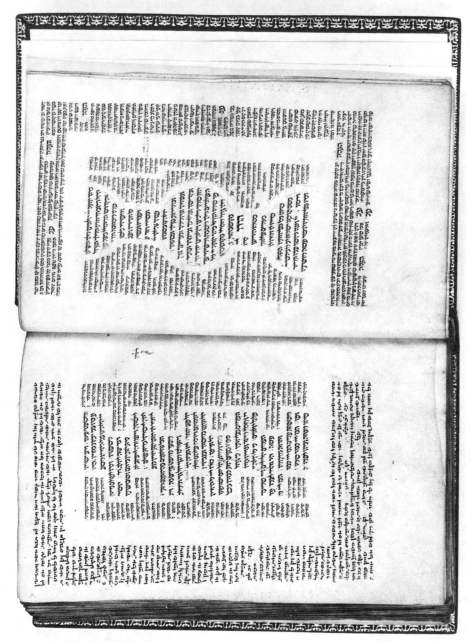

From Siddur Tsarafat, prayerbook from France, 14–15th centuries, done in calligraphy with commentary in margins.

CHAPTER EIGHT

Prayer
and the Prayerbook

ALAN MINTZ

J udaism is a civilization of remarkable persistences; perhaps the most remarkable is the case of prayer. Bestir yourself on a Friday evening or a Saturday morning anywhere in the world where there are Jews and you will likely find a congregation reciting Hebrew prayers several thousand years old. Nor is this a quaint vestige. Gathering for prayer is the preeminently central activity of most branches of Jewish life today, and it is within the roomy framework of the synagogue service that much else takes place: Torah study, rites of passage, political commentary, and even fund raising.

This combination of antiquity and centrality enjoyed by Jewish prayer is the result of its distinctively composite nature: Jewish prayer is both a text and an experience. As a text, Jewish prayer is a prayerbook, a classical written liturgy, a structure of words and ideas, which, like any text, is open to literary and theological analysis within the terms of the historical periods that produced it. As experience, Jewish prayer also incorporates the several means by which the text is brought to life: what takes place in the inner, subjective world of the worshiper during prayer; the communal arrangements and nonverbal techniques of the practice of prayer; and the contemporary interpretations of the meaning of the text of the liturgy.

Although there have been attempts at prayerbook reform in the modern period, the text of the liturgy has remained relatively stable over the ages. Not so with the experience of prayer. How Jews have prayed and what the ancient words have meant to them have differed at various

403

times, sometimes radically. The elaborate inner drama experienced in prayer by the mystics of sixteenth-century Safed (discussed in Chapter Six), for example, was something very different from the associations conjured up by the recitation of the same words by their contemporary coreligionists. The best analogy is to great drama. A play of Shakespeare's is not just the words of the play as Shakespeare wrote them. It comes to life only in the realization of those words by actors on the stage. Although the text has been little altered, through its production each age has given a different coloration to the play: the classical Shakespeare, the romantic Shakespeare, the absurdist Shakespeare, and so on. Similarly, the prayerbook exists only by virtue of its being prayed, that is, in the "realizations" of successive generations.

So, while most of what follows is devoted to explicating the text of the liturgy, it should be kept in mind that Jewish prayer exists at the same time along another axis. If this other axis, the dramatic-experiential one, were our principal focus, it would make sense to speak of the prayerbook as an orchestrating of a sequence of spiritual states, and then to identify these states by referring to categories in the phenomonology of religion. However, since the concentration here is on the prayerbook as text—reading it as opposed to praying it, as it were—the approach will be literary, which is to say, attentive to the ways in which words express ideas and the ways ideas are woven into thematic patterns. In analyzing the liturgy, the modern explicator unfortunately cannot make use of a rich history of traditional commentary. The Torah and the Talmud were always texts to be studied, to be puzzled out word by word, and each generation contributed its stratum of commentary. The prayerbook, in contrast, was not part of the curriculum; it was to be actively utilized in worship, not studied. With some exceptions, then (for example, the works of David ben Joseph Abudarham, who lived in Spain in the fourteenth century), attention to the prayers as objects of study in themselves began only with the rise of "scientific" Jewish research in the nineteenth century (see the bibliography).

The major features of the prayerbook crystallized during the first two centuries of the Common Era. Until that time, Jewish worship had been comprised of two activities that remained quite distinct: the spontaneous verbal prayer of the individual and the sacrificial ritual of the central cult in the Jerusalem Temple. The Hebrew Bible abounds with examples of individual prayers: Moses advocating the cause of the people after the sin of the Golden Calf (Exod. 32), the barren Hannah praying for a child at Shiloh (1 Sam. 1), David singing praises to God for saving him from his enemies (2 Sam. 22), Jonah crying out from the belly of the whale (Jon. 2), and of course, that great anthology of prayers, the Book of Psalms. These biblical prayers express a variety of functions: intercession, petition, and thanksgiving; what they have in common is their ad hoc nature. Their impetus is a moment of heightened awareness, either of distress or grace. They are spontaneous and voluntary prayers in the sense that they are undertaken neither as the fulfillment of an obligation, nor in accordance with a received formula, nor at a fixed time.

The divine service in Jerusalem was conducted in a different mode altogether. The order, procedures, and categories of the sacrifices are precisely defined in the Book of Leviticus. At the center of the ritual stood not words but a material act, the "offering up" of an ox or a lamb or the pouring out on the altar of precious oils. Sacrifices were offered on behalf of the people as a whole on a daily basis and on special occasions (see the elaborate rituals recounted in the Yom Kippur liturgy); individuals would dedicate offerings in the Temple for the purpose of expiating sins or acknowledging good fortune. Although individuals would dedicate their offerings, they would not themselves offer them upon the altar. Whether individual or communal, all sacrifices had to be performed through the intermediacy of the *kohanim* (priests), the hereditary religious professionals; and only in one central place, in the Jerusalem Temple, could a person undertake these acts of atonement and thanksgiving.

In 70 c.e. Roman legions destroyed the Temple, and after the suppression of the Bar Kochba Rebellion in 135, it became clear that the Temple would not be rebuilt for an indefinite time, perhaps only in a messianic era after the "conclusion" of history. With the destruction came the cancellation of the sacrificial system; the sanctioned channels through which man achieved communication and reconciliation with God were cut off. The measures taken by the rabbis to counteract the despair and alienation potential in the aftermath of the catastrophe—measures that had been evolving for some time—involved combining components of individual prayer and sacrificial ritual. Verbal prayer uttered by the individual—what the rabbis called "the service of the heart"—was declared to be a wholly adequate substitute for the sacrifices; it was, moreover, an experience open to all Jews, not just to members of the priesthood, and it could be engaged in wherever the individual found himself, not just in Jerusalem.

However, the rigorously regulated structure of the sacrificial regime was applied to the spontaneity of individual verbal prayer. A fixed liturgy was established, made up of scriptural verses and newly composed formulas which served as a minimum framework for prayer. This was the Siddur, literally "the ordering," and Siddur became the standard Jewish term for the prayerbook. Mandated, also, were the hours and frequency of prayer, corresponding to the great communal sacrifices in the Temple. Although a Jew did not have to be a priest to pray, one did have to be as careful as a priest in the fulfilling of these obligations. And although prayer did not have to be recited in a central place, a Jew was enjoined to pray in the company of other Jews rather than alone. One's congregation or synagogue *(bet kennesset),* wherever it was, would be a miniature of the lost sanctuary.

The genius of this fusion sustained Judaism in a moment of spiritual emergency. The medievals contributed certain elements (the Friday evening Kabbalat Shabbat service, the Simhat Torah celebration, the memorial prayers for the dead, and others), but the prayerbook remains to this day essentially a document of the early rabbis.

Two points should be made at this juncture. First, this fusion, as I've presented it, is a schematization of a complex process which is the subject of scholarly conjecture and debate. The attitudes of the rabbis to the Temple cult, while it was in operation and after its forced cancellation, are complex, and some would say ambivalent. This equivocation is expressed in the fact that while the liturgy for Sabbath and festivals enumerates precisely the sacrifices once offered in the Temple on those occasions, praying indeed for their restoration, *in the meantime* the rabbis viewed these verbal prayers as fully adequate spiritual substitutes for the lost sacrifices! Second, the dates for specific prayers can usually not be given with any certainty. Archeological reconstruction of the liturgy was a major task of nineteenth-century Jewish scholarship, which had to go about its work by evaluating references in Talmudic literature, whose dating is difficult as well, and by examining the contents of medieval prayerbooks used by particular individuals and communities. Although it is extremely useful to have a general awareness of what is of rabbinic origin and what is medieval, a religious or literary appreciation of the Siddur does not require more sharply refined historical knowledge. The essence of the experience of the Siddur has always been a timeless one.

BLESSING AND AFFIRMATION

The smallest and most crucial unit of the liturgy is the *berakhah* (plural: *berakhot*), the blessing or benediction. The *berakhah* is a formula that concludes a prayer, and sometimes begins it as well. The opening

of the *berakhah* is the fixed phrase: "Praised [also translated "Blessed"]
be You, Lord our God, King of the universe . . ."; the ending is varied
according to the particular value or concern at hand. Here is an example
from the morning service:

> *Praised are You, Lord our God, King of the universe,* who creates
> light.

One of the key features of the fixed part of the *berakhah* (above in italics)
is the double way God is addressed. When God is addressed as "You,"
implied is an intimate relationship with an individual pray-er, a relationship that is accessible and personal. When God is referred to as the "King
of the universe," the perspective shifts to a vast cosmic plane over which
God is the absolute ruler. The simultaneous immanence of God *within*
the world and His transcendence *of* the world expresses the rabbis' conviction of the fundamental nature of the divine mystery. Another word
which is strongly weighted in the formula is "our." Almost all the texts
of the Siddur are written in the first person plural; one is never allowed
to forget that it is not a God of one's own imaginings to whom the
worshiper prays, and that a person's prayer is efficacious only because
of one's speaking from within one's membership in a community.

The purpose of the *berakhah* is to acknowledge the primary connection between God and a phenomenon or process in the world. In the
example above, the creation of light stands for the miracle of creation as
a whole and for all that engenders amazement in the structure of nature
and reality. The *berakhah* first heightens the utterer's sensitivity to the
phenomenon itself, increasing awareness of the wonder of creation.
Then it bears witness to the source of the wonder; nature is not just
there, but owes its existence to God. The routinizing of experience and
the taking of the world for granted are the great enemies of the Siddur,
and the *berakhah* is an instrument for keeping them at bay. This is the
meaning of praise in Jewish liturgy. To praise God or to say, "Praised
are You," "Blessed art Thou," is not simply to release an emotional
outpouring or to describe some beatific aspect of God's nature. It means
making a connection between a phenomenon and its source; "praised"
means "deserving to be acknowledged" for this reason. The praise-
deserving action, it should be noted, is always phrased in the present
tense. The creation of light in the *berakhah* does not refer just to the one-
time event in the biblical account but to a process that is renewed daily.

The *berakhot* are distributed in two principal cycles, which make up
the major components of the daily morning service *(shaharit le'hol).* We
shall use the daily morning service for purposes of example because its

structure is the most inclusive. The service can be found in any traditional prayerbook; here page references will be given in the one compiled by Philip Birnbaum.* The first cycle is called the *Shema* (pp. 77–81); the second (pp. 81–97) goes by several names: the *Amidah* (The Prayer Said Standing), the *Shemoneh Esreh* (the Eighteen *Berakhot*), or simply *Hatefilah* (the Prayer). The two cycles represent, respectively, two basic modes of prayer: affirmation and petition.

In the Shema, the *berakhot*, composed by the rabbis, are constellated around three passages from the Bible, which form the theological center of the prayerbook. The passages are Deuteronomy 6.4–8 and 11.13–22 and Numbers 15.37–42. The first of these begins with one of the most famous and resonant statements in all of Jewish literature; during the service the pray-er recites it with eyes closed and in a moment of great concentration:

> Hear, O Israel
> *Shema yisra'el*
> The Lord is our God
> *Adonai eloheinu*
> The Lord is one!
> *Adonai ehad!*

The context for this verse in Deuteronomy reveals that it is uttered in a dramatic, interactive situation. The first phrase ("Hear, O Israel") is spoken by God to Israel; it carries no message, only the fact of being addressed by God, the experience of divine attention. Israel responds to being addressed by proclaiming that "the Lord is our God." In English this sounds like a redundancy; Hebrew differentiates between *Adonai,* which is the particular and proper name of God in the Bible (itself already an avoidance of the unpronounceable sacred name), and *Eloheinu,* which is the generic term for gods or divine beings. So Israel's response has the force of declaring that God, alone of all the claimants to divinity, is He Whom we choose. The last phrase, *Adonai ehad,* is understood by some interpreters to stress the exclusivity of the choosing of God (reading *ehad* as "alone"; "The Lord our God, the Lord *alone*") and by others to introduce a further concept: the oneness of God.

Exclusive fidelity to God and God's unity are the two major concepts of the Shema. The first demands that no system of value—not just another religion but an ideology, art, success, or personal happiness—be allowed to replace God as the *ultimate* ground of meaning. God's

* *Daily Prayer Book* (New York: Hebrew Publishing Co., 1977).

unity, conversely, asserts that all experienced moments of beauty, good, love, and holiness are not in and of themselves; they are disparate and scattered signals of the presence of the one God. Now, if this is the "message" of the Shema, the continuation of the passage from Deuteronomy, which completes the prayer's first paragraph, mandates what to do with the message: how to be loyal to it, how to transmit it, how to remain mindful of it:

> You shall love the Lord your God with all your heart and with all your soul and with all your might. Take to heart these instructions with which I charge you this day. Impress them upon your children. Recite them when you stay at home and when you are away, when you lie down and when you get up. Bind them as a sign on your hand and let them serve as a symbol on your forehead; inscribe them on the doorpost of your house and on your gates.

By using the term love, the text implies that these truths can be fulfilled less through cognitive affirmation than through relationship; this is a relationship that passionately transcends legal obligation and demands the mobilization of all the dimensions and resources of one's being. The question now becomes: how is this love preserved and guaranteed? The answer: by intentional, structured mindfulness. Children must be actively taught and rehearsed in the truths of God's ways rather than being left to the vagaries of nature. The adult, too, must not trust his or her nature; one must purposefully undertake to recall to mind God's unity within the coordinates of everyday life: morning and evening, at home and on the road. Symbols play an important role in this mnemonic regimen. The *tefilin,* the phylacteries, on hand and forehead, and the *mezzuzah* affixed to the doorpost, are in themselves the source of no totemic powers. They are concrete signs that remind one of larger truths. The function of the commandments as spurs to consciousness is elaborated in the third paragraph of the Shema (Num. 15.37–42), which mandates and describes the wearing of *tsitsit,* fringes on garments. The middle paragraph (Deut. 11.13–22) is monitory in tone: it warns that the enjoyment of God's grace, especially material prosperity and secure residence in the land of Israel, is absolutely contingent upon obedience to God's will as expressed through the commandments.

The Shema proper is surrounded by three extended *berakhot.* (As a unit within the prayerbook, the whole structure of the Shema plus its *berakhot* is itself called the Shema.) The three *berakhot* deal respectively with the themes of creation, revelation, and redemption; the Shema proper comes between the second and the third.

Berakhah One: Creation
Berakhah Two: Revelation
    Shema
Berakhah Three: Redemption

The sequence creation-revelation-redemption forms the essential theological drama of Judaism. There is a clear recapitulation here of the movement of sacred history as enacted in the Bible and interpreted by the rabbis: the formation of the world in Genesis, the giving of the Torah at Sinai in Exodus, and the messianic age-to-come as prefigured by the liberation from Egypt.

Yet history is only one level at which these prayers speak. Creation-revelation-redemption are presented not just as *events* located in the mythic past or the future, but also as *processes* ongoing within the life of the individual and the people. The first *berakhah,* for example, forcefully underscores this dimension when it declares that God "through His goodness daily renews the work of creation." Lest we lapse into an alienated conception of an Aristotelian prime mover, the text insists that the God of Israel continues in His moment-to-moment authorship of *our* reality.

The *berakhah* on Creation (pp. 71–72) is the longest, encompassing fragments of ancient poetic litanies and a depiction of the acclamations of the angelic choruses. It is also one of the places where the hand of the rabbis in shaping the liturgy out of biblical materials is most conspicuous. Take the opening statement of the *berakhah:*

> Praised be You, O Lord our God, King of the universe, Who forms light and creates darkness, Who makes peace and creates *all things*.

Now take its source in Isaiah 45.7; God is the speaker:

> I form light and create darkness; I make peace and create *evil*.

The rabbis have changed the Isaiah verse from the first person to the third and absorbed it into the *berakhah* formula. But they have gone further; they have done nothing less than tamper with the biblical text by emending *evil* into the euphemized *all things*. In truth this is not a gross violation. By setting up a series of antitheses (light/darkness, peace/evil), Scripture intends to convey the sense that God is the source of all phenomena, from A to Z, so to speak. The rabbis' "all things," then, is not far off the mark. The change, however, is more than a helpful gloss. While they too believed that God was the author of bad things as well as good, after the catastrophes that had befallen the Jewish people the rabbis felt that in the context of prayer it was appropriate to underscore God's merciful nature. The *berakhah* on Creation was supposed to inspire awe of the glory and plenitude of the world. For the rabbis "all things" told the truth, yet did not sound the minor chord of the original.

The shaping hand of the rabbis is also evident in the second *berakhah* of the Shema cycle, which begins, "With abounding love You have loved us, O Lord our God; with unshifting tenderness You have graced us," and concludes, "Praised be You, O Lord our God, who chooses His people Israel in love" (p. 75). The choice in love is the covenant at Sinai described in Exodus 19–23: the singling out of Israel of all the nations to enjoy the intimate protection of God in exchange for adherence to the regime of divine commandments and obligations. Of the covenantal transaction, what the rabbis select for emphasis is neither the transcendent awesomeness of the event nor the difficulty of keeping its terms but its basis in love: love expressed both in the choosing of Israel and in the granting of commandments, understood as opportunities for fulfilling His will.

If the primordial choosing of Israel is the historical event recalled in this prayer, the everyday experience described is the life of the Law, the living with and through the Torah. It is only through God's continuous love in the present, the pray-er acknowledges, that a Jew succeeds in keeping this discipline, and in keeping it with passionate devotion. God grants enlightenment, understanding, and learning; He is also the source of the will to take the further crucial step, to break through from cognition to practice. And through practice to love: God's love bestows the power to unify man's heart so that one can "cleave to the commandments" and offer back to God the love one has received.

With the sounding of the theme of reciprocal love between man and God, the Shema proper is now recited. Why the Shema is lodged here between the second and third *berakhot* can now be understood. Again, the reason relates to the dual levels of event and process at which the service operates. In the succession of theological moments from creation to revelation to redemption, the Shema belongs to the second because it itself is the *content* of revelation. It *is* Torah: biblical text and not rabbinic prayer. In their interpretation of the revelatory event at Sinai, the rabbis went a step further: they asserted that the assent given by the Israelites at that moment obligated all future generations, inasmuch as we were all present through our progenitors. Though we were pledged by that fateful "Yea!" we must nevertheless reconfirm the choice and make it our own. By reciting the Shema with passionate commitment we make true the rabbinic doctrine: we stand again at Sinai and take upon ourselves the "yoke of the commandments."

God is imaged as the creator of life and as the endower of life with meaning through the Torah. Now, in the third and final *berakhah,* God is presented as the protector of the community that keeps faith with the Torah (pp. 79–81). The immediate background is the recapitulation of the Covenant embodied in the second paragraph of the Shema proper. If Israel remains loyal to the oneness of God and to the way of life set down in the Torah, the Covenant stipulates, it will enjoy a special relationship to history. A small and vulnerable people, Israel cannot long survive within the power contests of the nations without the active protectorship of God. Whereas the previous *berakhot* stressed the divine attributes of mercy and love, the present context underscores power and force as the qualities displayed in the exercise of God's faithfulness to Israel.

The great archetypal instance of divine intervention is the liberation from Egypt, and it is the recollection of that event that is the main subject of the prayer: "From Egypt You redeemed us, O Lord our God, and from the house of bondage you delivered us. Their first-born You slew, and Your first-born You redeemed. You split the Red Sea so that the beloved would pass through and the oppressors would drown; the waters engulfed them and not one was left." Now the miracle at the sea was only one half of the Exodus event described in the Bible; it is completed by the great song of praise sung by Moses and the Israelites, which begins, "I will sing to the Lord, for He has triumphed gloriously" (Exod. 15). The liturgical evocation of the Exodus is similarly divided. Yet while the miracle at the sea is narrated like an event from the past, the Song at the Sea is not only narrated but, in part, *sung* as if it were taking place in the present (see the discussion of biblical poetry in Chapter One). The worshiping congregation momentarily merges with the ancient chorus, acclaiming together the words of Exodus 15: "Who is like You, O Lord, among the mighty?" and "The Lord shall reign for ever and ever."

This collapsing of past and present into a timeless moment of acclamation functions as a bridge to the final section of the prayer, which pushes the idea of timelessness into another dimension. The awareness of past redemption must of necessity coexist with the awareness of present *un*redemption. The liberation from Egypt in rabbinic thought is a prefiguration of a deliverance to come at the end of history, when the subjugation to the nations will be broken and the exiles gathered into the land through the agency of the Messiah. This is no fantasy, but God's recorded promise. By recalling the ancient redemption and resinging its hymn of praise, the pray-er reaffirms a belief not only in the future redemption but in the right to implore God to make good His pledge.

PETITION AND THE CYCLE OF RELIGIOUS EXPERIENCE

The invocation of the future hope brings to a conclusion the creation-revelation-redemption cycle of the Shema and forms the transition to the second major cycle of the service: the *Shemoneh Esreh* (The Eighteen Blessings, pp. 81–97). The difference between the two cycles is reflected in part in the different styles of recitation prescribed by the rabbis. The Shema is said seated and largely chanted aloud, with the leader ending units and conducting the congregation in antiphonal passages; the Shemoneh Esreh, in contrast, is said standing with feet together in a position of spiritual attentiveness, and it is recited silently—though, of course, not wordlessly—in what could be called a hushed internal whisper. Communal chant is the appropriate medium for theological affirmations; the individuated silence of the Shemoneh Esreh betokens a different purpose: petition. In the weekday Shemoneh Esreh, the pray-er *asks for things:* knowledge, forgiveness, prosperity, the messianic age, and other desirable gifts. Yet even here the function of petition does not operate independently; it is joined in each instance to the affirmation embodied in the *berakhah*. Take, for example, the fourth *berakhah* of the Shemoneh Esreh:

> You grant man knowledge and teach him understanding. O favor us with knowledge, understanding, and enlightenment. Praised are You, O Lord our God, who grants knowledge. (Birnbaum, p. 86)

The *berakhah* at the end makes the kind of characteristic affirmation with which we are familiar from the Shema. Man, it is asserted, is mistaken in assuming that his powers of cognition and discernment are self-generated. God is imaged as the source of knowledge in the world. (The three terms for knowledge—*de'ah, binah,* and *haskel*—may be taken as different varieties of knowing, say, instrumental, moral, and intellectual.) It is through the conduit of God's empathy for man that the faculty of understanding passes to us. While hardly flattery, this profession is not without ulterior motive. Acknowledging God as the source of knowledge puts us in the necessary frame of consciousness from which to make an appeal for some of that knowledge for ourselves. The appeal is based as well on an awareness of want. Every day we face the fact of our inadequate resources of mind for facing life responsibly and creatively.

Even though it is an individual who utters the appeal, the request is framed in the voice of the community. "O favor *us* with knowledge . . . ," "Heal *us,* O Lord . . . ," "Restore *our* judges. . . ." The first person plural is the nearly universal voice of Jewish liturgy. In the Shemoneh Esreh the "we" has a special role; it keeps the individual pray-er within the orbit of the community and of the Jewish people just at the moment when, immersed in a separate devotional silence, the individual is tempted to become absorbed in his or her private needs alone. At the very end of the Shemoneh Esreh after the recitation of the required *berakhot,* the rabbis did provide a place for purely private meditations. The Talmud brings examples of the private meditations of prominent scholars. One of them, a beautiful prayer for forbearance against the impulse to gossip and slander by a fourth-century rabbi, Mar, the son of Rabina, was early appended to the ancient text of the Shemoneh Esreh. It begins: "O my God! Guard my tongue from evil and my lips from speaking guile, and to those who curse me let my soul be dumb."

The idea of petition was made possible for the rabbis by a series of unambiguous convictions: God is in control of all reality; He is concerned both about mankind as a whole and those individuals who turn to Him sincerely; and He acts in the world as an expression of that concern. In other words, God listens to prayers, and when it pleases Him, answers them. For the modern Jew, the theological issues involved in this traditional petitionary aspect of prayer have raised considerable problems. Even in its classic distillation, it should be noted, petitionary prayer was never conceived of as a one-sided affair. Man, according to the rabbis, is God's partner in the work of creation, and it is essentially through the agency of man's actions that the divine purpose can be realized in the world. To return to our example: when a person prays to God for knowledge, one is simultaneously committing one's own best energies to sharpening, widening, and deepening one's powers of understanding and discrimination. To ask for something, in sum, presupposes the willingness to strive for it and to be the worthy beneficiary of it.

In the Shemoneh Esreh, as in much of the Siddur, structure is the key to meaning. You have to know how the pieces fit together in order to catch the interplay and progression of themes. Here is the order of the *berakhot* in the weekday service. (Although Shemoneh Esreh means "The Eighteen," there are actually nineteen; number twelve, the prayer against informers, was added during the period of the Roman occupation; yet the name of the prayer was not changed.)

1. God as the protector of the Forefathers
2. God as the power that makes for salvation
3. God as the source of holiness
    4. For knowledge
    5. For the strength to repent
    6. For forgiveness
    7. For relief from affliction
    8. For healing
    9. For the bounty of the land and material prosperity
    10. For the ingathering of the exiles into the Holy Land
    11. For the establishment of the reign of true justice
    12. Against slanderers and informers
    13. For the support and protection of the righteous
    14. For the rebuilding of Jerusalem
    15. For the coming of the Messiah
    16. For the acceptance of our prayers
17. For the restoration of the Jerusalem Sanctuary
18. Gratitude as man's response to God's work in the world
19. For peace

The first three and last three *berakhot* are the constant elements in the Shemoneh Esreh, present on Sabbath and holidays, as well as on weekdays. The *berakhot* they frame change with the spiritual requirements of the moment in time in which they are uttered; they register the rhythms of the Jewish calendar. While petition corresponds to the exigencies of ordinary time, for sacred time it is inappropriate. On the three pilgrimage festivals (Sukkot, Passover, and Shavuot), the New Moon, the New Year, and the Day of Atonement, it is this central core of the Shemoneh Esreh that concentrates and reflects the particular theological drama at hand.

Because they are a constant presence, the opening and concluding *berakhot* sound the most universal themes. The first *berakhah* invokes God's faithfulness to Abraham, Isaac, and Jacob and prays for the continuation of divine protection. The even more fundamental phenomenon of life itself is the subject of the second; God is acknowledged as the force that "uplifts the falling, heals the sick, and liberates the enslaved" and will eventually "grant eternal life to the dead." The third *berakhah* simply announces God's holiness: His sublimity, His otherness, His unassimilability to any other category. The concluding *berakhot* pray for the return of the Divine Presence—the *Shekhinah*—to Zion (seventeen), proclaim man's responsibility to give thanks to God (eighteen), and implore Him to bless His people Israel with peace (nineteen).

The main business of the weekday Shemoneh Esreh—the core of thirteen petitions—describes an ideal sequence of religious concerns, an arc of the normative Jewish spiritual life. The general movement is from individual needs in the here and now to the welfare of the people as a whole, especially as regards the redemptive process.

The beginning of the sequence (*berakhot* 4, 5, and 6) outline what for the rabbis was the fundamental mechanism of the moral life: the process of *teshuvah,* returning. A person prays for knowledge of God's will and an understanding of the world and insight into one's own nature in order to act wisely and justly. Yet man is imperfect, and despite this knowledge all people at times fall short of this goal. An individual's worth is judged by God less by one's sins than by one's capacity to recover from sin. The courage to return to the right path can be found only if there is a conviction that there persists a relationship with God to be returned to. This is the subject of the fifth *berakhah:* God is affirmed as the One who "delights in repentance," reaching out to man, desirous of reconciliation. Essential to the achieving of *teshuvah* is the verbal admission of wrongdoing, a self-recognition and an acceptance of re- sponsibility, which comes next: "Forgive us, our Father, for we have sinned." And if man completes the process by effecting a sustained change in his behavior, he has a right expectantly to praise God as "the gracious One, who abundantly forgives."

Once the pray-er has been reinstated within the covenantal relation- ship, one now has the right to appeal to God for the exercise of His blessings. The next three *berakhot* (7, 8, and 9) touch on the fundamental anxieties of everyday existence for the individual and the Jewish people alike. The redemption requested in the seventh *berakhah* refers less to messianic fulfillments than to the need for God's intermediate involve- ment in alleviating continual contention and persecution, personal and collective. The vulnerability of the body and the mind to natural afflic- tion is the subject of the prayer for healing, which follows. Although the appeal is general, an additional prayer may be inserted at this point for a particular person. The next *berakhah* asks God to "bless this year and all its crops for our welfare and bestow a blessing upon the earth." Although the formulation reflects the agricultural character of the society in which it was written, this is simply a prayer for material prosperity in any and all circumstances. There is nothing so spiritualized and refined about the religious world of the Siddur to prevent it from according a central place to the real human concern for livelihood.

The subject now shifts to the fate of the nation. The focus is binocular: the dismal present circumstances of the people and the hope for a transformation in the future. Putting aside for the moment the twelfth *berakhah*, the one added later on, numbers 10, 11, and 13 form a distinct sequence of petitions: for the termination of the exile and the ingathering of the dispersed into the Land (10); for the restoration to righteousness of the civil institutions by which Jews receive justice from other Jews and the world (11); and for the deliverance from suffering and the according of honor and reward to the spiritual elite of the people. the righteous, the pious, the elders, the teachers, and the true proselytes (13).

Between these last two is the *berakhah* concerning slanderers and informers, which was added to the "Eighteen Benedictions" to make them in fact nineteen. The prayer, which has many versions and has been the subject of much scholarly comment, has its origins in the sectarian strife of first-century Judaism and speaks of the fratricidal possibilities of Jews using the reigning regime against each other. Let the alien regime—the prayer implores—"the dominion of arrogance" that pits Jew against Jew, be speedily "crushed and uprooted." The messianic theme finally becomes explicit in the fourteenth and fifteenth *berakhot;* the return of God to Zion accompanied by the rebuilding of Jerusalem is one of the consummations to be ushered in by the Messiah, a descendant of the House of David, who will end once and forever the subjugation of Israel to the nations. The cycle of weekday petitions concludes with a prayer about prayer in which the pathos of God is affirmed: ours is a God who takes prayer and the human situation seriously. It is here also that the pray-er is given leave to insert private requests and meditations.

It should be said of the Shemoneh Esreh, in conclusion, that it is an important source for understanding the mind of the rabbis. Rather than being something apart, a pious or mystical transport, the liturgy was a vehicle for expressing the central value concepts of Talmudic civilization: *teshuvah* as the daily act of self-revision, the commitment to the establishment of justice and to the active pursuit of peace, a profound sensitivity to the power of rumor and slander in human community. These are the same values to be found in the codes and the commentaries; the difference is that in the Siddur these values function in a devotional rather than scholarly setting. That is, in prayer the task of mind and the soul is not to work out the why and the how, but to form a personal link of acknowledgment and responsibility to these fundamental categories.

SCRIPTURE AND PRAYER

The rabbis, we have noted, called the Shemoneh Esreh "The Prayer." In its origins in the experience of need and the appeal for help, the Shemoneh Esreh indeed corresponds to our most primitive and universal conceptions of what it means to pray. It is appropriate that this cry from the heart is cast in language that is very human. The Shemoneh Esreh, like much of the Siddur, is not the revealed word of God; it is not Scripture. Though biblical locutions are artfully interwoven, the texts of the prayers are humanly produced, with no attempt made by the rabbis to designate them as divine in origin. There are, however, several instances in the Siddur in which whole sections of Scripture are taken over with no rabbinic remolding and inserted wholesale into the service. The three scriptural paragraphs of the Shema proper, we have seen, form the creedal core of one of the main cycles of the Siddur. The recitation of a series of psalms and the reading of the Torah on sabbaths and holy days—before and after the Shema and the Shemoneh Esreh, respectively —are examples of important yet divergent uses of the Bible outside the main service.

The psalms are the last six chapters of the Psalter (145–150), and together they are called *Pesukei Dezimrah* (Songs of Praise). Their function is to prepare the pray-er for the Shema by setting a mood of spiritual concentration. The recitation of psalms in Judaism resembles meditation in the liturgies of other religions. It is a time more private than communal. As the members of the congregation collect in the synagogue they begin their prayers at different times, and it is not until the leader publicly announces the beginning of the Shema that all are joined together. As a variety of prayer, the Pesukei Dezimrah are at a polar extreme from the petitions of the Shemoneh Esreh. They differ from the Shema as praise differs from affirmation. The acknowledgment of God as creator, revealer, and redeemer in the *berakhot* of the Shema takes place through the vehicle of generalizing theological statements, which move the pray-er through a structured sequence of themes.

The praise of the Pesukei Dezimrah is more freestyle and spontaneous. Although there is nothing naive or unconstructed about these psalms, the point of their literary art is to make credible a religious impulse whose immediate response to the world is joyful intoxication with God's works. The form this enthusiasm takes is a nearly chaotic cataloguing of divine wonders, both natural and moral: "He lays down

snow like fleece, scatters frost like ashes. He tosses down hail like crumbs
—who can endure His icy cold? He issues a command—it melts them;
He breathes   the waters flow" (Ps. 147). The image of man reflected in
these psalms is radiantly optimistic. Rather than wanting and needful,
man's soul is assumed to be naturally receptive to God's actions and
transfixed in a permanent state of radical amazement. This is an art of
interjection and exultation; the word *hallelujah!* (Praise God!), which
opens and closes each psalm is less a substantive statement than a reflex-
ive rush of breath, the sound of wonder.

The progression in these psalms—which form both the culmination
of the Psalter and the introduction to the morning service—is from
justifications for praise of God to the experience of pure praise. Psalms
146 and 147 juxtapose the exhortation to sing praises to the Lord with a
vast inventory of the miraculous and redemptive ways in which God
works in the world; the psalms create a dazzling sense of the all-encom-
passingness of God's presence by switching back and forth between
humankind and the natural world, between great reaches of time and
space and the most humble local habitations. In the next psalm, these
reasons for praise become instruments for the expression of praise:
"Praise the Lord, . . . all sea monsters and ocean depths . . . all moun-
tains and hills . . . all kings and people of the earth . . . youths and
maidens alike, old and young together." The mute, reified world is
brought alive and urged toward articulation; things high and low, great
and small, are enlisted in a chorus of acclamation, whose dimensions
swell to incorporate all of reality. Psalm 149 introduces a national political resonance into this chorus; its praise is called forth by the occurrence
—or anticipation—of God's vindication of Israel before the nations.
"For the Lord delights in His people; He adorns the lowly in victory."

The movement of praise reaches its crescendo in Psalm 150. The
surge of jubilation can be contained in no space (neither God's sanctuary
nor the whole heavens), nor rationalized by pointing to specific acts. The
praise becomes wordless sound, as it summons forth and then outstrips
each of the instruments in the ancient orchestral repertory. Finally, life
itself is called upon: "Let all that breathes [literally, 'all breath,' *kol
haneshamah*] praise the Lord, Hallelujah!" *Neshamah* is the breath of life;
it is what God breathes into Adam's nostrils at the Creation: the difference between "dust of the earth" and a "living being." *Neshamah* is at
once the most elemental life process and the totality of all life. It is with
this exalting of life that the Psalter as a whole concludes. Yet for the
rabbis, who made the materials of the Bible part of their new composi-

tion, the Siddur, this is only the beginning. They made the conclusion to the Book of Psalms the introduction to the main service to come, the Shema and the Shemoneh Esreh.

There the focus of significance remains on weekdays. Yet on Sabbath mornings the focus shifts further, to what comes after the Shema and the Shemoneh Esreh: the Torah Service (Birnbaum, pp. 361–89). The Humash (Pentateuch) was divided by the rabbis into some fifty sections to be read weekly over the course of the year. With each weekly reading (*parashah* or *sidrah*) there was coordinated a brief passage from the prophetic books of the Bible *(haftarah),* which contained a thematic link to the Pentateuchal reading. Though not required, some form of exposition or homily *(derashah)* relating to the scriptural readings usually formed part of the Torah service, as well. As an instance of the utilization of the Bible in the context of prayer, the Torah service seems to stand conspicuously by itself and for itself. Its treatment resembles neither the absorption of scattered verses into the mosaic of rabbinic discourse, nor the wholesale incorporation of a block of texts, like Psalms 146–50, into the flow of the service.

Yet at the same time, the presentation of the Torah in the synagogue on Sabbath mornings is very different from the way in which it is studied outside a liturgical context. In the study house *(bet midrash),* the classroom, and in private study at home, the text is customarily delved into with its various commentaries; passages from many books are compared back and forth; questions are posed and answers sought; the pace of progress through the text is regulated by the incidence of problems and the acuity of discussion. In the synagogue, however, there is none of this. The Torah is read aloud at a uniform pace, with no provision for posing queries or lingering over a passage. Although individual congregants may privately peruse commentaries, the basic obligation is to listen attentively to the public reading.

The reading of the Torah, then, remains something of a special case in which the recitation of Scripture is set off as an event unto itself, yet one that is adapted to the prayer service of which it is a part. The reading of text, in short, becomes a liturgical act. The liturgical dimension comes into play in several ways. The consecutive linear reading of the Torah in its weekly units, repeated yearly, represents the ideal rhythm of the sacred time of the Jewish calendar. Each year at the holiday of Simhat Torah in the early autumn, the cycle of readings is closed and immediately recommenced. The reading of the Torah in the synagogue is a pulse of communal religious consciousness, around which, and in counterpoint to which, individual questionings and investigations of the text are conducted. The rhythm of individual existence has a role in the Torah service, as well. On Sabbath mornings seven or more members of the congregation are called to read from the Torah or to follow the reading in the Torah scroll as it is read by another. This ascent to the podium (called an *aliyah*) is the occasion for the public celebration or announcement of individual life moments. The Bar Mitzvah, in which the thirteen-year-old boy "comes into" his religious responsibilities in the community, is the best known of these. (The Bat Mitzvah, a similar ritual for girls, is observed in Conservative and Reform congregations.) Other such celebratory moments include the announcement of births and the naming of babies and the announcement of marriages to take place during the coming week. Moments of danger are registered here as well: the sick are prayed for, and the individual thanks God for being rescued from extreme situations.

It is in the ceremonial display and treatment of the Torah as a holy object that its liturgical role is most vividly highlighted. The Torah resides in a special cabinet whose ritual curtain and perpetual lamp *(ner tamid)* recall the ancient Israelite Ark of the Law and the Holy of Holies of the Jerusalem Temple. The opening of the ark, the retrieval of the Torah scroll, the procession with it around the synagogue, and the removal of its ornaments and vestments are dramatic rituals which attend the disclosure—literally, the unveiling—of the central symbol of Judaism. Characteristically, what lies at the sacred center of Judaism is not a hieratic mystery but the word, the possession of all Israel, whose public recitation and exposition are the main business of the Torah service. The difference between this reading of Torah and the study of Torah is underscored by the specialness of the physical object itself. One studies from any printed and bound edition of the text. The Torah as read in the synagogue is a parchment scroll written in highly stylized calligraphy by a scribe in a state of purity. For a Torah scroll to be fit for use *(kasher)* there cannot be even one letter misshapen or out of place. The same rule of correctness applies to the public reading: any mispronunciation of the unpointed Hebrew text is quickly caught and corrected. The reading itself is undertaken in a kind of chant or cantillation, according to musical notes that appear above and below the words in the Masoretic text.

CHANGE FROM WITHIN AND WITHOUT

Although it was set in its classical crystallization by the age of the rabbis, the Siddur, like the larger Judaism of which it is a part, has hardly remained unchanged during the subsequent fifteen hundred years. During this time three varieties of change have been dominant: (a) supplementation, (b) prayerbook reform, and, (c) *kavvanah,* meditative reinterpretation. Of these only the second involved the actual alteration of the words of the text or even the excising of whole sections. Until the emergence of Reform in Germany in the nineteenth century, under which these radical changes were undertaken, the authority of the text held sway. Even though the Siddur was acknowledged as a human rather than a revealed creation, its power was such that it could only be added to or at most reunderstood.

Supplementation was by far the most prevalent practice, and frequent recourse to it explains how the slight proportions of the rabbinic prayerbook swelled into the substantial compendium in use today. The Kabbalat Shabbat service Friday evenings, the processional *hakkafot* of Simhat Torah, the memorial prayers for the dead (Mourner's Kaddish, Yahrzeit, Yizkor), the various hymns and poems that take up the greatest part of the service on Rosh Hashanah and Yom Kippur—much that seems today to be standard parts of the service shrouded in antiquity—are in fact, relative to the rabbinic liturgy, late additions.

A striking example is the Kabbalat Shabbat ("Welcoming the Sabbath") service (Birnbaum, pp. 237–55). This consists of a group of Psalms plus a hymn which are universally recited in the synagogue before the commencement of the Shema on Friday evening. The hymn, the Lekhah Dodi, was composed around 1540 by Rabbi Solomon Halevi Alkabetz, and its recitation together with Psalms 95–99 represents the actual practice of a circle of mystics active at this time in the Galilean hill town of Safed. The mystics would put on white robes and at sunset walk into the field surrounding the town reciting psalms and meditating on the spiritual meaning of the moment. In the mystical doctrine of their teacher, Isaac Luria, the Sabbath was invested with a messianic resonance. It was a moment of union between the transcendent and immanent—masculine and feminine—aspects of God, a union that presaged the ultimate redemption. The theme of Psalms 95–99, accordingly, is the establishment of God's kingship as if it were already a present fact: "The Lord, enthroned on cherubim, is king, peoples tremble, the earth quakes" (Ps. 99.1). The Lekhah Dodi brings the sexual metaphor to the surface. The hymn celebrates the arrival of the Sabbath, pictured as a bride and a queen, who is about to be joined to God, her consort. The scene of this union is a rebuilt Jerusalem, whom the poet addresses and exhorts to bestir herself and be ready for the redemptive events when

Your plunderers will themselves be despoiled,
Your violators will be banished;
Your God will rejoice in you
As a bridegroom takes pleasure in his bride.

These mystical symbols are expressions of a religious philosophy that amounted to a major reinterpretation of Judaism and that gained wide acceptance in Jewry at the end of the sixteenth century, as discussed previously in Chapter Six. The brief Friday evening service in the received text of the Siddur was apparently felt to be too slight an armature to bear the weight of the newly defined Sabbath experience. The solution was to create a preparatory rite, which was new, though built out of traditional sources, and affix it to the established prayer service.

The dominant form of supplementation, the *piyyut,* was both less radical and less confined in its origins to a particular moment in history. A *piyyut* (plural, *piyyutim*) is a poem written for recitation in the synagogue on holidays and special occasions. Whereas additional prayers like the Kabbalat Shabbat stand as separate units introducing or succeeding the service proper, the *piyyutim* are always integral parts of the service. So, on the morning of the holiday of Shavuot, for example, a *piyyut* describing the revelation at Sinai was interpolated directly into the *berakhah* after the Shema and became part of an expanded version of the prayer. The composing of *piyyutim* began in Palestine at the close of the Talmudic period in about the sixth century and was a ubiquitous practice until the modern period, flourishing with the fortunes and gifts of the centers of Jewish life.

The volume of output in this genre was stupendous; tens of thousands of *piyyutim* have come down to us, and more are discovered daily in manuscript. *Piyyut* is the genuine and central art form of classic Jewish civilization, and it is the place to look for the vigorous continuation of the creative liturgical impulse after the close of the rabbinic period. The *piyyut* is poetry, yet poetry that is different from the lyric, romantic, expressive conception most of us have of the poem. The *piyyut,* to begin with, is always subordinate to its context in the synagogue service and has no meaning or function as a free-standing poem. Because the *piyyut* is an extension of the service, it is invariably public and collective in spirit, rather than revelatory of private inward moments. Finally, because *piyyut* is an oral, declaimed poetry, it puts an emphasis on elaborate sonal patterns and the virtuoso manipulation of poetic forms.

Piyyutim are found in *mahzorim* (sing.: *mahzor,* "collection" or "cycle") devoted to each of the holy days of the Jewish calendar. *Mah-*

zorim differ between and within the two principal geographical-historical groupings of world Jewry, Sephardim and Ashkenazim. Because *piyyutim* are an optional, extracanonical component of the service, they vary according to the spiritual style of a community; the choice of different *piyyutim* is the chief determinant in what makes for the existence of a number of different rites (called *nusah*). The *mahzor* for the Days of Awe, Rosh Hashanah and Yom Kippur, is by far the largest. The liturgy handed down by the rabbis is only moderately larger than an ordinary Sabbath; it is the *piyyutim* that make the Yom Kippur nearly an all-day affair. It was not the aim of the medieval liturgists, however, to make the service a trial of our endurance. They were responding to a need for materials to help sustain a heightened religious moment and to elaborate its central images and symbols. Yom Kippur eve, the Kol Nidre service, can serve as an example. This is perhaps the most charged religious moment in the Jewish year, yet the rabbis have left a remarkably spare service which could be dispatched in under an hour's time. While the interpolated *piyyutim* do not expand this compass overmuch, they perform the function of dilating upon the shared feeling of the awesome anxiety of the moment. One *piyyut* captures the role of Kol Nidre as the beginning of a twenty-four-hour spiritual journey whose happy conclusion can be hoped for but not guaranteed:

> May our words and deeds of penance rise at dusk,
> our pardon come to greet us with the dawn,
> and let atonement cleanse us all at dusk.
>
> May our prayers of confession rise at dusk,
> our anguish at our imperfection meet the dawn,
> and let reconciliation make us whole at dusk.★

Later in the same service another *piyyut* underscores the mortal vulnerability and contingency at the heart of the Yom Kippur experience:

> As clay in the hand of the potter, to be thickened
> or thinned as he wishes, are we in Your hand.
> Preserve us with Your love.†

In each of the seven verses the simile is repeated in terms of the work of a different craftsman: the mason, the blacksmith, the glazier, and so on, and after each there follows the same appeal to show mercy rather than

★ Jules Harlow, ed., *Mahzor for Rosh Hashanah and Yom Kippur* (New York: Rabbinical Assembly of America, 1972), p. 387.
† *Ibid.*, p. 395.

strict judgment. Like many *piyyutim,* this one is built less on a progressive development of themes than on the variations of one striking idea, whose accumulating repetitions spur the congregation's participation and pathos.

Before the Enlightenment, the idea of tampering with actual received words of the Siddur was unthinkable. To add or reinterpret— yes, but not to alter. With the rise of the Reform Movement in the nineteenth century the practice of prayerbook reform was inaugurated. In addition to the aesthetics of the service (decorum, length, the use of musical instruments), two kinds of issues were opened up concerning the text of the liturgy. Whereas prayers had hitherto been recited in Hebrew alone, there were now proposals either to eliminate Hebrew or mix it with prayers in German or English or whatever was the language of the larger culture. There was the further assumption that the text of the prayerbook should reflect doctrinal changes; objectionable beliefs such as the Siddur's nostalgia for the Temple cult should be excised, and new emphases, such as ethical universalism, forthrightly inserted.

A number of different Reform liturgies vied with each other until 1894–95, when they were harmonized into a unified rite in *The Union Prayer Book,* which went through several revisions in this century. With the publication of a new work, *Gates of Prayer,* in 1975, Reform returned to the model of pluralism by offering several alternative services within the same prayerbook. A smaller and more recent movement in American Jewish life, Reconstructionism, also produced a prayerbook which, while more traditional than Reform's, especially in its use of Hebrew, also insisted that ideology be reflected in liturgy. The Reconstructionist prayerbooks of 1945 and 1948, for example, reflect the denial of the idea of the chosen people and the diminution or deletion of supernatural and anthropomorphic references. Conservative Judaism, in contrast, has made few alterations in the traditional Hebrew text, choosing instead to supplement it with a wide range of suggested readings in English.

The third mechanism of change, *kavvanah,* is the least visible but the most pervasive. Rather than reforming the liturgy or adding new materials to it, the *kavvanah* bids the pray-er reunderstand the words that are already there. As such, *kavvanah* pertains more to the experience of prayer than to the text of prayer. *Kavvanah* has two different historical connotations. In rabbinic literature and classical Judaism generally, *kavvanah* means proper concentration during prayer. Although they could fashion a profound liturgy, the rabbis were aware that the success of prayer ultimately depended on the spirit with which those words were said by individuals. Whether a person concentrates on the religious message of the words and invests them with emotion and meaning, or whether one prays hurriedly and out of habit while one's mind wanders to other affairs—this is the difference between praying with *kavvanah* or without it.

With the popular diffusion of mysticism in the sixteenth century, the term in its plural form, *kavvanot,* came to have a more programmatic meaning. Prayer was obviously one of the principal opportunities for mystical experience; during prayer the soul journeys across a map of realms or *Sefirot. Kavannot* are both the itinerary and the travel instructions for the journey. Later on, in Hasidism, praying with *kavvanah* came to mean meditation on the letters and words of the prayers. The letters of the Hebrew alphabet represent spiritual forces that can be linked together in a process of unification, which works to overcome divine alienation. One Hasidic source explains as follows:

> For in every word there are worlds, souls and divinity. These ascend and become bound and united one to the other and with the divine. Then the letters become united and bound together to form a word and then they become truly united in the divine. A man must allow his soul to be embraced by each stage of the above-mentioned and then all the worlds become united as one and they ascend so that there is immeasurable joy and delight.★

These mystical journeys are but a particularly radical instance of the dynamic of interpretation and reinterpretation which has always operated in Jewish prayer. In a general sense, *kavvanah* indicates the interpretive axis of prayer, that which is heard and meant when the words are uttered, and how that meaning changes over time and among individuals and communities. *Kavvanah* is the means by which a fixed liturgy eludes routinization and retains vitality. It is the subjective margin that allows the prayerbook to be meaningful and useful at times of both national emergency and personal crisis, in confronting both collective responsibilities and the individual moral life. As our sense of what is sacred and ultimate evolves, the prayerbook, like the Torah itself, stands with one foot in the received historical text and the other in the world of contemporary experience. The question in the end is not whether Siddur is relevant to our age, but whether we possess the will to join our ancestors in the enterprise of interpretation.

★ Quoted in Louis Jacobs, *Hasidic Prayer* (New York: Schocken, 1973), pp. 76–77.

Where to Go from Here

Three, good, general, nonscholarly accounts of the whole field of Jewish prayer and the prayerbook are Evelyn Garfiel's *Service of the Heart* (New York: Burning Bush Press, 1958), Abraham Milgram's *Jewish Worship* (Philadelphia: Jewish Publication Society, 1971), and Hayim H. Donin's *To Pray as a Jew* (New York: Basic Books, 1980). Jakob J. Petuchowski's *Understanding Jewish Prayer* (New York: Ktav, 1972) combines an overview by the author with seven essays on specific topics by other authorities.

Detailed treatments of specific prayers can be found in several commentaries on the Siddur. *The Hirsch Siddur* (New York: Feldheim, 1969) contains the marginal comments of Samson Raphael Hirsch, the great nineteenth-century German Neo-Orthodox figure. Joseph H. Hertz's *Daily Prayer Book* (New York: Bloch, 1959) carries the commentary of the Chief Rabbi of Britain between the wars. B. S. Jacobson's *Meditations on Siddur* (Tel Aviv: Sinai, 1966) concentrates on the classic sources for various prayers, while Elie Munk's *The World of Prayer* (New York: Feldheim, 1954–63) is concerned with the theological themes embodied in the liturgy. Two helpful and lucid modern commentaries on the High Holy Day services are Max Arzt's *Justice and Mercy* (New York: Burning Bush Press, 1963) and Herman Kieval's *The High Holy Days* (New York: Burning Bush Press, 1959). The *Encyclopaedia Judaica* provides a wealth of historical information, which is presented in scattered entries according to the Hebrew names of individual prayers or parts of the service (Amidah, Shema, Kaddish, Shaharit, and so on). These articles have been gathered together and edited into a consecutive text by Raphael Posner, et al., in *Jewish Liturgy*. (Jerusalem: Keter, 1975).

Of scholarly works on the historical development of the text of the liturgy, the great one, Ismar Elbogen's *Der Jüdische Gottesdienst* has unfortunately not been translated into English. (The revised Hebrew version is the most important book in the field.) An overall account in English is A. Z. Idelsohn's somewhat dated *Jewish Liturgy and Its Development* (New York: Schocken, 1932). More recent studies include: Joseph Heinemann's *Prayer in the Talmud: Forms and Patterns* (Berlin, New York: de Gruyter, 1977); Lawrence Hoffman's *The Canonization of the Synagogue Service* (South Bend, Ind.: Notre Dame University Press, 1979); Eric Werner's *The Sacred Bridge* (New York: Columbia University Press, 1959) on the interdependence of liturgy and music in the synagogue and church during the first millennium; Louis Jacob's *Hasidic*

Prayer (New York: Schocken, 1973), and Jakob J. Peutchowski's *Prayer Book Reform in Europe* (New York: World Union of Progressive Judaism, 1968).

Philosophical and analytic treatments of Jewish prayer, as opposed to historical approaches, can be found in Max Kadushin's *Worship and Ethics* (Evanston: Northwestern University Press, 1964), Louis Jacob's *Jewish Prayer* (London: Jewish Chronicle Publications, 1962), and Abraham J. Heschel's *Man's Quest for God* (New York: Charles Scribner's Sons, 1954).

There are a number of useful anthologies of translated Jewish prayers which are not themselves prayerbooks. *Literature of the Synagogue* (New York: Behrman House, 1975), edited by Joseph Heinemann, contains excerpts from the classic liturgy with brief scholarly prefaces. *The Language of Prayer* (New York: Schocken, 1947), edited by Nahum H. Glatzer, is a beautifully designed and printed volume, which contains facing translations of especially expressive prayers drawn from non-standard as well as standard sources. *Your Word Is Fire* (New York: Paulist Press, 1977), translated and edited by Arthur Green and Barry W. Holtz, is a collection of poetic versions of prayers and meditations from the sources of Hasidism, the modern religious movement that transformed the experience of prayer.

As for prayerbooks themselves, there are as many versions as there are groupings of synagogue movements. In the traditional or Orthodox camp, notable compilations and translations have been put together by Philip Birnbaum (New York: Hebrew Publishing Co., 1977), Ben Zion Bokser (New York: Hebrew Publishing Co., 1957), and David de Sola Pool (New York: Behrman House, 1960). (Since the titles tend to be more or less identical, these prayerbooks are usually referred to by their compiler's name.) Whereas most prayerbooks in American Jewish life reflect the practice of Ashkenazic Jewry, *Prayers for the Festivals* and *Prayers for the New Year* (New York: Union of Sephardic Congregations, 1963), compiled by David de Sola Pool, represent the liturgical customs of Sephardim. One Hasidic rite in prayer, named for the Ari, Rabbi Isaac Luria, exists in a translation published by the Lubavitch movement: *Tehillat Hashem* (New York: Kehot Publications, 1978).

In the 1970s the Reform movement undertook a fundamental revision of their prayerbooks. The results, *Gates of Prayer* (Weekdays, Sabbaths, and Festivals) and *Gates of Repentance* (High Holy Days) (New York: Central Conference of American Rabbis, 1975 and 1978), edited by Chaim Stern, are distinguished by their clean translations and the plurality of formats offered to their users. Although the Conservative movement has made do since 1946 with a Sabbath and Festival prayer-book compiled by Morris Silverman, a fresh translation of the weekday service was produced in 1961. The most ambitious undertaking in this sector has been Jules Harlow's *Mahzor* (1972), which in addition to its elegant translation, deftly interweaves supplementary classic and con-temporary materials. All are published by the Rabbinical Assembly of America, which is currently working on a new version of the "com-plete" Siddur. The Reconstructionist movement, whose liturgy closely reflects a consistent theological stance, has its own series of prayerbooks: Sabbath (1945), High Holy Days (1948), and daily (1963). All are pub-lished by the Reconstructionist Foundation in New York.

Index

About the Contributors

BARRY W. HOLTZ is Codirector of the Melton Research Center at the Jewish Theological Seminary of America. He is also an Assistant Professor in the Seminary's Education Department. A graduate of Tufts University, he received his Ph.D. in English from Brandeis University and has taught in a variety of settings, including synagogues, adult study programs and New York's 92nd Street YM/YWHA. His writing has appeared in *Midstream, Present Tense, Response,* and *Teacher's College Record,* among other places, and he is the coeditor/cotranslator of *Your Word Is Fire: The Hasidic Masters on Contemplative Prayer* (Paulist Press).

JOEL ROSENBERG teaches Hebrew Language and Literature at Tufts University. His poems, essays, and reviews have appeared in *Moment, Midstream, National Jewish Monthly, The Melton Journal,* and other publications. His book on political allegory in the Bible will appear through Crossroad Press.

EDWARD L. GREENSTEIN is Associate Professor in Bible at the Jewish Theological Seminary of America. He is coeditor of *The Journal of the Ancient Near Eastern Society of Columbia University* and associate editor of *Prooftexts: A Journal of Jewish Literary History.* He has authored numerous articles, monographs, essays, and reviews in biblical and ancient Near Eastern studies and is coeditor of the forthcoming *The Hebrew Bible in*

Literary Criticism. He has taught at several institutions, including Columbia University Graduate School, Hunter College, and Hebrew Union College.

MURRAY H. LICHTENSTEIN is an Assistant Professor in the Department of Classical and Oriental Studies, Hebrew Division, at Hunter College. He received his Ph.D. in ancient Semitic languages and literatures at Columbia University and has published articles in the *Journal of the Ancient Near Eastern Society,* the *Catholic Biblical Quarterly,* and the *Encyclopaedia Judaica.*

ROBERT GOLDENBERG is Associate Professor of Judaic Studies and Director of the Center for Religious Studies at the State University of New York at Stony Brook. He received advanced training in the study of Judaism at the Jewish Theological Seminary of America, and at Brown University, where he studied with the noted scholar Jacob Neusner. His overall scholarly interest is the rabbinic transformation of early Judaism which enabled it to survive the loss of the Temple and the destruction of Jerusalem. He is the author of *The Sabbath-Law of Rabbi Meir* (Scholars Press) and of numerous articles and reviews.

NORBERT M. SAMUELSON is an Associate Professor of Religion and Director of the Jewish Studies program at Temple University. In addition he is the chairman of the International Academy for Jewish Philosophy. He has published more than thirty scholarly articles on Jewish philosophy. His published books are *Gersonides on God's Knowledge* (1977) and *Ibn Daud's Exalted Faith* (1983).

LAWRENCE FINE is Associate Professor of Religious Studies at Indiana University. His field of research is the Jewish mystical tradition, especially the kabbalistic community of Safed in the sixteenth century. In addition to having written a number of studies concerning techniques of mystical experience that were developed in Safed, he has translated a volume of texts called *Safed Spirituality: Rules of Mystical Piety and Elijah de Vidas' Beginning of Wisdom.* He is currently working on a full-length study of Isaac Luria and his mystical fellowship.

ARTHUR GREEN is a student of the history of Judaism, concentrating on the areas of Jewish mysticism and Hasidism. His major work is *Tormented Master: A Life of Rabbi Nahman of Bratslav.* In addition, he has translated Hasidic sources into English and has published various articles on the history of Jewish thought. He is currently editing a collection of essays entitled *A History of Jewish Spirituality.* He serves as Associate Professor of Religious Studies at the University of Pennsylvania.

ALAN MINTZ teaches Hebrew literature at the University of Maryland, where he is Director of the Meyerhoff Center for Jewish studies. He is coeditor (with David Roskies) of *Prooftexts: A Journal of Jewish Literary History* and author of *George Eliot and the Novel of Vocation* (Harvard, 1978) and *Hurban: Responses to Catastrophe in Hebrew Literature* (Columbia, 1984).